THE CHARTIST CHALLENGE

A PORTRAIT OF GEORGE JULIAN HARNEY

by

A. R. SCHOYEN

HEINEMANN

LONDON MELBOURNE TORONTO

KINGSWOOD BOOKS ON SOCIAL HISTORY
General Editors: H. L. Beales and O. R. McGregor

FIRST PUBLISHED 1958

PUBLISHED BY
WILLIAM HEINEMANN LTD
99 GREAT RUSSELL STREET, LONDON, W.C.1
PRINTED IN GREAT BRITAIN BY BUTLER AND TANNER LTD
FROME AND LONDON

CONTENTS

LIST OF ILLUSTRATIONS

PREFACE

THE impersonal nature of most of the available materials on Julian Harney, mainly newspapers and periodicals in which he wrote, leave one with no more than conjectures about some aspects of his life. Though Harney, like such other "typical" Victorians as Gladstone and Disraeli, was an extraordinarily prolific correspondent, of the hundreds of his letters which survived him only a handful were discovered. Almost as disappointing was my inability to find the invaluable hoard of correspondence from his friends—Marx, Engels, Louis Blanc, Ledru Rollin, Feargus O'Connor, and so on—to which he casually alluded in the 1890's as reposing in a Cambridge (Massachusetts) attic.

It may have been the lack of such personalia, or perhaps frustration at the impossible task of really knowing the man (which I suspect everyone who attempts biography feels) that led to a recurrent dream. In the dream, Harney was still living in the house at Richmond, Surrey, where he spent his last bedridden days, and I was taken there by one of his friends to be introduced. The friend rapped on the old man's door, and I could just glimpse the foot of Harney's bed as he entered, leaving me filled with an inexpressible anticipation. At last I should know the answers to all the questions left in doubt. Finally, after a long conversation within, in which I could hear the muffled, faintly irascible tones of Harney without being able to understand what he said, the friend came out. The old man was too ill to see me. Now I should never know—and never did, though I was to stand outside the door again in other dreams.

There remained, however, the materials for describing his political life and the movements in which he played a leading part: and for help in unearthing these I have to thank many people. Foremost among them is Mr. H. L. Beales of the London School of Economics, to whose fertility in imaginative generalization and knowledge of nineteenth-century English social history a generation of grateful students and scholars has paid due. I must also express my gratitude to the institution with which he is connected, the University of London, for a grant in aid of research.

One hesitates to select from those in the British Museum, the Public Record Office, and the provincial libraries, whose efforts make research in England a pleasure scarcely to be met with elsewhere, but I should like especially to express my appreciation to the staff of the Newcastle Central Library. I am grateful also to Dr. Alec Wilson, of the Adult Education Department of the University of Manchester; Mr. F. J. Patrick, the City Librarian of Birmingham; and Mr. William MacFarlance, the session clerk of Mauchline Old Church, for special information. The Trustees of the Bishopsgate Institute in London have been good enough to grant me permission to quote from manuscript materials in the Howell Collection.

And finally, I owe a great debt of gratitude to Professor Giovanni Costigan of the University of Washington for his unfailing support and advice.

A. R. S.

CHAPTER I

The Making of a Radical[1]

GEORGE JULIAN HARNEY was born by the Thames at Deptford on 17 February 1817. The "Great Wen" of London had not yet absorbed the dockyard community downstream; Deptford still retained its eighteenth-century character, the ship-building area along the river being an easy walk from the market gardens and farms which produced strawberries and vegetables for the London market. A harsher environment lay at Deptford's door, however, both in place and time. The Thames, where it ran beside the wooden hulls on the ways, was black with the sewage of London; with an indifference like Regency England's own it carried the coal barges in which the "whippers" worked away their short drunken lives, and the cholera which periodically decimated the London populace, as well as the great East and West Indiamen whose cargoes had enriched a portion of the nation. Back from the river below old London Bridge stretched neighbourhoods in which, as one contemporary newspaper described it, "both physically and mentally the rising generation is distinguished for its demoralized condition beyond that of any other part of the Metropolis". On one side were the rabbit warrens of Bethnal Green and Spitalfields, on the other the narrow streets and blind alleys of Bermondsey and Southwark. The open fields which separated Deptford from this atmosphere of squalor and violence were to disappear within a generation. Julian Harney plunged into that atmosphere before adolescence.

Both Harney's parents were of the working classes, but the household in which he spent his early years, though poor, was hardly dull. His father, George Harney, had carried on the family's sea-going tradition by serving in the transport service of the Royal Navy during the Napoleonic wars; and the boy heard the glorious echoes of that era at first hand, including such dubious incidents as the death of a soldier from the wind of a cannon-ball in his father's landing-boat, during Abercrombie's

[1] See bibliographical note, Appendix.

Egyptian landing of 1801. There were also stories at second-hand, for the Harneys' poverty did not prevent them from owning books. The inevitable *Pilgrim's Progress* gave him, as it doubtless had countless other small boys, nightmares—an effect which was not alleviated by the Gothic horrors of Walpole's *Castle of Otranto*. A blander diet was provided by *Robinson Crusoe*, over which, so he later wrote, he dreamed for hours. The boy also read Goethe's *Sorrows of Young Werther*, and to the influence of this tragic romance of youth was added in subsequent years the poetry of Byron, for which he formed a passionate attachment.

The thirst for knowledge which was to characterize Harney's entire life found little formal satisfaction. The few pennies necessary to send him to dame schools were scratched together, but this rudimentary schooling was all that he ever received. It was enough, however, to make him envy the rich for their ability to buy the books which he could not afford, a class-reaction not uncommon in a generation growing up barred from education and literature by poverty. Yet there were pleasures from which he was not excluded of a more colourful kind. On May-Days he watched the travesty of the old country custom done by chimney-sweeps in cast-off finery, dancing around the pole to the music of pipe and drum to extract coppers for beer; and at Easter and Whitsuntide there were the Greenwich and Deptford fairs—"Saturnalian revels", as he remembered them, in which pig-faced ladies and boa-constrictors competed for attention with thimble-rig tables, gingerbread stalls and wax museums amid a pandemonium of cymbals and gongs.

The boy's political education began very early. Both of his parents, in common with the majority of the metropolitan working class, were ardent supporters of Queen Caroline in the divorce proceedings which a suddenly pious George IV brought against her after his accession in 1820; and one of his first memories was of the news of the London rioting and deaths which were a consequence of the Queen's funeral. Even headier than the Greenwich fairs were the Southwark general elections, with the intensely popular General Sir Robert Wilson, a hero of the Napoleonic wars and champion of the unfortunate Caroline, bowing from his carriage like a Roman conqueror to the intoxicated mobs of non-electors. Nor was his experience with the political cliche long in forthcoming. As a boy of nine, he later recalled, "I was at first puzzled between the claims of 'Polhill and our glorious Constitution', and 'Farncombe, the Man of the People'. But 'Wilson and Reform' . . . captured me beyond recall." The pervasive influence of the Clapham Sect also enveloped the young observer:

"Among the many flags and banners carried by Wilson's supporters was one bearing an anti-slavery device—on a white ground the figure of a black man in chains, and with clasped hands, asking in the inscription above his head—'Am I not a Man, and a Brother?' There needed not the speeches of a Wilberforce or a Clarkson, or the writings of a Granville Sharp, to make me an Abolitionist forthwith." [1]

But it was the sea which exerted the greatest fascination on Julian. As a small boy he gazed through the balustrades of old London Bridge at the forest of masts which crowded the river past the Tower, and played in the Naval Dockyard. The latter place had a more morbid attraction in the wretched chained convicts who worked under the fixed bayonets of soldiers and slept in the dismantled hulks which he could see anchored in the stream—"their name was sufficient of a forbidding horror".[2] With his family's maritime tradition and the romantic proximity of sailing-ships it was almost inevitable that he should go to sea, and in 1828, at the age of eleven, he entered the Boys' Naval School at Greenwich for training as a merchant sailor. Very likely this was as a ward of Greenwich Hospital, a branch of the Admiralty which at that time was taking care of some 3,000 naval veterans as well as their dependants.

The illness which was to plague Harney for the rest of his life kept him in the infirmary for much of his time at Greenwich. Yet there were consolations: he was able to feed his hunger for books by reading such apposite works as Southey's *Life of Nelson*, as well as becoming familiar with a living character from that volume—Dr. Beatty, physician at Greenwich, who had been on the *Victory* at Trafalgar. But his illness had a more significant effect. Had he been more robust, Harney might well have ended as his father had, an obscure seaman. The appalling severity of the foc's'le life of the 'thirties was too much for him, however, and after six months as a cabin-boy on trips to Brazil and Lisbon

---

[1] Newcastle *Weekly Chronicle*, 15 November 1890. Unless otherwise noted, quotations from this source are taken from a literary column which Harney wrote from 1890 to 1897.

[2] *Ibid.*, 25 June 1896.

in 1831 he took a job as a pot-boy in London. The world must not have seemed a particularly fragrant oyster to this slight, brown-haired youth of fourteen, handicapped with congenital quinsy and impaired hearing.

Young Harney came ashore to the seething unrest of the Reform Bill agitation, and his political education now began in earnest. He had already heard of the Bill when his ship, on the way home from Lisbon, hailed another for news and was told that the Lords had thrown out the Bill, leaving popular feeling at a feverish pitch. Though his ideas of "Reform" were vague at this time, having been mainly derived from ballad-singers, he needed to look no farther than the windows of the radical book-sellers' shops which he began to haunt to find what the attitude of the middle and working classes was. Such posters as that showing a heroic Lord John Russell administering a huge dose of purgative—the "Russell purge"—to a recalcitrant "borough-monger" were secondary, however, to the news of near-revolu-tionary outbreaks in Bristol, Nottingham and Derby, and middle-class threats of a refusal to pay taxes and to "stop the supplies". With public feeling running so high that people had begun to lay in provisions for an expected upheaval, the Duke of Wellington was unable to form a Tory government to dam the tide and a triumphant Whig ministry under Earl Grey carried the Bill on 4 June 1832.

The political union of the middle and working classes which had achieved the Reform Bill was destroyed so thoroughly by its passage that it was not to be reconstructed for three decades. The limited extension of the franchise which had been achieved was regarded by the working classes as a betrayal, and the dis-illusionment which followed the passage of the Act was the more intense for the hopes which had preceded it. To this distrust of the middle class was added a belief in the effectiveness of direct pressure on government through threatening mass-action which sank deep, to re-emerge in the Chartist movement six years later. Many middle-class leaders of the Reform Bill agitation were then given an opportunity to remember the violence of their lan-guage and the semi-revolutionary character of their recom-mendations in 1831 and 1832.

These attitudes had a profound influence on young Harney. Moreover, he had been introduced into the main stream of advanced London working class thought by one of the anonymous cobblers who, with tailors, played such a large part in the radical movements of the time.[1] The majority of working-class support during the Reform agitation had gone to the National Political Union, dominated by such moderate Radical leaders as Sir Francis Burdett and Francis Place in London, and Thomas Attwood in Birmingham. But a predominantly working-class organization, the National Union of the Working Classes, which demanded manhood suffrage, the secret ballot, and abolition of the property qualifications for members of Parliament, had gained a considerable following, particularly in London. Among this group was Harney's radical mentor, and Harney himself joined the National Union early in 1833, after its period of most intense activity was over and it had begun to disintegrate. The first public meeting of the organization which he attended was sufficient to drive home some of the lessons of what was regarded as the "Whig betrayal". In May, a large and peaceful gathering convened in Coldbath Fields to plan a national convention was attacked and dispersed by the police. The meaning of this forcible repression of the right of public meeting, coming after the seating of a Parliament many of whose members had led more threatening demonstrations a scant year before, was not lost on the working-class participants and the new recruit.

From this time on the adolescent Harney became one of the regular spectators at the small political gatherings held at the "Crown and Anchor" and other taverns. Disillusioned by the results of political agitation, the main body of the labouring classes had turned to the co-operative and trade union efforts which coalesced in Robert Owen's "Grand National Consolidated Trades Union"; but Harney was now absorbed by another movement stimulated by the failure of broad franchise reform— the unstamped press struggle. Filled with a desire to become a printer, due to his belief that the makers of books and newspapers were the "intelligentsia of the working class", Harney had frequented the area around Lincoln's Inn Fields and the Temple, where B. D. Cousins, Richard Carlile and other radical publishers and booksellers had their shops. He had made no more impression on these Olympians than had his nose pressed against their windows as he read the opened books on display. The formidable Carlile, a "gentlemanly figure with a face of extreme

[1] This cobbler may well have been either Allen Davenport or Thomas Preston, for whom see below, p. 14.

pallor and intense blue eyes", remained a remote, if much
admired, person to him.[1] It was finally in meeting Henry
Hetherington, an Owenite socialist and political radical who had
been a leading member of the National Union of the Working
Classes, that Harney entered this desirable world as a shop-boy,
selling pamphlets and running out with parcels.

Hetherington, undeterred by the second six-month sentence
which he had just served for publishing the unstamped *Poor
Man's Guardian* in defiance of the newspaper tax laws, was ingenious in devising strategems to get the paper to its vendors.
Thus, for example, some of the bundles which were carried from
his shop were likely to be dummies over which the carrier put up
a strong resistance if intercepted by Stamp Office men, while
genuine bundles of the paper were made off with in another
direction. Harney had engaged himself in a lively and dangerous occupation. More than this, it meant his education in what
he later described as the "radical school of the 'thirties".[2]

The basic assumption underlying most of the writing in these
unstamped papers—a belief in the perfectibility of man through
reason—is evidence of the continuing effect of French revolutionary thought on the radical English working classes. A free
press meant the diffusion of knowledge, with the inevitable consequence of progress. This assumption became a credo with
Harney.

> "The liberty of the press once established" [he wrote in 1837],
> "a new age will commence, the standard of truth and science will
> be erected among the nations of the world, and . . . we may con-
> template, with heartfelt satisfaction, the establishment of the dig-
> nified empire of reason and the improvement and happiness of the
> human race." [3]

Such utopianism had a more practical consequence. The refusal of the Whig government to repeal the prohibitive four-
penny tax on newspapers—in radical jargon, the "blood-red,
knowledge-smothering mark"—was considered additional proof
of middle-class enmity toward the class which had just put them
in power. As Doctor Wade, a Warwick clergyman of extreme
views, told an audience after Hetherington's second arrest,
"From the conduct pursued by those in power it would appear

---

[1] Harney, letter in *Notes and Queries*, 8 October 1887.
[2] *Northern Star*, 22 December 1849.
[3] London *Dispatch*, 26 March 1837.

that they would rather that the people were kept in ignorance
. . . for by keeping them in ignorance they hope a little longer to
domineer over them." [1]

To further underline this conclusion there was the freedom of
"respectable" penny weeklies from prosecution. James Watson,
a radical bookseller with a background similar to Harney's
employer, found himself sentenced to six months' imprisonment
for selling the *Poor Man's Guardian*, though none of the other
penny weeklies which he sold—the *Penny Magazine*, *Penny Cyclo-
pedia*, *Saturday Magazine*, etc.—had ever been troubled, despite
their culpability under the law which had led to his conviction.[2]
The forbearance of the magistrates and the Stamp Office toward
these publications, issued under the patronage of such dignitaries
as the Lord Chancellor, Henry Brougham, and Bishops of the
Church of England, was obviously due to their containing what
was considered to be proper knowledge for the lower classes. It
was the "dangerous doctrines" preached in the radical penny
weeklies which caused the difference in treatment.

Hetherington's new shop-boy noted that the conductors of the
unstamped had nothing but contempt for such knowledge as that
purveyed by the *Penny Magazine*, a publication of the Society for
the Diffusion of Useful Knowledge, which had been founded by
Brougham and other Radicals. Instead of its pictures of old
abbeys and birds and its "useful" articles on science, they dealt
with factory exploitation, attacked Church rates, and reported
the progress of trade-unionism. "*True* useful knowledge", they
felt, lay in the exposure of the evils brought on the working class
by class legislation and the profit system.[3] Even the best of the
unstamped papers, according to Francis Place, a staunch
defender of *laissez-faire* economics, "constantly inculcated the
absurd and mischievous doctrines respecting the right to property".[4] This economic judgment was exactly reversed in the
attitude of the radical unstamped to its more respectable cousins.
As Harney wrote some years later in describing Charles Knight,
the publisher for the Society for the Diffusion of Useful Knowledge, "A political economist and Malthusian, he has hardly
issued a solitary publication in which he has not done his best to

---

[1] *Workingman's Friend*, 26 January 1853.
[2] Petition of Watson to the House of Commons, March 1833, quoted in W. J.
Linton, *James Watson: a Memoir* (Manchester: 1880), p. 3.
[3] Newcastle *Weekly Chronicle*, 20 June 1896.
[4] Add. MS. 27,819, fo. 27 (British Museum). Hereafter referred to as Place MS.

promulgate the damnable doctrines of the heartless political school to which he belongs." [1]

Thus in these formative years Harney was imbibing from the contents of the radical unstamped a belief in political democracy as a means to the social amelioration of his class, a belief which he had also heard from the speakers of the National Union of the Working Classes. The social doctrines which he read were generally Owenite in their tone, but he picked up such general concepts as the right of labour to its fruits and the virtues of co-operation rather than a systematic belief. Added to this was a growing awareness of the conditions being brought by the new industrialism in the factory districts, and with it, a growing class-consciousness. As a small boy, he had cheered the anti-slavery mottoes of Sir Robert Wilson, but the effect of reading such publications as the *Poor Man's Guardian* was to make him familiar with a more immediate grievance.

> "I discovered" [he wrote subsequently], "that a good many manufacturing 'philanthropists', whose sympathies had been enlisted on the side of the negroes, had been quite oblivious to the sufferings of women and children in their own factories, and had opposed, and continued unyielding opposition to the efforts of . . . champions of the factory workers . . . to redeem the white slaves of England from what was, in some respects, worse than Jamaica or Barbadoes slavery." [2]

The changing attitudes of the youth were symbolized in his other reading also. At Greenwich he had read Southey's *Life of Nelson*; now he read the Laureate's *Wat Tyler*, a panegyric on the leader of the Peasants' Revolt written in the first flush of enthusiasm for the French Revolution of 1789, and reprinted by Richard Carlile in the 1820's to a more conservative Southey's extreme discomfort.

It was not only the intellectual content of the unstamped press, however, that was shaping Harney's political character. He suffered directly from the attempts of the Whig government to suppress stampless papers. The danger of apprehension came both from Stamp Office agents and from informers, for the latter flourished as a result of the reward of one pound offered to those helping in the conviction of illegal vendors. Two ex-members of the "New Police" alone accounted for between 300 and 400

---

[1] *Northern Star*, 10 June 1848.
[2] Newcastle *Weekly Chronicle*, 15 November 1890.

victims by the simple and profitable method of the one providing some destitute person with illegal newspapers, and the other purchasing a paper—at which the dupe was seized. During Hetherington's struggle to publish the *Poor Man's Guardian* no less than 500 of his vendors were imprisoned, and in 1834 Harney first saw the grim interior of Coldbath Fields prison.

After a short term of imprisonment, he turned to hawking the unstamped in the streets. Cousins's and Lorimer's shops, as well as Hetherington's, became familiar to him, and even after the *Poor Man's Guardian* had been declared legal in a somewhat paradoxical court decision in June 1834,[1] there remained a host of other papers which were not so favourably regarded. In less than a year, Harney was once again behind bars in Coldbath Fields prison. The corrective power of this institution was something less than effective, however, for on his release the unregenerate young jailbird was sent by Cousins to Derby to sell his *Political Register*, the former vendor having begun a sojourn in Derby prison. With the skill gained from his mouse-and-cat experiences in the metropolis, Harney managed to evade his pursuers for some months. Living under an assumed name and aided by the local working-class Radicals, he was not arrested until February 1836, when nemesis appeared in the form of a Stamp Officer from London. Charged with selling a newspaper which did not contain the name and address of its printer, he was hauled before a special sitting of the magistrates on the evening of his arrest.

Here for the first time Harney emerged from the obscurity which shrouded him and the anonymous hundreds who sold illegal papers. It was but a partial emergence, as he refused to give his name. Only through the testimony of a young woman tried the next week for selling the same paper is it plain who the nameless young man was: it seemed that he suffered from "a quinsy". Both of the respectable Derby newspapers found his trial interesting enough to report fully, and it is apparent that Harney used his dock-rostrum effectively, defiantly declaring:

> "These laws were not made by him or his ancestors, and there-
> fore he was not bound to obey them. The government of Lord
> Castlereagh, of notorious memory, was the author of the laws

---

[1] An obedient jury found, in accordance with the instructions of the judge, that Hetherington was not guilty in publishing the *Poor Man's Guardian*, but guilty in publishing a similar twopenny paper, the *People's Conservative*.

B

against the press, but the Whigs, who had strenuously opposed their enactment, were now the parties to enforce them. In spite, however, of all their efforts, he declared that knowledge should be untaxed. He had already been imprisoned for selling these papers, and was ready to go to prison again, and his place would be supplied by another person devoted to the cause. He defied the government to put down the unstamped . . . He had no goods to be destrained upon, and if he had, neither his majesty or any of his minions should have them."[1]

This intransigent manifesto was hardly calculated to placate the magistrates; Harney was sentenced to a fine of £20 or six months' imprisonment, and for the third time in as many years he was inside bars. (The Derby magistrates evidently took defiance of H.R.M.'s revenue machinery very seriously: contemporary trial reports show that they felt a "rogue and a vagabond" merited but seven days' imprisonment, the assailant of a policeman only one month.)

It is apparent from Harney's remarks that he regarded imprisonment as a duty. If this principle had been common to the hundreds, who were jailed for selling the unstamped, the movement could be considered an early example of deliberate "passive disobedience". Hetherington seems to have been aware of the attritive effects of a campaign involving mass-arrests, and the fact that the Victim Fund which was organized was used to ease the imprisonment of convicted vendors rather than to pay fines might possibly be regarded as additional evidence.[2] But the majority of those who participated in this hazardous occupation were doubtless driven, as was Harney originally, by poverty rather than by the consciousness of being part of a movement whose success depended to such an extent on their being victimized. That it had become more to Harney was another indication of his political development.

This is hardly to say that he accepted imprisonment philosophically. After serving his six-month sentence, he was released in such a condition that he fainted on the road to London from weakness. His reaction was one of burning resentment: "If he ever forgave the scoundrels who caused his misery then, . . . might he never be forgiven himself." [3] And this desire for retribution was not mitigated by the Whig government's reduction

[1] Derby *Mercury*, 24 February 1836.
[2] For the working of this fund, see Place MS. 27,821, fo. 4.
[3] *Northern Liberator*, 28 December 1838.

I. Henry Hetherington

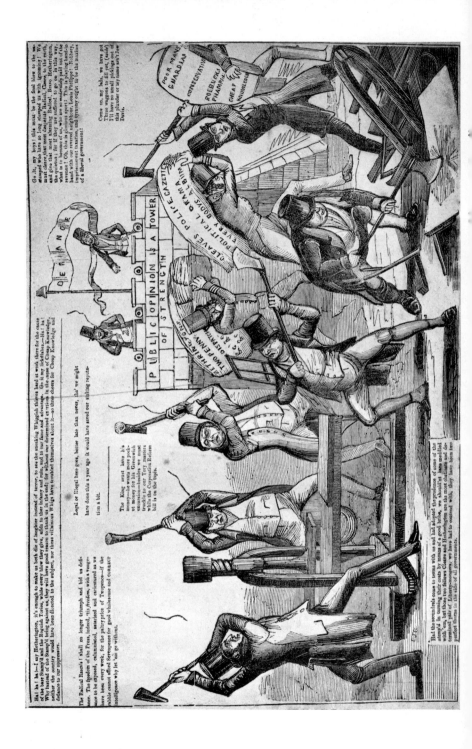

Ha! ha! ha!—I say Hetherington, it's enough to make us at both side of laughter instead of terror, to see the sneaking Whiggish thieves hard at work there for the cause of the base Stamp'd knowledge to strike blow after blow in shameful against the cause of the Unstamp'd. We can thank the Sulp! Bing against us, they will have good reason to thank us in the end; for without our determined crush in the name of Cheap Knowledge, neither the country would have been directed to the subject, nor these villainous Whigs have troubled themselves about it—so three cheers for Cheap Knowledge and defiance to our oppressors.

The Radical Rascals shall no longer triumph and bid us defiance. The freedom of the Press, indeed, its freedom, with a vengeance—to be exposed, calumniated, satirized and caricatured as we have been every week, for the paltry price of Twopence—if the rabble cannot afford Sevenpence for good wholesome and CORRECT intelligence why let 'em go without.

Logical or Illogical here goes, better late than never, for we might have done this a year ago it would have saved our sinking reputation a bit.

The King must have his money—he wants more pocket money for his Greenwich concubine—besides we must truckle to our Tory masters while the Corporation Reform bill is on the tapis.

Go it, my boys! this must be the final blow to the escamps who have so long stamped us with ignominy! We must clear that most desperate Radical, Carse, to the earth, and give that most shriving Radical, Bravo Hetherington, the quietus; for if they are not crushed at once in the reverse? Oh, this is glorious sport! This is playing hand-in-hand with our revered neighbour, Louis Philippe! Robbery, imprisonment, taxation, and tyranny ought to be the maxims of a liberal government.

Come on, my lads, we have got (smile) Three waggons to fill yet. I'll have no small pickings out of this plunder or my name ent Jew Davis.

Had the scoundrels come to terms with us and had adopted the prudence of some of the sharp'd in turning their coats by stealth and a good bribe, we could have managed well enough with 'em, but those two fellows Carse and Hetherington are the most obstinate and determined pair of Liberty-mongers, we have had to contend with, they have been two perfect thorns in the side of all governments.

of the newspaper duty to one penny in the month of his release, under the urgings of the Parliamentary Radicals and the unrepressed flood of unstamped papers. The new newspaper act, in fact, destroyed the unstamped press through its more rigorous provisions concerning enforcement and punishment, while it made a cheap press uneconomic by its retention of the taxes on paper and advertisements. To Harney, observing this effect, the passage of the act was but one more example of the "mock reforms" of the new government.[1]

"Mock reforms": Harney's use of the term was a common one and expressed the attitude which was taking form in the minds of many of the working classes toward the legislation of the new government. Such achievements as municipal reform and the abolition of slavery in the colonies, though laudable, had nothing to do with the real grievances of factory hands, hand-loom weavers, colliers and agricultural workers. Whig factory legislation had barely touched "wage-slavery". The Reform government had instead pursued a policy which working men could only regard as one of active hostility. The government's support of the strong counter-measures taken by employers to destroy the Grand National Consolidated Trades Union in 1834, climaxed by the savage sentence of transportation passed on the "Tolpuddle Martyrs", a group of farm-workers who had formed a branch of the Union, crystallized sentiment in a way no amount of abstract argument could have done. If additional evidence were needed of the intentions of their rulers, it was furnished by the speedy passage and introduction into the southern counties of the most thoroughly detested act of the nineteenth century from a working-class viewpoint—the New Poor Law.

That this sense of grievance and the collapse of the trades union–co-operative effort embodied in the Grand National led to no overt mass political expression in the years during which Harney alternated between prison and selling the unstamped may be attributed largely to the steady recovery of business following the depression of 1832. Plentiful harvests and the renewal of industrial activity gave some truth to the statement of a group of Birmingham manufacturers, referring to the period 1834–36: "Workmen have generally been placed in a condition of full employment and good wages, producing a general state of satisfaction and contentment among them." [2]

[1] *Ibid.*   [2] London *Mercury*, 26 March 1837.

Thus Harney returned to a London in which political activity was at low slack, with the activities of confirmed Radicals scarcely disturbing the surface tranquillity. In the following months he took a room in Horselydown Lane, a narrow street below London Bridge in Bermondsey, and renewed contact with his friends. Through these men, Harney had a living link with the radical working-class past: Henry Ross, a carpenter, had been involved in the Glasgow violence of 1819; Allen Davenport, universally respected by London democrats for his selflessness, was a disciple and propagator of the ideas of the land-reformer, Thomas Spence; and Thomas Preston, a colleague of Horne Tooke and Thomas Hardy in the London Corresponding Society of the 1790's, had evaded the noose twice, being tried on both occasions for high treason for his part in the disturbances following the Napoleonic Wars. Of these men, Davenport had the most direct effect on Harney, who was to avow himself a Spencean a few years later. But the strongest single intellectual influence of his formative years was James Bronterre O'Brien, a middle-class Irishman who had given up the study of law to devote himself to the working-class movement.

O'Brien had been the editor of the *Poor Man's Guardian*, and Harney's acquaintanceship with him probably dated from his employment as Hetherington's shop-boy in 1832. In the two years following Harney's release from Derby prison their contact was frequent, and his devotion to Bronterre was testified by his reference to him as his "guide, philosopher, and friend".[1] Brimming with bitterness at his Derby imprisonment, and with a sense of protest which had been steadily nurtured throughout his adolescence, he made an ideal pupil for the man who became known as the "Schoolmaster of Chartism". What were the ideas which now gave Harney's resentment toward society shape and direction?

Though sympathetic with the social aims of Robert Owen, O'Brien parted company with the Owenites on the means by which their aims were to be achieved. Socialism in the 'thirties and 'forties connoted the withdrawal of individuals from capitalistic society and their construction of communities based on co-operative effort and sharing.[2] Their conversion of the rest of

---

[1] *Operative*, 11 November 1838.

[2] In England by 1850 the term "socialist" was used loosely to describe not only the "associationists"—followers of Cabet, Fourier, etc.—but those who believed in

society would be by example and instruction. Like Marx and Engels later, O'Brien considered this viewpoint utopian; to gain socially desirable ends by such means was not only impossible but ignored historical fact.

Bronterre thought that the achievement of social and political equality—the ideal end of state policy—had been subverted by the land-owning and commercial classes' exclusion of the working class from government. Only through the conquest of political power could the working class create a society in which each man, while being guaranteed the product of his labour, would be prevented from appropriating the labour of others. Private property would exist, but not private capital, which he saw as accumulated labour. In his view, it was the expropriation of the fruits of labour, primarily by the middle class, which accounted for the miserable condition of the real producers of wealth. The potentiality for a life of plenty already existed through the advanced state of technical knowledge; but the realization of this potentiality would be deferred so long as the owning classes monopolized government.[1]

Bronterre found historical evidence for the accusations he levelled against the middle class in an analogy between French events of 1791 and English events in 1832. In both cases, the middle class, after achieving its ends, had excluded the masses from the franchise and begun a counter-revolution directed against the egalitarian aims of its onetime ally, the working class. Robespierre, the embodiment of the aims of the working class, had eventually been the victim of society's worst enemy, the "profit-monger". From these analogies, O'Brien drew the plainest of lessons for his readers: the English social revolution would succeed only if the power of the middle class was destroyed by the working class.[2]

---

the State as the logical instrument to replace the economy based on profit. See, e.g., W. J. Linton in the *Red Republican*, 19 October 1850. This usage will be followed here.

[1] For O'Brien's views at this time, see *Bronterre's National Reformer*, 7 January 1837; London *Mercury*, 9 July 1837; *Northern Star*, 2 June 1838. Bronterre's estimate of the productive capacity of the English economy is reminiscent of the claims of the American "Technocrats" a century later. He estimated that, given equitable distribution, three hours' daily work by everyone capable of producing would mean a return of £300 each per annum.

[2] *Cf.*, Buonarotti, *History of Babeuf's Conspiracy for Equality, Translated by Bronterre* (London: 1836), p. xiv; J. B. O'Brien, *Life and Character of Maximilian Robespierre* (London: 1838), pp. 276–84.

Bronterre, then thirty-one, was coming to the full flood of his powers in 1836. Francis Place, an acute observer, thought him more responsible than any other individual for the widening acceptance by the working class of "mischievous doctrines regarding property" in the late 'thirties.[1] This was due not only to the ease and logic with which he presented his ideas, but to one of the finest polemical styles of the period—Bronterre's invective could be both bludgeon and rapier. Thus his impact on young Harney was not surprising. In the next three years, the pupil in fact outdid his teacher in modelling his behaviour and his analysis of events on the actions of the Left during the French Revolution. The communism of Babeuf, with its stress on egalitarianism, the state as the mechanism of social change, and both the right and the obligation to labour, became an integral part of his thinking. And where O'Brien had to some extent identified himself with Robespierre, Harney took as his prototype Marat. "Hail! spirit of Marat! All Hail!" he declaimed rhetorically in 1839. "Thou whose imperishable title I have assumed; and oh! may the God of Freedom strengthen me to brave, like thee, the persecution of tyrants and traitors, or (if so doomed) to meet, like thee, a martyr's death!" [2]

It was not only in its French version that the doctrine of natural rights which underlay Bronterre's writings reached Harney. A belief in this doctrine and the arguments which proceeded from it was common among the Radical working-class leaders of the 'thirties.[3] That this had an English as well as French origin is evidenced by the programme of the first political organization in which Harney played a leading role. The East London Democratic Association, formed in 1837 by Harney, the Spencean cobbler, Allen Davenport, and Charles Neesom, a violently outspoken republican, declared in its manifesto that its object would be to promote the moral and political condition of the working class "by disseminating the principles propagated by that great philosopher and redeemer of mankind, the Immortal Thomas Paine".[4]

---

[1] Place MS. 27,819, fo. 24.

[2] London *Democrat*, 13 April 1839.

[3] See, e.g., the declaration of the National Union of the Working Classes, quoted in William Lovett, *Life and Struggles of William Lovett*, 2nd edition (London: 1920), p. 74.

[4] *Prospectus of the East London Democratic Association, No. 19, Swan Street, Minories.* Flyleaf dated January 1837, Lovett Collection, Birmingham Public Library.

The mixture of French and English elements in English radicalism is apparent in an address written by Harney some months later which set forth the Association's assumptions and aims more fully.[1] The great object of the Association, this address declared, was the achievement of a democratic and republican England—a natural society based on the principles of liberty, equality and fraternity. Such a society meant the restoration of a state of organization which had once existed, and the eradication of the institutions which had taken its place: "Kings, aristocrats, and tyrants of every description . . . are slaves in rebellion against the sovereign of the earth, which is the people, and against the legislator of the universe, which is Nature." The address also drew its economic conclusions from natural rights: the accumulation of private property violated natural law, for it meant that one class lived on the labour of others, thus causing all who laboured to be slaves. To achieve the change in society which they desired, they would adopt such means as were expedient to achieve the "five grand principles of Radical Reform": universal suffrage, vote by ballot, the abolition of the property qualification for Members of Parliament, equal electoral districts, and annual Parliaments.

The main group to which the Association turned for support in London was that which corresponded most closely to the French *sansculottes*: the Spitalfields silk-weavers, chronically poverty-stricken, and described by one observer as "not daring to show their half-naked squalid persons out of doors, lest they be taken up and committed as nuisances".[2] This section of London's population had been ignored by the existent radical organization, the London Working Men's Association, which had been formed in June 1836 by a deliberately select group of working men. The L.W.M.A., led by the men who had dominated the National Union of the Working Classes—Hetherington, Watson, and the indefatigable Cornish cabinetmaker, William Lovett—was exclusive in a double sense: middle-class men were specifically barred from any share of control in the organization, though they were permitted as honorary members; and of the working classes only the "intelligent and influential portion" was to be admitted. Composed for the most part of skilled working men, this group saw itself as an élite which by example

---

[1] London *Dispatch*, 4 June 1837.
[2] O'Brien, *Life and Character of Maximilian Robespierre*, p. 14.

and the dissemination of propaganda would raise the "vicious many" to the level at which they would be able to participate in the government.[1]

There was, superficially, no reason for dissension between the Working Men's Association and the East London Democratic Association. Their spheres of action did not impinge. One looked to the gradualist, educational efforts of a select group to extend their influence and achieve their democratic objects; the other occupied itself with the attempt to organize a mass following in the slums of the East End. But the formation of the East London Democratic Association was part of an alignment of forces which, though of no great significance at this time, was of considerable importance for the future. The key figure in this alignment was Feargus O'Connor, with whom Harney now had his first contact.

It is worth noting that O'Connor, who was to become a leader of unparalleled popularity among the English working classes, and Bronterre O'Brien, the dominant intellectual force in shaping the radical ideas of these classes, were both Irishmen. O'Connor, an ex-Member of Parliament who had lost his seat after a falling-out with Daniel O'Connell, the "Irish Liberator", was a tall, powerfully-built man of commanding presence, with a superb gift of mob-oratory, graceful manners, and what seems to have been an overpowering charm. Many years later Harney described him as an "inferior Cobbett", and a comparison of the two men's ideas, as well as their manner of writing and speaking, indicates that O'Connor owed much to Cobbett, if he did not indeed deliberately model himself on the great Radical editor. Without a doubt, too, Feargus had learned much from his one-time leader, O'Connell, about the most effective methods of crowd-appeal. What he did was to transplant the techniques used with the Irish peasantry to the English industrial classes. Francis Place regarded Feargus as an "unprincipled political adventurer"; possibly Clemenceau's cynical aphorism—"All great men are great frauds"—comes closer to the mark. Yet even in the bitter attacks which O'Connor's single-minded quest for dominance was to provoke subsequently a note of respect is to be found. Until he went mad, this mountain of a man was never considered a molehill save by one person, William Lovett

[1] Place MS. 37,773, fo. 3 (the minute book of the L.W.M.A., 1836–39); "Address and Rules of the London Working Men's Association", *ibid.*, 27,819, Appendix.

—and Lovett was a man who, eye-to-eye with God, would have obstinately persisted in looking for a cast.

While Harney had been selling unstamped newspapers and suffering imprisonment in Derby in 1836, Feargus had been attempting to form radical associations of working men in the North as well as in London, where he was prevented from playing an active role in the Working Men's Association by his middle-class background. Now, early in 1837, O'Connor resumed his effort, this time in conjunction with O'Brien and John Bell, the editor of a struggling ultra-radical weekly newspaper, the London Mercury.[1] It would seem that the strategy of this group, with whom Harney's connection was close, was two-fold: Harney and his associates of the East London Democratic Association were to attempt a union with the Working Men's Association, with the object of control; and, following this, a new organization was to be formed which would unite all the radicals of the metropolis. But Lovett, the canny secretary of the Working Men's Association, as well as other members, responded coolly to the E.L.D.A.'s overtures and the attempt—the first of many—came to nothing. Shortly after this, the "Central National Association" made its appearance, and with this organization Harney and the other leaders of the E.L.D.A. allied themselves.

The Central National Association was, in some respects, an early form of "Tory Democracy". As its name implied, it was intended to be nation-wide in its appeal, taking the form of an alliance between the industrial working class and the agricultural interest. The latter was represented by James Bernard, an eccentric Cambridgeshire farmer and currency-reformer (with heavily mortgaged property) who had made unsuccessful overtures to the Working Men's Association in the preceding year. The result of the alliance was a catch-all programme which included not only universal suffrage, the repeal of the New Poor Law, and an eight-hour factory day, but Bernard's panacea for farmers who were suffering from high fixed rents and debts due to the fall in the price of wheat. Bernard's scheme consisted basically of currency inflation and protection for both agriculture and industry, the result of which was to be high prices and wages. The only loser in this scheme would be the "Moneyocracy"

[1] According to Place, Bell had lost a considerable fortune publishing Radical newspapers.

—that is, the industrial and commercial middle classes. Bernard was elected the first president of the Association, an action with unfortunate results.

It quickly appeared that the new president was as thriving an egomaniac as the English public was to be afflicted with until David Urquhart took the limelight in the middle 'fifties, being possessed as well of an obdurate self-conviction which paled that of Robert Owen. Universal suffrage had been virtually attained, he assured the audience which listened to his inaugural address; his control of the agriculturists of England—they had been unable to withstand the irresistible logic of his proposals—made this certain. It was difficult, he admitted, to explain his conviction that power would be theirs within six months: "My views take, of necessity, a far more extended range than those of other people, and are impossible to be rendered intelligible in the present state of human understanding, until events actually occur to confirm them." Apparently it was within their feeble powers to comprehend that the coalition of powers which he had achieved, plus the imminence of the Bank of England's collapse, would make necessary his assumption of national control. In this crisis, he would not shrink from the "responsibility of issuing a proclamation that . . . would settle the whole affair in twenty-four hours".[1] What the reaction of his audience was can only be imagined; one workman at least was not so sanguine about national bankruptcy, "being of opinion that the people of England would take the paper of the government in lieu of money even if it bore the mark of having been used in the King's closet".[2]

O'Connor, keeping discreetly in the background of the new association, was not one to bother overmuch about principles, and Harney was a very junior partner in the new undertaking. But the spectacle of O'Brien and Bell, both mature, sincere, and intelligent men, stomaching Bernard's nonsense is difficult to explain other than on the ground that he had promised financial support to the London *Mercury*, then on the verge of bankruptcy. Bronterre was installed as joint-editor with Bell; and shortly after Bernard's election in early April 1837, it was announced that he was the new publisher of the *Mercury*.

Henry Hetherington's London *Dispatch*, the spokesman for the London Working Men's Association, fell on Bernard's messianic

---

[1] London *Mercury*, 26 March 1837.   [2] *Ibid.*, 30 April 1837.

revelations with gusto, and Bronterre and Bell, though defending
the principle of protection for native agriculture and industry,
made at best a weak reply. The Central National Association did
not, in fact, fully recover from the attacks in the *Dispatch*, which
went on to quote some of Bernard's anti-democratic expressions
which had already reached print. This newspaper bickering,
besides resulting in the washing of a certain amount of dirty
linen in public—a seemingly inevitable accompaniment of such
polemics—also brought the basic hostility between the main
groups of London Radicals into the open.

This hostility was more than a matter of personalities. The
disagreement between the rival organizations was primarily one
of means and not ends. Bernard's currency notions, for example,
received only a politer disdain from O'Brien than from Lovett.
With the Working Men's Association's political credo—the
familiar "Six Points" of universal suffrage, payment of M.P.s,
equal electoral districts, abolition of property qualification for
M.P.s, annual Parliaments, and secret balloting, which found expression later in the "People's Charter"—there was entire agreement. But Lovett's group had also indicated that its method to
achieve these aims would be strictly legalistic. Parliament would
be petitioned and a cautious co-operation entered into with the
Radical M.P.s who were sympathetic to reform. Yet these
Parliamentary Radicals, several of whom were honorary members of the Working Men's Association, were also strong proponents of the New Poor Law. Alliance with such men seemed
to O'Brien and Harney a repetition of 1832 and a betrayal of the
working classes; Lovett and his group had become the "tools of
the Malthusian sham-Radicals". The issue was a fundamental
one: was it possible to have any political co-operation, however
limited, with those whose legislative actions showed their economic and social incompatibility with the working classes?

This dissension in London took place in a near-vacuum of
popular interest. But in spite of the lack of spectators, here in
dress rehearsal were the main characters and ideas which were to
result in dramatic conflict two years later, splitting the national
movement of the working classes into two opposing factions. The
leaders of the Working Men's Association had no more reason
than their more extreme rivals to believe in the trustworthiness
of the middle-class Radicals, but their policy of education and
gradualism depended in the last resort on the Parliamentary

Radicals implementing it. Harney was already in the extreme camp, being fully in agreement with his mentor, O'Brien, in believing that political concessions would come only as a result of coercion. "Petition the base, money-mongering Whig Parliament?" cried Bronterre. "He was for bolder measures . . . and would, if he were disposed to petition at all, do so after the fashion of the character in Le Sage's story of Gil Blas, who presented a petition to his victim with one hand, while pressing a blunderbuss to his head with the other." [1]

O'Brien, thinking in French Revolutionary terms, suggested instead the election of a people's parliament, which, strongly supported by perhaps 200,000 working men, "would have no difficulty in legalizing their proceedings". To this revolutionary strategem Harney vouched the readiness of the men of Derby; but London remained stubbornly deaf to the plan and to the efforts of the Central National Association in general. It was not without significance that, very likely due to O'Connor's continuing trips to the north, resolutions of support for the Association came from radical organizations in Northumberland, Yorkshire and Lancashire; but the Association's attempt to introduce the issue of universal suffrage into a great anti-Poor Law meeting in Yorkshire in April met with indifference. In spite of this, following William IV's death in June 1837 a half-hearted effort was made to put O'Brien's election plan into effect in the ensuing General Election.

The delegates to a people's parliament—who, in Harney's phrase, were to decide upon the best means of "co-operating with or superseding (as circumstances may permit) the existing assembly miscalled the house of commons" [2]—were to be chosen by a show of hands at the hustings. Bell offered himself for Coventry, O'Connor for Preston, and Bronterre for Manchester; and the Central National Association endorsed J. R. Stephens and Richard Oastler, the leaders of the anti-Poor Law agitation in the North, for Ashton-under-Lyne and Huddersfield. Harney found the men of Derby less ready than he thought: he received no invitation from them, though this had been suggested in the London *Mercury* by Bronterre.

The result was, inevitably, disappointing: O'Connor's growing influence in the north was shown by his success in receiving the show of hands at Preston; but, refusing to share the hustings

[1] London *Mercury*, 21 May 1837.   [2] *Ibid.*, 23 July 1837.

expense, O'Brien did not stand at Manchester. Bell—reported by an optimistic Feargus just prior to the Coventry election as being a certainty for election—made a miserable showing, receiving but 43 votes in nomination, and this, as he said, in a city with the closest thing to universal suffrage in England. Stephens and Oastler were the most successful of the candidates, the latter being beaten by but 22 votes in a total of 624; but neither had accepted the endorsement of the Central National Association. If any lesson was to be learned from these dismal results, it was that the New Poor Law and not manhood suffrage was the real issue in 1837 in the working-class mind.

The plan had obviously failed, and with this proof of public disinterest the Association began to disintegrate. Bernard, now absorbed in a plan for the regeneration of Europe, found that his usefulness so far as his colleagues were concerned was at an end when he sold the London *Mercury* in August. Lacking a public organ, the Association vanished in little more than a month; and by September, Feargus having departed for the greener radical pastures of the North to start a new paper, the *Northern Star*, the East London Democratic Association and the Working Men's Association remained alone in the metropolitan field.

The failure of the Central National Association to start a national political movement may be attributed not only to its essentially incompatible elements and its failure to gain a following in London—which was, and remained, comparatively apathetic—but to the fact that it was so far removed from the areas where unrest was beginning to develop and political agitation might have had listeners. The relative prosperity of 1836 had continued into 1837, but by March it was becoming apparent that the direction of the economy had sharply changed. A group of Birmingham manufacturers put the situation succinctly in a memorial to the Home Secretary:

> "Orders for goods are countermanded . . . both for the foreign and home trade. The prices of goods are falling, so as in many cases to occasion a loss . . . Unless remedial measures be immediately applied, a large proportion of our population will shortly be thrown out of employment." [1]

---

[1] *Ibid.*, 26 March 1837. Contrast this with the statement of the Birmingham middle-class Radical leader, Thomas Attwood, two months before: the working class was in work and contented, and "it could not be expected that they would indulge in political excitement" (*ibid.*, 5 March 1837).

It was at this time that the proponents of the New Poor Law, taking the prosperity which had obtained until then (and a large saving in the rates) as proof of the efficacy of the law, urged its quicker extension; and the Poor Law commissioners turned from their successful efforts in the south to the factory districts of Yorkshire and Lancashire. Thus at the same time that a commercial crisis and unemployment were swiftly spreading, the system of outdoor relief was to be superseded by a new system which, in effect, treated the unemployed as criminals. The effect was a reaction so violent and widespread that the Commissioners were forced to delay their measures. In such an atmosphere the political movement in the North rapidly germinated.

It was Lovett's group, rather than Harney's, which benefited from the growing unrest outside of London. The successful effort of the Working Men's Association to promote similar, though autonomous, organizations in other cities through the use of "missionaries" and correspondence was marked by a steady rise in the number of such Associations as autumn drew on and the decline in economic activity spread. What had seemed remote in the general political passivity of 1836 no longer seemed so, and Lovett's group was forced by the pressure of events to devote more attention to the co-ordination of a national effort and agitation than to the gradual educational methods which had been envisaged originally. The increasing influence of the Working Men's Association was not matched by a similar progress on the part of the East London Democratic Association. Their efforts to organize a mass-following in the East End having met with little response, Harney and his colleagues turned to their more successful rivals. The episode which followed was still another lesson in practical politics for the twenty-year-old.

Due to the doubts of Lovett and other moderates, it was only with difficulty that the East London leaders were able to gain admission to the London Working Men's Association in October 1837. Lovett's uneasiness about their motives was not baseless. Harney had sacrificed none of the views with which the Working Men's Association were in fundamental disagreement; and in his subsequent actions it became clear that, with the loyal support of his "junta", he intended to discredit the Association if he failed to change its policy of middle-class collaboration. His opportunity arose almost immediately.

The Working Men's Association had steadily pursued its aim of gaining the co-operation of the Parliamentary Radicals, the most powerful of whom was Daniel O'Connell. The famed Irish agitator was the epitome of the "sham-Radical" so detested by Harney, combining as he did sympathy with some extension of the suffrage with a strong defence of the New Poor Law.[1] Factory legislation, in his view, was an infringement of the worker's as well as the capitalist's freedom; the usual methods of trade unions appeared to him as a violation of the freedom of contract. These were hardly popular views in working-class eyes—the "paternal, interfering principle of government" which he desired to eradicate was precisely what they wished to reinstate by a return to the old Poor Law—but his connection with the L.W.M.A. might have gone unnoticed except for a few London radicals like Harney had it not been for his involvement in the trial of the Glasgow Cotton Spinners, which began in September 1837.

The Spinners' union committee had been arrested for alleged crimes, including the murder of a "blackleg", which had grown out of a bitter strike begun in the spring. The strike, a protest against a fifty per cent cut in wages, had little to differentiate it from the general pattern of industrial strife in the developing crisis of 1837, as manufacturers cut their costs and workmen struggled to protect their gains of the preceding years. But the arrest of the committee and the nature of the indictment against them changed their case, giving to it the symbolic importance of the "Tolpuddle Martyrs' " trial three years before. The charge, originally conspiracy to murder, had been altered to include simple conspiracy, the administration of unlawful oaths, and the secret transaction of union business. The analogy with the Tolpuddle trial was obvious, and was frequently drawn by speakers at the working-class protest meetings which became widespread in the latter part of 1837. In the deepening commercial depression, the working class was convinced that the state was once again moving against them in combination with the masters—also a common interpretation of the New

[1] See, e.g., O'Connell's speech of January 1837, which sums up the attitude of New Poor Law exponents toward relief given outside the workhouse: "Poor laws encourage idleness, improvidence, early marriages, seduction, prostitution, and crime. . . . Society is bound to protect the property of its members, and . . . no individual or class of society has any right to relief out of the earnings of other individuals or classes."

Poor Law [1]—and the Glasgow trial confirmed them in their belief.

In December, a few weeks after he had participated in a banquet with the London Working Men's Association, O'Connell made his position with regard to the trial clear by declaring to the House of Commons his intention to call for a parliamentary commission to inquire into the whole subject of unions. His speech placed the Working Men's Association in a dilemma: if they did not disavow their connection with a notorious opponent of trade unions, the accusation of being "middle-class tools" which had been levelled against them by such men as Harney and O'Brien would gather force; if they did disavow O'Connell, their carefully-planned policy of conditional co-operation with the Parliamentary Radicals would be damaged, perhaps irreparably. Keeping to its policy of non-participation in issues other than political reform, the Association did nothing, and Harney's opportunity had arrived.

After giving notice that he would bring O'Connell's conduct before the Association and prepare a resolution of denunciation, Harney wrote a letter to O'Connell, liberally sprinkled with such epithets as "apostatizing miscreant", demanding that he deny his statements in the Commons. This red rag had its desired effect. The furious Irishman informed his baiter that he had sent his reply to the Working Men's Association with his permission to publish it or not, as they saw fit.[2] Harney had forced an issue on the Association which they had hoped to avoid. In the events which followed one fact remained apparent; the Association did not want to publish O'Connell's reply, nor in fact did they. Harney's motion of censure on O'Connell was buried in committee, and the correspondence was, in effect, suppressed.

After a trial conducted in such a way as to cause its condemnation by Brougham in the House of Lords as a "miscarriage of justice", the Glasgow Spinners were convicted and given a severe sentence of seven years' transportation on 11 January 1838. Considering the great outburst of working-class indignation which followed, and more particularly, the upper-class hostility

---

[1] With outdoor relief withdrawn they would be forced to work for starvation wages.

[2] For this correspondence, see *The Times*, 13 February 1838; letter from O'Connell to John Cleave (n.d.) in the Lovett Collection.

toward trade-unionism which had been evoked through the publicity given to the violent actions of the Glasgow Spinners during their strike, the action taken by Lovett and the Association at this juncture appears to have been a tactical error. Toward the end of January they petitioned the Commons for an inquiry into the subject of associations, or the Glasgow Association. Obviously their intention was to have the conduct of the Glasgow trial investigated, but their demand showed a strange lack of grasp of events. Francis Place, who had been a prime mover in getting the restrictions on combinations removed thirteen years before, wrote in a public letter to Joseph Hume that such an inquiry would be dangerous; and, after a delegation from the Association had called on O'Connell the same day to find out his intentions, the L.W.M.A. took a new line toward the inquiry which O'Connell succeeded in getting.[1] But their first recommendation had already brought down a chorus of execration on their undoubtedly well-intentioned heads.

Augustus Beaumont, the leader of the Newcastle radical movement, accused the L.W.M.A. of being corrupt middle-class coadjutors; and O'Connor, who with his new and highly successful *Northern Star* had attempted to make himself the leader of the agitation against the trial of the Spinners, now returned to London and attacked the Association as "tools of the Whig-Malthusians" in speeches before the Radical Association of Marylebone and the London trades. Harney, in an address printed by the London *Dispatch*, made the line of attack even plainer: the interests of the genuine working class were incompatible with those of the middle class—thus those who attempted any sort of co-operation with the latter were not true working men. This accusation of anti-proletarianism was echoed by O'Connor in the *Northern Star*: "Let those with unshorn chins, blistered hands, and fustian jackets, read . . . [the L.W.M.A. members'] occupations."

On 13 February, Harney's correspondence with Daniel O'Connell appeared in *The Times*, with a postscript by Harney denouncing the leadership of the Association for shielding an enemy of the working class. On the same day the House of Commons responded to O'Connell's pressure, and voted for an inquiry into combinations. It seemed apparent, both from the parliamentary committee's membership, and a searching

[1] For a tacit admission of their error, see Place MS. 37,773, fo. 97.

C

questionnaire sent to manufacturers all over the country, that the misgivings of the trade unions were well-founded. As events turned out, no legislation followed on the committee's hostile findings as the wave of political excitement which washed over the country in the following years absorbed the government's attention; but the whole incident had had its effect.

Events could hardly have been more fortuitous with regard to Harney's determination to disrupt the London Working Men's Association's policy of co-operation with the Parliamentary Radicals. In his attempt to discredit the Association, he had a more mixed success. Lovett's probity was too well known in London to be questioned, as his selection as the secretary to the trade unions' defence committee during the inquiry into combinations showed; but with the powerful propaganda organ of the *Northern Star* giving wide circulation to the charges against the L.W.M.A., its reputation had been clouded to some degree in the north. The Edinburgh Trades Committee, for example, strongly condemned the Association's actions. The main effect of Harney's actions, however, was to bring the internal antagonism in the embryonic working-class political movement farther into the open. Up to this point, O'Connor had remained an honorary member of the L.W.M.A. Now his attack on it as a non-representative élite and Lovett's counterblast, which condemned Feargus as a power-hungry liar who wished to become the dictator of the radical movement, clearly showed the schism which was to divide that movement so fatally.

Obviously there was no question as to where Harney stood in this division. Moreover, his adroit use of the O'Connell correspondence to emphasize the dual nature of the Parliamentary Radicals was evidence not only of the principles which activated him, but of a shrewd and ruthless political sense as well. Harney had only just reached legal manhood when he resigned from the L.W.M.A. following a vote of censure. He did so not only as O'Connor's lieutenant in London, but as the leading exponent of the "true proletarians" of the Metropolis. It was to them that he now turned again to organize a mass following. The events of his youth had given him, in the description of a contemporary, "a bitterness of spirit which breathed in nearly every word he uttered and every line he penned".[1] His new organization was

---

[1] R. G. Gammage, *History of the Chartist Movement*, 2nd edition (London and Newcastle-upon-Tyne: 1894), p. 53.

to embody the beliefs and attitudes which he had absorbed from the miserable streets of Bermondsey, the contents of the unstamped press, the prisons of London and Derby, and the teaching of Bronterre O'Brien.

CHAPTER II

The New Jacobins

ALTHOUGH the activities of the East London Democratic Association had ceased during the stormy period of its leaders' membership in the L.W.M.A., it had never formally dissolved. On its reactivation in May 1838, however, it was evident that Harney, Neesom and Davenport had decided to extend their efforts. The East London Democratic Association now adopted the more inclusive title of the London Democratic Association. Harney emphasized their expansive plans in a letter to the *Northern Star* after his resignation from the L.W.M.A.: "Bronterre has too often been under the necessity of upbraiding the men of London for their disgraceful apathy," he wrote. "Let us hope this lamentable state of things is near its close; *a new organization of the Proletarian Classes of the Metropolis is in progress.*" [1]

In the series of addresses which Harney wrote for the new Association O'Brien's influence was unmistakable. England, Harney declared, was a land of potential plenty, where no person who worked should want—and yet thousands, through no fault of their own, perished for lack of the common necessaries of life. The reason for this lay in the preservation of an artificial state of society through the medium of bad laws, laws which had been passed and were defended by the propertied classes to protect themselves in their "plundering of the productive classes". This evil state of society would never be eradicated until the proletarian classes took their places in parliament and ensured the end of class legislation. [2]

The achievement of political power was, however, but a means to the end of social equality. "We are generally branded as levellers," Harney wrote of the Democratic Association, "to which term—if by it is meant the destruction of inequality, occasioned by the enactment of bad laws—we plead guilty." Only through the abolition of the profit system, the "usurers'

[1] 19 May 1838.
[2] *Operative*, 13 January 1838; *Northern Star*, 24 March, 21 July 1838.
28

exaction of the fruits of the labourers' industry", could social equality be achieved.[1]

As to the economic institutions which would characterize the just society, Harney was not explicit. It was the principle of social equality embodied in Babeuf's doctrine and the substitution of co-operation for competition espoused by Robert Owen, not the systematic organization of society put forward by these men, to which Harney gave expression. "Did he mean that they all should have their food dressed alike, their houses built in parallelograms, their coats having one uniform cut?" he asked an audience in 1839. "God bless you, no such thing. He only meant that all men should have what they earned, and that the man who 'did not work, neither should he eat'." [2] Harney's social criticism was, in essence, destructive; the power of the Association's addresses came from their protest against the capitalist ethic and the exclusion of the working class from political power rather than from specific economic proposals.

The young leader of the London Democratic Association had obviously not been dozing in the "radical school of the 'thirties". The influence of still another teacher is unmistakable, both in Harney's polemical style and certain of his attitudes. The outraged voice of William Cobbett and his hatred of the "Scotch feelosofers"—the *laissez-faire* school—echoed from the past in his pupil's vitriolic attacks. In a characteristic address in the *Northern Star*, Harney described the "political economy" of the middle-class Radicals as

"... a philosophy that reigns in all its hideous supremacy throughout our manufacturing and commercial systems, deforming and slaying labour's sons and daughters, seeking to seduce our young men and maidens from the land of their sires—that they may toil in the swamps of Canada or perish in the wilds of Australia. A pretended philosophy that crushes, through the bitter privation it inflicts on us, the energies of our manhood, making our hearths desolate, our homes wretched, inflicting upon our heart's companions one eternal round of sorrow and sickening despair; nor is this all. When that we shall have arrived at a premature old age, our only reward for all our cares and toils is to be a horrible bastille, where, separated from all that is near and dear to us, we may pine out the remaining period of our existence, exposed to all the brutality which demons could conceive . . .; and then the pauper's funeral, consigned to the earth like dogs, or delivered over to the dissecting knife of the surgeon for the benefit of the rich! Thus does

---

[1] London *Dispatch*, 1 July 1838.   [2] *Northern Star*, 13 June 1839.

this hypocritical, Malthusian philosophy outrage the decrees of heaven, trample upon the best feelings of humanity, and violate all the principles of justice and morality—thus do our scoundrel tyrants pursue us from the cradle to the grave, inflicting upon us all the bitterness of poverty, and then punish us for being poor!" [1]

Why did such a philosophy rule their lives? Harney asked. The answer was the main theme of the Association's propaganda: "The masses are socially, because they are politically, slaves."

Any form of co-operation with the men who held "Malthusian" views thus constituted class betrayal. In a direct attack on the London Working Men's Association's policy of collaboration with the middle-class Radicals Harney put this conclusion bluntly: "Depend upon it, Fellow Democrats, that which our enemies will not yield to justice, they will not yield to *moral persuasion*." The belief in the efficacy of education was equally illusory—"The ruling class will never grant the working class that kind of education by which they will learn their political rights." In short, any means or system which had the support of the middle class would have for its object the perpetuation of the people's slavery.[2] The inescapable conclusion, so far as Harney and the other leaders of the Democratic Association were concerned, was that the working class would achieve a democratic state only through force, or the threat of force. Their recommendation as to one of the first steps which should be taken was boldly printed on their membership cards: "He that hath no sword, let him sell his garment and buy one."

With this programme, the London Democratic Association emerged as one of the most militant of the radical political associations which were springing up as the commercial crisis became more acute. In violence of language such leaders of the burgeoning anti-Poor Law agitation as Richard Oastler and Joseph Rayner Stephens more than equalled that of the Association's leaders, but this movement had not yet been channelled into the demand for political reforms, and neither leader had any faith in democracy as the solution of economic distress. As to the powerful radical political organizations which were coming into being in the summer of 1838—the Edinburgh Radical Association and the Birmingham Political Union, the latter re-activated by its leader during the Reform Bill agitation, the M.P. Thomas

[1] 13 October 1838. *Cf.* Cobbett, in *Cobbett's Two-Penny Trash*, October 1830, p. 31; March 1831, p. 213; July 1831, pp. 20–21.
[2] *Northern Star*, 24 March 1838.

Attwood—middle-class men dominated in their leadership and their policy of action was generally moderate and legalistic. Even Feargus O'Connor, whose recently organized Great Northern Union spoke for more outright measures, considered himself, at least publicly, subordinate to the middle-class Birmingham leaders until the winter of 1838.[1]

The attitudes to which the Democratic Association gave expression were not unique, however. It is true that they found acceptance only among a fraction of the London working classes, but the Metropolis remained a relatively tranquil backwater in the political storm which was now gathering. In the sections of the country where homogeneous working-class groups were found, both those whose occupations lay in relatively large-scale production and those whose skills were being superseded by machinery, anti-Malthusian and "physical force" doctrines found a wide acceptance, as events were to show. Two such disparate observers as Francis Place and Bronterre O'Brien agreed that a large number of the working classes believed the reason for their misery lay in the employing class taking too much of the produce of their labour. This belief, reinforced by the introduction of the new Poor Law—which was considered to be another device to drive down their wages—and brought to a fiery pitch by their increasing misery, led these groups to the same conclusions which Harney was expressing for the Democratic Association.

London, with its greater diversity of occupations acting in some degree as a cushion, never felt the profound shock of the misery which enveloped such groups as the cotton-mill hands of Lancashire, the handloom weavers of Yorkshire, and the iron and colliery workers of Northumberland, Durham, and Wales in the late 'thirties. It was for these men rather than for the relatively well-off artisans of the Metropolis that the Democratic Association spoke. Not that the "true proletarians" to whom Harney directed his addresses did not exist in London. It is doubtful whether an occupational group more miserable and long-suffering than the Spitalfields silk-weavers could have been found anywhere in England. Nor was the new organizational drive of the Democratic Association confined to the weavers. A sampling of one of the Association's meetings made possible by a police raid in the following year reads like a summary of the

[1] Place MS. 27,820, fos. 134, 191.

most oppressed groups of the capital. Among those who gave their occupations when arraigned were a coal-whipper, boot-maker, tailor and porter. Reporting on an East End Chartist procession, a constable laconically assured the Home Office that they were unarmed, for "their clothing was so thin that had they any dangerous weapons about them, I must have observed them".[1]

In the rising political excitement of 1838 these men began to join the Democratic Association in such numbers that within a year the membership was asserted to be over 3,000. From its headquarters—first at 19 Swan Street, Minories, and later at the Ship public house, Temple Bar—three main divisions were organized: the City, Tower Hamlets, and Southwark. These in turn were subdivided into sections which met, as *The Times* reported, "in public houses of a very inferior description". Compared with the deliberately limited nature of the London Working Men's Association, which never exceeded something like 200 members, the new Democratic Association could claim with some justice that it was the mass-party of the Metropolis by the autumn of 1838.

The political efforts of the Association did not preclude their participation in a minor *cause célèbre* which occupied the press in June. The incident, though obscure, throws some light on the state of feeling of both the "respectable" and working classes in that summer of 1838, as well as indicating the depth of ignorance with which working-class leaders were to struggle in the rural districts. Following the attempted arrest of one William Courtenay, alias Thom, who had gained a considerable following among the agricultural workers about Canterbury due to his attacks on the New Poor Law, a pitched battle between the farm labourers and a detachment of troops had resulted in the death of ten of the working men, including Courtenay. This outbreak was the more startling in view of the fact that the southern agricultural districts had been so thoroughly subdued following the unrest there in 1830–31 that they had remained passive amid the growing excitement of the rest of the country.

It was the medieval aspect of the affair and not the economic grievance expressed by this abortive rising which engrossed the attention of Parliament. Courtenay, a man of some education who had been at one time confined in a lunatic asylum, had

[1] Home Office Papers, 40/44, 1839. Hereafter cited as H.O.

represented himself not only as a political and religious reformer, but as a new Messiah, invulnerable to shot and steel. "So completely has he deluded numbers in the neighbourhood . . .," wrote one newspaper correspondent, "that they even now fancy that though he appears dead he will rise on the third day, and lead his followers on to victory." [1] The existence of this "appalling ignorance" almost exclusively monopolized the discussion of the incident in the Commons, one member recommending that "if any unfortunate lunatic should happen to be discharged he should not be allowed to go at large in East Kent, where so many ignorant and fanatic people dwelt".[2] The fact that Courtenay had gained almost 1,000 votes as a Tory candidate in the General Election of 1837 seems to have been tacitly ignored by the M.P.s after its mention in the Commons, but it did not go unnoticed in another quarter.

Bronterre, now writing a weekly letter in the *Northern Star*, noted the fact with mordant pleasure; but he was more concerned with what he saw as the main implications of the affair. Ignoring the messianic aspects of the rising, he pointed out with great force that the bloodshed had followed a series of anti-Poor Law meetings which had been disturbing the quiet of Canterbury for some days previous to the attempted arrest of Courtenay. In the following week's *Northern Star*, a letter appeared from Harney supporting Bronterre's interpretation:

> "We deny that it was fanaticism which caused this gathering of the labourers—it was distress and misery . . . So far from the labourers being 'brutally ignorant', they know too much for their oppressors, and hence this united yell about fanaticism . . . [T]he object in view was to strike terror into the hearts of the peasantry, that without further resistance they may submit to the infamous Poor Law and prepare the way for a rural police." [3]

The Democratic Association followed Harney's letter with a petition to both Houses which stated that the labourers' action was the result of their unbearable misery and prayed for the release of the prisoners being held. Presented in the House of

---

[1] *The Times*, 1 June 1838. This belief was still current almost a year later (Kent *Herald*, quoted in *Northern Star*, 26 May 1839).

[2] Mr. Handley, *Hansard*, 3rd series, vol. XLIII, p. 1116. Cf. speeches by Lord John Russell and Sir Vivian Hussey, *ibid.*, pp. 1101, 1107. Henry Vincent, one of the L.W.M.A.'s missionaries, described the Gloucestershire villagers as being "steeped in ignorance, beer, and superstition" (*English Chartist Circular*, vol. I, no. 18).

[3] 17 June 1838.

Lords by Earl Stanhope, an opponent of the New Poor Law, the petition found one supporter, also an opponent of the New Poor Law. Laughter greeted the mention of the "London Democratic Association" and Lord Teynham's suggestion that the death of ten men deserved an inquiry met with indifference. Without a division the petition was rejected.

It was not to be expected that the prayer of the petition would be granted, but this cursory disposal of the issue was not one to mollify the readers of the *Northern Star*, which had printed the proceedings in detail. As Harney pointed out in one of a series of attacks in the following weeks, this was simply one more example of the justice to be expected from the "class of tyrants of which both the House of Lords and the Kent butchers are made up". William Hill, the editor of the *Northern Star*, drew a similar moral: the working class would get nothing without striking fear into their rulers; moral suasion on their part would be met by force on the government's part.

The incident was an isolated one in the southern rural districts; during the ensuing political excitement they remained unaffected. But while the affair was soon submerged by the flood of events in the agitated areas, to many of those who read the *Northern Star* it had furnished another instance of the callousness of the ruling classes. Whatever the truth in representing the Canterbury incident as one of the increasing number of outbreaks against the New Poor Law, the fact remained that it had been accepted to some extent as such. At an Oldham anti-Poor Law universal suffrage meeting early in July, for example, Courtenay was alluded to as an example of a typical "physical force", anti-Poor Law leader—not the lunatic playing on rural gullibility which he had been depicted in the "respectable" press. This difference epitomized perhaps the most important aspect of the incident; the *Northern Star*, with its national circulation among the working classes now more than 12,000 weekly, had made the "Kent massacre" general knowledge and part of a pattern. In its columns such isolated incidents gained an added significance as part of a larger whole, and working-class Radicals scattered about the country could see themselves for the first time as part of a great movement of men with like ideas.

The affair in Kent shared space in the radical press with news of greater importance. A number of mass meetings in the north indicated that the economic grievances which had found ex-

pression in the anti-Poor Law and Ten Hours' agitations were
taking a specific political form. The "People's Charter", largely
the work of William Lovett, had been published in May 1838 and
widely approved by public meetings and local radical organizations about the country. At a great public gathering early in
August, the Charter was adopted by the Birmingham Political
Union, with whom the L.W.M.A.'s liaison had been close. The
two organizations had already agreed that the Birmingham
Political Union's "National Petition" should embody the Six
Points of the Charter, and resolutions of the Birmingham Political
Union during July gave a definite form to the idea of a national
convention of popularly elected delegates which would present
such a petition to Parliament signed by millions. This organization now set up an executive committee to implement the plan.
The committee was to act as the repository of funds to be raised
by popular subscription—the "National Rent"—and called on
localities to elect delegates at public meetings. A time early in
1839 was set for the National Convention to meet in London and
present the Petition.

The struggle which ensued between the Democratic Association and the L.W.M.A. to control the metropolitan delegation
to the Convention foreshadowed a larger struggle between the
extreme wing of Chartism, headed by O'Connor, and the more
moderate wing represented by the Edinburgh, Birmingham and
L.W.M.A. leaders. O'Connor, however, was as yet preserving
the attitude of neutrality toward the L.W.M.A. to which he had
returned following their altercation early in the year; and a letter
which Harney seems to have written attacking the L.W.M.A.
leaders late in August was refused publication by the *Northern
Star*, which recommended only that "sham patriots of any
description" be avoided as delegates. With this slight comfort,
the Democratic Association turned to the intensification of its
organizational effort.

Meanwhile, Lovett's group, in its usual experienced and
methodical way, had set the time and place for the London election meeting—to be held in Palace Yard, Westminster, on 17
September—and taken precautions to ensure their control. The
content and proposers of the resolutions to be presented to the
meeting were decided on and seats on the platform limited to
ticket-holders. Among those holding tickets were a number of
Radical M.P.s; among those excluded were not only the leaders

of the Democratic Association, but Feargus O'Connor. Compared with this tight efficiency, the efforts of the Democratic Association were amateurish. Finally, in desperation, they tried to persuade Lovett's group to adopt a compromise slate of candidates, but their overtures were rebuffed and the meeting went off as planned.

For the most part the arrangements worked smoothly. The crowd, estimated to number 15,000, listened to sober speeches on the necessity of unity and legality from a succession of moderate delegates representing Edinburgh, Birmingham and Sheffield, and the L.W.M.A. candidates were quickly elected. O'Connor, claiming to speak as the delegate of forty or fifty Scottish and English towns, slowed this smooth-running mechanism briefly through a veiled attack from the crowd on the "moral force men"; and the Newcastle delegate, Robert Lowery—also speaking from the crowd—echoed O'Connor's sentiments in a speech which included a curious metaphor: "The men of the Wear and the Tyne would not draw their swords against their enemies, until their enemies drew upon them; but having put their hand to the plow, they would not look back." [1] But it was obvious that Lovett's group had achieved their aim of speaking for London radicalism in the National Convention with an expert display of organizational skill.

One result of their victory was to bring the thwarted O'Connor's support of the Democratic Association, which had remained covert up to this event, into the open. In speeches at mass-meetings in Manchester and Liverpool in the following week, he described himself as representing not only thousands of men in the north but the Democratic Association. Even more significantly, the powerful influence of his *Northern Star* began to be exerted in the Association's favour. Harney's organization was hailed as the advanced party of the Metropolis and the similarity of its members to the men of Yorkshire and Lancashire heavily stressed; they too were men "with fustian jackets and blistered hands". And, noted the *Star*, they had a larger following than had been thought—a fact which may have influenced Feargus's open espousal. Harney was singled out as the leader in the Association's struggle against the "base and sneaking opposition" which had driven Feargus from London and was trying to split the Chartist movement.

[1] *Champion*, 23 September 1838.

Harney had made himself the leader of left-wing London Chartism, such as it was, and with this new turn of affairs, he began to acquire a national reputation. The value of the *Northern Star's* publicity was immediately proven by an invitation to the Democratic Association from the Norwich weavers and mechanics, which asked that a member might be sent to stand as a Convention candidate. At an Association meeting in late October attended by the ubiquitous O'Connor, Harney was selected. A similar invitation had been extended to the L.W.M.A., which accepted with alacrity and despatched one of their leading members, the radical publisher, John Cleave.

With these invitations to the rival London organizations, the struggle between moderate and extreme Chartism emerged still more openly. There was little question about the issue involved. Lovett, writing to a friend in Hull, declared that they were sending Cleave to oppose "Feargus's man" and subvert O'Connor's attempt to pack the Convention.[1] The struggle between two divergent policies was being transferred from the relatively calm precincts of London to a locality whose atmosphere was that of Yorkshire and Lancashire.

The difference between working-class feeling in London and in Norwich was dramatically illustrated by the manner of the delegates' reception. The procession of 10,000 men which escorted them in a carriage to a meeting-hall carried caps of liberty on poles and strongly-worded banners, and was obviously in no mood for the sort of moderate talk which had gone down so well in Palace Yard. In the carriage with Harney and Cleave rode J. R. Stephens, the ex-Methodist minister who had built up a great popular following as a leader of the anti-Poor Law agitation. Stephens, whose power of impassioned mob-oratory was unparalleled among his contemporaries, responded to the feeling of the meeting with a violent appeal for physical resistance to the New Poor Law. "England stands on a mine—a volcano is beneath her!" he cried, and then in effect exhorted the volcano to explode if further attempts were made to introduce the law into new areas: "Men of Norwich, fight with your swords, fight with pistols, fight with daggers. Women, fight with your nails and your teeth, if nothing else will do . . . husbands

[1] For this letter and Feargus's vehement denial of its accusation, see *Northern Star*, 8 May 1841,

and wives, brothers and sisters, will war to the knife. So help me God." [1]

Harney, an inexperienced orator at this time, could not match Stephens's eloquence, but the tone of his remarks was almost equally sanguinary. Where his speech differed fundamentally from that of Stephens was in its emphasis on political power. To the passionate exponent of resistance to the New Poor Law, political change was incidental—the real remedy for distress lay in the spiritual regeneration of the upper classes. To Harney, the seizure of the state was primary. "They had petitioned too long, they had prayed too long, they now demanded," he told his cheering audience. "They would have the Charter or die in the attempt to obtain it. . . . Petitioning had always failed unless the people backed their petitions by *arguments* not to be misunderstood." [2]

What the *arguments* were Harney made as plain as the tricolour ribbon which he was wearing around his neck; in June 1792 thirty thousand Frenchmen had petitioned for a redress of grievances with pikes and muskets in their hands, and in August the people had arisen *en masse* to support them. The parallel, one which Harney was to use repeatedly in his speeches, was unmistakable; the Chartists should petition as a strongly armed force and revolt if their petition failed. Harney concluded by advising the meeting that they should elect delegates to the Convention who were men "prepared to carry their heads to the scaffold".

With Stephens and Bronterre O'Brien (who was not present), the young incendiary was unanimously elected to represent Norwich. Cleave, it appears, was almost entirely ignored. [3] With this crushing defeat of the L.W.M.A.'s effort, Harney returned to London and began another attempt to arouse the stubbornly apathetic metropolis, in company with O'Connor. Some success attended their effort in the next two months, though compared to the huge demonstrations which were taking place in the north their meetings were very small. But these events were of little moment compared with the open division which threatened the Chartist movement.

Alarmed by the increasingly revolutionary character of the

[1] *Ibid.*, 10 November 1838.
[2] *Operative*, 11 November 1838.
[3] The main accounts barely mention Cleave's activity. This may well have been due to deliberate suppression by the *Northern Star* and by Harney, who seems to have reported the meeting for Bronterre's new paper, the *Operative*.

agitation, the middle-class leaders of the Birmingham Political
Union had strongly condemned the tone of the speeches made
by Stephens and Harney at Norwich; and on 27 November the
entire "physical force" faction was publicly castigated by them—
O'Connor, Oastler and Stephens being condemned by name for
their defence of open arming. Shortly after this, a central meeting of the Scottish Radical Associations on Calton Hill in Edinburgh, dominated by the Edinburgh moderates, repeated the
Birmingham denunciation of physical force. These Calton Hill
resolutions in effect split the Chartist movement, though a
superficial unity continued.[1]

The issue was not one between revolution and legalistic
means. O'Connor was no more ready than Attwood and the
Edinburgh men to make a revolution. It was a question rather
of how pressure short of revolution could best be brought to bear
on Parliament. Men like Attwood and Lovett believed that a
course of mass-petitioning, peaceable meetings and determined
propaganda, with the help of sympathetic Parliamentary Radicals, would eventually accomplish their aim. The function of
the National Convention, as Attwood envisaged it, was to co-
ordinate such a campaign. And while it was true that he spoke
of a "National Holiday" (a general cessation of labour) as a last
resort if other efforts failed, his belief that such an action could
be peaceable and orderly seems to have been sincere. The
moderates believed that exhortations to arm, inflammatory
banners, and such slogans as "peacefully if we can, forcibly if
we must"—by this time an ultra-radical cliché—would alienate
not only Radical support but that of the small-propertied class
which remained unenfranchised.

To the extreme wing, coercion rather than persuasion seemed
the only means to their end. Pleas against actions which would
alienate the middle-class Radicals seemed specious to men who
had seen these Radicals carry out a legislative policy which they
interpreted as one of enmity to the working class. The Radicals
were attempting to take away their right of subsistence under
the old Poor Laws; they refused to "spread work" by their resistance to the Ten Hours' Bill. The Radicals were, in short, the
employing class—the men who took the fruits of their labour

---

[1] Harney wrote twelve years later that the resolutions worked an amount of
evil which could not be recognized at the time, but was never forgotten later
(*Northern Star*, 2 March 1830).

and left them in abysmal poverty. Attwood saw democracy as a means to currency reform; the unemployed cotton-mill operatives saw it as a means to basic social change, however vague and ill-defined. Thus when Daniel O'Connell, the embodiment of economic Radicalism, warmly eulogized the Birmingham leaders for their denunciation of O'Connor, there was no doubt whom these operatives would support. The Birmingham leaders, as the *Northern Star* reiterated, were "O'Connellites"—that is, enemies of the working class.

Economic status had a great deal to do with the division of opinion in the Chartist movement. The moral force exponents, in many cases, did not feel the whip of poverty which was driving such groups as the Yorkshire weavers to desperation as the commercial depression showed no signs of abating. It was this rising feeling to which O'Connor and Harney were giving expression. O'Connor, power-hungry without a doubt, but with a sincere emotional sympathy for suffering, and Harney, conditioned by poverty and soaked in the French revolutionary tradition, were as much followers as leaders of the hordes of suffering men whose great meetings were taking on such a menacing aspect. And it was not the sensible means expounded by Lovett but the threat of physical force which seemed to the unemployed and underpaid to promise immediate relief.

The effect of the Birmingham and Calton Hill denunciations was to unite this support behind O'Connor. Resolutions condemning the attacks flooded in to the radical press from Manchester, Newcastle, Bristol, Leeds, Macclesfield, Carlisle and smaller localities. What was more, schisms appeared where unity had hitherto existed. In Scotland, the Ayr Chartists condemned the central meeting of Scottish Radical Associations which had passed the resolutions on Calton Hill, and the Midlothian Chartists denied the representative nature of the meeting. In Glasgow, O'Connor succeeded in having the condemnatory resolutions rescinded; and even in the stronghold of the Scottish moderates, Edinburgh, he won great applause from a public meeting while the Calton Hill leader, Abraham Duncan, received a mixed reception.

No such disunity affected the Democratic Association over the issue. Harney heatedly attacked the Birmingham and Edinburgh men for dividing the working-class movement and predicted that government coercion would follow this weakening of a united front. But the virus of dissension infected the moderate London Chartists. Within the Working Men's Association, invulnerably united up to this time, Lovett's efforts to take a strong line against Feargus were thwarted; and such leading members as Hetherington, Robert Hartwell, and Vincent—whose contact with the militant Welsh movement had made his views indistinguishable from those of O'Connor—now appeared with Feargus at London meetings which the *Northern Star* reported as being sponsored by the L.W.M.A. Hartwell and Vincent also began an effort to unite the L.W.M.A. with Harney's organization, and a few members, resigning in protest against Lovett's attitude toward physical force, joined the Democratic Association.

The conflict between Lovett and O'Connor and their respective policies came to a head in a public meeting held on 20 December at the Hall of Science, Commercial Road. With the leaders of both the L.W.M.A. and the Democratic Association on the platform, the meeting was also in effect a test of the rival organizations' strength in London. In spite of Lovett's threat during the stormy proceedings to leave the Chartist movement, O'Connor carried the meeting. Within the following weeks the swing of active London working-class opinion away from the L.W.M.A.'s policy was attested by the passage of resolutions supporting physical force—"The Charter, peacefully if we can, forcibly if we must"—by radical associations in Hammersmith, Chiswick, Kensington and Wandsworth. The drift toward extremism was further evidenced by the election of William Cardo, a cobbler with violent opinions, as a delegate to the Convention by the Marylebone Radical Association. Thus when Feargus and Harney sat as the guests of honour at a Democratic Association dinner at the "Ship Tavern" in Bermondsey on 22 December, they could look with some satisfaction at the events which had followed the low point of the Palace Yard meeting two months before. The following evening, Harney left for Newcastle, where the Northern Political Union had invited him to stand as a delegate for the Convention.

Harney's journey to Newcastle conveys something of the hardships which working-class leaders suffered in these years. Leaving London at eight in the evening of the 23rd, the coach did not toil up the steep incline from the Tyne until early in the morning of Christmas Day. During this time, stops were made

D

only to change horses and for meals—which Harney could not afford. Riding on top of the coach through two nights and a freezing day in which snow fell, with only a leather apron buckled across his knees for warmth, he arrived in Newcastle exhausted.[1] After a few hours' sleep Harney made his first real contact with the "men of the North" at a great mass-meeting.

The fact that his revered prototype, Jean Paul Marat, had visited Newcastle some sixty-five years before might have stimulated Harney had he known it;[2] but the political atmosphere of Tyneside, as well as the neighbouring collieries and iron-works of Northumberland and Durham, was sufficiently exhilarating. In the small villages lying out from Newcastle the exhortations to arm were being taken literally. At Winlaton, where the great Crowley works had made a community of iron-workers, a strong tradition of owner-paternalism had been replaced by an extremely class-conscious Chartism, and fowling-pieces, small cannon, stoneware hand-grenades, pikes, and "craa's feet" or caltrops—four-spiked irons which could be strewn in a road to disable cavalry horses—were being turned out in quantities. It was localities like this which, on hearing rumours that troops would be present at the great meeting in Newcastle on Christmas Day, sent couriers to find out if they were to bring their arms with them.

Harney's host, the Northern Political Union—which was to prove one of the best-organized and most resilient of Chartist associations—extended through these villages, and had its headquarters in Newcastle. Here the organization was more complex from a social viewpoint. A greater degree of middle-class participation in the Chartist movement existed in Newcastle than in any other locality in the country, according to O'Connor;[3] a judgment borne out, for example, in the occupation of the Union's treasurer and ardent protagonist, Thomas Horn, who owned a prosperous music store. This political radicalism was not a new thing; the Union had played a very active part in the Reform Bill agitation, on one occasion sending 300 stave-armed men to Durham to break up the Tory opposition at a Reform

---

[1] Augustus Beaumont, whose physical-force *Northern Liberator* had done much to consolidate the Chartist movement in Newcastle, had died from the effects of such a trip in the preceding winter (Place Newspaper Collection, set 56, vol. I, fo. 94).

[2] "Jean Paul Marat in Newcastle", *Monthly Chronicle of North-Country Lore and Legend*, April 1887, pp. 49–50.

[3] *Northern Star*, 29 June 1839.

meeting.[1] It would also seem that the Newcastle working-class Chartists were comparatively well-off in the winter of 1838–39, as they undoubtedly were later in 1839, when no appreciable improvement had taken place in the British economy as a whole.[2] This, one Chartist leader explained, was due to the diversity of "mechanical employments" in which most of the people were engaged. An additional factor in the relative prosperity of the town was the great building programme being carried out in the construction of the beautifully planned Grey and Grainger Streets.

On any simple economic or social grounds one would expect Newcastle's reaction to the Chartist agitation in 1838–39 to have been similar to the tepid participation of London—where comparative prosperity also obtained among the artisans—or a strong moral force line of action. The fact was that Newcastle Chartism was dominated by extreme advocates of physical force, and the town was to prove one of the most revolutionary localities in England. The answer possibly lies partly in what sort of condition constituted "relative prosperity" in this period. In any case the character of Newcastle Chartism was apparent in the appearance and actions of the crowd, an estimated 60,000 to 80,000 strong, which stood in the bright cold weather of Christmas Day and listened to hours of speeches.

This great meeting was typical of those taking place all over the north in the winter of 1838–39. Contingents had marched to the gathering from as far away as Hexham. Colliers and ironworkers from the many small villages up and down the Tyne mingled with delegations of the trades and benefit societies under banners with such slogans as "Liberty! or I shall make my arrows drunk with blood, and my sword shall devour flesh!" and the familiar "He that hath no sword, let him sell his shirt and buy one." The violence of these slogans was matched by the speeches which were unanimous in their condemnation of the Birmingham and Edinburgh moderates. That Harney's reputation as an opponent of the moderate party had reached the north was evident in his introduction to the meeting, his proposer declaring that Harney had "bearded an association in

[1] Ironically enough, this excursion of force had been led by John Fife, the mayor of Newcastle in 1839, who was later knighted for his firmness in handling the Chartists.

[2] *Cf.* H.O. 40/49, Northumberland to Russell, 27 February 1839; Harney, letters in the *Northern Star*, 15, 29 June 1839.

London, which, though it might be honest enough, followed an imbecile and impracticable plan of operation". The *Northern Star's* campaign to discredit the L.W.M.A. as non-proletarian had also had some success, this speaker adding that "those men were well fed, and therefore they relied on moral force; but let them labour for one week, and be ill-fed and clothed, and it would soon convert their moral force to physical force".[1]

Harney's speech, well-salted with French revolutionary allusions, continued this attack on the moral force wing of the movement. Only by the direct action of the men of the north would the Charter be theirs in twelve months, he declared; arms, not petitions, would gain them their ends. And—with a certain amount of prescience—he expressed the Democratic Association's lack of faith in the usefulness of a convention in which two parties of divergent views would be represented: "one party to do for the people, one party to do for themselves".

What the attitude of delegates to the Convention should be Harney had already indicated in his letter accepting the Northern Political Union's invitation: "I go to the Convention determined (so far as I have the power) that the question of universal suffrage shall be finally settled, for I have sworn the oath of a democrat— . . . 'To live free or die!' "[2] The Convention, he had told a meeting of Polish democratic exiles just before his departure from London, should be analogous to the French National Convention of 1793—a revolutionary body which would accomplish by force if necessary, the political demands of the Charter. This was the gist of his speech at Newcastle, as it had been at Norwich, and it was clear in both instances that he was expressing the feeling of those who listened to him. As his Newcastle seconder rather mildly put it, "In that Convention they wanted men of a peculiar character, for the circumstances in which the members might be placed were not those which would be most agreeable. He thought the constitution of Mr. Harney's mind was such as would highly fit him for such a position."[3]

The immense meeting evidently agreed with him, for Harney was unanimously elected with two other strong advocates of physical force, Robert Lowery, a young crippled tailor, who like Harney had been to sea, and Doctor John Taylor, a one-time

[1] *Northern Liberator*, 28 December 1838.
[2] London *Dispatch*, 13 November 1838.   [3] *Northern Star*, 29 December 1838.

naval surgeon from Ayr, and the most exotic figure in the Chartist movement. Taylor—later described by Harney as "a cross between Byron's Corsair and a gypsy king, with a lava-like eloquence that set on fire all combustible matter in its path" [1]— had spent a fortune in his involvement with the Greek revolution of 1829, according to one account.[2] Harney's tricolour sash was conservative by comparison with Taylor's striped coloured shirts, which he wore open at the neck. One of the most determined and popular of the Chartist leaders, Taylor's language was as colourful as his shirts; his Newcastle peroration had concluded with the promise that his last action would be to "write his epitaph upon a tyrant's brow, in characters of blood, with a pen of steel".

The breach between the left and right wings of the Chartist movement discussed in the speeches at this Newcastle meeting had already been widened by the first of a series of cautious steps taken by the Home Office to curb the mounting excitement. Earlier in 1838 Lord John Russell, the Home Secretary, had remarked at a Liverpool dinner that "He did not think the demonstrations [led by O'Connor, Stephens and Oastler] dangerous or blameable; they were nothing more than the natural consequence of the people being released from Tory tyranny and would pass off without mischief if not molested." [3] But by December he had changed his mind sufficiently to ban torchlight meetings—a blow to the Chartists in that it curtailed the number of meetings those in employment could attend. Both Harney and O'Brien had prophesied that such coercive measures would follow the weakening in Chartist unity caused by the attacks on the left wing, and this step seemed to bear them out. The schism between the two sections of Chartist opinion was now further deepened by the arrest of J. R. Stephens, an event which was immediately put down to the divisive efforts of the moderates.

The intensity of working-class reaction to the arrest makes it a nice question if Stephens at large or Stephens in custody was the more dangerous to public order. In the Newcastle district, for

[1] Newcastle *Weekly Chronicle*, supplement, 5 January 1889. Taylor's father, a member of a good Ayrshire family, had married an Indian, according to Harney.

[2] W. E. Adams, *Memoirs of a Social Atom*, 2 vols. (London: 1903), vol. I, p. 211. Francis Place claimed that Taylor had squandered his fortune in the "wildest debauchery", but Place's judgments on all of the physical force leaders show an inveterate prejudice.

[3] Quoted in Derby *Mercury*, 9 January 1839.

example, delegates were dispatched from the villages to the central council of Chartists in Newcastle to find out if they were "to begin"; and even the middle-class Radical press condemned the arrest as either bungling or illegal. The moral force London *Dispatch*, which had somewhat optimistically stated early in December that the exponents of physical force had had their doctrine "exploded", now declared: "Lord John Russell has . . . roused the sleeping lion; let the fault be placed at his door, if its fangs are felt."

If the danger of rioting existed, it was quickly controlled by the physical force leaders themselves. The line taken was shown in a speech by Harney shortly after the arrest. The government's action was an effort to provoke a premature revolution, but "if there is to be an insurrection, it shall be when it suits us, not when it suits them".[1] Yet if no immediate effects of importance followed Stephens's arrest, the long-range effect was unmistakable. Stephens, according to one sour observer of these events, had been throwing O'Connor in the shade in some localities, and his removal left Feargus a clear field.[2] Moreover, the result of the government's action was to increase the strength of the extreme wing of the Chartist movement, both by its example of "Whig repression" and in its removal of an advocate interested rather in the repeal of the New Poor Law than in the Charter.

In this atmosphere of growing tension Harney toured Northumberland and Cumberland in the next weeks, speaking almost daily to the crowds who came to hear and cheer the "delegate of Northumberland and Norwich". It was, he wrote many years later, the "dream-time of his life".[3] Not yet twenty-two, Harney had grown into a slender, intense man with rather delicate features, plainly-marked dark brows, and brown hair, worn long in the fashion of the time. With the tricolour sash or riband which he affected, he presented an appearance not unlike that of the dashing Doctor Taylor; and he seems to have possessed something of Taylor's charm for women. The element of vanity in Harney's character was particularly apparent in his appearances before female audiences, when allusions to his past sufferings were apt to be frequent; but mixed with this appeal was a more solid intellectual argument. Harney's thoroughgoing

---

[1] *Operative*, 13 January 1839.
[2] Place MS. 27,820, fo. 267. [3] Newcastle *Weekly Chronicle*, 30 January 1892.

egalitarianism, like Bronterre's and that of many Chartists, included the belief that women should participate as fully as men in society. And that the attention which he gave to "the fair women" of this or that locality could have concrete results was evidenced by the fact that shortly after his speech at a Newcastle *soirée* on the evening of Christmas Day, in which he exhorted the "women of the north" to participate in the struggle for the Charter, he was the guest of honour at a meeting which saw the birth of the female branch of the Northern Political Union. The plaid presented to Harney on this occasion—"I shall wear it to the National Convention," he said gracefully—was not the last from similar groups.

In winning the approval of the Winlaton iron-workers he was equally successful. These men were to be his warmest supporters, a support which seems to have come from affection as well as respect. Harney, in the words of one contemporary Winlatonian, was "intelligent, pleasant in manners, sanguine in temper, and daring in the execution of projects". Another never forgot his buoyant youthfulness and hearty laughter, as well as his love of singing. For a moment the youth, rather than the political leader, is glimpsed:

> "Nothing pleased him more than to take his partner for a dance at the Highlander Inn. . . . On these occasions he would frequently place his red cap, which he usually wore, on the head of his fair partner and conduct her along the room, delighting the company by his gallantry." [1]

But such idyllic interludes were rare in the month preceding the Convention, which had been scheduled to begin on 4 February. There was nothing light-hearted about his speeches or the temper of his audiences. The men at a moonlight meeting at Winlaton were armed; at Dalston in Cumberland his appearance was advertised by two men accoutred with musket and sword, who marched about playing a fife and drum to attract a crowd which carried heavy sticks and knives to the gathering. Harney spoke to these men as an unequivocal exponent of

[1] William Brown's letter, *ibid.*, 13 February 1897; Isaac Jeavons, quoted in Richard Heslop, "A Chartist Spear", *Monthly Chronicle of North-Country Lore and Legend*, April 1889, p. 149. "He reminded me of the Grecian heroes of whom one used to read," wrote an old Carlisle Chartist more than fifty years later, adding that the memory of Harney's vivid remarks was still fresh in his mind (William Farish, in Newcastle *Weekly Chronicle*, 21 January 1893).

physical force. At Carlisle on New Year's Day he declared to an enthusiastic audience:

> "Rather than live as we now live . . . I will call upon my countrymen to weave no more for their tyrants but their winding sheet—to dig no more but their graves. Three months will bring about the change we seek; and 1839 shall be as memorable in the annals of England as 1793 is in the annals of France."

Returning a week later, he advocated the use of the fire-brand, and gave expression to a belief which had a wide currency: "The soldiers were not to be relied upon; the government knew that they were with the people." [1]

After a brief stop at Hexham, Harney went on to Lancashire and Yorkshire, speaking to meetings at Preston, Bury, Ashton, Stalybridge and Leigh—a short list of the most affected areas of the north. At Bradford, in the middle of January, he was to be found marching at the head of a procession, with a band playing and cottagers cheering, to a meeting with the local Chartist leaders, after which, with O'Connor, he shared the honours at a banquet in the evening. And sometime during these weeks he attended a pre-Convention meeting of northern delegates at Manchester, the proceedings of which were reported only in outline. It seems likely that this was a pre-Convention caucus of the O'Connorite forces.

This tour of the northern counties was climaxed by Harney's arrival in Derby on 21 January. Not until a few months before had a radical association been formed there, and it was due to the desire of this organization for a speaker who could rouse the town that he was invited. After addressing a small group on his arrival, Harney and the association turned to agitating the town and a week later held a mass-meeting. According to a contemptuous leading article in the Tory Derby *Mercury*, the local workmen were too content with their lot to listen to "mercenary agitators" and only 1,200 of the "curious" paraded through town after a band to the meeting. Whatever the objectivity of this report, there was a striking contrast in the circumstances of Harney's return to Derby and his six months' sojourn in the local gaol in 1836.

His speech on this occasion was a typical example of the mix-

---

[1] London *Dispatch, Operative*, 13 January 1839. "The best of the working men with very few exceptions became convinced . . . that in a general outbreak the soldiers would be with them," wrote Place (Place MS. 24,821, fo. 3).

ture of vituperation and sometimes vivid imagery with which he
had regaled his audiences of the preceding weeks. After describing to the meeting the condition in which he had left Derby
before, Harney declared, with what was doubtless a considerable
satisfaction, that he had returned "to look the tyrants in the teeth
in the proud character of a leader of the people". He then went
on to attack the Malthusian creed, to which he attributed the
misery of the working class and the rise of the popular movement:

> "They say we are too many—that population increases faster
> than the means of subsistence. If so, let those leave the land who do
> not labour—let those who work not leave the country, and when
> the Aristocracy betake themselves to Van Dieman's Land, and the
> moneymongers to the devil, take my word for it there will be
> enough for you and me . . . [O]ur country may be compared to a
> bedstead full of nasty, filthy, crawling Aristocratic and Shopo-
> cratic bugs. In answer to our calumniators who say we wish to
> destroy property, I answer that we will not destroy the bedstead,
> but *we will annihilate the bugs*. . . . My friends, we demand Universal
> Suffrage because it is our right, and not only because it is our right,
> but because we believe it will bring freedom to our country, and
> happiness to our homesteads: we believe it will give us bread, and
> beef, and beer. What is it that we want? Not to destroy property
> and take life, but to preserve our own lives, and to protect our own
> property—namely, our Labour." [1]

This expression of the political and economic rights of the
working classes concluded with an inflammatory exhortation to
prepare for violence:

> "Universal suffrage there shall be—or our tyrants will find to
> their cost that we will have universal misery. . . . We will make
> our country one vast, howling wilderness of desolation and destruc-
> tion rather than the tyrants shall carry out their infernal system.
> I have given you to understand that the men of the north are armed.
> I invite you to follow their example. . . . Believe me, there is no
> argument like the sword—and the musket is unanswerable."

For the third time a mass-meeting signified its agreement with
such sentiments by electing Harney its delegate to the Convention. An attack on his violent language by a new radical
organization in Bethnal Green the following week received the
angry reply from a Derby Chartist that Harney's tour through
the north had been "one continued march of triumph, and . . .
his reception in Derby, even in hitherto apathetic, degraded,

[1] *Northern Star*, 9 February 1839.

priest-ridden Derby has been most enthusiastic". The young firebrand had roused them from a "slavish sleep".[1]

Harney had left London little more than a month before. During that time he had advanced considerably toward a national reputation as a leader of the extreme left wing. During his absence the efforts of Vincent and Hartwell to unite the L.W.M.A. and the Democratic Association had proved abortive, but the organizational effort in the East End had not flagged. Furthermore, their actions in January had revealed something of the role which the L.D.A. leaders thought their organization should play in the Convention. Their proposal that all of the London divisions should select candidates in the event of "division in, or secession from" the Convention was a plain indication that they had not accepted the Palace Yard election as the final word in their struggle with the London moderates.

As early as December 1838, in his speech before the Polish exiles, Harney had made his idea of the functions of the Democratic Association during the Convention clear: "Be assured that as the Gallic Convention of 1793 required a Jacobin club to look after it, so will the British Convention of 1839 require the watchful support of the Democratic Association." [2] "Watchful support" obviously meant more than the protection he had told the Christmas Day mass-meeting in Newcastle the L.D.A. would give to the Convention. His organization would act to ensure the Convention's revolutionary action, if that were necessary. He had frequently expressed doubts about the courage or willingness of the moderates to lead the movement in the event that legal measures failed, a contingency he regarded as inevitable. It seems evident from this, as well as from their future actions, that Harney and the Association saw the Convention as purging itself—or being purged—of the moderates, at which time they, as the extreme left, would supplant the London delegates and in combination with the other advocates of physical force make the Convention the leader of the revolution which would follow.

The "Jacobinism" of the Democratic Association on the eve of the Convention was not limited to its determination to act as a "Mountain". With the possible exception of the L.W.M.A., it was also the most internationally-minded of the English radical associations. This was evident not only in the tricolour and cap of liberty under which the Association marched to its demon-

---

[1] *Operative*, 3 February 1839.   [2] *Ibid.*, 9 December 1838.

strations and with which it decorated its meeting room in Ship Yard, Temple Bar, but in its actual connection with the main body of political exiles in London, the Polish refugees of the revolution of 1831–32. Harney's association with the Poles—one of the most profound influences of his life—had begun four years before, and during the interim he had become a member of the Polish Democratic Society, apparently the only Englishman ever to do so.[1] As early as July 1837 the two organizations had spon-sored a joint meeting and by the summer of 1839, if not before, at least two members of the Polish Democratic Society had be-come active in the L.D.A.[2]

The addresses exchanged between the Poles and Harney's organization in 1837 had stressed the international community of working-class interests, and conversely, the solidarity of the ruling classes. An incident late in 1838 provided what was con-sidered to be a convincing illustration of this concept. The Polish exiles, split into democratic and conservative factions, were supported in cases of need by a Treasury fund, which until the autumn of 1838 had been administered by the Literary Society of the Friends of Poland, headed by Lord Dudley Stuart and closely connected with the aristocratic faction under Prince Czartoryski. At that time the Treasury decided to take over the fund's administration, and Stuart was asked by the government to provide them with information on those Poles who ought not to receive further relief. The result was that the Poles who were participating in Chartist affairs were struck from the aid-roll. The government's refusal to support refugees who were aiding an increasingly threatening political agitation is understandable, but to the democratic Poles and the Democratic Association the implications of Stuart's and the government's actions were too obvious to be missed. As Harney dramatically put it as the lead-ing speaker at the Polish banquet of 3 December:

"[The Polish and English aristocracy] have established a verit-able reign of terror, under which every Pole who dares to avow himself a democrat and assert the universal rights of man, is per-secuted to the death. I denounce Dudley Stuart as a false friend and a real enemy of Poland, because he is the enemy of the working-classes of England, and no enemy of the English working-man can be a friend of the exiled Pole." [3]

[1] *British Press and Jersey Times*, 24 April 1863; *Northern Star*, 26 December 1846.
[2] H.O. 40/44, police report of 3 May 1839; *Operative*, 16 June 1839.
[3] *Operative*, 9 December 1838.

Also present at this banquet was a delegation from the Working Men's Association. So far from the Democratic Association on domestic issues, the L.W.M.A. was at one with it in international views. Written by Lovett, the addresses of the L.W.M.A. to the European working classes dated from 1836 and may well have formed the model for Harney's first address. Their messages were the same: "Fellow-producers of wealth", stated one of Lovett's declarations, "seeing our oppressors are united, why should not we too have our bond of brotherhood and Holy Alliance?" [1]

Both the Polish Democratic Association and another body of exiles, the Union of French Democrats, saw in the upsurge of working-class political agitation in England a harbinger of European revolution [2]—as did Marx and Engels some years later. How widespread the reciprocal feeling of being part of a European movement was, outside of the Democratic Association and the L.W.M.A., is difficult to assess. Scattered evidence of internationalist sympathies in the provinces in 1838–39 does exist, and Harney's references to the Chartist role of *avant-garde* to the European working-class and nationalist movements elicited applause at the meetings he addressed. [3] But it can hardly be said that the Democratic Association's advanced internationalism was typical of the Chartist movement as a whole.

The French revolutionary influence which was so marked a characteristic of the Democratic Association was more pervasive. Many of the Chartist leaders had been among the young men who had drawn inspiration and hope from the July Revolution of 1830; and the petitioning of the French National Guard for an extension of the suffrage in 1838—interpreted by the Chartist left-wing as an example of "petitioning with sword in hand"—had received wide publicity in the Radical press. [4] The common belief that the soldiers would be with the people in the event of a rising probably owed as much to its propagation during the Reform Bill agitation as to the example of 1793 or 1830; but an

[1] Place Newspaper Collection, set 56, vol. I, fo. 103. The earliest such declaration seems to have been the L.W.M.A.'s "Address to the Workers of Belgium", printed in the *Constitutional* (London) and translated and distributed in Belgium despite police repression (Place MS. 27,819, fo. 45).

[2] *Charter*, 28 July; *Northern Star*, 17 August 1838.

[3] For evidence of this kind, *cf. Operative*, 11 November 1838; *Northern Star*, 9 February, 11 May, 15 June 1839.

[4] Place MS. 27,820, fo. 197.

alternate belief—that armed civilians could defeat trained troops —was common among the more extreme Chartist leaders, and the French example here was likely the main influence. Certainly the caps of liberty on poles at Chartist meetings and the common appellation for the new poor-houses—"Bastilles"—had their origin across the Channel; and negative evidence of French revolutionary influence is indicated by the fact that it was thought worth while to publish counter-propaganda which stressed the baneful effects of the Revolution of 1789 on the French workers.[1]

But Harney and the Democratic Association were without doubt much more extreme in this respect, as in their international views. The Charter and the amelioration of their misery, and not the achievement of the "liberty of a world of republics and the happiness of the human race", which Harney put as the ultimate aim of the L.D.A., absorbed the attention of the great majority of Chartists. This latter-day Jacobin club could therefore look on itself with some justice as the representative of the extreme left in the events which now followed. As their main spokesman, and representing the extreme opinion of Newcastle, Norwich and Derby, Harney stood as the leader of the most radical wing of the National Convention when it met on 4 February 1839 in London.

[1] See, e.g., *The People's Charter and Old England Forever* (Cheltenham: 1839). Pamphlet in H.O. 40/57. This copy states "22,000 printed".

CHAPTER III

Legalism and Revolution

THE anonymous artist who sketched the "General Convention of the Industrious Classes" as it met for its first sitting at the British Coffee House, Cockspur Street, saw a long, high-ceilinged council room, with the winter sun streaming in through tall windows, and a fire burning in a huge fireplace.[1] The sedateness and respectability of the room was matched by the soberly-dressed, predominantly middle-aged men who either sat about the table which stretched the length of the room or stood chatting seriously in small groups, indistinguishable in appearance from a meeting of the English and Foreign Bible Society. If he had expected to see here the "horny-handed, clothed in fustian", the appearance of the gathering must have surprised him. The contrast between this group and the starving and turbulent mass of men it represented was an incongruous one—and this impression persists in the gulf between the subsequent actions of the delegates and the urgency of the conditions which had brought the Convention into being.

Unanimity was lacking from the first in the delegates' ideas of what the real function of the Convention was to be. The Birmingham men, who had originally envisaged themselves as the dominant force in the Convention, had seen the control of the movement drift steadily into the hands of the more extreme wing under O'Connor. They were not, in fact, to play any significant role in the Convention, participating in its proceedings only sporadically and resigning when they found themselves unable to play the role they wished.

Yet this inability of the strongest section of the moderate wing of Chartism to dominate the Convention did not indicate that a "physical force" group with an integrated organization and an agreed policy existed. It was apparent that O'Connor, the leader with the greatest national following, had no plan. He had not even a consistent body of principles on which to base his

---

[1] This drawing is reproduced in Adams, *Memoirs of a Social Atom*, vol. I, p. 154; and Gammage, *History of the Chartist Movement*, frontispiece.

actions, unless this was the principle of personal power. Even Bronterre O'Brien, without doubt the most brilliant of the Chartist delegates, found himself forced by events to negate whatever was consistent in the Convention's directives. Harney's forebodings as to the usefulness of a body composed of such divergent elements were well-founded.

The lack of unity in the Convention made itself evident almost at once, the initial majority of moral force delegates electing Lovett secretary over the protests of O'Brien and Harney's associate, Neesom.[1] Lovett, O'Brien said, was a fine man personally, but ". . . it was notorious that the Working Men's Association, to which Mr. Lovett belonged, differed very considerably from large masses of the people in the north, as to the means by which the objects of the Convention should be carried out." Well aware of the danger of schism, he added that as an exponent of unity he would also have protested against a London Democratic Association candidate, as being unacceptable to other delegates in the Convention.[2]

Harney took no part in this argument, nor in the debates over organizational matters which followed. With Doctor Taylor, he had experienced some difficulty in taking his seat due to a committee ruling that only representatives whose constituents had provided either National Rent or signatures to the National Petition should be recognized as delegates. Forty delegates out of the fifty-four elected had presented more than half a million signatures and over £1,000 "rent"; but Harney, though now on salary from the Northern Political Union, had presented neither.[3] Through O'Brien's intervention the two men were finally accepted on condition of their qualifying under the rule within a month, and Harney took his seat as the delegate of Northumberland, Derby and Norwich.

His non-participation in the initial meetings of the Convention did not preclude more significant activity, however. Sometime during these first days Harney was allying himself with William Rider, the Yorkshire extremist, and Richard Marsden, a weaver and delegate from Preston. When the Convention moved to Bolt Court, Fleet Street, and the delegates found habitual seats,

[1] Neesom had been elected from Bristol, thus giving the Democratic Association two delegates in spite of their having been ignored at Palace Yard.

[2] *Charter*, 10 February 1839.

[3] The poorer delegates were evidently paid by their "constituents". The two pounds a week which Harney received was a comfortable sum for the time.

Harney and these two men, along with Neesom, sat as a group
on the extreme left of the Chairman's table—a position deliberately chosen for its historical associations. The young radical
had wasted no time in forming a "junta" which could act as
representative of the Democratic Association's viewpoint.

The critical or destructive role of the Association as a Jacobin
club was held in abeyance until it was seen what the Convention
intended to do. In an address of 19 February the Association
pledged its intention to defend the Convention "with its blood,
if necessary"; and, in fact, the first real decision of the Convention gave no cause for criticism from Harney's viewpoint. A
week after the first sitting, J. P. Cobbett, William Cobbett's son
and one of the Manchester delegates, moved that the Convention
should discuss no measures but the actual presentation of the
Petition, which meant that in the event of the Petition's rejection,
the Convention should dissolve. The vote against the motion
was overwhelming, an indication of the almost unanimous belief
that the Petition would be rejected and further measures necessary to achieve the Charter. Cobbett then resigned, the first of
a number of defections which followed as the Convention slowly
swung to the left.

For the time, however, the potentially divisive problem of just
what measures were to be taken on the Petition's rejection was
postponed, the Convention turning its attention to the agitation
of London. The apathy of the capital had obviously come as a
shock to the provincial delegates, who laid this condition to the
better wages and more regular employment of the London
artisans. Harney had little faith in more meetings and resolutions—his belief was that action alone would rouse the London
working classes—but he could scarcely oppose the attempt to
arouse the metropolis, and the Democratic Association co-
operated in the plan.

The response to the delegates' efforts was disappointing. It
was the "better classes" rather than the artisan class which
attended the meetings; those held in predominantly working-
class districts were scantily attended. A police observer of a
meeting held in a small public house reported one of the Convention delegates as speaking "in a desponding tone of the want
of sympathy displayed by the London working men".[1] Harney's
following, however, remained intact and enthusiastic. The

[1] H.O. 40/44, report of 25 March 1839. *Cf., ibid.,* reports of 19, 29 March.

Democratic Association's meetings were large, and their speakers took advantage of the situation by constantly emphasizing the point that support for the Convention could best be accomplished by joining the Association. Harney, as the leader of the only mass-organization in the metropolis, was ensuring that it remained an effective amplifier for his voice in the Convention.

Their failure to arouse the London working classes doubtless increased the delegates' awareness that support for the Charter was not as broad as they had believed. In the mood of optimism which characterized the first weeks of the Convention, such proposals as O'Brien's plan to have a joint meeting of members of the Convention and Members of Parliament had seemed to hold much promise. Even Harney backed this proposal, doubtless due to the way in which it was presented: the members of the true "People's Parliament" would meet the "sham Parliament" as equals. But the sanguine atmosphere in which such plans seemed fruitful steadily evaporated, and by the end of February, with signatures to the National Petition being added very slowly, it was decided to delay its presentation while missionaries were sent to rouse the dormant areas. Harney was not one of those chosen, obviously due to his extreme views and language; but the Convention's decision to peacefully propagandize for a longer period convinced him that the time had come to exercise his Jacobin role and to force the Convention to consider what seemed to him the really vital problem of direct measures.

At a meeting on 28 February held by the Democratic Association at the Mechanics' Hall, Harney, Rider and Marsden introduced resolutions directed at the Convention which were unanimously passed. Harney's resolution declared without preamble that the Charter could become law in a month if the people and their leaders acted, and called for immediate resistance to all acts of oppression. Rider emphasized this urgency, concluding: ". . . we hold it to be the duty of the Convention to impress upon the people the necessity of an immediate preparation for ulterior measures".[1]

Uproar and an almost universal condemnation of the resolutions and their authors followed in the Convention. One of the Manchester delegates, J. R. Richardson, excoriated those who were trying to involve them in a revolution not of their making.

[1] *Operative*, 10 March 1839. *Cf.* Marsden's letter in the *Northern Star*, 4 March.

E

"There were individuals in the Convention who formed a junta," he cried, "a band of conspirators, who held ulterior measures independent of the Convention as their principle objects." Harney's waving of a dagger over his head at one of the London meetings was attacked by another member; and a third declared that Harney had sworn before a crowd "By God, London was ready . . . and if the Convention meant to trifle away any more time, he would tuck up his sleeves and begin." [1]

The virtual unanimity of the Convention in condemning Harney's actions was not due only to the fears of the moderates. The presumption of the young extremist and his clique in forcing consideration of the crucial matter of direct action antagonized more extreme members. Among others, Bronterre and Whittle, the editor of the *Champion*, were in no position to throw stones at those who advocated arming and coercive measures. But O'Brien believed that discussion of the resolutions by the Convention at this juncture would destroy its unity. The value of a unity which so effectively hamstrung the Convention—which was the gist of Harney's viewpoint—Bronterre did not attempt to describe. The fact was that Harney's junta stood in a stronger position than many of the Convention wished to admit: their resolutions might be impolitic, but what, after all, was the Convention's policy?

This weakness reflected itself in the final upshot of the affair. Asked to apologize to the Convention, Harney answered flatly, "I distinctly and deliberately state that I will not make any such apology"; and so with Rider and Marsden. The reaction to Hetherington's attempt to have a vote of censure passed on the three men and Whittle's motion that they be expelled revealed that there was an increasing amount of support for Harney's group; and the final act, in which the Convention accepted "apologies" which contained no word of regret or disclaimer, really solved nothing.

Harney's unregeneracy was even more blatant in a "Manifesto to the Democracy of Northumberland, Norwich and Derby" which appeared in the *Northern Star* and the *Operative* soon after. An uncompromising reiteration of the need for force, it showed that he had become even more openly the advocate of direct action. The proposal that delegates confer with some

[1] *Morning Chronicle*, quoted in Harney's letter to the *Operative*, 31 March; *Northern Star*, 9 March 1839.

of the Radical M.P.s—to which he had given his support in Bronterre's version of the plan—was now condemned as a miserable farce and dangerous delaying tactics. And, answering those who had attacked the violence of his language the previous week, he sarcastically referred to delegates who had "one set of speeches for the north, another set of speeches for the metropolis". This defiance was repeated in a speech which he made to a meeting of 3,000 at the "Crown and Anchor" on 16 March. The date of the presentation of the National Petition to Parliament, 6 May, should be the last day for doubt or hesitation, Harney declared. "The people should then set about asserting their rights in earnest and should have before the end of the year universal suffrage or death." [1]

Although Harney had been unable to force the issue between the two factions in the Convention to a head, the public meetings and resolutions attacking the procrastination of the Convention exerted an indirect pressure which brought about another of the Democratic Association's ends: the "purging" of some of the middle-class delegates. According to Lovett, it was this pressure which caused Feargus O'Connor to propose the "Crown and Anchor" meeting of the 16th. Harney's remarks on the occasion were matched in violence by those of men who had attacked the junta's resolutions an inconsistency of behaviour which did not escape some of the readers of the Convention's proceedings— with the direct result of the resignation of the Birmingham moderates from the Convention. The actions of Harney's group had been well-timed in their expression of a growing popular discontent with the "empty speech-making" of the Convention. He could now point to his prophecy that the men of property within the Convention would desert when they thought their property was in danger.

The ambivalence of men like O'Brien and Doctor Taylor— their moderation within and extremity without the Convention —may have been due not only to their desire for unity, but to their scrupulousness about endangering the delegates as a whole. Signs of a growing governmental watchfulness were becoming apparent. The opening of delegates' mail, a process almost impossible to conceal, had been going on in the case of the old radical Warwick clergyman, Doctor Wade, as well as Richardson, Hartwell and Vincent since February; and the public meetings

[1] *Charter*, 24 March 1839.

in London were being reported upon by police-spies.[1] The activity of spies was an old story to most of the delegates, and the realization that they were once again being employed engendered an atmosphere of increasing fear and suspicion. When to this is added the anxiety of the moderate Chartists about being involved in an insurrection and their belief that those who preached violence were little short of criminal, it is not strange that the use of the epithet "spy" became increasingly common.

At one time or another almost all of the extreme Chartist leaders were to be so labelled, but Harney enjoyed the dubious distinction of being first. The accusation, a direct outgrowth of the furore caused by the junta's physical force resolutions, was levelled by a short-lived Radical paper with strong moral force views, the *Chartist*.[2] The opinion was getting about, a leading article claimed, that Harney was a paid government agent. As proof, the anonymous writer could only give "guilt by association":

> "We do not pretend to be able to prove this charge by regular testimony—it is a charge which, from its very nature, cannot be so proved; but we look to his acts, we look at his conduct, at his headlong violence, at his insane harangues. We ask what object the man can possibly have? why should he wish to bring us all within the power of the police?"

The only answer, the *Chartist* concluded, was that he was being paid to do this.

The acceptance of such grounds for the accusation would automatically have rendered almost all of the speakers at the "Crown and Anchor" meeting of 16 March, to take one of many instances, liable to the same charge. Harney, in Norwich to consult his supporters when the attack appeared, could only reply scathingly, "The vile scribe in question unblushingly avows that he has no means of proving his charge," and with no specific accusations, no specific rebuttal was possible.[3] Short of a libel action, scarcely the resort of a man with the temporary income of two pounds per week, and in any case a ridiculous course in the rough and tumble of Chartist politics, he had no recourse.

Public reaction to the *Chartist's* charge was slight. The

[1] H.O. 79/4, Entry Books, secret and private, contain the warrants for opening mail. Copies of the delegates' letters are to be found in H.O. 40/53.

[2] 15 March 1839. Not to be confused with the *Charter*, the new organ of the L.W.M.A.

[3] *Operative*, 31 March 1839.

Northern Political Union did not see fit to comment, though a resolution of support came from the Newcastle female radical association, as well as that of Norwich; and the Heywood Democratic Association and the Heyworth Chartists rebutted the accusation. But the insidiously damaging nature of such attacks was shown by the persistence of the rumour. When Harney was charged with seditious speech in Birmingham four months later, four out of six men who testified in his defence stated that they had gone to hear him speak because they had heard that he was a spy. His speech had been sufficient to convince them of the falseness of the rumour, but the incident showed that the seed sown by the *Chartist* was not barren.

The only inference by which the charges of the *Chartist* could have had any substance would be that the Home Secretary was using *agents-provocateur* to precipitate a premature uprising in the early months of 1839. On the contrary, Lord John Russell was bending every effort to limit, not extend, the power of the extreme leaders. Shortly after the "Crown and Anchor" meeting, for example, he inquired of the law officers of the Crown if speeches delivered by certain Convention delegates made possible their prosecution; and a few months later he moved against the *Northern Star* after similar inquiries as to the possibility of quashing its reports of violent speeches.[1] In this light Harney's next action was hardly that of a government agent, for on 13 April, in conjunction with J. C. Coombe, the secretary of the Democratic Association, he brought out the first issue of the London *Democrat* the most extreme of the Chartist papers.

A small penny weekly which was unstamped and thus carried no current news, the London *Democrat* was Harney's first essay at journalism, apart from his reports which had been printed in the radical press. Coombe seems to have acted as the business manager and later the publisher, but Harney's influence was dominant in the four issues with which he was connected.[2] While he admitted semi-apologetically in an introductory leader that he was "uneducated, in the usual meaning of the term", his journalistic talent was apparent. In the contemporary radical style—a style which suggests modern Communist propaganda—his writing was somewhat over-loaded with invidious descriptive

---

[1] H.O. 49/8, 6 April, 25 July 1839.
[2] Although the London *Democrat* was published until 8 June, Harney's connection with it ceased after the issue of 4 May.

terms: "blood-stained kings", "tyrant aristocrats", "hypo-critical, lying, persecuting priests", and "scoundrel-cannibal usurers" were flayed weekly in his articles. But Harney's columns were vivid and readable; his flair may be noted by comparison with Coombe's efforts, which were pathetically dull and limited.

The tone of the London *Democrat* was revolutionary and inter-nationalist. Major Beniowski, the Polish democrat who had joined the Democratic Association, wrote a history of the Polish revolution of 1830–31 in the first numbers, while Harney con-tributed a series on the first French Revolution. No advocate of the Ranke school of history, Harney frankly stated that his purpose was to show these deeds of the past "so that in the revolution which will speedily take place in this country, my countrymen will learn to avoid the errors and to imitate the heroic, god-like deeds of the sons of republican France". His analysis of the revolution and its analogy with the conditions of 1839 admittedly derived in part from O'Brien:[1] if the English middle class did not concede working-class demands, they, like their French counterparts, would be responsible for provoking the bloodshed which would follow.

The most interesting of the ideas expressed by Harney in the *Democrat* was a rudimentary statement of the class-struggle in history. Instead of the Cobbettite (and O'Connorite) nostalgia for a golden age which had been superseded, Harney described the past as a long process of exploitation, "one never-ending conspiracy" against the working classes in which priests, kings and aristocrats had finally been succeeded by the "profit mon-gers". "In all ages, in all countries, with but rare and mo-mentary exceptions, the many have been slaves of the few," he wrote. The lesson was obvious: the many would end their slavery only by overthrowing their latest rulers, the middle class.

Direct armed mass-action was the policy repeatedly advocated by the London *Democrat* to achieve this end. When in the latter part of April a dissolution of Parliament was rumoured, Harney took the opportunity to advocate Bronterre's old election plan: the selection of a real People's Parliament at the hustings by the entire population, with a body-guard of thousands of armed men to see that they were seated. In the same issue, Beniowski, who was to figure in a shadowy way in the insurrectionary plans of

[1] His other main sources: Arthur Young, Shoberl, and the "liberal, stock-jobbing, mountebank Thiers".

late 1839, began a series of articles on military science, in which his theorizing was illustrated by such apt examples as that of an attack on London from the north. All this was dangerous enough, but even more so was the *Democrat's* printing of a letter signed "Irish Soldier" which requested that an organizer be sent to Woolwich by the Democratic Association, and a report of a Chartist meeting presided over by an army sergeant, at which seventy soldiers had declared that they would not fight the people.[1] Harney pointed the moral of this dubious evidence of military disaffection by recalling the revolutionary role of the French National Guard.

The London *Democrat's* advocacy of revolution was matched by the Democratic Association's actions. As early as April their preparations for participation in an armed demonstration had begun, the date selected being 6 May—that is, immediately after the presentation of the National Petition. There was nothing clandestine about the significance Harney attached to this date; in the *Democrat* of 20 April, he told his readers, "The Sixth of May is approaching ... Listen not to the men who would preach delay ... ARM! ARM! ARM!" The record of the L.D.A.'s actual arming, however, exists only in the reports of police-spies to the Home Office.

The lack of caution on the part of those plotting against order is one of the most surprising aspects of these reports—a generalization which is even truer so far as some of the outbreaks in the winter of 1839–40 are concerned. The Democratic Association had been infiltrated in January 1839, at which time a member of the Metropolitan Police, one "P.C. 113", became a member.[2] In the debate over the junta's resolutions in the Convention, Harney had been told by one delegate that his organization contained police-spies, a declaration which he heatedly denied. Yet it seems that in addition to the regular policeman there was another paid informer—Edward Goulding, who later played a leading part in the affairs of the Association and acted as an *agent-provocateur* early in 1840. Under these circumstances, the leaders of the L.D.A. were almost asking for the noose or transportation in the case of any actual outbreak,

[1] The authenticity of the letter is questionable, as is the report, which was in a letter from Harney's colleague, William Rider.
[2] H.O. 61/22, Metropolitan Police Correspondence, 4 January 1839. *Cf.* report of Bethnal Green court hearing, *Northern Star*, 25 January 1840.

although the possession or manufacture of arms in itself was not illegal.[1]

At a meeting on 13 April of the Association's council an anonymous seller of pikes brought a sample to be examined; and a week later at the "Hole-in-the-Wall", a public house in Fleet Street, Harney, with Coombe, Ireland and Beniowski, again met the man. " 'P.C. 113' overheard Harney say on the staircase to this man that he must have them all ready by the next Thursday [25 April]," the report stated.[2] At a meeting of the council on the same evening, Harney discussed the public demonstration which was to take place on 6 May—the "Great Day"—and told those who wished to form a defence in case of police attack to meet him at his house in Kennington Cross to make arrangements. It would seem, however, that it was an armed demonstration and not a deliberate uprising which was contemplated on 6 May. Though rumours of a national demonstration were widespread, so far as can be told from spy-reports Harney was not in contact with any other locality; and his actions were probably directed to rousing the "brown jackets" of the Metropolis, an effect which he believed would be produced only by demonstrations of force.

While these preparations were going on, Harney and the Association did not relax their efforts to achieve complete control of London Chartism and to influence the Convention. The methods used were simple but ingenious, and showed that Harney and his colleagues had learned much about political infighting since the Palace Yard meeting. At a mass-meeting of all the London radical associations held on 16 April to create a Metropolitan Radical Association—a union which had been strongly urged by some of the Convention delegates—Harney and his followers swamped the other delegations and succeeded in having a motion passed which threw the whole organization of London into their hands. Three days later, Coombe announced that the West London Democratic Association, also

[1] See, e.g., the instructions of the Home Office to the magistrates of Cockermouth: they could not prosecute pike-manufacturers or seize stores of arms unless they had proof that the weapons were to be used for purposes dangerous to the public peace (H.O. 41/14, 15 July 1840).

[2] H.O. 40/44, 14 April 1839. This pike-seller was also a profiteer, asking four shillings each—an exorbitant price for a pike, which could be made for one shilling. For profiteering in pikes, cf. W. Napier, *Life of Sir Charles Napier*, 4 vols. (London: 1857), vol. II, p. 6. The starving Loughborough weavers were running penny-a-week clubs to buy arms at this time (H.O. 40/44, 20 March 1839).

a physical force group, was to pool their finances and membership with them. But this was the high-spot of the effort. The
other small groups, including the L.W.M.A., refused to accept
the decision of the mass-meeting, founding instead a rival organization, the Grand Metropolitan Charter Association. Nevertheless, the effort had not been entirely fruitless. Not only had an
alliance been set up with the West Londoners, but Harney had
also demonstrated that in a public show of strength the L.D.A.
was the dominant London working-class organization.

This strength was shown again in the Association's attempt to
increase their representation in the Convention through the
election of new delegates. Their opening gambit was a letter
written by Thomas Ireland which appeared in the *Operative* of
14 April, raising again the representative nature of the London
delegation. A few days later, at a meeting held on Kennington
Common under the aegis of the L.W.M.A. to elect a new delegate for East Surrey, the Democratic Association, which had
marched to the Common in thousands with banners flying, succeeded in completely dominating the proceedings and elected
one of their leaders, Joseph Williams.

The introduction of Williams to the Convention provoked a
storm of protest, in which much of the L.D.A.'s manœuvring
came to light. Lovett revealed that the Democratic Association
was planning to elect delegates from Stepney, Smithfield and
other localities; and Fletcher, the Bury delegate, claimed to have
proof that there was a conspiracy of "self-styled Jacobin clubs"
to pack the Convention. The occasion was taken for a renewal
of personal attacks on Harney, Cleave decrying the "Marats" of
the Convention, and another delegate deploring Harney's wearing of a red cap at the public meetings which the L.D.A. was
holding. Harney met the attacks frontally. He was proud to
wear the red cap—"an emblem under which mankind had won
the most glorious victories over tyranny"; and, so far as the
elections were concerned, the Democratic Association had never
accepted the mode in which the L.W.M.A. delegates had been
admitted.[1]

O'Connor backed Harney in the admission of the new delegate, remarking that "if Jacobin clubs or the Democratic Association could infuse fresh zeal into the Convention, so much the
better". That his support was sufficient to win Williams a

[1] Debate of 23 April, *Operative*, 28 April 1839.

conditional seat was an indication of the weakening of the Right in the Convention. Throughout April the strength of the moderate party had steadily diminished through resignations; in some of the sittings barely twenty of the original fifty-four members who had been elected were in their seats. But those who remained were by no means united under O'Connor, as the last act in Harney's attempt to "Jacobinize" the Convention showed.

When, on 6 May, the junta introduced a newly-elected delegate from the Tower Hamlets, the Convention refused by a large majority to allow his seating. This result was in part due to the opposition of the moderates, but the number of provincial delegates of all shades of opinion voting against the new member suggests that the already disproportionate number of London representatives was also a factor. The same day also saw the failure of Harney's attempt to arouse the "brown jackets" of the Metropolis by a display of force.

The mass-meetings of the Democratic Association in the City during the latter part of April had been sufficiently threatening to lead the raising of questions in the House of Commons and the despatch of special instruction to the Lord Mayor by Lord John Russell; but the "Great Day" demonstration which had been the subject of the L.D.A.'s clandestine plotting proved to be a fiasco. Though much of the significance of 6 May had disappeared with the impossibility of presenting the National Petition due to a cabinet crisis, and in spite of a ban on the mass-meeting by the Lord Mayor, the plan was persisted in. After marching to Islington Green in regular formation, the meeting was told by Harney that they should all arm—"They would shortly be called on to act." Cheers greeted this pronouncement, but Harney's request that those who were armed should hold up their hands was responded to by fewer than a score of his listeners, and a further request that those who were determined to acquire arms should give a similar indication was answered, as the police observer present reported, "by a few hands rather timidly raised".[1] The crowd was obviously too timid to express whatever they might have felt—Harney's demands had evoked cries of "Oh! oh! that's going too far!"—and their cautious response must have been a crushing disappointment to him, in view of the hopes he had entertained for the demonstration. He had only to remember the thicket of

[1] H.O. 40/44, report of 6 May 1839.

weapons which were upraised in the north in answer to such requests to realize the extent of the L.D.A.'s failure to arouse the London working class.

This dismal proof that London provided sterile soil for a militant movement doubtless had much to do with Harney's support of the growing demand within the Convention for a change in location. The apparently hopeless attitude of the capital was one of the main factors in the Convention's decision to quit London for Birmingham. O'Brien's condemnation of the "deadening atmosphere" of the metropolis, backed by O'Connor and a majority of the delegates, including Harney, was sufficient to override the main opposition to a move, which came from Lovett's group. There were more pressing reasons as well for the decision. The arrest of one of the best-known Chartist leaders, Henry Vincent, came as a confirmation of rumours that the government had decided on a more determined course. The rumours were indeed solidly based on fact, and the advantages in being among a militantly Chartist populace under such circumstances were obvious.

Moreover, there was the influence of the mounting violence of feeling in the provinces. Evidence of working-class militancy was furnished by a rising of the Llanidloes Chartists in late April, in which they delivered some of their members from arrest and held control of the town for several days. In the Convention's isolation from the real centres of the agitation there existed the danger of their losing control over the popular movement. The realization that decisions would have to supplant oratory had already led the Convention to begin the discussion of what ulterior measures were to follow on the rejection of the Petition; and, as Bronterre bluntly put it, "they would be safer under the guns of Manchester or Birmingham" when the decision on these measures was taken.[1]

The Convention adjourned on 8 May; on the 13th they were to reconvene in Birmingham. Two days after the adjournment, the police struck at the Democratic Association, raiding its headquarters at Ship Yard, Temple Bar, and arresting Thomas Ireland and twelve others, most of whom were not members. The Association's papers, a number of banners, and two pikes were seized; and the suspects' homes were then searched. At least one member of the Association—a shoemaker named Cornish—

[1] *Northern Star*, 4 May 1839.

had taken the Biblical exhortation on the L.D.A.'s cards to sell
one's shirt for a sword almost literally: his miserable room contained no bed, but it did contain a cutlass. (Cornish's wife
asked the police "if they thought it would come to a battle".)[1]

The incident of the raid was a most peculiar one. Russell's
policy as Home Secretary was to arrest leaders while avoiding
mass arrests. Yet, with the exception of Thomas Ireland, those
taken into custody at Temple Bar were either of the rank-and-
file or not members at all. Nor, apparently, had the police any
evidence to connect those arrested with the ownership of the
pikes or, what was essential, to show that they intended to use
the pikes to disturb public order. Coombe wildly called for an
invasion by the "men of the North" to free the prisoners, who
had not a chance if they came to trial; as it transpired the
arrested men, after being warned by the magistrates to quit the
Association, were simply bound over in security of thirty pounds
for six months and told that they would be watched. According
to *The Times*, this leniency was due to the intervention of the
Home Office; according to the *Operative* it was due to a complete
lack of evidence of seditious proceedings. Apart from the possibility that the police had bungled the job, the only reasonable
hypothesis for the arrests would seem to be that the government
wished to frighten the membership of the Democratic Association. The police had already been pursuing a policy of repression toward the Association, warning publicans that they were
to refuse to allow Section meetings.

If this was the intention of the raid, it was partially successful.
Subsequent police reports of Association meetings spoke of the
"subdued tone" of the speeches delivered, and the frightened
Coombe left the movement. But this was a temporary quietude,
as events of the winter were to demonstrate. The militant
leaders such as Joseph and David Williams lost none of their
fervour, and Harney, addressing the huge crowd which had
greeted the delegates in Birmingham on 13 May, made a violent
attack on the government's action: "It might be if the government began the reign of terror, the people would end it. . . . It
might be that the people should oppose them with the musket
and the pike."[2]

The escape of Harney and the main Democratic Association
leaders from arrest did not pass without comment. The *Chartist*

---

[1] *The Times*, 13 May 1839.   [2] *Northern Star*, 18 May 1839.

blamed their "stupid and dangerous proceedings" for the incident, and noticed that they had "managed to be out of the way" when the arrests were made. The spy rumours about Harney also seem to have been strengthened by his absence from Ship Yard on the night of the raid. Those who knew him best denied the rumours; and it was soon obvious from the action of the Birmingham magistrates, who were acting under the close supervision of the Home Office, that he occupied no favoured position. Still the fact remained that some suspicion concerning his integrity as an extremist leader was entertained in Birmingham by the time of his arrival there.

Birmingham had reached a state of ferment in the fortnight preceding the transference of the Convention. Brown and Fussell, two of the local leaders who had come to the fore after the middle-class leaders' resignation from the movement, were the key figures in an agitation which had grown to such proportions that the Riot Act had been read and the central place of meeting, the Bull Ring, forbidden to public gatherings. Lord John considered the situation serious enough to instruct the Birmingham magistrates to arrest immediately any members of the Convention who used seditious language.[1] While the delegates could not have known this when they resumed their sittings, they did know from the Chartist press that the government had offered to arm the "principal inhabitants of disturbed districts"—that is, the propertied classes. The situation was beginning to take on literally the aspect of class-struggle.

Thus it was in an atmosphere of local and national tension that the Convention turned to the crucial question which had been avoided in the relatively stagnant backwater of London: what positive measures were to be taken when the Petition was rejected? The Convention's answer was equivocal. While a definite programme was drawn up, a plebiscite was to be conducted on these recommendations by the delegates at mass-meetings of their "constituents" during the Whitsuntide holiday. The Convention would then finally determine its policy when it came together again on 1 July. It was clear from this procrastination that considerable doubt was entertained by the delegates as to the unanimity of support their programme was likely to obtain.

Most of the measures proposed stemmed directly from the

[1] H.O. 40/50, 13 May 1839.

Reform Bill agitation of 1831–32. Such were a run on the banks, trading exclusively with sympathizers, the refusal to pay rent, rates and taxes, and the election of Chartist candidates at the expected General Election. In addition, arms were to be acquired and, as a last resort, there was to be a general strike—the "sacred month". Toward all these measures but the last two, Harney's attitude was contemptuous. Arming was to him the crucial measure; the "national holiday" was inseparably bound up with this. In the last issue of the London *Democrat* for which he wrote (4 May), Harney had lavished his scorn on those delegates who, following Attwood, believed that a general strike could be a peaceful economic weapon. On the contrary, it would mean insurrection within a week, he wrote. The people would find it impossible to lay by food; therefore they would attempt to take it by force. It was not the insurrection which would follow that he objected to, but that those who were the loudest advocates of the plan at the same time denounced the arming of the people, for without arms the strike would inevitably fail.

With the quasi-endorsement of arming by the Convention, Harney became a protagonist of the national holiday. Using the familiar Biblical allusion of the originator of the concept, William Benbow, Harney told a Birmingham crowd on the night of 14 May: " 'The thousand hills, and the cattle thereon, are the Lord's, and what is the Lord's is the people's' . . . He would not tell them to steal the cattle . . . [but if the owners] would not lend them an ox or a sheep, borrow it yourself." [1] The speech was significant in more than its expression of opinion, as the next few days showed.

On 17 May the Convention adjourned to seek the public decision on the ulterior measures. Harney took no part in their last deliberations—a fact not without importance, for in the early morning of the 17th Brown and Fussell, the Birmingham leaders, were arrested, and, as *The Times* reported, "Two other Chartists, against whom warrants are issued, the officers were unable to meet with". One of these Chartists was Harney, who had left to report to Newcastle. Included in the crowd which had listened to his remarks on the national holiday had been a London police officer; and that speech had formed the basis for a charge of seditious utterance.

[1] Police evidence, *Charter*, 14 July 1839.

Harney may not have known that he was wanted by the Birmingham magistrates when he travelled north, but he very probably soon found out. Doctor Taylor, who with other Chartist leaders had managed to control a riot after the arrest of Brown and Fussell, arrived in Newcastle a few days later. In view of the non-secretive and inefficient nature of the Birmingham police it is likely that the names of the two Chartists who had escaped arrest were well known by this time, and that Taylor communicated the news to Harney. In any case, there was no necessity for Harney to go to ground, for, as he doubtless well knew, local authorities were not keen on pursuing wanted men outside their own bailiwicks.

The Birmingham magistrates reckoned on Harney's return when the Convention resumed on 1 July, and decided to wait until then to arrest him.[1] Their behaviour illustrates the curious provincialism of local law-officers of the time. It was well known that Harney was one of the most extreme of Chartist leaders; it was also well known within a short time that he was pursuing his "seditious activities" in the north. Yet, like the town sheriffs in the American West of a later period, local authorities seem to have felt that their responsibility stopped when an undesirable had departed. As noted by Sir Charles Napier, the commanding general in the north, the borough magistrates "take no cognizance of what passes out of their jurisdiction".[2] The main technique to avoid arrest under such conditions was mobility, and in the next few weeks Harney's ceaseless travelling from one small town to another in Northumberland, Durham and Cumberland amply satisfied this requirement.

Newcastle had been in a state of extreme excitement for a week before 20 May, when Harney, Lowery, and Taylor addressed a great mass-meeting on the Convention's resolutions. The preceding Saturday a pitched battle had occurred in which more than 2,000 Chartists had engaged a force of police and special constables, being dispersed finally only by the alerting of the military. On the 20th, in spite of threats and intimidation by factory-owners, a crowd estimated variously at 15,000 to 100,000 gathered from twenty miles around to the sound of firing guns to hear their delegates. Harney's address was concerned

---

[1] *The Times*, 11 July 1839.
[2] Quoted in Napier, *Life of Sir Charles Napier*, vol. I, pp. 98–99.

mainly with the General Election scheme: the Chartist candidates who were elected by a show of hands at the hustings should, supported by an armed people, actually take their seats in Parliament and begin to legislate—a version of the Convention's recommendation which would have shocked the moderate delegates. How far ahead of the Convention the Tyneside Chartists were was demonstrated by the tremendous enthusiasm with which this recommendation and the rest of the ulterior measures were adopted. In Carlisle the following evening a cheering gathering of 10,000 who listened to Harney and Taylor echoed the resolution of the Tynesiders.

Harney's itinerary during the next weeks was an exhausting one. In the last seven days of May he convened and spoke at meetings in no less than ten localities, sometimes alone, sometimes with Doctor Taylor. As in the previous winter, there were lighter moments; bands, long processions and festive dinners in the evenings greeted him. Perhaps thinking of Charlotte Corday, the young latter-day Marat's attention to his female listeners was as assiduous as ever; to his collection of scarves he now added two of "magnificent silk". In an outrageously flattering speech to the Newcastle Female Political Union, for example, he told his auditors that, like Burns, he believed women to be superior to men. But as before such treatment had a practical result in the formation of a new female political organization— this time at Cockermouth.

If Harney knew of the warrant for his arrest the fact did not cause any moderation in his speeches. Joining O'Connor in Newcastle on 17 June for a meeting which had as its object a defence fund for the growing number of arrested Chartists, he told a crowd which had fervently applauded his entrance that they should first try to ransom their friends with gold, but if the government persisted in its arrests they should pay the ransoms with cold steel. His influence and popularity in Northumberland had in fact reached its zenith, as O'Connor's fulsome praises on this occasion indicated. "It is but justice to this young man (whose over-zeal has done less mischief than the over-caution of his more discreet friends) to say that his mission has been productive of incalculable good," commented the *Northern Star*. (His missions had also had a more personal effect: Harney had "very much improved in public speaking".) One could hardly find better evidence of his popularity, as well as of the grip

Chartism had in Northumberland, than that of an incident at Bedlington, a small coal-mining and iron-working centre, a few days later. The engine-wrights of the iron-works turned their backs on barrels of free beer doled out by the management and joined the colliers in a meeting held by Harney. In this town he remained due to the illness which fatigue seemed to bring on after protracted activity; and the Convention reconvened on 1 July without him.

Events now moved swiftly to one of the many climaxes of the summer of 1839. Acting on its mandate from the popular meetings the Convention concerned itself with the date that the ulterior measures, in particular the national holiday, should be put into effect. Neesom, Marsden and Taylor proposed that the date for the strike be 15 July. While agreeing on the usefulness of the measure Lovett asked that a committee be set up to devise the most efficient plan, and argued that the people's attitude should be tested more fully by a preliminary subscription of funds. On the 3rd of July a compromise was reached by which certain of the measures—a run on savings-banks, the abstention from exciseable luxury articles, and arming—were to be put into immediate operation, while the final decision on the strike date was to stand over until the Petition had been considered by the House of Commons on 12 July.

Now, however, the choice of action was taken out of the Convention's hands by the Birmingham rank-and-file Chartists. On the evening of the 4th, a large and peaceable crowd assembled in the Bull Ring listening to Chartist orators was charged by a force of Metropolitan Police which had just arrived from London, under the direction of Scholefield, the local mayor. The police, wielding cutlasses and bludgeons indiscriminately, enjoyed a momentary success, but the infuriated crowd rallied and drove them from the Ring. A troop of dragoons and a rifle brigade arriving opportunely at this moment, the crowd was dispersed temporarily; but shortly after midnight they marched on the town armed with clubs, and were halted only by the efforts of Doctor Taylor and Peter McDouall—who were promptly arrested for their services.

Under these turbulent conditions the Convention met the next day and, with Lovett playing the leading role, determined to attack the actions of the magistrates and police in a public proclamation. Signed by Lovett, the address was placarded

F

about Birmingham on the 5th, with the result of Lovett's immediate arrest along with John Collins, a Birmingham delegate
who had seen to the printing. The Convention, unable to find a
meeting-room in the alarmed town, adjourned on 7 July to meet
in London in two days' time. On the morning of the next day,
Harney, guarded by a Birmingham constable, arrived and was
confined pending a hearing. His arrival intensified the already
violent feeling in the town, and in the evening the dragoons were
again charging crowds.

The circumstances of Harney's arrest throws light both on the
state of feeling in Northumberland and Cumberland and on the
regard in which he was held. There is little doubt that his arrest
could have resulted in an extensive outbreak in the north-east
had he so wished. That the authorities were well aware of this
is also evident. In spite of the presence of a contingent of London police in Bedlington, sent there shortly before in response
to the urgent pleas of the inhabitants, the magistrates who
arrested Harney took the double precaution of providing themselves with the escort of a troop of dragoons and making the
arrest in the very early hours of the morning.[1] "Torn from the
arms of his wife in bed," according to the *Morning Chronicle's*
reporter (Harney was not yet married), he was hurried through
Newcastle in the dawn and taken by rail to Carlisle. The crucial
part of his circuitous journey occurred here. His presence becoming known, a large and threatening crowd surrounded the
hotel where he and his guard had put up for the night, and
demanded his release. Harney did not encourage his delivery,
but aided in devising the stratagem by which they got away.
While the crowd was engaged in front of the hotel, he and the
police-officer got into a post-chaise at the back and drove off.
Had their stay been prolonged until the mill-workers came out
for their midday meal, order could probably not have been preserved; and his guard was convinced—probably with some
justice—that Harney had saved his life.[2]

There was a more extensive reaction which shows even more
clearly what might have happened had he allowed the Carlisle
crowd to rescue him. The news of his arrest was placarded in
Newcastle on the following day, and an intense excitement

---

[1] H.O. 40/46, 19 July; 40/53, Sir Charles Napier to Russell, 10 July 1839.
[2] *Morning Chronicle*, 17 July 1839. *Cf.* Adams, *Memoirs of a Social Atom*, vol. I,
pp. 220–21; Newcastle *Weekly Chronicle*, 10 May 1890; *Northern Star*, 13, 20 July 1839.

gripped the town and countryside. Business came to a standstill as some of the trades came out; the mines closed and colliers generally expected that the rising had come and that they were to march on London. The senior magistrate of Newcastle wrote to Russell at the Home Office that the men coming to protest-meetings were armed with pikes, and the police were refraining from any interference through fear of provoking an outbreak.[1] In Bedlington the state of feeling was equally feverish, and it was found necessary to dispatch a troop of dragoons there to keep order, although a large number of special constables had just been sworn in.[2] The mood in these districts was definitely revolutionary and there seems no question but that Harney might have provoked bloodshed had he pursued a different course in Carlisle.

Why didn't he precipitate this violence? Prior to the "Great Day", 6 May, his actions in London had been unsuccessfully directed at just such a *dénouement*. But here at his hand were Chartists who, unlike the "brown-jackets" of London, needed no more conditioning by armed demonstrations for the final step, being already roused to a near-insurrectionary pitch. From his subsequent actions it would seem that Harney did not wish to provoke a premature outbreak. Believing that the National Convention would declare the national strike and that a national insurrection would follow, he may well have hesitated to provoke a sectional outbreak in Northumberland and Cumberland. All of which assumes that Harney was able to examine the alternatives rationally, and very possibly he was not. From his appearance at his two hearings before the Birmingham magistrates on 11 and 15 July it was obvious that he was ill, and this may have had something to do with his actions.

In any case, the actual hearings were farcical, considering the dangerous feeling aroused by his arrest. The charge against him —that of seditious speech at the Birmingham meeting of 14 May —was supported only by the evidence of a London policeman. His testimony that Harney had recommended a "musket in one hand and a petition in the other" to his auditors was contradicted by six witnesses, with the unlikely tale that he had recommended not "muskets" but "biscuits", and that his subject had

[1] H.O. 40/46, 11 July 1839.
[2] *Ibid.*, 10, 13 July. *Cf.* H.O. 41/14, 11 July, for special precautions taken in Cumberland to control popular feeling.

been the "biscuits and oatmeal" for the sacred month.[1] Two witnesses for the prosecution were necessary; they could produce but one. And, luckily for Harney, the meeting at which his speech had been delivered had elicited only two lines in the entire press, so far as can be told. There could be no recourse to a reporter as an additional witness—a common practice in the Chartist trials which followed.

The magistrates were not unfriendly to Harney, and the clerk of the peace, George Edmunds, went so far as to cast considerable doubts on the policeman's testimony. Perhaps this was due to the obvious weakness of the case or the statement of Harney's escort that his prisoner had saved his life in Carlisle. More likely it was because of the awkward position of the magistrates themselves. They and Edmonds were staunch Radicals and had been leading figures in the Birmingham Political Union, the organization which had originated the National Petition. One member on the bench, Salt, had actually been among the original Birmingham delegates to the Convention. And possibly there were uncomfortable memories in some of their minds about the language and threats they had used to obtain the franchise for their class in the Reform Bill agitation of 1832. Certainly there seemed to be a lack of decisiveness in the magistrates' first dealings with Chartist agitators.

So at least thought a highly irate Duke of Wellington. The riots at Birmingham had become the subject of a party fight at Westminster, with the Tories attacking, and the Whig government defending, the Birmingham magistrates.

"Their Lordships knew," the Duke told the House of Lords on 18 July, "that those were most to blame who had deliberately made a party appointment of magistrates, not only in Birmingham but in all parts of the country. He just begged leave to mention one circumstance to the House . . . the clerk of the peace . . . of this very bench of magistrates, was the person who defended one of the persons taken up for these disturbances, before the magistrates." [2]

Within the next few days the Home Secretary communicated his views on this revelation in no mild terms to the Birmingham magistrates: they were to cease any such "objectionable proceeding" and "give all the assistance in their power to procure further evidence in the case of those to be prosecuted".[3]

---

[1] *The Times*, 12 July; *Morning Chronicle*, 17 July 1839.
[2] Parliamentary report in *The Times*, 19 July 1839.　　[3] H.O. 41/14, 22 July.

The Birmingham bench had undoubtedly bungled their instructions to proceed strongly against the Convention delegates. Harney had been arrested for a comparatively mild speech which was not even properly witnessed. Doctor Taylor, another of the most violent of the delegates, had been arrested for what amounted to aiding the forces of order, a fact so obvious that binding him over to the Summer Assizes (in August) was no more than a gesture. Lovett and Collins alone of the top-flight leaders were firmly in the magistrates' grip, and, prodded by Lord John, the magistrates made no mistake about them.[1] By the time that Wellington made his speech, however, Harney had been bound over to the Summer Assizes and released on bail of one hundred pounds.

Harney had been in Warwick Gaol for almost a week when he was released after the hearing on the evening of 15 July. He came out into a fiery recrudescence of Birmingham violence in which the Chartists burned several shops about the Bull Ring, assaulted the Public Office, and—largely through the lack of co-ordination between the various forces of order in the town—demonstrated without hindrance for several hours. The demonstration was the more ominous in that no looting took place, an indication of a disciplined rank-and-file. Harney evidently witnessed this disorder, and, remaining in Birmingham for the next week, absorbed the state of feeling which Muntz, one of the magistrates, described to Russell as a "general disaffection of the working classes and strong feeling in favour of a conflagration".[2] When, shortly after 20 July, he left Birmingham for the Convention he must have realized that if the delegates did not now lead, at least part of the movement would go on without them.

[1] H.O. 40/50, Russell to Scholefield. Lovett and Collins were sentenced to a year's imprisonment.
[2] *Ibid.*, 23 July.

CHAPTER IV

The Resort to Force

THE National Convention had at last come to the question which had underlaid every other from its optimistic first meeting five months before: if all other means of achieving the Charter failed, was it prepared to lead a revolution? Due partly to events beyond its control, partly to its vacillation, the Convention had delayed decision, using as an excuse the still-to-be presented National Petition. When at last, on 12 July, the House of Commons refused by an overwhelming majority to consider the Petition, the delegates could not have felt surprise; but the last veil shrouding reality had been pulled away. Their constituents had voted for ulterior measures; those who had opposed a resort to such measures had long since resigned; and, most fundamental of all, the Birmingham outbreak had revealed the feverish state of Chartist feeling. If the Convention was to control the movement, the time for decision had come.

Harney had equated the National Holiday with insurrection in May, and by the time the delegates reconvened in July there was no real disagreement about what a general strike entailed. Perhaps Lovett thought otherwise—he seems to have believed that thorough preparation would make violence unnecessary— but he was occupied in preparing for his trial and took no further part in the deliberations. Osborne, the physical-force Brighton delegate, said plainly that the sooner they began, the better would be their chances of success; and even Moir of Glasgow, who had generally stood with the moderates, demurred only to the extent of advising delay until the crops were in. Thus when the Convention voted on 16 July for the "sacred month" to begin on 12 August the issue was clear. They were risking revolt.

But the vote—13 to 6 with 5 abstentions—showed how far from agreement the delegates were, and in spite of the decision having been taken, the debates on the subject continued. The Convention's indecision was epitomized by Bronterre's actions in this crisis. On 15 July he told a cheering Stockport crowd that the sixty meetings he had just finished addressing in Scotland and Cumberland supported the National Holiday unanimously; yet little more than a week later in the Convention he succeeded, with the aid of O'Connor, in reversing the strike-vote.

By the time Harney reached London late in July an impasse had been reached. The Convention's lack of purpose was embodied in a resolution which, if it meant anything, meant that another sampling of public opinion would be taken. Harney had been instructed in unequivocal language by the Northern Political Union to stand with Taylor and Lowery for an immediate commencement of the general strike—the Newcastle Chartists were getting out of hand and beginning to lose faith in the Convention. Speaking in reply to a plea by O'Brien for more information before a decision was taken, Harney put for the last time to the delegates the views which he had held throughout these long months. That those views were in large part derived from the man whom he was attacking was an irony which could hardly have escaped pupil and teacher. Curtly dismissing O'Brien's caution—"Information wanted, forsooth! What then, were all the simultaneous meetings a farce?"—Harney demanded that the Convention call the national holiday. The forty meetings which he had addressed in Cumberland and Northumberland had shown the temper of the people, and Yorkshire, Durham and Lancashire were as fully prepared. If the Convention did not do its duty "by calling upon the people, and placing them in collision with their tyrants" they would not be roused again.[1]

To lead the people to "collision with their tyrants": this was placing the Convention's dilemma squarely before it. O'Connor's angry branding of Harney as a fool who was attempting to mislead the people had more to it than resentment at the independence of one whom he had considered a follower. The inescapable fact was that if Harney was not speaking for all of the Chartist movement he was speaking for the advanced section of it, a fact of which Feargus and the others were well aware. Without doubt, as some of the delegates said, their followers were not ready for a general strike and revolt. Knox, the Durham delegate, denied that his county was in favour of such a course, a statement flatly contradicted by Doctor Taylor. In the confusing interchanges of these crucial days such disagreements as to

[1] *Charter*, 28 July 1839. Harney's speech was not printed by the *Northern Star*.

the mandate the delegates had received in the simultaneous meetings of June became increasingly common. Who was closer to the truth? And further, what were the prospects of revolution?

So far as Harney's "constituency" was concerned, there was strong evidence to show that the men whom he represented would attempt to rise with or without the Convention's leadership. Something has been said of the preparations which had been going forward in Newcastle since the previous winter, and the reaction of this district to the Birmingham riots and Harney's arrest had shown how close insurrection was. The Newcastle magistrates now informed the Home Office that they had no doubts about the Convention's power to cause a widespread cessation of labour, and they were well aware of the consequences that would follow. What these consequences would be was made obvious in the brief rejoinder of a local Chartist leader when the plan of waiting to strike until the crops were in was raised at a meeting: "There was plenty of bacon and flour to be obtained." [1]

Before Harney spoke on 26 July, a preliminary skirmish had taken place in Newcastle, shops being plundered and a bank broken into before the dragoons arrived. More threatening still was an outbreak on 30 July, which developed into a hard-fought struggle—later called the "Battle of the Forth"—involving some 6,000 Chartists, half of whom were armed, and a force of two companies of infantry, a troop of dragoons, and 500 police and special constables. [2] This was almost on the scale of regular warfare. And when it is noted that the closest reinforcement to Newcastle was a small contingent of troops sixty miles away at Carlisle, and that the Chartists involved were only a portion of the thousands in the colliery and iron-working villages clustered around Newcastle, it is hardly overstatement to describe the situation as being potentially revolutionary.

As for others of the affected counties, Harney's belief that they needed only determined leadership to rise is borne out in part by the testimony of the general commanding in the north, Sir Charles Napier. "The spirit of revolution is strong and increasing," he informed Lord John Russell on 16 July, empha-

---

[1] H.O. 40/46, letter of 19 July. *Cf.*, for the magistrates' alarm, letters of 11, 13 July.

[2] *Ibid.*, Fife to Russell, 31 July. *Cf.* Newcastle *Weekly Chronicle*, 19, 26 July 1890; letters of Peter Doyle and "Old Chartist", *ibid.*, 27 September 1884, 9 August 1890.

sizing this two days later in a dispatch which stated that the people were "ready to rise".[1] If, in the quiet of the Home Office, Russell thought Napier an alarmist, the thought must quickly have fled, for the post on the 23rd brought news not only of the initial outbreak in Newcastle but of a renewal of incendiarism in Birmingham. Just one week later the Home Office found it necessary to send instructions to the magistrates in more than forty localities on the measures to be taken against Chartists who threatened storekeepers or attempted to stop men from working.[2] It would seem that the government took the state of feeling in the country more seriously than did the people's delegates.

Although a concentration of leadership with perhaps greater power than it was aware of existed in the Convention, it was true that the Chartists were still disorganized from a national standpoint. But the government was by no means strong so far as the co-ordinated exercise of force was concerned. For all practical purposes, the mechanism of public order still rested where it had in 1815; England was still to a large extent "a country governed without police".[3] This was true of the provincial towns, few of which had come as yet under the Municipal Corporations Act of 1835 with its compulsory regulations concerning efficient police forces (apt to be disregarded in any case, as Birmingham demonstrated),[4] and it was even truer of the countryside. Local jealousy and parsimony, coupled with the fear of a central bureaucracy and the association of regular police with "Continental despotism", had left the Home Secretary with a system in which he was forced to depend heavily on local

[1] H.O. 40/53.

[2] H.O. 41/14. The threatening of storekeepers is an example of the way in which a peaceful "ulterior measure"—in this case, exclusive dealing—was transformed by heated feelings into something quite different from what the Convention had envisaged. One could plot a map of the most disturbed areas from the localities mentioned: the majority lay in Northumberland, Durham, Cumberland, Lancashire, Yorkshire, Derby and Warwick.

[3] Elie Halévy's phrase, in *England in 1815*, 2nd edition (London: 1949), p. 44. Halévy's further comment—"the public was prepared to put up with a certain amount of disorder if it was the price of freedom"—loses its pertinence only during the Chartist struggle.

[4] Birmingham, incorporated in October 1838, was still without an adequate police force during the violence of July 1839, due to the Town Council's doubts about the legality of levying rates for this purpose. Only by direct act of Parliament were these doubts overcome; not until November 1839 was the small number of constables and watchmen directed by three separate local bodies replaced by a regular force. (For this information I am indebted to Mr. F. J. Patrick, City Librarian of Birmingham.)

magistrates of varying abilities, and the magistrates, in turn, dependent on minute forces of watchmen and constables. Faced with this problem, Lord John in effect armed the middle class in the guise of "special constables"; but no significant increase of strength seems to have accrued from this step. The special constables distinguished themselves neither for their courage nor for their effectiveness. The inescapable impression received from the Home Office dispatches is of an extraordinarily inept system of control and a central guiding policy exerted only with difficulty, the passage of much time, and a consequent vast increase in disorder. It was to take the threat of revolution to overcome the almost universal English distrust of a regular rural police.

The maintenance of public order in 1839 thus depended almost entirely on the army, a force hampered by its rigid subordination to the civil power in such matters. It was the army which Harney considered the main danger when he spoke of the "contest which would set the fatherland free". His belief that such a contest could have a successful result was based on his reading of French history: from the Revolution of 1830 he drew the conclusion that civilians could defeat trained troops; from the events of 1792, that the soldiers would go over to the revolutionaries. This was perhaps calling both sides of the coin, but it was not sheer foolishness. At Lane End (near Newcastle-under-Lyne), for example, an action between rioters and cavalry in May had ended in a stalemate after confused fighting in which the rioters used firearms and brought their opponents to earth in the dark by the use of low barricades erected in the streets. As to the potential disloyalty of the regular troops—a belief widely held by the working class—Sir Charles Napier's testimony indicates that this was not without some slight basis. Napier warned the Home Office in late July that small detachments of troops spread widely were doubly vulnerable to "corruption" by the Chartists, and cases of doubtful loyalty had come to his attention. It is significant also that in requesting that more troops be sent to him from Ireland, he specified that regiments with the highest percentage of Irishmen be selected: "The difference of religion and of country form additional barriers around the fidelity of the soldier." [1]

Events three years later proved that the working class, rising over a great enough area and using hit-and-run tactics against

[1] H.O. 40/53, report of 29 July. *Cf.* reports of 29 June, 31 July.

regular troops, could meet with at least a temporary success.[1] But neither then nor in 1839 did the army, with a few dubious exceptions, provide any evidence for Harney's and the working classes' belief that they would prove disloyal to the established order in a conflict with the people. Napier's caution in this respect did not alter his confidence in the ability of the troops under his command to quell any civilian rising. In this assumption, then, Harney was wrong; and while there might have been more substance in his belief in the prowess of armed civilians, a rising of such elements could have had a chance of success only if leaders commanding local followings had acted with unity and decision. It was precisely in these qualities that the delegates were most lacking.

This can be attributed in part to the variety of aims which the Charter embodied, a factor of fundamental importance so far as the unity of force was concerned. A skilled engineer in a Manchester mill might support the Charter because he thought it held the means of achieving a ten-hour day—but he was unwilling to revolt for it. On the other hand, a starving handloom weaver saw in the Charter salvation from an intolerable existence and might well feel that the lives of his oppressors were worth no more than his own. To Harney the problem seemed clear, but he represented a part of the country almost unique in its unanimity and determination to resort to force if that proved necessary.

His advocacy of the general strike rested on still deeper considerations than this, however. He was convinced that the active minority of Chartists could act as a sort of "revolutionary vanguard", a conviction which had been implicit in his concept of the Democratic Association as a Jacobin club and his role in the Convention as leader of the extreme left wing. Harney had preached that a Chartist revolution would mean an English revolution; the advanced forces of armed Chartism would precipitate a national rising. Implicit too in his thought was the self-immolation which would very likely be the lot of the

---

[1] The comment of Mayor Scholefield of Birmingham on the incessant Chartist demonstrations in July 1839 is worth quoting in this context. After remarking on the exhaustion of the soldiers due to the necessity for their constant patrolling, he goes on: "If the tactics of the mob should tend to this sort of guerrilla practice for months (as they may do) it is not easy to forsee by what means the disorganized condition of society may be put an end to" (H.O. 40/50, 22 July). General Napier would probably have agreed with him.

revolutionary leaders, a recurrent theme which may be traced
through many of his public speeches in the preceding year.

But the Convention was prepared to initiate neither a revolution nor their own martyrdom. With some possible exceptions,
their actions were not dictated by personal fear; no one had
known better than this group of men from the first the latent
violence of the force they were directing. What they did fear
was the responsibility of provoking an action which would result
in fruitless bloodshed. And doubtless they were right. On
3 August a committee dominated by O'Connor and O'Brien
which had been set up to consider the sacred month equi-
vocally recommended that no strike should take place, but that
the 12th should be the first of two or three days devoted to public
demonstrations. The Convention accepted the plan, and after
determining to again "consult the country", adjourned until
1 September. Their action was the abandonment of control.
What would have been the result of a decision to back the
national holiday is a matter for conjecture; by dissolving itself in
the crisis, the Convention destroyed whatever hope there was of
solidarity in the general strike. The strike was not stopped by
their action, it merely lost its cohesion.

This effect may be briefly described in the district with which
Harney had had so much to do since the great Christmas meeting of 1838. The Newcastle mayor noted in a report to Russell
on 10 August that the feeling in favour of a strike did not appear
so strong among the local Chartists as it had a few days before—
i.e. before the news of the Convention's decision had reached
them. On the very day he wrote, the Northern Political Union,
acting on the decision of a delegate-meeting representing more
than forty localities, placarded the town with notices of a
national holiday to begin on 12 August. Though the placard
stressed the peaceable intentions of the strikers there is little
doubt that the leaders believed that violence would result. The
apprehensions of the magistrates, which had led to an accelera-
tion of middle-class arming, proved baseless so far as Newcastle
itself was concerned; but in the surrounding colliery villages the
strike was almost total, an estimated nine-tenths of the miners
coming out.

The result of this disunity was tragic. Accompanied by
dragoons, the magistrates dealt with the strikers piece-meal,
arresting bound pitmen and charging them with having violated

their bond. With no backing from Newcastle the strike quickly disintegrated—and with it, for a time, the Northern Political Union. The same pattern was evident in other sections of the north. Napier reported that the Nottingham Chartists lacked only the "word from Headquarters" to begin, and that Carlisle, Barnsley, Sheffield, Macclesfield and Manchester were in a state of ferment; but it was only at Bolton that an outbreak occurred. There the Chartists fought the troops for three days with guns and pikes and destroyed machinery in the mills before they were put down. Ten days after the strikes had begun all was quiet again, and Napier could report to Russell that "the campaign is over *at present*".[1]

Harney had time to think of these events, for during the outbreaks he was again in Warwick Gaol, awaiting his trial. Conscious that the judicial atmosphere was unpropitious, on 8 August he exercised his right and traversed until the Spring Assizes, though he remained imprisoned for another week while sureties were forthcoming. It is possible that he visited Newcastle before returning to London to rejoin the Convention, for his last speech to that body indicated an intimate knowledge of the bitterness against the Convention which now filled the Tyneside Chartists.

The last sessions of the Convention were a sad affair, only 21 of the original 52 members participating in what was really a post-mortem. The *Champion* disingenuously asked what had happened to O'Connor's repeated boast to the men of Lancashire that he would lead them to "death or glory" if the Charter was not theirs by 1 September. Never the man to be bothered by what he had said the month before, O'Connor ignored this awkward question and bent his efforts to preventing the dissolution of the Convention. Harney's argument against this policy was an alloy of sarcasm and disillusionment:

> "It had been urged that the Convention had no power to dissolve itself without the consent of the constituencies, but that was a mere quibble, for he was quite sure that if the majority of them went to sleep for a year they might do so without the slightest fear of being disturbed or called upon by the people to resume their functions in the Convention."

His constituents, through the Northern Political Union, had

---

[1] H.O. 40/53, 22 August. For the preceding events, *cf.* Napier's dispatches of 15, 16 August; Colonel Cairncross's of 15 August.

withdrawn their confidence from the Convention and were using their funds to support the families of those who had been imprisoned due to the Convention's "imbecile conduct". That imbecility, he declared, had in two weeks broken down the organization of two years in Northumberland, Cumberland and Durham.[1]

The vote for dissolution showed the schismatic nature of the Convention persisting to the last: the steady process by which members of the left had joined members of the right in resigning had left a core which in turn split neatly in half. Even the two members of the Democratic Association, Harney and Neesom, found themselves in opposition, and it was only through the deciding vote of the chairman that the Convention came to an end.

The Convention had lasted seven months since that day in February when the optimistic delegates had sat for the first time in the British Coffee House in London. They had accomplished none of their aims. The Six Points were, if anything, farther from acceptance than they had ever been. Yet to call this complete failure would be to overlook the fact that the Convention had, after all, remained in existence for seven months. Here for the first time a body representing the working classes, with a national following and a compact programme of political reform, had met and deliberated. And while no part of its programme had become law, short of a successful revolution or a miraculous change in the minds of the governing class such an accomplishment was not possible in 1839. The rationalizations of hind-sight are not given to contemporaries of events, however, and this was the way it was regarded at the time. While the achievement of the Charter—and with it, the social ameliora-tion that gave these political principles their compulsive force—might have been impossible, the great mass following which had sent their delegates to the Convention had expected nothing less than success. And, as in the fight for the Reform Bill of 1832, disappointment was as extreme as hopes had been.

Whether any policy put forward by the Convention in September would have stopped the drift of mass-support away from Chartism which now began is doubtful. O'Connor, still the most influential man in the movement, argued for what was possibly the best interim policy: the Convention "rump" should

---

[1] H.O. 40/44, police report of 8 September.

continue to sit as a symbol of solidarity while replenishing the movement's strength through the setting up of a national organization and the intensification of Chartist propaganda. The dissolution, which was the result of a coalition between men like Taylor, who were thinking of a direct resort to force, and men like Harney, who were temporarily disillusioned, made this impossible; and the events of the next few months saw the policy of reorganization superseded by one of violence.

In the course of his last scathing attack on the Convention Harney had touched on a more personal grievance: his efforts to bring the Convention to a determined course of action had caused his denunciation as a traitor and a spy. That he should bring up an accusation which (so far as can be ascertained) had appeared in print in the radical press but once indicates that the rumours refused to die. Doubtless his moderate treatment by the Birmingham magistrates revived this talk, the harsh sentences on Lovett and Collins providing a sharp contrast. There was evidence of another kind, however, which the public could not see. Reposing in the files of the Home Office was a letter from W. C. Alston, a Birmingham magistrate, which might have been interpreted as proof of Harney's complicity in a spy-ring.[1] The letter, which asked the Home Secretary's consent to the hiring of some volunteer spies, contains a puzzling reference to Harney: "I may add that I sent Thomas to London at the desire of Julian Harney on Thursday last [29 August] and that I have had no communication with him (Harney) whatever or have I seen him." A postscript makes it plain that Thomas was a spy who was to use the name Wilkins in London.

If the assumption is made that Harney *knew* that Thomas was a spy, the passage is damning evidence of his guilt. But Alston emphatically denied either personal or written communication with Harney. This would seem to indicate his desire to make it unmistakably clear to the Home Secretary that Harney was unaware that in telling Thomas to go to London for some purpose—perhaps to contact the Democratic Association leaders— he was in fact helping a spy. In this context, rather than proving Harney was an agent the letter shows that he was an unwitting abettor.

Even if a judgment on Harney's integrity depended solely on

[1] H.O. 40/50, 31 August. Mark Hovell, *The Chartist Movement* (London: 1925), incorrectly identifies Alston as the Police Commissioner.

the interpretation of Alston's phrase it would be difficult to share the suspicions of his contemporaries. But other evidence from the Home Office papers leaves no doubt that both before and after Alston's letter Harney was considered an enemy of public order and a dangerous agitator. Due to the Home Office's careful practice with correspondence, it is unlikely that other official letters incriminating Harney have left no trace. Yet if Alston had followed the ordinary procedure in hiring a spy of Harney's calibre it is extremely doubtful that something like the discussion regarding other informers would not have taken place. Spies' salaries came from Secret Service funds; Harney's price would also very likely have included an arrangement about his trial, which was a Crown prosecution. No such correspondence concerning Harney exists. Furthermore, the many references to him in these and the following months leave no question about the belief of the government and the local authorities (including those of Birmingham) that the young radical was a menace. Not only were his movements under close observation by the Home Office, but his mail was being opened and read. When all this has been said, however, the fact remains that the stigma of suspicion clung to Harney during this period, and while his subsequent actions in time cleared his name, the old accusation was apt to be thrown at him years later in the bitter controversies which characterized Chartism.

Possibly because of these suspicions, more probably because the quick crushing of the sporadic outbreaks in the summer of 1839 and the August strike had convinced him that anything short of a thoroughly organized revolution on a national scale was futile, Harney played no part in the clandestine plotting of the next months. Even before the Convention's demise such plotting was rife in Birmingham and London, the latter evidently involving Harney's old friend, Major Beniowski. Though it is not possible to estimate the extent of the secret planning in the affected areas, it was sufficient to arouse some of the Convention delegates to attacks and warnings. These went unheeded; the conspiracies continued.

Alston's letter reveals that the extremist movement in Birmingham was riddled with spies, and in almost every trial which grew out of the attempts at violence in the winter of 1839–40 these gentry played an important part. Their corruption was in many cases voluntary; the grinding poverty which forced some men to revolt forced others to betray them, and offers to spy from former Chartists are numerous in the Home Office correspondence of these months. (The price of betrayal could not have been a heavy drain on the Secret Service fund: the average wage was a guinea per week.) Others betrayed their colleagues through fear of the consequences of their actions, turning Queen's evidence under pressure. And a small minority volunteered information with the sincere motive of preventing violence. Such perhaps was "Arthur S. Wade, D.D.", who can hardly have been other than the Church of England clergyman who had played a leading role in London radicalism. From these different levels, starting at the top with conscience and descending to hunger, fear and greed, the Home Office drew its voluminous information. Birmingham's movement, the most corrupted of any, was like a bucket of worms, with spies winding blindly around each other.[1] As the semi-secret activities of the extreme Chartists grew more dangerous, so suspicion increased; in the fog of betrayal even familiar faces grew indistinct and sinister— Doctor Taylor and other sincere exponents of force, as well as Harney, were stigmatized.

There remained, however, a good deal of activity which was so secret as to elude the vigilance both of the government and of the local authorities. Some of this came out later in the mutual vilification of the Chartist leaders and in memoirs, but the stories told are so contradictory that the only certain conclusion which may be drawn is that a number of plots existed and that attempts were made to link them into more than local uprisings.[2] These activities fall into two phases: the events of September and October which culminated in the Chartist attack of 4 November on Newport in South Wales, and a second period of preparation which ended with the Bradford and Sheffield risings of January 1840.

Of the many accounts dealing with these events, only one mentions Harney—that of David Urquhart, an ex-diplomatic official who carried his Russophobia to an almost pathological extreme. By all odds the most fantastic of the accounts, it contains enough elements of fact to indicate that he may have come

---

[1] E.g. William Tongue, reported by one spy as a leader in the plotting, was himself an informer.

[2] An attempt is made in Appendix A to correlate these stories with other sources of fact.

G

into contact with the fringe of the clandestine movement in the winter of 1839. According to his story, Harney and Doctor Taylor were the ostensible leaders in plotting a rising which was to occur in the "long dark nights before Christmas". Twenty towns were to be seized by 100,000 armed Chartists, who had been organized pyramidally in groups of ten with a Council of Five at the top. Harney and Taylor were in reality the dupes of this council, which included Major Beniowski and a high official in the police. So efficient an organization—"like a piece of machinery with every groove and cog in perfect working order" —could only be Russian, the somewhat unpatriotic Urquhart believed; and a Russian fleet stood ready to sail for England to aid Beniowski when he began the insurrection in South Wales. However, getting wind of all this a few days before the rising, the indomitable Russophobe had convinced two of the council of their stupidity and, aided by twenty faithful followers, quelled the revolution. Unhappily, the messenger sent to South Wales arrived an hour late and the Newport rising could not be stopped.[1]

This rhodomontade would hardly bear repeating were it not for the fact that Harney was mentioned as playing a role in the conspiracy. Some of the facts to which Urquhart gave his rich Muscovite colouring were of course true. Organization in "classes" of ten was being widely adopted in the winter of 1839, though for the most part this was done openly as a means of improving local associations. To Urquhart, such groups of ten connoted the Greek *Hetairia*, the revolutionary organization with close Russian connections which had precipitated the Greek struggle for independence in the 1820's. That models for such organization existed closer to home in Methodism and earlier working class associations—e.g. the National Union of the Working Classes—evidently escaped his attention. There is a substratum of historical fact to other parts of Urquhart's myth as well. That a rising was to take place in the "long nights before

---

[1] *Diplomatic Review*, July 1873. His account is based in part on a number of letters between Chartists which Urquhart printed in the Sheffield *Free Press* in 1856, and as a pamphlet ("The Chartist Correspondence", *Free Press Serials*, no. 13, 1856). Other contemporary evidence indicates that some of these letters may be genuine. Urquhart did in fact convert—at least to the point of employing them as paid lecturers—such staunch Chartists as Lowery, Cardo, Ayr, "Daddy" Richards and Warren; and managed to split off portions of the Chartist movement in Newcastle, Carlisle and Glasgow (Gammage, *History of the Chartist Movement*, p. 189; Harney, in the *Northern Tribune*, December 1854).

Christmas" was a subject of comment in the radical press as early as October; and other later accounts, from which Urquhart probably got much of his information, indicate that a national insurrection was being talked of in London before the dissolution of the Convention, though the persons involved were not those of Urquhart's tale.[1] But it is clear from Harney's actions that Urquhart's description of him as a leader in the insurrectionary plotting rested on no more substantial grounds than his reputation as an advocate of violence.

During the period in which the active revolutionists moved toward the first tragic climax of 4 November, Harney occupied himself in speech-making in Northumberland and Birmingham. While some of these speeches caused concern to the Home Office, he was not involved in the arming and drilling which was going on in both localities. Spies reported that the "secret" plotters in Birmingham were talking, late in October, of the imminence of a rising; and a considerable underground movement seems to have centred on Newcastle. If the story of Thomas Devyr, sub-editor of the ultra-radical *Northern Liberator* and a participant in the Northumberland movement, is accepted, some 60,000 pikes were manufactured on the Tyne between July and November and communication existed with Wales and Birmingham.[2] Whatever the reality of these inter-connections, the misadventure in South Wales early in November brought an end to this first period of revolutionary action. On the morning of the 4th, John Frost and a body of armed Chartists descended on Newport, engaged in a brief skirmish with a small contingent of soldiers in which ten or more Chartists lost their lives, and retreated in disorder into the Welsh hills. Within a few days the leaders and a portion of the rank-and-file were in prison charged with high treason.

Frost's rising evoked almost no popular support, and the lesson of his fiasco—if lesson were needed—confirmed the apathetic attitude of the great majority of Chartists toward revolution. It was not that misery and disaffection became less acute. Napier, a humane observer of working-class suffering, warned the government that if the wealthier classes in Nottingham did not "in prudence, if not from compassion" help the thousands

---

[1] *Cf.* Ashton's and Hill's stories, *Northern Star*, 3, 17 May 1845.

[2] Thomas Devyr, *The Odd Book of the Nineteenth Century* (Greenpoint, New York: 1882), pp. 177, 195-98.

starving, those plotting violence would make great gains. "When men beg in *bodies* they will soon do worse." [1] His fears reflected his good sense, but he was wrong in believing that distress would cause a widespread rising under the aegis of Chartism. While the plotting which resulted in a second outbreak of violence in January 1840 did not cease, the conspirators worked for the most part in isolation.

In this second phase of insurrectionary activity Harney played a much more ambiguous role than he had in the preceding months. Joining Doctor Taylor in December, he came for the first time into the circle of those who were thought to be organizing a revolution. Taylor, "as mischievous a man as any in the Kingdom" in the view of the Home Office, was just free on bail under a charge of seditious speaking when Harney and he managed to convert a Carlisle sabbatarian meeting into a Chartist demonstration. The following weeks saw both addressing Cumberland crowds in terms of thinly-veiled violence. The reports of the informers in these crowds repeated a theme which was filling the ears of the Home Office from many parts of the country: if Frost were convicted of treason in his January trial, a revolution would result. Nor would this be limited to the North. Spy reports indicated the existence of conspiracies in Wales, London and Birmingham, as well as in Bradford, Dewsbury, Newcastle and Manchester. What was even more alarming was the considerable evidence showing that an attempt was being made to concert these efforts through couriers and conferences. [2]

What Taylor planned to do and Harney's part in his plans are difficult to determine. Certainly this is not due to any lack of information. To the reports of spies and trial evidence may be added the recollections of contemporaries and the letters printed by the addled Urquhart. All of the versions are bizarre in the extreme, ranging from Taylor's claim that a rising in France had been arranged to coincide with that in England, to plans for the seizure of the main towns of northern England and their control by his lieutenants, perhaps including Harney. Major Beniowski is mentioned by three independent sources as being the potential military commander for operations in the North; trial testimony

---

[1] H.O. 40/53.
[2] *Cf.* H.O. 40/50, 11, 26 November 1839; 40/44, 15 December 1839; 65/10, 19 November 1839, 26 February 1840; Ashton's account, *Northern Star*, 3 May 1845; Porter's speech, *Morning Herald*, 1 January 1840.

contains the assertion that a Chartist army was to march south to
the aid of simultaneous risings in Yorkshire. As with the events
preceding the Newport rising, just what actuality lay behind this
evidence can only be conjectured. The extravagance of the tales
is no proof that some truth does not lie in them (perhaps the
plots leading to successful revolutions only seem meaningful and
logical because they *were* successful). In any case nothing came
of the plans, though the Home Office took them seriously enough
to have Harney's and Taylor's letters opened, and one of the
men associated with them, Robert Peddie, was actually to lead
the rising at Bradford.

From their subsequent actions it would seem that Taylor and
Harney were indulging in the rhetoric of revolution rather than
seriously planning it. According to one account, Taylor was now
drinking heavily. When Frost was convicted in January and his
sentence commuted to transportation for life, Taylor spoke of an
armed ship which, under his command, was to intercept the
vessel carrying Frost to Australia—a plan odorous of spirits.[1]
Taylor's tippling, if it occurred, may well have influenced
Harney. Certainly the presence of Robert Peddie, whom he and
other Chartists distrusted as an *agent-provocateur*, and the obvious
evidence of the government's close surveillance, augured ill for
any outbreak. Conscious of the "apathy of no inconsiderable
portion of the people" Harney had probably even now lost his
faith in the prospects of an immediate revolution.

The sombre events of the next few weeks convinced him.
During the first fortnight of 1840 the revolutionary plotting came
to an end in a number of pathetic outbreaks, crushed without
difficulty by the government. In all of the risings, the force mus-
tered by the authorities seems in retrospect to have been dis-
proportionately large. Harney's old organization, the London
Democratic Association, was faced with a total mobilization of
all the police and troops in and near London. Churches, docks
and ships were heavily guarded, and when no overt action took
place, the Association's leaders were seized at an armed meeting
in Bethnal Green. A few days before, a rising of the Sheffield
Chartists, armed with guns and spears, was put down by a force
of dragoons and the leaders quickly arrested. At Dewsbury, a

[1] Here again, the plan was not entirely as incredible as it might appear, for it
was said that Taylor had lost the small fortune he had inherited by outfitting and
commanding a warship in the Greek struggle for independence.

projected outbreak which was supposed to have co-ordinated with the Sheffield rising amounted to no more than a demonstration; and the Bristol Chartists, reports of whose planning had alarmed the local authorities, did not even demonstrate. So also at Newcastle, where less than 70 armed men met instead of the 700 expected. The last despairing outbreak of violence occurred at Bradford on 27 January, where Napier had taken his precautions a month before.

In the subsequent testimony of spies and frightened Chartists who turned Queen's evidence allusions were made to measures of co-ordination between localities; but even if such testimony is accepted fully, it is not possible to say that anything like a national insurrection had come close to fruition. The planning was even on a local level pitifully inadequate; the plotters were remarkable only for their rashness. Robert Peddie, for example, had carried out his missions with a disregard of elementary caution so pronounced as to lead to a general suspicion of his motives among Chartists and his denunciation as a government agent after the Bradford rising. Even Harney, whose experience as a target of calumnies equally baseless should have taught better, got some of his own back by joining in the hue-and-cry.

The government's effortless blotting-out of the last embers of revolt was observed by Harney from a calmer atmosphere, for he had crossed the Scottish border on foot just before the New Year, bearing a letter of introduction from Doctor Taylor, an old Ayrshire man. If his reputation for violence or the suspicions attached to his name had preceded him it was not apparent in Dumfries, where he spent New Year's Eve as the guest of a leading local Chartist in the company of Robert Burns, the poet's eldest son. Temporarily, at any rate, the gloomy struggle to the south must have seemed far away; Harney was immersed not only by his lawyer host's whisky—of which he drank too much—but in listening to the younger Burns singing his father's songs. And while the plotting of the English Chartists moved to its fateful end in the first weeks of 1840, he was travelling and addressing meetings in Ayrshire. This first direct contact with Scottish Chartism, combined with the failure of the resort to force, exerted a powerful influence on his ideas.

The Scottish Chartist emphasis on organization, education, and sound financing had impressed such a veteran radical as Francis Place in the early days of Chartism; and following the virtual secession of the Scots from the English movement in August 1839, these characteristics became more pronounced. Condemning those who had caused dissension in the National Convention—an unmistakable reference to Harney's junta—the dominant moderate element had recommended that Scottish "missionaries" be "not firebrands, but men possessed of calm, correct judgment". It was not likely that such an organization would look with friendly eyes on Harney's lecturing in southern Scotland, nor did they. One of their organs, the *True Scotsman*, told him repeatedly to take himself back to England; and his appearance in Glasgow under the sponsorship of a small extremist organization had resulted in an uproar. Yet the young Radical had enjoyed a considerable popular success in the smaller towns of south-western Scotland, and in spite of the attacks of the moderates had developed a warm admiration for the Scottish movement.

The influences of Scottish Chartism and the fiascos to the south found expression in an address to the "Democrats of Great Britain" which Harney wrote prior to his departure to stand trial at the Warwick Assizes in March. The address, which appeared in the *Scottish Patriot*, reviewed the events of the preceding year and set forth his recommendations as to the course which English Chartism should pursue. The failure of the national holiday in August 1839, he wrote, had been due to the disunity of the National Convention and a "want of sterling patriotism on the part of no inconsiderable number of the people". Its effect had been to destroy the strong organization built up in Northumberland, Durham and Cumberland, which under a strong leadership might well have precipitated a decisive struggle. This had ended the "first campaign of Chartism", following which had come the projects involving secrecy and their failure. These events had led to the current state of English Chartism—a spectacle of "disorganization, apathy, distrust, and despair".

What, then, was to be done? Harney's answer anticipated much of later Chartist action. The English working classes should follow the example of the Scots. In addition to a permanently-sitting national executive there should be locally elected Chartist "tribunes" whose function would be to organize systematic petitioning, the moving of Chartist amendments at Anti-Corn Law, sabbatarian, and other public meetings, and the

replacing of conventional religious services on Sundays by Chartist services. Finally, the Chartist aim should be to build from
the bottom a national structure which would make possible the
election of a people's parliament and the implementation of the
Charter.

With the last point Harney reverted to his old conviction: "I
still believe it is physical force, or the fear of it, to which in the
end we shall be compelled to resort—with me it is question of
time only." But the programme of action he recommended
showed a great change in emphasis from that of the past, which
might be summarized in his exhortation to "Arm! Arm! Arm!"
Yet, while recognizing the necessity of a period of organization
and propagation of the principles of the Charter, Harney had
lost none of his old class-consciousness. It was the "vile shopo-
cracy" who were responsible for the continuing "cannibal state
of affairs" and who constituted their main enemies in the "war
of class against class". And it was in the financial difficulties of
the system on which the middle classes depended for their existence that the working classes' main hope lay: "their ruin is our
salvation".[1]

Ten days after writing this address, Harney appeared in Birmingham to prepare for his trial. Long before the doors of the
court opened on 1 April the news of his appearance with two
other defendants, Wilkes and Brown, had packed the avenues
leading to the court with people. As with his previous hearings,
Harney's trial itself was something of an anticlimax, both he and
Wilkes being released after the Crown Counsel had stated that no
evidence against them would be offered. According to the
Counsel, this was due to the fact that the accused had conducted
themselves in a "becoming manner"—that is, they had refrained
from Chartist agitation—since their first hearings. Harney had
obviously done nothing of the sort, as he was at pains to explain
to the readers of the *Northern Star*—the government's case could
not stand because there was insufficient evidence of the seditious
speech with which he had been charged.

The fact seems to have been that the grand jury had thrown
out the bill of indictment against him on the basis of the deposi-
tions of his first hearings. But the manner of his acquittal was
scarcely one to decrease the suspicion which clung to him, particularly at a time when the main Chartist leaders, almost with-

[1] *Scottish Patriot*, vol. II, p. 177.

out exception, were either in or on their way to prison. Whittle, the editor of the *Champion* and an old enemy of Harney, wrote in effect that his freedom was proof of his having been an *agent-provocateur*. And it is doubtful that the indignant repudiation of Whittle's charges by the ever-loyal Winlaton Chartists and Fear-gus O'Connor effectively counteracted the accusation. "Was the honesty of a public man to be tested by his going, or not going to prison?" Harney asked. In the early months of 1840 the answer was not likely to be rational. It remained only for him to answer his accusers by his future actions.

The stormy events of the first period of Chartism left their mark on Harney. "He was," as he admitted to a Glasgow audience in January, "much wiser in the year 1840 than he had been at the commencement of 1839." [1] This was a matter not only of changed intellectual convictions, but of personality as well. The suspicions which attached to him must have been galling, and doubtless had much to do with the creation of a man whom an unfriendly contemporary described as gloomy and vindictive, but passionately loyal to his friends. He had not been alone in his belief that the political and social system which tolerated so much misery might be eradicated and a more just society born overnight. The youthful fervour with which he had entered the National Convention little more than a year before had been characteristic of the working-class movement as a whole. The ardent feeling that anything was possible was not to return either to him or to Chartism.

[1] *Ibid.*, p. 73.

CHAPTER V

Interregnum and 1842

LATE in 1839 there had been a faint lightening of the economic gloom. Trade improved slightly; there were isolated instances of wage-increases and a lessening of unemployment. It was a false dawn, however, and few among the working classes were even aware of it. In the following three years the price of bread fell slowly, but whatever benefit to the operatives might have resulted from this was negated by a steady process of wage-cutting, as employers struggled desperately to cut costs. Lock-outs, strikes and riots provided the sombre background of these years, and finally in 1842 discontent crystallized in a single convulsive reaction which assumed the proportions of an insurrection in some sections of England. Perhaps the most expressive comment on the conditions which gave rise to the General Strike of 1842 lies in the original demand of its participants: they wished a return to the wage scales of *1840*.

Whether the extension of the suffrage sought by the Chartists would have led to an amelioration of the widespread suffering may be debatable; but certainly it would have been impossible for a Chartist representation to have done less than the Whig and Tory governments of the period, which regarded their function as being limited to dealing with the symptoms, not the causes, of discontent. With order assured by troops quartered on the country and the imprisonment of more than 400 Chartist leaders, the Government, acting in the spirit of Victorian morality, turned to the spiritual welfare of its citizens. The equation of ungodliness and unrest was a common one, and the pressure of the clergy, linked with the predilections of the cabinet accounted for the only positive "social" policy which may be discerned in 1840.

An apt illustration of this is to be found in London's East End, where the Democratic Association had gained its greatest following. The perusal of a copy of Harney's London *Democrat* had prompted a horrified minister to write to the Home Office that order and religion were the prime requisites for the miserable

slum-inhabitants, for "although some of them are very poor I
believe they are well disposed to the present order of things".[1]
The agreement of the ruling classes with this analysis was demonstrated by a new church-building programme in Bethnal Green
in 1840—whether with reduced pew-rents is not apparent. A
further illustration of this concern for the spirit may be found in
the wave of prosecutions for blasphemy, in which those secu-
larist-economic critics of the *status quo*, the Socialists, were the
main targets.

Needless to say, such a policy neither converted Chartists nor
eased unrest. Indeed, it may have increased the dislike of the
clergy as defenders of the established order which in times of
stress was evidenced by attempts to fire churches and the singling
out of clergymen's dwellings for attack.[2] Harney, in a phrase to
be more succinctly expressed by Karl Marx, thus summed up the
government's policy of alleviation: "This is the good old remedy
for social ills—give 'em more church—give 'em more parsons—
more Bibles—and more bullets—they are the remedies war-
ranted, like Morrison's Pills, to cure all popular diseases." [3] Religion as the Morrison's Pills of the people had its limitations as
policy.

Despite the need for an organization to express working-class
protest against their continuing misery, Chartism recovered but
slowly in 1840. With the exception of Harney and the Scottish
leaders, almost every Chartist of importance was in prison by
March. The effect of this decapitation of the movement was to
be found in a diffusion of the political effort which had reached
such formidable proportions in 1839. New organizations developed which stressed the achievement of the Charter in terms
of temperance, education or religion; in some cases, such tactical
survivals as exclusive dealing had the effect of diverting attention
to the promotion of Chartist co-operative stores. A broader trend
may also be discerned, the effect of which was to further weaken
Chartism temporarily. Thwarted by the failure of political
action, many of the working classes turned again to direct
economic action, as they had after the disillusionment of 1832.
In Yorkshire and Lancashire, as Harney later wrote, the desire

[1] H.O. 44/32, 24 May 1840.
[2] E.g. in 1842. See P. C. G. Webster, *Records of the Queen's Own Royal Regiment of
Staffordshire Yeomanry* (Lichfield and London: 1870), pp. 125–42.
[3] *Northern Star*, 11 September 1841.

for social reform found expression increasingly through the medium of trade unions.[1] And the widening gap between Socialists and Chartists may well have been due to the confirmation of Socialist distrust in political action which they found in the events of 1839. How many trade unionists and Socialists had been active Chartists as well in 1839 cannot be determined, but the defection of many such men was doubtless a factor in the temporary *malaise* of the movement.

Equally difficult to measure is the direct loss of many of the most vigorous and intelligent of the Chartist rank-and-file through emigration. This "political emigration", as Harney subsequently described it,[2] included not only men who distinguished themselves in other countries—e.g. M. M. Trumbull, a general in the American Civil War; James Charlton, the manager of the Chicago and Alton Railway; and (an ironic example) Allan Pinkerton, whose private police agency became notorious for its American anti-labour activities—but such essential local leaders as Wolstenholme, the Convention delegate from Sheffield, who emigrated with twelve other highly-skilled Chartist workmen late in 1839.

There was, however, a more hopeful sign for the revival of Chartism. In July 1840 the English Chartists followed the example of the Scots and set up a national organization, the National Charter Association. Financed by the contributions of local associations, an executive of five with headquarters in Manchester (always a stronghold of Chartism) was to direct the activities of paid lecturers and the movement as a whole. The indispensable propaganda organ with a national circulation lay to hand in the *Northern Star*. Yet it was apparent that the effort to re-create a political mass movement waited on the future, when such leaders as O'Connor, O'Brien and Lovett would emerge from prison.

Meanwhile, having "escaped the fangs of the Whigs" at his trial, Harney had returned to Scotland. There he remained for nearly a year, travelling over two thousand miles and addressing hundreds of meetings, varying from great crowds in such militant working-class centres as Aberdeen to small groups of crofters in the Highlands. Something of the manner in which a radical agitator managed to live in those hard years emerges from his day-by-day experiences. For his living expenses Harney de-

---

[1] *Friend of the People*, 18 January 1851.   [2] Newcastle *Weekly Chronicle*, 6 May 1882.

pended mainly on the collections ordinarily taken at meetings, probably augmented by small sums for his reports in the *Northern Star*, which paid ten shillings a column to its regular contributors. His expenses were in any case minute, travelling as he did on foot and enjoying the hospitality of local Chartists. Obviously it was a life of extreme discomfort at times. To cover nearly three hundred miles through the Highlands by foot in the bitter weather of November and December was a rigorous experience for a city-bred youth whose health had never been robust. That he should, for example, walk eighteen miles in a driving rain immediately following a week's illness in Aberdeen suggests a certain indomitability—as does the Pepysian casualness of a later reference to his method of self-medication after such experiences: "Drenched myself with physic . . . applied leeches to my throat, which did me some good." [1]

Yet this itinerant life was not always so bleak. The exuberance which he felt in traversing southern Scotland and speaking to village crowds on the warm summer nights of 1840 is unmistakable in his terse comments. And such an experience as the night trip he made on a boat specially hired by the Dundee Chartists to Perth, where they paraded at dawn with band and banners flying to the startlement of the local burghers must have compensated for much suffering. There was also the pleasure he derived from the natural beauty of the countryside: the prospect of the River Doon in Ayrshire was, he wrote a few years later, "A scene lovely as Eden and beautiful as Elysium . . . I gloated on its charms." [2] All this was a far cry from the squalid Thames-side backstreets where he had spent his adolescence. Nor was it necessary to look so far for contrasts: not all of Scotland was an Eden. As something of an expert on slum life, Harney's reaction to Glasgow is worth quoting: [3]

> "Of all the wens of corruption and misery it has ever been my lot to visit, surely Glasgow is the worst. I have seen London, Manchester, Birmingham, Leeds, and other great hives of human crime and human agony; but for undisguised profligacy, offensive brutality, squalid wretchedness, and unbearable filth, Glasgow, to my mind, excels them all . . . I know of no remedies for the horrors of Glasgow but that of blocking it up at one extremity and setting fire to it at the other."

---

[1] *Northern Star*, 26 June 1841.
[2] *Ibid.*, 26 August 1843.   [3] *Ibid.*, 2 September 1843.

Harney's experience as a travelling agitator in Scotland also conveys a good deal about certain aspects of the working-class movement north of the border. Scottish Chartism had weathered the stormy events of 1839 and early 1840 more staunchly than had English Chartism, but it was by no means free from the divergences of opinion which had plagued the latter. Harney's reputation as an advocate of violence still rendered him suspect to the moderate element which dominated the Universal Suffrage Central Committee for Scotland, though he was active in organizing new branches under its aegis. There was, however, a larger physical force element in the Scottish movement than such admirers as Francis Place had noticed, and with this group Harney's reputation was not a handicap. While the majority of Glasgow Chartists remained hostile, the extremists of the Glasgow Democratic Club elected him their president. And, as he travelled to the east in the summer of 1840, he found a welcome which contrasted sharply with the general coolness of Clydeside, particularly with the militant working-class organizations of Dundee and Aberdeen. Here the response to his speeches which stressed the ultimate necessity of coercion was enthusiastic.

The advanced nature of the Chartist movements in these localities finds striking evidence in the anti-war demonstrations which they staged in the late summer and autumn of 1840, when hostilities with France seemed imminent. With a working-class internationalism which could trace its roots to the ill-fated Scottish Convention of 1793 Harney was in utter sympathy; and as the leading speaker at both mass-protests he stressed the class nature of national conflicts. "In spite of all the arts and intrigues of usurping rulers, may the people of Britain and France ever be united," he declared to a cheering crowd of Aberdeen working men who had paraded in thousands wearing tricolour ribbons. "We, the working-people, are their friends, not their foes." The common enemy of the European working class was the European ruling class and—drawing his Chartist moral—a foreign policy that involved them in wars would be changed only when they had changed the political system which gave their rulers power.[1]

Aberdeen and Dundee Chartism, it is apparent, differed in degree from that of Glasgow. Harney's speaking tour north into the Highlands in the winter of 1840 revealed a much more funda-

[1] *Northern Star*, 17 October 1840.

mental cleavage. In southern Scotland as a whole his audiences possessed a considerable degree of political sophistication; he could range from such subjects as emigration and Corn Law repeal to proletarian internationalism and find a ready response. But in addressing his small gatherings of farm-labourers and weavers in the Highlands, he was forced to the simplest type of political exposition, soon confining himself to explaining the principles of the Charter—which were comparatively unknown —and finally concentrating his efforts on the promotion of newspaper clubs. In a report to the *Northern Star* which summarized his findings, he suggested that in the same way the English Chartists sent their used radical papers to Ireland, so should the southern Scots to the Highlands. The implied comparison is an illuminating one.

That the labourers of the Highlands were comparable in political enlightenment to their Gaelic brothers across the Irish Sea was not due only to their isolation. The aristocracy, the Church of Scotland, and the middle classes exercised an obscurantist power in the Highlands for which there was no counterpart in the larger towns of southern Scotland. Harney conducted his tour as a "Candidate for the Representation of Aberdeenshire" in the forthcoming election, but he was left in no doubt from the first that the enfranchised classes considered him a dangerous interloper. After walking all day across unsettled country he would arrive at a small village where, more likely than not, the local laird or shopkeepers would not permit a public meeting, thus forcing him to utilize sheds or the homes of courageous local radicals. At Inverness, he reported, the middle-class Corn Law Repealers were deterred from physically attacking him only by the menacing aspect of the "workies". Most repressive of all, in his experience, were the "black slugs" of the Kirk, who denounced active Chartists from their pulpits. Harney had frequently attacked the Scottish clergy as supporters of the *status quo* —evidently a popular practice among Scottish Chartists [1]—and on his journey back from the Highlands the "Auld Kirk" got back a little of its own, the young agitator being gaoled briefly

---

[1] Harney, writing in 1892, estimated that in 1840 half of the Scottish Chartists had cut loose from connection with any kind of church. The other half looked on Christ as a great Radical reformer, and regarded most ministers as false to this ideal. Hence the success of Christian Chartist Churches in Scotland (Newcastle *Weekly Chronicle*, 24 August 1892).

in Stonehaven for riot after he had come into collision with a
"non-intrusion" meeting.

This incident, taken lightheartedly by its victim, did his
reputation no harm. In retaliation for his imprisonment, the
Dundee Chartists stormed a local "non-intrusion" meeting,
several going to gaol as a result. In Forfar, he was received with
an ovation; a fortnight later, having traversed the width of Scotland once again, his arrival was the occasion for a ball at
Greenock. The "smart, good-looking little gentleman", as the
Scottish Patriot described him, had in fact re-established himself in
Chartist esteem by his indefatigable efforts. His two-thousand-
mile walk and hundreds of speeches had made him a familiar
figure to Scottish Chartists and the excellent press that he had
received in the *Northern Star* doubtless had done much to restore
his prestige in the English movement. That the industrious
agitator and the reporter who so sedulously chronicled his
activities were the same person hardly alters this fact.

The year in Scotland gave him more than a reburnished
reputation. Before his Highland journey Harney had married
Mary Cameron, the daughter of an Ayrshire weaver with a long
record of radicalism, and a "tall, beautiful woman of high
spirit", according to a contemporary.[1] If Harney had been a
lonely young man—and there is much in his behaviour and
utterances to indicate this—Mary Cameron more than filled the
void, for their marriage was a rare compound of love and
intellectual sympathy.

Thus his return to England in April 1841 was quite different
from his departure a year before. It was, in fact, something of a
triumph. As he journeyed toward Manchester, the seat of the
English Chartist Executive, it was evident that his activities in
Scotland had been followed in the *Northern Star*. Processions and
bands greeted him at Carlisle and the surrounding villages and
he was quickly in demand to speak at meetings in Lancashire
and Yorkshire. The "Malthusian calculation" of keeping a wife
—Harney's phraseology was incorrigibly political—was solved
when he became the "West Riding lecturer", a position with a
salary of £6 per month paid through the district organization's
levy on its local branches.

The regular lecturers were key men in the Chartist movement

---

[1] G. J. Holyoake, *Sixty Years of an Agitator's Life*, 2 vols. (London: 1893), vol. I,
p. 106.

of 1841, building a grass-roots organization by speaking regularly in out-of-the-way villages and binding their districts together through incessant travelling. For the ambitious young Chartist unknowns with some intelligence and eloquence the position offered an entrance into the national counsels, and such rising new men as Jonathan Bairstow and R. G. Gammage, later the historian of Chartism, began in this way. Harney had himself become a fluent and effective speaker, and certainly his duties made extreme demands on his talent, it being nothing unusual for him to lecture seven or more times a week. That his salary and the contributions made at meetings for travelling expenses enabled him to travel sometimes by rail rather than by foot was not an unmitigated advantage: third-class coaches in the West Riding of the early 'forties were without covering or seats and the passengers rode standing up, exposed to the weather. Seemingly they were lacking in other facilities as well, in Harney's brief phrase being "detestable pig-pens on wheels".

In August the itinerant life which had occupied him since his trial came at last to an end, when, after a visit to the imprisoned O'Connor at York Castle, he became the Sheffield correspondent of the *Northern Star*. Among the primary reasons for O'Connor's continued ascendancy in the Chartist movement was his control of its main source of publicity, and to this could be added the fact that his main correspondents constituted a personal political machine. In the larger towns the position was held by his lieutenants; thus Harney's appointment confirmed his return to the front rank of Chartist leaders. He lost no time in taking over the local Chartist organization—not very tactfully, if his critics may be credited, one claiming that he threatened to annihilate through the medium of the *Northern Star* anyone opposed to him. Yet, after a preliminary period in which the opportunity for self-advertisement proved too heady a draught —e.g. "The inimitable manner in which Mr. Harney showed up the hypocrisy and knavery of the priesthood well-nigh convulsed his hearers with laughter . . ."—he became a fairly impartial, as well as lively, correspondent.

Harney's life in Sheffield was one of intense activity. His duties as agent and correspondent of the *Northern Star* (including the sale of the quack nostrum, "Chartist Pills", a small percentage of which went to the National Executive!) took up only a portion of his time. His activities included the presiding over the

H

regular meetings of the Sheffield Chartists two or three times a week at their rooms in Figtree Lane, the organization of public demonstrations in Paradise Square, and the capturing of Anti-Corn Law meetings for Chartist propaganda. He also found time to carry out his concept of a Chartist leader's duty "to stand between the people and their oppressors". When one Noakes, for example, was taken up by the police for loitering, it was the ubiquitous Harney who secured his release, had him lodge a complaint against the police, and suggested a boycott of the tradesman responsible for the arrest. Nor were his efforts confined to Sheffield. Harney also found time to make frequent trips to the adjoining villages and towns re-activating moribund Chartist associations.

All this was perhaps the small-change of radicalism, but it was through the multiplication of such efforts, made effective by the unrelieved distress of the working classes, that Chartism recovered from its first numbing shock. By the autumn of 1841 the National Charter Association included almost two hundred local organizations, in contrast with less than forty a year before. This growth occurred in spite of a renewal of internal criticism in the movement, the main source of which was O'Connor, whose incarceration in York Castle did not prevent him from inveighing against "Teetotal, Church and Household Suffrage Chartism". Particularly baneful in the *Northern Star's* view was "Knowledge Chartism", a reference to the recently-freed William Lovett's plan to convert Chartism into a national educational system. The attack on Lovett revealed the recrudescence of a more basic issue as well: that of Chartist co-operation with the middle-class radicals. Francis Place and the Parliamentary Radical, Joseph Hume, had made overtures to Lovett about pooling forces in a new organization—a "New Move" represented by the *Northern Star* as a middle-class plot to destroy Chartism. The accusations of deviationism and bourgeois-collaboration flung by O'Connor have a modern ring, as do the public recantations of many Chartists who had initially favoured Lovett's educational plan. But while that plan was buried under the invective of the *Northern Star* the issue of Chartist-Radical co-operation was far from dead.

To follow the "party-line" as laid down by O'Connor entailed no soul-searching for Harney, who remained irreconcilably opposed to any form of collaboration with the middle classes. As

he told a South Lancashire delegate meeting, while he deplored
Lovett's leaving them, "If O'Connor himself had proposed the
'New Move' he would have been flung overboard." [1] It was at
this juncture that political events—the fall of the Whig ministry
and the General Election of 1841—projected the issue of Chartist-Radical union on to the national stage, making it something
more than a disagreement between two old Chartist rivals.

As defined finally by the National Executive, Chartist policy
in the election of 1841 was a compromise between the conflicting
recommendations of O'Connor and Bronterre O'Brien. Feargus
advised support of the Tories on the ground that a Tory victory
would force the Whigs to woo working-class support through
concessions; in O'Connorese, "the galled jades [would] put their
sore necks to the collar and pull the Chartist wagon up Constitution Hill".[2] Events were to prove that there was considerable
political shrewdness in this reasoning, but Bronterre attacked the
policy in his most polemical vein as "a gross lump of Cobbet-
tism", recommending instead that Chartist candidates use the
hustings solely to protest the unrepresentative nature of the electoral system. The upshot was that the twelve Chartist candidates selected, among them Harney, utilized the campaign for a
democratic propaganda which in practical terms amounted to
an attack on the Whigs.

There is little doubt that an anti-Whig policy reflected working-class feeling. Many factors contributed to this antipathy: it
was a Whig government which had imprisoned hundreds of
Chartist leaders; the detested New Poor Law had been passed
during their occupation of office; the factory-owners who were
cutting wages and fighting the Ten Hours' Bill were associated
with the Radical wing of Whiggism. That, despite the fact that
many Tory candidates attacked the New Poor Law, no distinction could be drawn on lines of party on this measure—or on
almost any other measure which affected their condition, for
that matter—meant little to the working classes. The pot and
the kettle might in reality have been indistinguishable in hue,
but one was very much more in view. " 'We will be revenged
upon the Whigs' " became the Chartist slogan.[3]

The West Riding election, in which Harney stood as a Chartist

---

[1] *Northern Star*, 22 May 1841. [2] *Ibid.*, 6 February 1841.
[3] Thomas Cooper, *The Life of Thomas Cooper, Written by Himself* (London: 1872),
p. 148.

candidate with another one-time member of the National Convention, Lawrence Pitkeithly, epitomized in many ways the General Election of 1841. Consistent party principle was notable chiefly by its absence. On the important issue of Free Trade, for example, the young spokesman for the Whig landed interest of the West Riding, Lord Milton, assured his listeners that the Whigs would "drive the free trade gentlemen from the field", while the speeches of his confrère, the former Whig minister, Lord Morpeth, identified him as just such a gentleman. Nor were the Tory candidates, J. W. Wortley and Beckett Denison, more consistent, one attacking Free Trade, the other embracing it as a Tory policy initiated by Peel and Huskisson in the 1820's. Harney did not concern himself with this extreme elasticity of party policy, other than to impartially damn both "titled Aristocrats and wealthy Commoners" as the authors of class-legislation, the cause of the people's misery. But the main object of his attack was the party of Lords Milton and Morpeth. In a style more than suggestive of the candidate's own, the *Northern Star* reported, "He castigated the Whigs, laying bare their sophistries and exposing them to the public gaze in all their hideous deformity."

To say that the West Riding candidates "fought" the election is not indulgence in political cliché. Harney's first attempt to address a crowd was the signal for mounted Whigs to ride into his Chartist supporters, who retaliated with brickbats. Great efforts were devoted to mustering a show of force at the hustings on election day. The Whig landlords of the Riding "requested" their tenants to appear and vote for their candidates, while thousands of working men were bribed or cajoled into support of the Whigs or Tories. From Leeds, Bradford and Huddersfield (where bludgeons had been in production for weeks) factory owners dispatched their employees to Wakefield by wagon and train in platoons of twenty, with a day's wage in their pockets and overseers to ensure the distribution of food and beer—and the massing of their men under the right banner. These strategical preparations were matched by the Chartists, one group of six hundred Huddersfield men marching the thirteen miles to the hustings carrying stout staves. When Harney's opening remarks were drowned out by the noise of the Whig contingent a "forest of oak-saplings" was raised—a scene he was never to forget—and "from their ranks rose one long deafening shout of defiance which quelled the Whig mercenaries".[1] Taken amid such excitement the show of hands proved indecisive, but the poll of electors on the following day showed that the Tory candidates had triumphed.

This result came as a profound shock to the Whigs, who had held both seats in the West Riding since 1832. More shocking were the national returns, which gave the Tories a majority of more than ninety. It was apparent that popular revulsion from "Whig" policy had swept them from office—and the Chartists had formed the vanguard of popular discontent. Though some discomfited Whigs attributed this support to Tory gold (a charge not entirely without foundation), the Radicals looked deeper into the election result and drew another conclusion from it: to go on with their reforms it would be necessary to enlist the aid of the unenfranchised. The *Morning Chronicle* put the position of the extreme Free Traders unequivocally: they would not achieve repeal of the Corn Laws in the existent state of the representation. Thus the effect of the Tory victory with Chartist help was to infuse fresh vigour into middle-class Radical attempts to concert their efforts with the Chartists, a result which to some extent bore out O'Connor's prophecy.

The effort to organize a mass-movement of Chartists and Corn Law Repealers quickly gained momentum. By the early months of 1842, under the leadership of the selfless Birmingham Quaker, Joseph Sturge, and Edward Miall, editor of the powerful Radical *Nonconformist*, the more democratic section of the Anti-Corn Law League had declared for manhood suffrage. So far as the Chartists were concerned, the National Executive had indicated its approval of some form of joint action and one of its members had furnished a model for future action by merging the Chartists and Repealers of Bath. When in April representatives of the two movements met in Birmingham a formidable coalition of forces seemed in the making. On the one hand, Sturge and Miall were joined by John Bright, destined to become the most brilliant orator of Repeal; on the other, such long-time advocates of class-collaboration as Lovett and Vincent had combined forces with the quondam advocate of class-struggle, Bronterre O'Brien. And when, further, the delegates came to an agreement on the basis of the Six Points and decided to call a national convention in September to concert the new movement, the prospect of a

[1] Harney, quoted in W. E. Adams, *Memoirs of a Social Atom*, vol. I, p. 183.

united radical organization appeared closer than at any time since the Reform Bill "betrayal" had split working- and middle-class Radicals two decades before.

One essential element of success was still lacking, however: the support of Feargus O'Connor and the *Northern Star*. That Feargus still enjoyed an unquestioned primacy in the estimation of the majority of rank-and-file Chartists was attested by the celebrations on his release from York Castle in August 1841. *Feux de joie* were fired at the exact moment of his liberation and the hero himself rode through cheering York crowds like a giant black pearl (wearing a fustian suit specially made by the Manchester Chartists) in a triumphal coach of green and pink velvet shaped like a sea-shell. Harney, representing Sheffield and Barnsley, was one of fifty-eight delegates who then heard Feargus hint broadly at a union with the "little middle class"—shopkeepers and small tradesmen—against the "steam producing class". But O'Connor's attitude toward subsequent developments in this direction was even more than usually ambivalent, veering from outright denunciation of the Sturgeite conference of April to mild approval of Sturge's "Complete Suffrage" movement. This schizophrenic behaviour was a clear indication of a division of opinion among Chartists with regard to the new policy; O'Connor, with his instinctive demagoguery, was trying to divine the feeling of a working class body with two minds.

One has only to turn to Harney's experience in Sheffield to see the national division of opinion in microcosm, for what went on there was typical of the majority of the manufacturing towns. Unlike O'Connor, his Sheffield lieutenant was unremittingly hostile to the move toward union with the middle-class Radicals. Sturge's Birmingham conference in April he condemned as an attempt to destroy the N.C.A. and the old leadership of Chartism. "If the middle class are honest," he declared at one of many Sheffield meetings, "let them adopt our Charter and join our Association." [1] At the same time—in language which was doubtless partly responsible for the Tory Sheffield *Mercury's* wistful recollection of the days when such talk had led to the gallows —he continued to denounce all compromise with men whose democratic overtures were merely a means to their own class-aims, that is, the repeal of the Corn Laws and a consequent cutting of wages when bread became cheaper.

[1] *Northern Star*, 30 April 1841.

This uncompromising stand led in Sheffield, as it did in a similar way all over the country, to a splitting of the movement. In part the split was due to the influence of Lovett and Vincent, and above all, of Bronterre O'Brien, whose prestige, though waning, was still great. But the composition of the dissident Sheffield Chartists, who now organized in the "Political Institute", reveals a more basic division on class lines within the unenfranchised. The Political Institute men were the relatively well-off Chartists, both operatives and small shopkeepers—or, as the Whiggish Sheffield and Rotherham *Independent* characterized them, "the more rational and enlightened Chartists". Furthermore, the Institute men could look for support to the working-class élite—the "acting and leading-men and secretaries, and speakers of the trades", in Harney's terms—who were, he was convinced, not Chartists but Corn Law Repealers.[1] Yet, as even the unfriendly *Independent* reluctantly admitted, Harney commanded the main mass-following in Sheffield, a following made up of the same *sans-culottes* type which had once marched under the banners of the London Democratic Association. The Political Institute members, the *Independent* reported of a great Chartist meeting in June 1842, "made a much more respectable appearance than their companions of Fig-Tree Lane"; the appearance of the latter "betokened the distress that prevails". That distress now temporarily swept the issue which had divided Sheffield and English Chartism into the limbo of abstractions; the question of a union of the classes was forgotten in the great tide of violence which rolled over the Midlands and North in the summer of 1842.

In the preceding autumn Harney had observed furtive humans in the fields near Sheffield dragging ploughs to turn up potatoes to eat. During the winter the streets had been full of increasing numbers of unemployed and emigration had been heavy. As 1842 drew on the distress became even more acute, one alarming symptom being a sharp increase in crime which made it necessary to hold a double session of the Sheffield Assizes in June. Out of 30,000 employables in the town, some 24,000 were entirely destitute or on half-time; and though Sheffield had raised its poor-rate twice since 1840, the totally indigent still received but slightly more than a shilling weekly, an amount

[1] Sheffield *Iris*, n.d., quoted in Feargus O'Connor, ed., *The Trial of Feargus O'Connor and Fifty-Eight Others at Lancaster* (London: 1843), pp. 236–37.

impossible to consider in terms of subsistence. What conditions were like elsewhere may be gathered from the fact that the rate of dole in Sheffield was higher than that paid in all but one of the hundred most distressed localities in England—in some cases, ten times higher. Faced with this appalling spectacle of suffering, the government did nothing, unless the Queen's appeal to private philanthropy is excepted. And it was apparent that the state did not intend to do anything. As summed up in Macaulay's well-known peroration on the presentation of the second Chartist Petition to the House of Commons in May 1842, no government "ever had been or would be able to . . . dispel poverty from the land". In short, the desperate condition of the working class was irremediable.

One reaction of that class to the twin goads of economic distress and the passivity of the government was a great revival of Chartism—a fact which demonstrates once again the social dynamic of the movement. "Circumstances are doing what argument failed to effect," wrote Harney of the accession of members in the winter of 1841–42;[1] and the startling number of 3,317,752 signatures on the second Chartist petition attested to this generalization. Macaulay, in his attack on the petition, put the propertied classes' awareness of the social nature of the demand for universal suffrage succinctly when he declared that political democracy would mean economic democracy. This was precisely the essence of the matter from the Chartist standpoint. "I conceive that civilization rests on the security of property," said Macaulay, and property necessarily rested in the hands of a few. While it would be too much to claim that Harney's public reply to Macaulay in the *Northern Star* expressed the considered beliefs of the more than three million signers of the petition, without doubt he gave form to the inarticulate feelings of many in declaring that "the wretchedness, starvation and fearful despair of the operative classes loudly proclaim that *their property*—their labour and its fruits, are not secured to them; but on the other hand are the common prey of all the legal plunderers of society". It was to ensure a rightful return to *this* form of property that the Chartists sought political power.

The correlation between sharpening distress and Chartist resurgence can be clearly observed in Sheffield in the summer of 1842. Where previously the joining of a half-dozen new members

[1] *Northern Star*, 27 November 1841.

had been the occasion for congratulations, the weekly intake now numbered hundreds. Less than 200 strong in June, by August there were more than 1,500 registered Chartists under Harney's leadership, and an apprehensive Sheffield press estimated the attendance of the Chartist meetings held morning and evening in Paradise Square as being well in the thousands. Harney's reports in the *Northern Star* became very brief: "We don't write now, we work," he noted.

The death in prison of Samuel Holberry, who had been a leader in the abortive Sheffield rising of January 1840, further excited the town in midsummer. The depth of the feeling of indignation at this event—"murder it is considered here", Harney wrote to the Chartist spokesman in the Commons, Thomas Duncombe[1]—was due in part to the horror with which the new "scientific" penal systems of the time were regarded. Holberry had spent most of his time at Northallerton Gaol, where the system of silence and solitary confinement was in effect —a system which, though abandoned in some cases due to the high incidence of incurable insanity, was being extended in such new prisons as Holloway. Faced with living conditions which made life almost intolerable, the 20,000 people who attended Holberry's funeral could ponder what the consequences of revolt against those conditions were.

In a powerful funeral oration Harney drove home the political lesson of Holberry's fate.

> "Tyrants have in all ages and all countries strove by persecution to crush liberty; and by torture, chains, and death to prevent the assertion of the rights of man . . . We bid them defiance!" he cried. "Here, by the graveside of the patriot, . . . swear to unite in one countless moral phalanx, to put forth the giant struggle which union will call into being . . . If ye do this and act upon your vow, our children will rejoice that he died not in vain but that from his ashes rose, phoenix-like, his dauntless spirit. . . ." [2]

Despite the note of defiance in his speech, Harney's emphasis was upon the necessity for thorough organization: the working classes must first weld a "countless moral phalanx" before challenging the governing classes. And it is apparent in his public addresses during the following weeks that the lesson of the

---

[1] Thomas H. Duncombe, *The Life and Letters of Thomas Slingsby Duncombe*, 2 vols. (London: 1868), vol. I, p. 306.

[2] *Northern Star*, 2 July 1842.

failure of violence in 1839–40, of which Holberry had been a victim, was uppermost in his mind. In a typical speech late in July, Harney, following the inflammatory remarks of the physical force leader of Leicester Chartism, Thomas Cooper, stressed the necessity for "unwearied prudence and caution" until their organization was complete. Nor was he alone in emphasizing the danger of precipitate action: the same note of caution is to be found in the *Northern Star's* leading articles and in the warning of the National Executive against "insurrections and secret conspiracies".

These exhortations indicate the growing uneasiness of the Chartist leadership as outbreaks of violence became more frequent. Sporadic violence could be considered the "normal" background of events since 1840, but in these new outbreaks a definite pattern was to be discerned. At Dudley in April, for example, wage cuts had led the nailers to strike and riot, following which they had marched about the countryside stopping others of their craft from working and cutting the bellows of those who refused to co-operate. By late July the same pattern was to be observed in the Potteries, where colliers and ironworkers resorted to violence to extend their strike and the Staffordshire Yeomanry were called up to restore order. Finally, early in August, these scattered outbreaks of violence merged in a great spasm of protest which quickly assumed the form of a general strike. Beginning as a reaction against wage-cuts in Stalybridge, the cessation of labour rapidly spread to Manchester, South Lancashire and through the West Riding and Staffordshire, accompanied by rioting, attacks on mills and private houses, and battles between troops and strikers.

Though the resorts to direct industrial action which culminated in the "Plug Riots" or General Strike of 1842 involved many rank-and-file Chartists, they were in no way linked to the central leadership of Chartism. And so with the General Strike itself: its initiative came from below; its origin lay in a spontaneous outburst of rage against the last of an interminable series of wage cuts. These facts explain the confusion and disunity of subsequent Chartist policy, a policy which was shaped by events and never rose above expediency. It was a convention of trades' delegates meeting in Manchester on 12 August which introduced an entirely new aim into the strike by declaring that it would continue until the Charter became law. For this decision the national Chartist leadership could scarcely be held responsible; they met only after the step had been taken.

By the time Harney left for the Chartist convention which was to meet in Manchester on 17 August the strike had assumed frightening proportions, extending north (though not solidly) as far as Glasgow and Dunfermline, and south into Warwick. In the Potteries the military exerted control only sporadically; due to the great range of the affected areas, as the *Evening Star* reported, the troops were "quite unequal" to the task of dispersing the insurgents. The problem of maintaining public order in the event of mass disturbances, which had last been posed in the summer of 1839, had now to be dealt with, and it was plain that in spite of the new rural police, the yeomanry, and regular troops, the forces of order were temporarily not up to their task. In Sheffield no overt action had yet taken place, though the state of feeling there was such as to cause the magistrates to request troops. In Manchester too, by the time Harney arrived there, an ominous calm reigned, ensured by the presence of the 8,000 special constables and 2,200 regular troops who had managed to restore order. But no smoke rose above the "City of Long Chimneys" and the situation remained explosive.

About sixty in number, the Chartist delegates met on the morning of 17 August, after reaching their hall through streets patrolled by cavalry and horse-drawn artillery. The majority of delegates were from districts already on strike, and it was obvious as they briefly summarized the feeling of their districts that they were in favour of continuing and extending the strike to achieve the Charter. McDouall, the most forceful member of the Executive, and Thomas Cooper of Leicester, who had just come from addressing the huge and turbulent mass-meetings in the Potteries, were the strongest advocates of this course, the latter declaring that "The spread of the strike would and must be followed by a general outbreak." [1] O'Connor—who, according to one participant, had appeared frightened before the meeting—protested against the talk of fighting, but waited to learn the sense of the convention before taking a stand.

It was his editor, the Reverend William Hill, who led off in attacking the majority, denouncing the strike as a machination of the Anti-Corn Law League. "Fighting!" Hill cried, "the people had nothing to fight with and would be mown down by

[1] Cooper, *Life of Thomas Cooper* . . ., p. 208.

artillery if they attempted to fight." Harney's speech, following that of Hill, was the sensation of the debate. Cooper recalls the scene vividly:[1]

> "Nothing caused so much amazement in the Conference. . . . He supported Editor Hill—even he, Julian, the renowned invoker of the spirits of Marat, Danton, and Robespierre, in the old Convention times!—Julian the notorious advocate of physical force, at all times! 'What! Julian turned "moral-force hum-bug"!—what will happen next?' was said by the advocates of the strike. And yet, Julian had supported Editor Hill in a very sensible manner; and a more sincere and honest man than Julian, perhaps, never existed."

The situation must have seemed paradoxical. Once again Harney stood with the minority in a Chartist Convention, but this time as an advocate of moderation. The fact was that Harney was no longer "the notorious advocate of violence at all times". Though still convinced that the working class would ultimately gain power only through coercion, two elements now seemed to him indispensable for success: thorough preparation and a unified mass-support. The first element was obviously lacking in the existent situation; his intimate knowledge of the Sheffield working class made him extremely dubious of the existence of the second. The majority of delegates felt otherwise, however, and on the afternoon of 17 August voted overwhelmingly to endorse the strike policy.

There was a fatal inconsistency in their decision. The Convention's first address strongly cautioned against violence, yet it was obvious that merely withholding labour from employers who were actually saving wage-costs in a time of severe depression could exert no pressure. Thomas Cooper was at least consistent in arguing that the general strike "must and would" become an insurrection. Perhaps the National Executive did not believe that it was playing with revolution when it issued a second address couched in much stronger language than the first, but the government was of a different mind. One member of the Executive was immediately arrested; the three others fled, McDouall out of the country to France. Already hampered by an inconsistent policy, the movement thus immediately lost its head. The co-ordinating body for the strike had, in fact, dis-

---

[1] Cooper, *Life of Thomas Cooper* . . ., p. 210.

appeared before it had begun to function, for the delegates had already dispersed and O'Connor, though he had voted with the majority and might possibly have given some direction to events, had quickly made off to London where he remained *incommunicado*. There remained but one effective organ of control, the *Northern Star*. But Hill, doubtless aware of his employer's real feelings and still violently opposed to the majority decision, gave those who waited for instructions no lead at all, instead playing down the events at Manchester to the fullest extent compatible with not ignoring them altogether.

These events did nothing to lessen Harney's foreboding, yet, as the local press reported of his address to a meeting on his return to Sheffield, "Though he thought the course unwise, if the people of Sheffield decided to strike he would act with them." [1] It was plain, however, that the "people of Sheffield" were sharply divided on the strike policy. During his absence a popular meeting had endorsed the Convention's decision, but in response to his announcement of a mass-meeting on the 21st to decide the issue, six of the Sheffield trades placarded the town with a declaration of non-participation and only five attended. This disunity decided Harney's course of action. Well aware of the strong current of support for militant action, he arose to attack a pro-strike resolution at the great meeting on 21 August. "Let them think about what they were to do!" he demanded. "Were the trades of Sheffield Chartist already? If they were, would they, at the fiat of that meeting, turn out to a man?" Though the majority of some trades were Chartist, he declared, more were not, and their leading men were Corn Law Repealers rather than Chartists. And, he went on, "Men who turned out, not for the Charter, but for fear of having their heads broken, when the turnouts had left them, or when military protection was offered them, would resume their labours in spite of the turnouts."

Angry cries greeted these statements: "Cut it short and run home," shouted one voice. Harney refused to accept this advice and tumult followed. "Will O'Connor support the strike?" he was asked. "O'Connor supports the strike and I oppose it," Harney replied, unaware perhaps of Feargus's discreet retreat to London. Men were already starting to return to work in other towns, he declared, why then should they go out? But it was his

[1] Sheffield and Rotherham *Independent*, 20 August 1842.

repetition of what he considered the crucial aspect of the general strike that was decisive. "Are you ready to fight the soldiers? You may say that this is not the question but I tell you that it would be the question. I do not think you are. I am ready to share your perils but I will not lead you against the soldiers." [1] Only faint cheers greeted the end of Harney's speech, but he had won the meeting, as a show of hands indicated. He had not won the pro-strike faction, however, and in the following days so violent was feeling against him that he was forced to close his shop temporarily and police protection was given him.

Events had already begun to bear out Harney's analysis of the strikers' weaknesses. The day before his speech the trades' delegates in Manchester had declared the strike at an end. Hunger and the lack of central control and mass support limited the total duration of the movement to less than a fortnight, though it persisted in isolated cases for some time longer. With enough troops concentrated in the affected areas to restore order, the ranks of the strikers broke. Those who had been captive rather than willing participants returned to work, a process possibly hastened by the government's pressure on manufacturers to refrain from imposing conditions on re-employment and to reach an accommodation over wages. And with the subsidence of the fever came the application of the government's usual method of aiding convalescence: arrests and imprisonments.

A more lasting consequence of the General Strike of 1842 was the turning away of trade-unionists from Chartism. The way in which this came about was quite natural, if hardly logical. In its inception the strike was economic in character. It had then adopted a political object—the achievement of the Charter. Not the formal Chartist leadership, but trades-Chartists were responsible for this step; and it was these men whose voice had really dominated the Manchester Convention and led it to endorse the strike. The real irony of the situation, and the tragedy for Chartism, lay in the fact that the trades-Chartists, when confronted with the dismal failure of their policy, blamed the formal Chartist leadership for a course of action which it had not initiated, and a powerful element of Chartist strength fell away.

There was another consequence as well, having to do with the attempt at middle and working-class union which had appeared so promising before the events of the summer. Certainly the very

[1] Sheffield *Iris*, n.d., quoted in *The Trial of Feargus O'Connor* . . ., pp. 236–37.

wide currency given in the popular, as well as Chartist, press to accusations against the Anti-Corn Law League as the instigators of the strike made some Chartists more antipathetic to middle-class Radicalism in general. And, conversely, the identification once again of Chartism with near-revolutionary disorders confirmed many of the middle-class Radicals in fears which had been lulled by the respectability of the movement since the violence of 1839–40. Typical of this reaction was the comment of the *Free Trader* on Sturge's renewed efforts to effect a union of Chartists and Repealers in the months following the strike: "He who asks the help of such a rabblement of scoundrels as the Chartists is the biggest jackass who ever brayed for thistles."

The effort thus delicately described furnishes the concluding theme of Chartism in 1842. With the restoration of order, Sturge called for a conference to meet in December in which half of the representatives were to be electors—i.e. middle-class Radicals, and half non-electors—i.e. Chartists. O'Connor's first reaction was to call for a boycott on the "humbug conference" and for a time it seemed that he, with Harney, the Reverend Hill, and eighteen other participants in the Manchester Convention, would have no choice in the matter, for on 29 October they were arrested for their part in the strike. Their enforced activity was brief, however. Charged with riot and conspiracy, they were able to traverse to the February Assizes instead of standing trial immediately before a special Liverpool Commission—a fortunate occurrence in view of the severity of that body in dealing with those who came before it with the events of August still fresh in the public mind. Feargus, with one of his characteristic about-faces, then dropped his plan of boycotting the conference and instructed the Chartists to ensure that delegates elected at the public meetings were not predominantly middle class.

That this meant packing the conference with O'Connorites went without saying. In Birmingham, the electoral meeting presided over by Sturge himself was overwhelmed by O'Connor's local lieutenant, George White, and—as the *Nonconformist* noted uneasily—four Chartists and two Sturgeites were elected. Harney was even more efficient in Sheffield. When the Complete Suffrage Union, a body composed of middle-class Radicals and the "cream of the working class" with a Nonconformist minister as chairman, boycotted the public meeting which elected Harney and three other Fig Tree Lane men, Harney in turn zestfully swamped their private meeting with his followers and the Chartist delegates were reaffirmed.

Nevertheless, when the 400-odd delegates representing 146 localities in England, Scotland and Wales met on 27 December, the O'Connorites constituted no absolute majority. While the Chartists outnumbered the Sturgeites by almost three to one, Lovett's party of moderates made up a significant portion of this group. In fact, as one participant later wrote, the hope of conciliation and a new party was so strong that had the Complete Suffrage men evinced a sincere desire for complete union, "not even O'Connor himself could have prevented the great body of working-men delegates from uttering shouts of joy".[1]

As events transpired, it was unnecessary for O'Connor and his lieutenants to play any decisive role in wrecking the Convention. Not the least of the paradoxes of 1842 was the fact that that role was played by the staunchest Chartist advocate of co-operation with the middle class, William Lovett. It was his adamantine refusal to discard the name of the Charter, even when its Six Points were accepted, that constituted the rock on which the Convention split. The symbolism of the Charter had much to do with this. To the Chartists (as Lovett said) it represented imprisonment, transportation and death in a cause which had absorbed their lives for four years. To the Sturgeites its associations were those of violence, strikes and clandestine plots—an insuperable handicap in rallying middle-class support. But there were deeper irreconcilabilities hidden in this disagreement. In the high temper of debate which preceded the Sturgeite withdrawal from the conference, such incidents as that in which Lawrence Heyworth, a wealthy Free Trader and prominent Sturgeite, pointed his finger at O'Connor while addressing the Chartist delegates and shouted, "We don't object to your principles or your name; what we want to get rid of is your leaders!"[2] indicated one aspect of antagonism. Still another was assiduously propagated by Harney in private conversations with the Chartist members. Cobden was the head of the group of which the Sturgeites were the tail, he argued, yet Cobden not only denounced the name but the principles of the Charter. How

[1] Cooper, *Life of Thomas Cooper*. . . . p. 222. Henry Solly and William Lovett, both participants, appear to have annotated the account of the conference which appears in the copy of Gammage's *History of the Chartist Movement*, 1854 edition, in the British Library of Political and Economic Science.

[2] *Evening Star*, n.d., quoted in *Northern Star*, 7 January 1843.

then could they trust such men? And perhaps deepest of all lay the economic incompatibility of the two forces. The strong socialist element in Chartism was anathema to the Sturgeites, as one of them made clear in a furious outburst against "levelling".

The hopes blighted by the ruin of the conference were not to find fruition until the 1860's. A more immediate effect of its failure was a further weakening of Chartism. Disillusioned or disgusted, Lovett and a body of well-intentioned men dropped from the movement. Thus, the fateful year of 1842 saw two grievous wounds inflicted upon Chartism: the large-scale defection of trade-unionists as the result of the General Strike and the loss of many moderate leaders through the failure of the Sturgeite conference. From these wounds Chartism was never to fully recover.

CHAPTER VI

"All Men are Brethren"

THE sorry legacy of 1842 was not yet paid in full. The failure of the Sturgeite conference was followed by an ugly mood of recrimination in which charges and counter-charges between the defenders of the Executive and the O'Connorites reached a nadir of pettiness. Such response of the Chartist body as there was indicated that it had sickened of internal dissension, however, and Feargus finally gagged the most vituperative of the controversialists, his editor Hill, bringing an exhausted calm. Like a good latter-day Communist, Harney declared, "It was denunciation which had kept the movement in its present sound and healthy condition";[1] but in view of Chartist apathy in January 1843 the claim was a dubious one.

For what it was worth, a kind of unity had finally been achieved. Feargus stood without any serious rivals. The Chartist giants of the past—Lovett, O'Brien, Attwood, Frost—were gone, casualties of the government, of disillusionment, or of O'Connor's climb to power. Mokannah—Bronterre's bitter epithet for the man who, like Thomas Moore's Prophet Chief in "Lalla Rookh", had been raised to his throne by the "blind belief of millions"—ruled supreme. But where were the millions? Unlike the period after the Chartist debacle of 1839–40, in the months following the Sturgeite conference there was no revival of popular political interest. Travelling in Scotland in the late summer, Harney observed that organized Chartism in Ayrshire and Dumfries had vanished; Glasgow, Dundee and Edinburgh, onetime strongholds of the movement, were politically lifeless. Even the Sturge faction was defunct, he reported, "gone out like the last smoke of a farthing rushlight, leaving nothing behind but the stink of its bad name".[2]

Luckily for Harney and the fifty-eight other Chartists who stood trial at Lancaster in March for their connection with the General Strike, this abatement of the previous summer's fever characterized their prosecution as well. Instead of the summary

[1] *Northern Star*, 14 January 1843.   [2] *Ibid.*, 2 September 1843.

treatment which those tried immediately after the strike had suffered, the defendants were treated with an impartiality and mildness which caused the splenetic *Times* to accuse the judge, crown counsel and jury of a flagrant dereliction of duty. The case against those whose connection with the strike was limited to participation in the Manchester Conference was not, in fact, a strong one. As Harney pointed out in an ably reasoned defence, the conference had met only after the strikers had declared for the Charter; their only private meeting prior to the conference had been at a tea-party, where the sole sign of "conspiracy" evident was the "apparent universal determination to get rid of the tea and toast as soon as possible".[1] While he reviewed his opposition to the strike policy, he emphasized his solidarity with his co-defendants by defending the legality of the Convention's decision: what, after all, had been illegal about it? Baron Rolfe, summing up for the jury, was by no means sure, intimating that the Court of Queen's Bench would have to consider the matter. So it transpired. Although Harney and O'Connor, with thirteen others, were convicted on one count, their appeal two months later resulted in a reversal of the verdict on the ground of the charge's ambiguity.

The Chartist leaders returned to a movement of which only a solid core of the faithful remained active. In Sheffield, the organization held together better than in many localities, though Harney admitted that they were "not making much noise". From that somnolent Sheffield summer some of the homely detail of Chartism emerges. The Chartist rooms in Fig Tree Lane served much the same all-embracing function as did the Methodist chapel to its communicants. The meeting-place was the centre of intellectual life for the members, weekly discussion groups meeting under a bust of the martyred Holberry to hear Harney or others discourse on such topics as "The Working Class in Roman, Saxon and Norman Times". On the walls hung home-made banners inscribed with the names of working-class heroes, ranging from Wat Tyler to Byron and Shelley; and a small library was started. The rooms served also as a focal point of social life. There were frequent dinners and teas to which entire families came—perhaps a conditioning factor of some importance for the children's beliefs. This secular counterpart of Methodism finds a particularly striking, and quite

[1] O'Connor, ed., *The Trial of Feargus O'Connor* . . ., p. 232.

amusing, illustration in the singing of Chartist hymns and the
recitation of the "Chartist Litany", a portion of which reads:[1]

12. And he [O'Connor] opened his mouth and taught them
    saying:
13. Ye Chartists are the salt of the earth:
    Ye are the light of the world: let your light so shine before men
    that they may see the truths of the Charter, and seeing
    believe.

*   *   *

20. And the names of a few of the great apostles of Chartism were
    F. O'Connor . . . and George Julian Harney . . .

Possibly gripped by the piety induced by such recitations, Harney went so far as to propose that the Sheffield Chartists take the
teetotal pledge, but this aberration was only temporary. "Charles
Mackey's philosophy is ours," he wrote a little later. "Little fools
will drink too much, but great ones not at all." [2]

It is indicative of the stagnation of popular interest in Chartism
that the major public activity of Harney's group in 1843 was
devoted to the agitation for Irish independence. With his ready
sympathy for nationalist movements—Ireland, he commented,
was the "Poland of the West"—Harney was the first Englishman
in Sheffield to join the Repeal Association. But this connection
was as short-lived as O'Connor's, Daniel O'Connell, the leader
of the Repealers and old enemy of both men, soon making it clear
that he did not relish their association. All this, needless to say,
had little to do with Chartism. The frustrating fact remained
that the movement was being smothered by the increasing complacency of the working classes; and about this they could do
nothing, for its basic reason lay in economic improvement. After
five frightful years of working-class suffering (it is this period that
has been misnamed the "Black Forties") industry had slowly
begun to recover. By May of 1844 the *Northern Star* was discussing "prosperity", albeit in inverted commas, and reporting
such facts as a "great rise" in miners' wages. With this gradual
improvement of economic conditions acute distress lessened, and
with it disappeared temporarily the social dynamic of Chartism
as a mass-movement.

An accurate index of this is to be found in the declining circu-

---

[1] *Penny Democrat and Political Illuminator*, n.d., quoted in H. U. Faulkner, *Chartism
and the Churches* (New York: 1915), p. 125; *Northern Star*, 5 November 1842.
[2] *Northern Star*, 19 December 1846.

lation of the *Northern Star*. By the summer of 1843 its weekly
sale was only 10,000 copies, a quarter that of 1839. Further
evidence lay in the fact that Editor Hill, who had wished to see
the Chartist movement "purged of the ranting, mouthing locusts
who have done it so much harm" was himself purged by O'Connor in July after a particularly virulent outburst against the
exiled McDouall. The time for internecine warfare was past,
as local Chartist resolutions made plain; Feargus could afford the
alienation of no more of the faithful. It is difficult to believe that
many felt sincere regret at Hill's departure—in Graham Wallas's
phrase, he "appears to have had a perfectly extraordinary talent
for making himself nasty".[1] Hill's misfortune was Harney's gain.
When Joshua Hobson, the publisher of the *Star*, took over as
editor, Harney moved to Leeds as sub-editor. He had finally
penetrated to the heart of that working newspaper world at
which he had once gazed so longingly through the windows of
radical printers.

Although the *Northern Star* had seen palmier days it still remained the working-class equivalent of *The Times*, and its new
sub-editor, now twenty-six, was firmly placed in a position of
influence. In the two years that followed his part in the direction
of the paper steadily grew, and he had become editor in fact
before he became such formally in October 1845. Some measure
of his influence may be gained from the recollection of an obscure
radical a half-century later, whose Saturday task as a boy had
been to read the *Northern Star* to his illiterate parents. "As soon
as the paper came, my father would say, 'Come, take up the
paper, and see first of all if George Julian has owt to say this
week.' George Julian was my father's high priest." [2]

Comparing the *Northern Star*—or, indeed, most of its contemporaries—with the average modern newspaper should give any
blind exponent of the inevitability of progress second thoughts.
Here was no pabulum with an admixture of dubious spices, but
solid fare meant for mature appetites. At the same time it must
be admitted that "stolid" rather than "solid" was at times more
descriptive of the contents of the *Star*, and Harney's natural
journalistic talent was soon evident in the added liveliness of the
paper. The regular arrival of Victoria's progeny, for example,

---

[1] "The Chartist Movement", *Our Corner*, vol. XII (1888), p. 118.
[2] John Arlom, in Newcastle *Weekly Chronicle*, 27 August 1892. *Cf.* an analogous
letter from Thomas Hayes, *ibid.*, 7 November 1896.

evoked his impious suggestion that, rather than reciting national prayers of thanksgiving, congregations should sing "hymns of despair for their misfortune in being saddled with another addition to the brood of Royal Cormorants". There was also his gift for the telling phrase: Carlyle was characterized as "that sword-worshipper, one half a great man and one half a humbug". And occasionally, doubtless to the entertainment of his readers, he completely lost his temper, never equable at best. Thus, in answering a critic's assertion of Burns's damaging effect on Scottish morals, Harney curbed himself so far as to present a great collation of sources to disprove the allegations against his hero; but this done, ended by suggesting that the offending writer was very probably a eunuch.

In addition to the two or three leading articles which he wrote weekly, he soon expanded the literary review section into a sort of second editorial page where he held forth in a controversial fashion, giving the *Star's* audience great draughts of his favourite Byron as well as the less heady Eliza Cook, and titbits of such diverse poets as the obscure Scottish weaver, Willie Thom, and the fashionable Monckton Milnes. Naturally, his was literary criticism with a strong political flavour. Long extracts of Disraeli's *Coningsby*—"by far the most popular novel of 1844", Harney commented—were printed in his columns; but he took care to point out the insidiousness of the siren-call of "Young England". "It is not a return to the 'good old times' when the baron and the priest, or the parson and the squire, were the local gods in every town and hamlet, that is now wanted to regenerate England," he wrote. "It is equality, not feudalism, which is the hope of the many . . . the 'golden age' is before, not behind us." While they might receive parks and baths from the great landowners, they could never expect really sincere social legislation from a class whom such measures would destroy. Such as it was, Harney ventured, Disraeli's movement was the offspring of Chartism, but the mountain had laboured and brought forth a mouse[1]—a judgment scarcely to be disputed with the passage of a century.

In the same forthright, sometimes mordant, way he introduced his readers to such odd sects as the "mystical communists" of Ham Common (near Richmond-on-Thames). This ascetic group, with its vegetarianism and partiality to Roman togas,

---

[1] *Northern Star*, 9 November, 14 December 1844; 14 February 1845.

was treated kindly by the *Star*; but Harney could not forbear a remark or two at the expense of the "Concordists' " views on marriage, which entailed a trial period in which no consummation but that of the intellect was to take place. "This 'prothetical' and 'metaphysical' love may be enchanting to those who can understand it and divest themselves of human passion," he commented, "but we are not of that number: the *Giaour's* love is the love for us." More to his taste were the novels of Eugene Sue, with their mixture of romance and biting social criticism—a formula to which G. W. M. Reynolds, the radical novelist and publisher, was to add a dash of pornography with such phenomenal success.

Directly attributable to Harney was a more significant change in the *Northern Star*: the increasing attention to certain events abroad which gives the paper a unique claim to having been the first mass-circulation organ of international socialist movements in England. Prior to Harney's employment the usual practice of the *Northern Star*, like most contemporary weeklies, was simply to condense the foreign reports of the metropolitan dailies, which dealt conventionally with political events—i.e. like the history of the day, from the governing classes' viewpoint. His innovation lay in a concentration on popular radical news, in order, as he wrote early in 1844, to counteract the insularity of Chartism and "to make the English Democrat aware of the part that was being played by his brethren on the different stages of the political world". The *Northern Star* had given the English working-class radicals a sense of their solidarity in the late 'thirties by gathering local reports in one national organ; Harney's object was to make the paper perform a similar function for the English operative on the international level.

Much of the young sub-editor's political views, and those of the extreme wing of the English working class, emerge from the foreign news columns of the *Star*. In part his attitude was that of the typical European liberal of the 'forties. He regarded the United States, for example, as a beacon for all those struggling against repressive or non-representative governments. "America is still the hope of the nations," he declared, ". . . on her, from the first hour of her independence, has the eye of patriotism been fixed . . . in her we find a surety for the final and universal enfranchisement of mankind." [1] But from this point on his views

[1] *Ibid.*, 17 October 1840.

diverged sharply from the bourgeois liberalism of the time. The new republic also demonstrated the fact—harped on constantly by anti-democratic critics—that political equality had done little to close the gap between extremes of wealth and poverty. "Experience has proved—bear witness America," he wrote, "that kingcraft and lordcraft may be abolished and the people remain practical slaves. The classes commanding the wealth of the country can always by force and fraud ensure the slavery of the millions." [1] Property controlled politics; American independence had simply changed the nationality of the exploiting ruling class. From these propositions Harney drew a scarcely Mazzinian conclusion: the only equality which could ensure a "veritable and lasting liberty" was social equality.

Thus the new American agrarian and socialist movements so effectively publicized by Horace Greeley of the *New York Tribune* and Charles Dana of the *New York Post*—both Fourierites—were warmly welcomed by Harney; and the social criticism of the American radicals was passed on to his readers with gusto. "The heartless, selfish, over-gorged luxury of the New York profitocracy, existing by the side of the misery of the toilers and wealth producers . . . is a crime against humanity," he commented typically. [2] The initial success of the New England *literati's* attempt at communal living, Brook Farm; the activities of agrarian reformers, whether "free-landers" or neo-Spenceans like Thomas Devyr (a quondam Chartist now editing a Virginia newspaper): all were evidence to Harney that the model of world political democracy was at last "carrying out the revolution which was begun but never finished in 1776". [3]

The trans-Atlantic circulation given to the American Radical press by Harney's copious extracts was not a one-sided affair. A cross-fertilization of American and British radicalism, however limited, took place with the quotation of the *Northern Star* by such organs as *Young America* and the *Working Man's Advocate*. Chartism had been a "theme for scoffing and denunciation prior to 1844" in the United States, according to Harney. [4] Now, at any rate to the American reformers, the social and political

---

[1] *Northern Star*, 26 September 1846.
[2] *Ibid.*, 4 October 1845.
[3] *Ibid.*, 26 September 1846.
[4] *Ibid.*, 14 September 1844. Very likely this judgment came from Devyr, for whom see comments on the Williamsburg (Virginia) *Gazette*, in *ibid.*, 20 April 1844.

objectives of their English cousins became clearer; Chartism was even honoured by the efforts of an earnest, if poorly endowed, American radical poet.

While America remained the "hope of the nations" to him, Harney's main interest remained in European developments. Heretofore, due to his close association with the Polish exiles in London, his attention had centred on their struggle for liberation. With the publication in November 1843 of two long articles on Continental socialism in the *Northern Star*, it was apparent that he had hit on a new vein.[1] In the author of the articles, Friedrich Engels, he had also found a friend whose path was to lie in much the same direction as his for the next eight years. The first meeting between the two occurred in the autumn of 1843, when Engels called on Harney at the *Northern Star's* office in Leeds. The young German bourgeois, who had arrived almost a year before in Manchester to complete his commercial training in a cotton mill partially owned by his father, had not seen the social revolution which he had so confidently expected on his arrival; but his unbourgeois leanings had already led him to close contacts within the Chartist movement in Manchester, and it was possibly a mutual friend, James Leach, a former member of the National Executive, who sent this odd member of the propertied classes to see Harney.

The two young men—Engels was three years the junior and, as Harney later described him, a "tall, handsome young man, with a countenance of almost boyish youthfulness"[2]—make an interesting study. Temperamentally, they were not unlike. Both possessed a ready sense of humour, likely to be edged with malice at times, and love of conversation and company, preferably with the accompaniment of a bottle of wine. Intellectually, they shared a sense of mission: a passionate desire to improve the miserable condition of the working class. But the ways by which they had arrived at this feeling made for a significant difference between the two. Harney had experienced that misery; the Barmen manufacturer's son had observed it from the vantage-point of the educated owning-class. From whatever springs Engels's sympathy with the working class came—whether from a subconscious sense of fraternity with others dominated by his

---

[1] *Ibid.*, 11, 25 November 1843. The articles first appeared in Robert Owen's *New Moral World*, 4, 18 November 1843.

[2] Newcastle *Weekly Chronicle*, 17 August 1895, obituary on Engels's death.

father or from objective motives of humanitarianism—it took a more intellectual form than did Harney's.

There was a great deal that this young foreigner, with his German training in philosophy, could, and did, learn from such radical leaders as Harney. Immersed from early youth in the struggles of a working class confronted for the first time with the problems of industrialism, Harney was saturated with ideas and attitudes which were new to Engels. When, for example, Harney told an average Chartist meeting that profits and wages, and thus the interests of the middle class and the working class, were diametrically opposed, neither he nor his audience considered these concepts anything out of the ordinary. But Engels, still filled with abstractions, was only in the process of realizing such concepts; he had just recognized the dominance of interests over principles in Manchester.[1] And he could still write, in his articles on socialism in the *Northern Star*, that in Germany communism was such a "*necessary* consequence" of the New Hegelian philosophy that no opposition could keep it down. To Harney, the idea of a historical necessity which made the German propertied classes desire the destruction of private property because of their "love of abstract principle" and "disregard of reality and self-interest"—which was the gist of Engels's view—must have been as sensible as looking to "Young England" to lead a communist revolution in Britain.

Though Engels was to discard the doctrine of a "philosophical revolution" in Germany within the next few years, the difference in attitude of the two men persisted. Both were socialists, but Engels already thought the communism of the German Democrats in London naïve;[2] while Harney's belief, always vague from a doctrinal viewpoint, was precisely of that kind—that is, a Babeuvian egalitarianism based on natural rights. The habits of thought which impelled Engels to systematize his observations and fit them into a philosophical framework were foreign to Harney, whose attitude was always basically empirical. As he was to write later,[3] his reaction to abstract thought was much the same as that embodied in Byron's lines in *Don Juan* on Coleridge

"Explaining metaphysics to the nation—
I wish he would explain his Explanation."

---

[1] Gustav Mayer, *Friedrich Engels*, translated by G. and H. Highet (London: 1936), p. 50.   [2] *Ibid.*, p. 45.   [3] Newcastle *Weekly Chronicle*, 25 July 1896.

The difference between the two young men was symbolic of much in the development of Marxian socialism and British socialism: as Engels may be considered a prototype of the former, so may Harney of the latter, with its inveterate empiricism and indifference to theoretical system-building.

On such differences their friendship was eventually to split, when Engels had become infected with some of Marx's intolerant sincerity, but in the winter of 1843 this lay years in the future, and the two became warm friends. Engels, with his first-hand knowledge of the Continent, had much on his part to give Harney; and when he volunteered to write on German affairs for the *Northern Star* his offer was accepted with alacrity.[1] "Our Own Correspondent", as the *Star* by-lined him, proved an excellent commentator. A strike of the Breslau weavers in June 1844, for example, was explained by an analogy to English conditions which any Yorkshire weaver could have grasped without difficulty. A pleasant light-heartedness was also evident in the new column. Others beside Harney, with his distaste for organized religion, must have relished Engels's report of the growth of "parsonocracy" in Prussia: he instanced a Berlin parson who refused to marry couples on Saturday, "alleging that the parties would in all probability not rise on Sunday morning in a fit state of mind for the celebration of the Lord's Day".[2]

That Harney was able to work a significant change in the tone of the *Northern Star* was certainly not due to any sympathy for his objectives on O'Connor's part. Like his famous predecessor Cobbett in this, as in so many ways, Feargus was anti-socialist and anti-internationalist. And while, strangely enough considering his dictatorial habits, there was considerable truth in his boast that his editors were given a free hand, it was due rather to O'Connor's increasing interest in a new scheme that Harney's policy was relatively unrestricted. This scheme, the Chartist Land Plan, had as its main features the purchase of land through the mass-subscription of operatives, and the allocation through periodical drawings of small plots of a few acres to be tilled by

---

[1] Although the letter volunteering his services (*Northern Star*, 4 May 1844) was unsigned, as were his articles, the style and content leave little doubt that their author was Engels. (*Cf., ibid.*, reports of 18, 25 May; 15, 29 June; 27 July 1844.) The correspondence then lapsed until the autumn of 1845, when it resumed until 8 November, with some interruptions. His next report was then in April 1846.

[2] *Ibid.*, 25 May 1844.

"spade-husbandry". Though O'Connor's objectives were originally limited, even in its nascent form the plan reveals once again the Cobbettite nature of his thought: the ultimate solution to the operative's plight lay in a return to the land. This was to become apparent when the recurrence of a commercial depression in 1846 and 1847 gave his arguments force; meanwhile a rising labour market and the dubious legality of the scheme led to a generally indifferent reception. Harney, sharing this indifference, was able to follow his own predilections without objection from O'Connor, and devoted more of the *Northern Star's* space to the American agrarian and socialist movements than to the Land Plan. Such news was, in any case, effective propaganda for the scheme. The lesson of what was presented as the comparatively prosperous American worker turning to the land as a solution to an over-crowded labour market, coupled with O'Connor's persistent editorializing, very likely played a part in preparing the minds of the paper's readers for acceptance of the idea. The main goal, however, was to be that of economic circumstances.

Both Land Plan and Chartism were side issues in the period 1843–46—another reason for Harney's growing preoccupation with the internationalist movement. To the common accusation of the anti-O'Connorites that the Plan was distracting working-class attention from the Charter, he might have replied, "What attention?" Knowing as much of local organization as anyone in the movement, Harney saw that Chartism was drying up at the roots. "A lecturer lectures in one town, and has a meeting to listen to him," he observed, "but ten miles off there is no lecturer and therefore there is no meeting. It was not so in the days of 1837–38–39. *Then* men met, whether they had lecturers or not." [1] To blame advocates of the Land Plan for Chartist apathy was as logical as to blame the colliers, whose union movement monopolized more of the *Northern Star's* attention in 1844 than either Chartist news or the Land. Still the greatest working-class paper despite a falling circulation, the *Star's* distribution of domestic news was a sensitive reflector of the shift in interest among its readers. If more of its contents was devoted to the Ten Hours' Bill agitation or analyses of the proposed Masters and Servants Act than to Chartism, it was because the working class had turned its attention from political agitation

[1] *Northern Star*, 18 January 1845.

to such issues as higher wages and shorter hours. The most pertinent evidence of this lay in the changing of the paper's name in November 1844 from the *Northern Star and Leeds General Advertiser* to the *Northern Star and National Trades Journal*.

Equally significant was the *Star's* removal from Leeds to London at the same time, indicating as it did the shift in the centre of active Chartism from its old centres in the north. The National Executive had already moved from Manchester to the metropolis; and, as Feargus frankly admitted, the main reason for the *Star's* quitting Leeds was to restore its circulation, now barely over the break-even point at 7,000 copies weekly.[1] Yet London Chartism, though it had retained its organization fairly successfully, was active only by comparison with the indifference of Yorkshire and Lancashire, and Harney's return did not divert him from the course which was to make him the leading English internationalist of the 'forties. It projected him instead into one of the main focal points of the European revolutionary movement.

A considerable foreign colony existed in London, composed mainly of Germans, Frenchmen and Italians, with a sizable body of Poles. The majority of the immigrants were politically passive; but a minority, in great part political refugees from repression on the Continent, constituted a concentration of revolutionary potential matched only by the exiles in Paris. Organized in national groups and in contact with the clandestine movements in their homelands and Paris, they engaged in incessant plotting as Europe moved toward the "Year of Revolutions", when many of them were to return to play leading roles. At the time of Harney's arrival in London these groups were, in the main, independent of each other.

Ideologically, the *émigré* societies fell into two categories. All were revolutionary, but while the German Democratic Society and the Union of French Democrats called for *la république démocratic et sociale*, the Italians opposed any socialist aims. Dominated by Mazzini, "Young Italy" was a liberal bourgeois organization devoted primarily to the liberation and unification

---

[1] Estimating from figures given by O'Connor in *ibid.*, 26 August 1848, the break-even point of the *Northern Star* was about 6,200 copies weekly. During 1845, the paper lost money; in 1846 it generally paid its way; in 1847 it made a profit of £8 to £12 weekly. In 1839, with a circulation of 40,000 weekly, the annual profit amounted to £13,000; in 1841, £6,500. Yet O'Connor, with his usual habit of exaggeration, claimed to have lost money during those years! (*Ibid.*, 21 November 1846.)

of Italy. Within each of these national groups a large measure of unanimity prevailed; but the Polish emigration remained irreconcilably split into aristocratic and democratic factions.[1] The Polish Democratic Society, if not as advanced in its programme as the French and German groups, espoused land reform as well as liberation, and tended to orient itself toward the social-democratic societies. It was the left-wing groups which Harney brought together in the first international organization of any permanence in England.

He was not alone among the old Chartist leaders in his interest in the cause of the revolutionaries. William Lovett was a close friend of Mazzini, and his National Association—a small group composed of the remnants of the London Working Men's Association and a strong middle-class Radical element—had gained considerable prestige among the *émigrés* by the leading part which they had played in a *cause célèbre* of the summer of 1844, which had arisen from the English government's interception of Mazzini's mail and the communication of its contents to the Austrian government. Following this incident, Lovett had launched the first international society in London, the Democratic Friends of All Nations, which combined Polish, German, French and English elements.

The Democratic Friends' first address proved to be its swan-song. Lovett's appeal for international amity was directed to all classes; reflecting the middle-class element of his English backing, its social message could have offended no one. What was even more fatal for the longevity of the society was his explicit repudiation of outbreaks of violence. Moral force might have been all very well for English radicalism, but it could scarcely appeal to the Continental revolutionaries. The address mortally offended the "physical force party" in the organization and with the withdrawal of the exponents of revolution the society quietly expired.[2]

It was into this situation that the *Northern Star's* removal to London brought Harney. Considering the fact that his connection with the Polish Democrats had now existed for a decade, it is not surprising that his first contact with the emigration should have

[1] For a thorough discussion of the Polish factions, see Peter Brock, "Polish Democrats and English Radicals 1832–1862: A Chapter in the History of Anglo-Polish Relations", *Journal of Modern History*, vol. XXV, no. 2 (June 1953), pp. 139–56.

[2] Lovett, *Life . . . of William Lovett*, p. 314.

been with the leaders of the Polish Democratic Society, two of whom—Stanislaus Worcell, the "father of Polish socialism", and Karl Stoltzman—became frequent visitors to his den in the *Northern Star's* office in Great Windmill Street. To these were soon added another Polish Democrat, the sabre-scarred veteran of the Polish Revolution, Louis Oborski. By the summer of 1845, Harney had become acquainted with the leaders of the German Democratic Society, possibly through the intercession of Engels, possibly due to the fact that their meeting-place, the "Red Lion" tavern, was also the public house most convenient to the *Northern Star's* office. With the establishment of similar contacts with the French Democrats his plans were complete, and at a banquet held on 22 September to celebrate the French Republic's constitution of 1792, the Fraternal Democrats came into being.

The reason why Harney succeeded where Lovett had failed is not far to seek. It lay in the compatibility of his views with those of the European revolutionaries whom he had brought together. While it was true that he no longer believed that physical force was necessary or practical to achieve Chartist aims, his attitude toward insurrection on the Continent was quite different: "He is but a knave or fool who denies the right of the oppressed to release themselves from oppression, even by force," he wrote. As to the subject of private property, which Lovett had skirted in such a gingerly fashion, Harney and the Fraternal Democrats were quite openly—if rather vaguely—communist. If a single dominant intellectual influence among the leading members is to be singled out, it was undoubtedly that of Babeuf. Jean Michelot, the French professor of literature who headed the French contingent of the society, as well as Harney and the German Democrats, was a thorough Babeuvian; and Harney's statement of the principles on which the organization was founded was explicit. Politically, the Fraternal Democrats believed in "Governments elected by, and responsible to, the entire people". But their democratic belief was not limited to politics.

"We believe the earth with all its natural productions to be the property of all; we, therefore denounce all infractions of this evidently just and natural law as robbery and usurpation," Harney declared. "We believe that the present state of society which permits idlers and schemers to monopolize the fruits of the earth and

the productions of industry . . . to be essentially unjust. The
principle of universal brotherhood commands that labour and
rewards should be equal." [1]

"Universal brotherhood" also meant the condemnation of the
national hatred of which the ruling classes had taken advantage
"to set them tearing the throats of each other when they should
have been working for the common good". Due to the governing
classes' monopoly of the press, Harney told the first anniversary
meeting of the Fraternal Democrats, democrats of every country
had remained ignorant of each other's progress—a state of
affairs which led to their acting separately and sometimes even
in opposition. The primary function of the society would be to
create a mutual knowledge among the members so that democrats of all nations would "act in concert, and move at one and
the same time for the triumph of their common cause".

The international proletarian unity of the Fraternal Democrats was no mere figure of speech. Although only two *émigré*
groups formally belonged to the society—the French Democrats
and the German Democratic Society—the six secretaries who
came to direct its affairs included also representatives of the
Swiss, the Hungarians, and the Scandinavians. Very likely the
three latter[2] were members of the German Democratic Society,
which included Bohemians, South Slavs, Russians and Alsatians
as well. Even the Mohammedan world was represented in a
"Turkish democrat", who entertained the celebrants at the
founding banquet of the society by singing until morning.

Possibly due to their financial support by the English government—which had been withdrawn from those who became involved with Chartist affairs in 1839—the Polish Democratic
Society avoided a formal adherence to the Fraternal Democrats.
Yet, in spite of the middle-class Radical *Weekly Dispatch's* warning to them about the "infernal Democrats" and the society's
"sword, blunderbuss and bludgeon" activator, Poles formed,
with Germans and Frenchmen, the bulk of the membership; and
Louis Oborski acted as their unofficial secretary. This advanced
section of the Polish emigration was in general agreement with

[1] Speech on first anniversary of the Fraternal Democrats, *Northern Star*, 26
September 1846.
[2] Henri Hubert, August Nemeth and Peter Holm, respectively. Michelot was the
French secretary, Karl Schapper the German. Harney was, of course, the English
secretary.

the Fraternal Democrats' attitude toward nationalism, set forth
by their usual spokesman. Poland and Italy, Harney declared,
were two countries where the spirit of nationality could be
beneficially invoked; but their freedom from Russian and Austrian domination was not all that was required—they must rid
themselves of their exploiting class as well.

Mazzini's reaction to this view is not recorded, though there
is no question what it would have been. "Young Italy" stood
aloof from the society; members were bound to join no other
organizations. Even had this rule not existed, the egalitarian
principles of the Fraternal Democrats precluded any close connection with the great Italian, to whom communism was
anathema. In addition to this fundamental ideological difference,
Mazzini could have had little desire to alienate that respectable
literary and Radical society which lionized him, by aligning
himself with the "levelling" wing of Chartism. It was indeed this
wing, made up largely of Harney's old confreres in the now-
defunct London Democratic Association, which formed the Chartist complement of the Fraternal Democrats.

Very likely the slowness with which the society took an overt
form—six months passed after the founding date before Harney
mentioned its name in print—was due to an awareness on the
part of the émigrés that the government which gave them asylum
might be less tolerant of their connection with extreme English
radicalism. They were, after all, known conspirators whose aim
was to overthrow the European *status quo*. There could have been
little mystery, for example, about the fact that Karl Schapper,
Joseph Moll, and Heinrich Bauer, the main leaders of the German Democratic Society, had participated in the abortive Paris
insurrection of 1839. Perhaps their connection with the ultra-
revolutionary League of the Just—in effect, a branch of Barbes's
and Blanqui's "Society of the Seasons" in 1839—was not known;
but the Home Office had only to read Engels's articles on
socialism in the *Northern Star* to know that such an international
organization, with a London branch, was in existence; and
public report showed that Wilhelm Weitling, another of its
leaders recently arrived from Switzerland, had addressed the
Fraternal Democrats. So also with those international couriers
of revolution, the Poles, and the French Democrats: both had
direct connections across the Channel. Certainly the English
government condoned their activities with a toleration which

K

today seems extraordinary; but, as 1848 was to show, that tolerance had limits.

Conversely, Harney moved cautiously in the developmental
period of the society—stressing, in fact, that the Fraternal Democrats were not a "society" at all, but an "assemblage for mutual
information". Another reason for his reticence during these
months of early 1846 lay in the suspicions of Chartists about the
nature of the new organization to which so influential a person
as the editor of the *Northern Star* was devoting his main efforts.
"They feared it was an attempt to supersede the movement—to
create a party within a party," wrote an observer of these events
later.[1] That such suspicion existed is not surprising; the first
English members of the Fraternal Democrats were, after all, the
self-same veterans of an earlier attempt to create a party within
a party—that of Harney's junta in the National Convention of
1839.

The way in which Harney allayed this distrust and converted
other leaders of Chartism to his international views, at the same
time using the invaluable sounding-board of the *Northern Star*
to propagandize the Fraternal Democrats' principles, is evidence
of the tactical sense he had developed in his long radical experience. Every effort was made to associate the views of the Fraternal Democrats with popular causes. In his dual role as editor
of the *Northern Star* and author of the society's addresses, Harney
constantly stressed the thesis that events abroad had a direct
effect on the every-day lives of the English working class. Thus
when the government proposed a Militia Bill early in 1846, the
reason for which was popularly believed to be the crisis with the
United States over the Oregon boundary question, the *Northern
Star* not only thoroughly publicized the series of great Chartist
meetings of protest held in England and Scotland, but incessantly hammered on the theme embodied in the demonstrators'
slogan: "No Vote! No Musket!" "When henceforth the masses
—the impoverished, unrepresented masses, are called upon by
their rulers to fight for 'their country' . . . ," Harney wrote,
"they will answer . . . 'if you will monopolize all, fight for the
country yourselves'." At the same time the Fraternal Democrats
utilized the popular reaction to emphasize what they saw as the
underlying issue: neither the American nor the British working
classes had anything to gain in an imperialistic war for territory

[1] Ernest Jones, in *Northern Star*, 5 February 1848.

or the China trade; such a war would benefit only the owning classes.[1] (This highly political and class-conscious treatment of the issue is even more marked when contrasted with the "respectable" middle-class agitation against the Militia Bill led by the Quaker Joseph Sturge, which was mainly pacifist in its inspiration.)

A greater opportunity to allay Chartist suspicion and propagate the society's views was provided by the Polish rising in Cracow early in 1846, an insurrection which revolutionaries and reactionaries alike saw as the overture to a general European revolution. Once again the technique employed was that of skilfully exploiting popular feeling—in this case, the Russophobia common to the working class in the 1840's—to advance the Fraternal Democrats' principles. In the Militia Bill agitation they had attacked war; now they called for English military intervention against the Russians. This difference in reaction was due to the fact that the Cracow rising was "no mere national war". The main forces involved in the proclamation of an independent Polish government were the Austrian and Prussian branches of the Polish Democratic Society; their programme called for the abolition of feudal privileges and the granting of lands to its cultivators as well as national liberation. It was these social provisions which led the aristocratic Czartoryski's Polish Committee to disavow the "wild theories of government" of the revolutionaries and *The Times* to deplore the Pole's adoption of the "horrible principles of Communism". And it was precisely these social-democratic aims, added to the issue of national freedom, which made the Polish cause so appealing to the Fraternal Democrats.

The society could not hope to bring about British intervention; but it made extremely effective use of its opportunity to popularize its views and enlist the support of the Chartist leadership. Philip McGrath, the president of the Chartist Executive, was persuaded to take the chair at a highly successful mass-meeting organized by the Fraternal Democrats at the "Crown and Anchor". More singular was the fact that O'Connor, always indifferent, if not actually hostile, to foreign causes, made a speech linking the Polish rising with the achievement of Chartist

[1] *Address to the Working Classes of Great Britain and the United States on the Oregon Question*, flyleaf in the British Museum; printed also in *Northern Star*, 7 March 1846. This was the usual practice of publicizing the society's views.

aims. It was an indication of the enthusiasm generated by the Polish cause that Feargus, with his sure instinct for the popular, even conquered his xenophobia so far as to become treasurer of a new organization which Harney now launched, the Democratic Committee for Poland's Regeneration. However tenuously, O'Connor had associated himself with the aims of the Fraternal Democrats.

Such demonstrations and Harney's persistent propaganda in the *Northern Star* had wider repercussions as well. The Democratic Committee for Poland's Regeneration—which was in effect a sub-committee of the Fraternal Democrats, Harney writing most of their addresses and the same leaders figuring in each group—expanded to almost thirty localities within six months. By the middle of 1847, Fraternal Democrats were to be found in twenty towns scattered from Dundee to Reading; and the growing acceptance of the international proletarianism which absorbed Harney's waking hours was also attested by the fact that Philip McGrath and two other members of the Chartist Executive became active members of the society.

Not all of the Chartist leaders looked with favour on this growth of militant internationalism, however. Thomas Cooper, who had built up a considerable following in London following his release from prison, denounced the Fraternal Democrats' efforts as a "new wild-fire scheme" to divert Chartist attention from the suffrage. With his usual startling completeness, the foremost exponent of physical force in the turbulent strike-days of 1842 had embraced a peace doctrine in which love and nonresistance constituted the only means of human advancement; and was now, with his usual vehemence, attacking revolution and interventionism. The insularity of the Chartist movement had by no means disappeared, and Cooper's challenge might have had serious consequences for the Fraternal Democrats had not his non-violent creed brought him into direct conflict with Feargus. What began as a disagreement over O'Connor's refusal to disavow physical force quickly developed into a challenge to O'Connor's dominance. It was a priceless opportunity for the Fraternal Democrats to strike down this attack on their principles and at the same time to demonstrate their loyalty to the most powerful of Chartist leaders. Harney moved quickly and decisively: in the columns of the *Northern Star* he called for Cooper's expulsion as a traitor to the N.C.A., and the Fraternal

Democrats harshly censured the rebel and re-affirmed their support of O'Connor. An international flavour was added to the controversy with Harney's publication of a letter from the "German Democrats of Brussels", signed by Marx, Engels and Philip Guigot, which flayed the "disguised bourgeois" in a fashion so detailed as to suggest a Julian inspiration. By this time, Cooper was overwhelmed in the uproar, and in the August convention of the N.C.A. was summarily expelled.

Besides confirming O'Connor's domination of the movement, the incident had served the Fraternal Democrats well. Cooper's loss of power meant that one of the strongest critics of the international wing of Chartism had been, for all practical purposes, silenced. It meant also that the society had established a lien on O'Connor's tolerance, if not his active support. By exploiting Feargus's insatiable desire for popularity through frequent expressions of loyalty in the following years the Fraternal Democrats maintained this fragile relationship. Certainly O'Connor was not converted. His dislike of communism remained unaltered; and when on one occasion in 1847 he attacked the creed, Harney thought it necessary to reply that calumniation of beliefs improperly understood smacked of the intolerance of radicalism from which the Chartists themselves had suffered. But whether as a result of the Fraternal Democrats' tactfulness or his belief that the working classes were becoming increasingly internationalist, O'Connor remained tractable, and sometimes more. In a remarkably eloquent speech at the first anniversary banquet of the Fraternal Democrats, for example, he spoke in a tone indistinguishable from that of Harney and Karl Schapper.

Harney's efforts on behalf of the new international society exhibit that extraordinary industry which seems peculiarly characteristic of Victorian leaders of all classes. Despite the bouts of illness which occasionally prostrated him, he spoke frequently at public meetings, wrote most of the addresses of the Fraternal Democrats, and corresponded voluminously with the provincial members of the society and the Polish Committee, of which he was also secretary—all this in addition to his regular duties as editor of the *Northern Star*. The trial period of the Fraternal Democrats having passed, his intent was to give their ideas as wide a circulation as possible. Harney was catholic enough about their audience to include the Home Office, which, he assured Lord Palmerston, did not have to maintain surveillance over the society, as he would be pleased to submit reports of their meetings. Yet even these activities did not consume all of his energies. The Home Office may well have been interested in an organization about which Harney was less frank. This was the Communist Corresponding Society—in Gustav Mayer's phrase, the "earliest Communist International".[1]

With their theoretical principles coalescing, Marx and Engels, now in Brussels, had begun to organize a Communist workers' party. Possibly preliminary advances had been made to the London German Democrats in the summer of 1845, when Engels had brought Marx to England to observe industrial conditions at first hand and to read the English economists, at the same time renewing his acquaintance with Harney. A certain coolness characterized the relationship between Engels and Harney's German friends—a coolness arising from Engels's attitude of "philosophical arrogance" toward Schapper, Bauer and Moll, and the suspicion on their part of "intellectuals".[2] One barrier, if not all, between them disappeared with Engels's disavowal in the *Northern Star* of his old reliance on the bourgeois intellectuals to achieve communism in Germany; communism, he now believed, could be achieved only by the proletariat.[3] It was to further this aim that they had organized the Communist Corresponding Society in Brussels, which by May 1846 had a London branch which included Bauer, Schapper and Moll, as well as Harney.

Initially, at any rate, Harney appears to have been the most important member of the London committee so far as Marx and

[1] Mayer, *Friedrich Engels*, p. 76.

[2] Engels, quoted in D. Ryazanoff, *The Communist Manifesto of Karl Marx and Friedrich Engels* (London: 1930), p. 3; Mayer, *Friedrich Engels*, p. 71. Ryazanoff claims certain inaccuracies exist in Engels's account, written for the edification of the German Social Democrats in 1885. E.g. Engels claimed that the League of the Just continued to exist after 1839; Ryazanoff denies this on the basis that the League issued no manifestos, etc., after that time which have been discovered. Engels, however, in his article, "The Progress of Social Reform on the Continent", *Northern Star*, 25 November 1843, describes an organization which may well have been the League of the Just as still in existence, with branches in Switzerland, Paris and London. Wilhelm Weitling was the leader in Switzerland, and a report of the committee of the Executive of the Swiss Republic showed that he communicated with Paris and London, as Engels points out. Ryazanoff, in his correction of Engels's 1885 account, is quite vague about Engels's first contact with Chartist leaders, giving the visit of 1845 as very probably his first acquaintanceship with Harney and Ernest Jones. Harney had by this time known Engels for almost two years; Jones did not enter the Chartist or internationalist movements until 1846.

[3] 13, 27 September, 25 October 1845.

Engels were concerned, a position due not only to his editorship of the main English working-class newspaper and his prestige in the Chartist movement, but to the still-existent coolness between them and the old leaders of the League of the Just. Indeed, it is quite likely that the two "scientific Socialists" had swallowed the Babeuvian "naïveté" of the German *émigré* leaders to ensure Harney's adherence;[1] and it was only the London Germans' proletarian reputation in Germany, possibly in conjunction with Harney's loyalty to them, which prevented Marx and Engels from breaking with them at the end of 1846.[2] The crisis passed; the German Democrats, persuaded by Marx's pamphlets, warmed to the theoretical views of the two "intellectuals", and in June 1847 the leaders of the old League of the Just and the Corresponding Committees merged in the Communist League.[3]

Unlike the Fraternal Democrats, the Communist League was a clandestine propaganda organization. Thus Harney's part in its inner working remains obscure, though his usefulness was unquestionable: the League now had an English outlet for its "scientific socialist" views. The propagation of their principles was mainly the work of Engels, who once again became a correspondent of the *Northern Star*; and his new attitude is clearest in his discussion of such English matters as Corn Law Repeal. Here he went directly contrary to the general Chartist position held by Harney and O'Connor; i.e. the Anti-Corn Law Agitation was simply a means of distracting the working classes from their political aims, and Repeal would inevitably mean lower wages if it brought cheaper bread. Engels, on the other hand, espoused Repeal, arguing that this would mean the fulfilment of the middle classes' revolutionary function: *"Let the Corn Laws be repealed today, and tomorrow the Charter is the leading question in England."* [4]

In spite of Harney's increasing contact with the ideas of Marx and Engels, neither now nor later is there evidence to show that they had any important theoretical influence on him. The difference in their attitudes toward historical development is particularly apparent with regard to events in France. The

---

[1] Ryazanoff, *The Communist Manifesto of Karl Marx and Friedrich Engels*, p. 19.

[2] Karl Marx and Friedrich Engels, *Briefwechsel*, 4 vols. (Berlin: 1929), vol. I, p. 59–60, Engels to Marx, end of December 1846.

[3] Franz Mehring, *Karl Marx* (London: 1936), pp. 138–39.

[4] *Northern Star*, 4 April 1846. Cf. the Brussels Communists' address to O'Connor, *ibid.*, 17 July 1846.

three men agreed that the French bourgeoisie was a "vampire class" which battened on the proletariat through the capitalist system; they united also in calling for social revolution. But Harney, still faithful to the teaching of Bronterre O'Brien, regarded French history from Robespierre's death and the crushing of Babeuf's conspiracy as a long process of reaction, in which the existent government under Guizot was the ultimate step—not as an historically necessary process in which the victorious bourgeoisie had now almost created the conditions for its own destruction. Judicious quoting might show a Harney with rare historical prescience, as in his prophecy of a day when the principles of "German Communism" would "overshadow the thrones of the earth";[1] but at the time of this prophecy (1846), to Harney "German Communism" connoted not Marxian Communism but the Babeuvian Communism which he and Karl Schapper had imbibed in the 'thirties. Ironically enough, the most important English colleague of Marx and Engels was not a disciple.

In these years following his return to London, Harney emerged as the pre-eminent figure of the internationalist wing of Chartism. When, late in 1846, the middle-class radical *Weekly Dispatch* attacked him, along with the "infernal Democrats", the Chartist Executive rallied strongly to his support. One member, just returned from a trip through the principal provincial towns, declared that no man stood higher in the estimation of the "real movement party" than did Julian; another spoke of the unique esteem for Harney he had heard expressed during an extensive Scottish tour. Nor was this growth of stature limited to England. The Central Committee of the Democratic Poles in Paris was well aware of his efforts on their behalf, and their *Polish Democratic Journal* had caustically reprehended an attack on him by the aristocratic faction's *Three Days*. His addresses written for the Fraternal Democrats and the Polish Regeneration Committee had also appeared in the Paris press in such left-wing journals as the *Réforme*. Perhaps the most effective bit of evidence for his growing international reputation lies in a minor incident: when establishing contact with the ultra-radical *Réforme*, Engels introduced himself to the editor as "Harney's representative", an act which gained him a warm and immediate entree.[1]

[1] *Northern Star*, 26 September 1846.

The period between 1844 and 1848 was the fullest and hap-
piest of Harney's life. His periodic illness impaired but slightly
the vitality which expressed itself in politics, in journalism, in the
zest with which he lived. Behind the sometimes drab detail of
the organizations to which he devoted his brimming energies
glimpses may be caught of less serious affairs. There was his
participation in the small group which met weekly at the "Crown"
tavern in Fleet Street and helped Willie Thom, the Inverury
weaver-poet, to sing and drink himself to death, though these
men were not in his real *milieu*. Both Thom and Thomas
Cooper, another of the participants, had been taken up by the
fashionable literary society, including Dickens and Douglas
Jerrold, the editor of the *Illuminated Magazine*, which circulated
in such salons as that of the Countess of Blessington and patron-
ized Mazzini. More to his taste were outings with his colleagues,
such as the boating trip which the Fraternal Democrats made
up the Thames, picnicking at a small inn, and singing national
songs as they rowed back in the warm night. And, a scene which
evokes for a moment the happiness of a fine summer day in
1846, there was the German Democratic Society's picnic on
Hampstead Heath, vividly described by Harney: below them,
the "huge Babel of bricks" swimming in a heat-haze; beside
them "immense German sausages, enormous piles of bread, and a
butt of beer almost rivalling the far-famed Heidelberg tun";
and, replete with beer and food, the men and women stretched
out on the grass being pleasantly harangued by those who
shared their principles and prejudices. It was a full life indeed,
of which the climactic years were now approaching.

¹ Engels to Marx, 25–26 October 1847, *Briefwechsel*, vol. I, p. 80.

CHAPTER VII

1848

THE correlation between economic conditions and Chartist activity is so marked as to need little elaboration. It is mainly to the soporific effect of fuller stomachs that the political quiescence of the working classes between 1843 and 1846 may be attributed. But disquieting signs that all was not well with the economy became clearly apparent in 1846; and by the spring of 1847 the trend downward from the relatively high level of production and employment reached in 1845 had assumed an alarming aspect. Once again such headlines as "Distress in Manchester" became common in the press; and the *Northern Star* began to juxtapose comparative accounts of the working-class diet and that of the Royal hounds, to the obvious disadvantage of the former. The commercial crisis gained a particular intensity from the disastrous crop failures of 1845–46 which, while littering the roads of Ireland with the starving and accomplishing in a few months what seven years of intensive agitation against the Corn Laws had failed to do, were by no means limited to that unfortunate island. In a single issue of the *Northern Star* (22 May 1847) food riots were reported in Devon, Somerset and Cornwall; and such governmental actions as the proclamation of a day of national fasting for Ireland to propitiate an offended Deity did little to stop people from thinking about the causes of their renewed suffering. Once again the instructive powers of unemployment and hunger were demonstrated in the revival of Chartist interest.

Feargus attributed the renascence of Chartism which began in 1846 to his Land Plan; but the real reason lay in the closing of factory doors. It is true, however, that reviving Chartist interest was channelled to a considerable extent into the Land Company; and as the commercial crisis deepened the Company experienced a phenomenal rise in subscriptions. As in the American depression of the 1930's, thousands turned from a system which seemed incapable of guaranteeing them security to dreams of "a little plot of land and a cow". O'Connor, with his almost infallible

insight into the working-class mind, had indeed struck a deep
well of feeling in the land-hunger which from first to last
accounted for some £112,000 subscribed in operatives' pennies.
Few of the subscribers would have disagreed with his date-lining
his letters from Herringsgate (later O'Connorville), the first
estate purchased, "From Paradise"; and it is not difficult to
imagine with what thirsty attention a miserable factory-worker
or collier read the lyrical descriptions of the estate, with its rich
earth, small wood, and clear stream running across the fields.
"O'Connor bid a village rise,/And a village rose instanter,"
declaimed Harney's old mentor, Allen Davenport. In another
poem entitled "O'Connorville", Ernest Jones, a bankrupt
Chartist recruit from the upper-classes now rising rapidly to
power, captured much of working-class feeling:[1]

> "In crowded town the poor mechanic wakes.
> But why today, at twilight's earliest prime,
> When moon's grey finger points the march of time,
> Why starts he upwards with a joyous strength
> To face the long day slavery's cheerless length?
> Has freedom whispered in his wistful ear,
> 'Courage, poor slave! deliverance is near?'
> Oh! she has breathed a summons sweeter still:
> 'Come! take your guerdon at O'Connorville!' "

In addition to worsening economic conditions, two factors
seem to have combined to give the Land Plan the impetus it
received in 1846. The first of these was O'Connor's decision to
change the tenure of the allocations from leaseholds to freeholds,
in the hope that the Land Company might achieve a legal standing. Though this hope was never realized, the change evidently
did much to remove doubts as to the soundness of allottees' titles
to the land. A more vital factor was the purchase of the first
estate in Hertfordshire in March 1846 and the selection by lot of
the first "fustian landlords". The dream was becoming reality,
it seemed; weekly receipts from operatives' subscriptions, less
than £200 in January 1846, rose to more than £1,300 in
December, and by May of 1847 were flooding in at the rate of
£3,200.

With this extraordinary increase in receipts, O'Connor's
belief in the potentialities of the plan expanded beyond the
bounds of reason. What he had originally described as no more

[1] *Northern Star*, 22 August 1846.

than an experiment which might benefit perhaps 5,000 operatives grew into the grandiose dream which had probably lain in
his mind from the beginning. He would achieve what Cobbett
had advocated: the salvation of the English working classes
through the creation of a "nineteenth-century yeomanry".
Feargus began to live in a "state of joyous excitement", as Jones
later recalled;[1] his absorption in the plan became an obsession.
Through a system of progressive mortgaging, based on the increased value he believed would accrue to the allotments
through intensive hand-cultivation, he thought to work a social
revolution. His claims for the Land Bank, launched in December
1846 to implement the self-multiplying mortgage principle,
showed how his mind was running: "If those with money to
lend would lend it [to the Land Bank] at three-and-a-half per
cent., on the best security in the world, I would change the whole
face of society in TWELVE MONTHS from this day. I would make a
paradise of England in less than FIVE YEARS." [2]

Harney's response to such claims was tepid. From its inception
to its dismal end, the Land Plan never seemed a concept of more
than limited potentiality to him. Unlike Ernest Jones, who
became a trustee of the Land Company and co-editor with
Feargus of a new journal, the *Labourer*, which was devoted
primarily to the plan, he took no active part in the new movement. His lack of enthusiasm was due primarily to a basic
divergence in his view toward land-ownership and that of
O'Connor. Feargus specifically repudiated the principle of communal ownership: "My plan has no more to do with Socialism
than it has with the comet," he wrote.[3] What he wished for was
a "large class of small and well-remunerated capitalists". But
Harney approached the problem of land-ownership from an
entirely different position. "His creed was—and Thomas Spence
had taught it—that 'the land is the people's farm', and that it
belonged to the entire nation, and not to individuals or classes,"
he told a meeting of London Chartists in mid-1845.[4] If, through
self-help, a certain number of impoverished weavers could be
put upon the land, so much the better; but this came no closer
to being the answer to the fundamental illness of society than had
the allotment scheme opened at Bingley in 1844 by those two
spokesmen of the "selfish and Sybarite lords of the soil", Disraeli

---

[1] *People's Paper*, 16 April 1853.
[2] *Northern Star*, 8 May 1847.
[3] *Ibid.*, 15 April 1843.
[4] *Ibid.*, 30 August 1845.

and the Tory M.P., Busby Ferrand. The state, according to his Spencean creed, must be the instrument of the "restitution" of the land to the people, being vested with its ownership and receiving its rent. In the meantime, a few operatives becoming self-sufficient through spade-husbandry was laudable but hardly revolutionary.

It would seem that the more doctrinaire Marx and Engels would have taken a stronger position against the plan. The most penetrating criticism from the socialist viewpoint, however, came from Bronterre O'Brien, who pointed out that the creation of a large class of smallholders would strengthen the forces of conservatism. Marx and Engels had, in fact, broken with Wilhelm Weitling and his disciple Kriege, now the leader of the German Communists in New York, over just such an issue, attacking small-ownership as "ostensibly hostile to communist principles".[1] Yet Engels's criticism of the Land Plan was mild: it was "unfortunate" that it called for a division, not community, of goods.[2] At the same time, the *Deutsche Londoner Zeitung*, in which Schapper's influence was dominant, was unrestrained in its praise of the scheme. Doubtless this curious ambivalence on the part of the German communists is attributable to motives of expediency. Like Harney, less concerned with doctrinal matters, they could scarcely attack the plan without coming into conflict with the formidable O'Connor and the formal Chartist leadership, as well as having the columns of the *Northern Star* closed to them. That this would have been the case seems unquestionable. Completely under O'Connor's domination, the members of the National Executive had become less political leaders than functionaries of the Land Company—a development which was to have important consequences for the Chartist movement in 1848.

The absorption of Chartist energies in O'Connor's scheme was not complete, however, as the General Election of 1847 showed, when twenty Chartist or Chartist-supported candidates stood for

---

[1] See Engels, quoted in Ryazanoff, *The Communist Manifesto of Karl Marx and Friedrich Engels*, p. 244. For Kriege's action, see *Northern Star*, 11 April 1846. Kriege had allied the New York German Communists with the National Reformers, an organization which called for free land grants to smallholders.

[2] *Communist Journal*, no. 1 (September 1847), quoted in full in Ryazanoff, *op. cit.*, Appendix E. *Cf.* Engels to Marx, 26 October 1847, in which he writes admiringly of O'Connor's defence of the Plan against the Radical press's attacks (*Briefwechsel*, vol. I, p. 84).

office. Harney's candidacy may have come as something of a surprise to him. Following a scathing attack at a close-packed London meeting on Palmerston's intervention against a popular insurrection in Portugal, he had appealed to the Foreign Secretary's constituents in Tiverton against their member's policy and offered to meet his redoubtable opponent "teeth to teeth on the hustings". The Tiverton radicals took him at his word (which had been circulated in 1,000 flyleafs in the borough); and late in July Harney arrived in the small Devon town, where he immediately began his campaign from a friendly draper's window after having dissuaded the enthusiastic crowd which greeted him from drawing his carriage by hand.

Harney's audacity in challenging one of the great Whig ministers in a borough which had returned him for the price of a few dinners since 1835 was a stroke of publicity which gave him a national audience. Palmerston's adventurous foreign policy was leading even in the summer of 1847 to an opposition which by the end of the year included such diverse elements as the Queen and Prince Consort, Richard Cobden, the Tories and *The Times*; and the leading London journals, aware of Harney's intention to attack Palmerston's policy, sent special reporters to cover the election.

In his address to the crowd of 3,000 gathered before the Tiverton hustings Harney once again stressed the Fraternal Democrats' theme, which he had put so succinctly in his original attack on Palmerston: "The people are beginning to realize that foreign as well as domestic questions do affect them, that a blow struck at liberty on the Tagus is an injury to the friends of freedom on the Thames. . . ." [1] The Foreign Secretary was an archetype of the international ruling classes. In Britain he stood for the New Poor Law and the coercion of Ireland; while abroad, "He everywhere allies himself with despotism and does the work of despotism, though sometimes in the name of 'Liberalism'." Those whom he had supported in Europe, Harney declared, were—like the English bourgeoisie—the most efficient plunderers of the people. In Asia, he had used armed force against the Chinese in a "murderous and immoral assault for purposes of trade"; in Afghanistan, British policy had made allies for Russia in the war which must inevitably come. ("Lord Palmerston bit his lip and looked even whiter than usual.") Finally, Harney

[1] *Northern Star*, 19 June 1847.

argued, imperial expansion was a process which benefited only the owning classes: "What a farce it is to speak to you [working men] of *our* Indian Empire, and *our* colonial possessions, when you have not one foot of soil in your own country to call your own." [1]

Stung by a two-hour review of his conduct which stretched back to his Tory days under Perceval and Canning, Palmerston replied in a manner described by one journal as "fit for the explanation of a minister to his sovereign". His rejoinder, which occupied five columns in *The Times* (against one paragraph for Harney—a procedure reversed, of course, by the *Northern Star*) was convincing enough from the Whig viewpoint; though his explanation of the Opium War was somewhat disingenuous. The Chinese had been arbitrary, it seemed; but in spite of themselves were now enjoying the benefits of free trade with England. Besides, he added, they liked opium. The main point of interest about his speech, however, is the fact that Harney had elicited from Palmerston the "most lengthy and plain-spoken account of his stewardship ever given to the British public", as one Radical leader-writer put it.

The debate on the hustings between the intense young Chartist leader, soberly garbed in black, and the urbane, cynical old Regency beau, a "jaded Cupid" with his dyed whiskers, bright blue coat and white pants, is a striking incident in more than one way. Palmerston was for the most part at ease in the novel situation, giving frequent vent to the odd, deliberate ejaculations which Henry Adams was to recall as "a laugh of the Congress of Vienna". Yet the laugh was somewhat strained at times; and not the least significant thing about that tableau in 1847 is the impossibility of such a scene having occurred in the year of the Congress—graphic evidence of the change which British politics had undergone in the intervening years. There is also the fact that, had there been a democratic franchise in 1847, Harney would have been elected. On the show of hands Palmerston was overwhelmingly defeated, certainly a shock to a man so conscious as he of public opinion. His demand for a poll, from which Harney withdrew, brought to his support the 264 stalwarts who alone in the crowd possessed the vote; but Palmerston's already

[1] *Ibid.*, 7 August 1847. The bulk of this account is taken from the reports of two eye-witnesses of the events, one of them Harney, in F. J. Snell, *Palmerston's Borough* (London: 1894).

strong opposition to any extension of the franchise—a major factor in preventing electoral reform in the last decade of his life—could scarcely have been weakened by his experience.

By giving Palmerston a "thorough thrashing on foreign policy" in the opinion of the Tiverton non-electors and the working-class radical press, Harney had gained a great deal of prestige for himself and his views within the Chartist movement. In a burst of generosity, Feargus wrote that the events at Tiverton had been the most important of the election—a grand gesture in view of his startling victory at Nottingham over the former Whig minister, John Cam Hobhouse. And not only in Tiverton and Nottingham had the General Election shown a sharp revival of political radicalism. Thomas Clark, a member of the National Executive, had won the show of hands at Sheffield, as had Ernest Jones and the Chartist-endorsed Edward Miall at Halifax, though all lost at the poll. More important still was the new alignment of forces which had manifested itself. While O'Connor's election was due mainly to Tory support—"Lord Radcliffe, the two principal bankers, and most of the clergy voted for me and asked me to dine," he wrote to the long-time spokesman for Chartism in the Commons, Thomas Duncombe[1]—in general the Chartists had joined forces with the middle-class Radicals rather than with Tories.

This rapprochement, once seemingly so shattered by the fiasco of the Sturgeite conference in 1842, had in fact been going on quietly since 1846, mainly in the form of the movement for registration of voters led by Duncombe.[2] With the success of the anti-Corn Law agitation, fought by the Chartists as a distraction from political objectives, one of the main grounds for dissension had disappeared; and by the end of 1847 both O'Connor and Ernest Jones, now a leader in the Chartist movement, were publicly expressing their sympathy toward a coalition of Chartists and Radicals. Moreover, this drawing together had taken an internationalist form in the People's International League, organized under the aegis of Mazzini, and combining in its

---

[1] Letter of 1 August 1847, quoted in T. S. Duncombe, *The Life and Correspondence of Thomas Slingsby Duncombe*, vol. I, p. 373.

[2] For the registration agitation, see *Northern Star*, 25 May, 22 June 1844; 26 April 1845; 3 October 1846; 20 January 1847. Thomas Duncombe was president of the Central Registration Committee, which directed the agitation on the same lines advocated by Peel and the Anti-Corn Law League for their purposes. Both O'Connor and Harney were members of the committee.

membership a strong element of influential middle-class Radicals and working-class dissidents from O'Connor's domination.

To these evidences of increasing class-fraternization Harney turned a cold eye. His unchanged belief in the political incompatibility of those whose economic interests were opposed led him to such gaucheries as his caustic criticism of middle-class collaboration at a public meeting held in December 1847 to congratulate the "respectable" pro-Chartist M.P.s who had been recently elected. As to the People's International League, their "namby-pamby Liberalism" was the subject for a bitter attack by their social-democratic critic which disturbed the tranquillity of their first public meeting. While he did not quarrel with their object of promoting the cause of nationalism on the Continent, Harney declared, holding up the "middle-class freedoms" of England as a model to the European nations was insulting, in view of the widespread distress prevailing at home under those freedoms.

But it was for another and more powerful organization with internationalist aims, the newly-formed Peace League, that he reserved his most acid scorn. This combination of Quakers, manufacturers, and Cobdenite M.P.s espoused an idealistic version of free trade, seeing in it the best means to prosperity for all classes and permanent world peace. To Harney, their pacifism—"a weak washy flood of 'moral' twaddle"—amounted to the condonation of the despotic *status quo* in Europe, which it was futile and foolish to believe could be changed peacefully. Typical of them, he wrote sardonically, was their protégé Elihu Burrit, the American blacksmith, who was preaching pacifism in England while his own country was embarked on a war (with Mexico) which was a "sore discouragement to the advocates of democratic institutions".[1]

The rapid international development of the Peace League, with its liberal, free-trade, pacifist aims, found an international organization already in existence to dispute its programme. A dramatic illustration of this lies in the fact that the first effective rebuttal of its claim to speak for the English operatives came not from London but from the Continent. At a Free Trade Congress of more than 300 delegates held in Brussels in September 1847, in which the Peace League formed the dominant contingent, George Weerth, a member of the Brussels branch of the Communist League who had lived in Yorkshire for some years, caused

[1] *Ibid.*, 1 May 1847.

L

a sensation by denying that free trade was a panacea for working-class distress, or that it would arrest the progressive pauperization of the operatives under capitalism; and concluded by declaring that he, and not the Peace League, spoke for the English working class. The speech, fully reported in the *Northern Star* by Engels, was unmistakably "Marxist" in its tone.[1] Equally obvious in it was what *The Times* correspondent labelled "Chartist common-place"—a phrase gratefully passed on to his readers by Harney. The Fraternal Democrats declared that Weerth was, in fact, their spokesman; and Harney pointed the moral of the whole incident a few weeks later in declaring to a meeting held in honour of George Thompson, an M.P. and active member of the Peace League: " 'All men are brethren' is becoming something more than a string of words, when a German, at a conference of delegates from several nations, is seen to rise in defence of the much-wronged people of England." [2]

The most important repercussion of these events was the Fraternal Democrats' decision to call for an international pro-letarian congress in answer to the Free Trade Congress. Where that body (and the Peace League) were liberal and pacifist, the working men's assembly would represent a union of socialist and revolutionary elements. Its purpose was to be the creation of branches of the Fraternal Democrats in the European nations and America. The response of Engels and Marx to this proposal was immediate. The Brussels Communists anticipated the action of international congress by forming a Brussels society "*à la* Fraternal Democrats", as Engels wrote in late September;[3] and a month later Marx and Engels arrived in London to cement the alliance of the societies at a banquet of the Fraternal Democrats commemorating the Polish Revolution. In the mood of en-thusiastic fraternity induced by speeches of Marx (in German) and Engels, both stressing the cardinal importance of the English

---

[1] "Our German Correspondent", *ibid.*, 9 October 1847. Marx was prevented from addressing the Congress, though the gist of his address was printed in the *Northern Star* (*ibid.*) and delivered to the Brussels Democratic Club early in January 1848. *Cf.* K. Marx, *Free Trade*, translated by F. K. Wischnewetzky (Boston: 1889). For an interesting anticipation of Marx's argument that free trade, by stimulating competition and production, would hasten the ultimate crisis of capitalism, see Charles Bray, *Essay upon the Union of Agriculture and Manufactures* (London: 1844).

[2] *Northern Star*, 30 October 1847.

[3] Engels to Marx, 28 September, *Briefwechsel*, vol. I, p. 75. The Brussels Society took the name of the Democratic Association for Promoting the Fraternity of All Nations.

working-class movement to that of the Continent, the meeting adopted by acclamation Harney's resolution to summon the international assembly when the "Fraternal Democratic Societies of London and Brussels" called for it. (The meeting preserved its international character to the end, concluding with "Three terrible groans for *The Times*, *Journal des Débats*, and the *Austrian Observer*" and three cheers for the *Northern Star*, *Réforme* and *German Universal Gazette*.)

The first step had been taken. It may be noted also that a public alliance between the ultra-radical groups in London and Brussels now supplemented the clandestine alliance of the Communist League, the same leaders being found in both organizations. Engels and Marx had, in fact, come to London for a dual purpose. Besides establishing a connection with the Fraternal Democrats they had attended the second congress of the Communist League, where they were directed to write a statement of principles which subsequently appeared as the *Communist Manifesto*. And it was Engels, still pursuing the double object of extending "scientific socialism" and promoting the international working men's congress, who was the main agent in gaining French participation in the plan. The young German had already met Flocon, the editor of the socialist *Réforme*, the organ which supported Louis Blanc and Ledru Rollin; and by late October had become the English correspondent for that paper, in addition to writing for the *Atelier*, a socialist journal run by working men. Chartist news now became a regular feature in both, with particular attention being paid to Harney's speeches. A month later Engels achieved something of a "scientific socialist" monopoly of the exchange of ultra-radical news between England and France by becoming the *Northern Star*'s French correspondent—as well as providing the *Deutsche Brusseler Zeitung*, now under Marx's control, with both French and English news. In his other mission he was equally successful. By January 1848 Flocon had indicated his willingness to "march together" and Ledru Rollin had publicly called for a "congress of Democrats of all nations".[1]

Thus in the opening months of 1848 the outlines of a new international socialist organization were beginning to take shape. In France, there was the powerful *Réforme* group (as well as a

[1] "Our French Correspondent", *Northern Star*, 8 January 1848. Engels to Marx, 14 January 1848, *Briefwechsel*, vol. I, pp. 91–92.

new branch of the Fraternal Democrats at Rochefort-sur-Mer, probably composed of British mechanics); in Belgium, the Brussels "Fraternal Democrats"; and in England, a steadily growing bloc within the Chartist party, the Metropolitan Delegate Council joining the entire Chartist Executive in backing the plan. If one includes the Polish contingent in the Fraternal Democrats it is clear that here in the making was an international organization more diversified in the nationalities it represented than the First International founded in 1864—and, it may be added, much more militantly social-democratic. Though there were wide differences between the socialist beliefs of those now drawing together, the tone of the nascent organization was unmistakably revolutionary. In an eloquent address that anticipates the tone of the *Communist Manifesto*, Harney set forth the ideas on which they were all agreed, declaring in part:[1]

"It is in the interest of land-lords and money-lords to keep the nations divided; but it is the interest of the Proletarians, everywhere oppressed by the same sort of task-masters and everywhere defrauded of the fruits of their industry by the same description of plunderers, it is their interest to unite. And they will unite. From the loom, the anvil, and the plow, from the hut, the garret, and the cellar, will come forth, are even *now* coming forth, the apostles of fraternity and destined saviours of humanity."

What might have been the consequences of the Democratic Congress can only be hazarded; the revolutions for which it intended to become the spokesman now swept the plan away and the reaction which followed made it impossible of fulfilment.

The growing hopefulness of the revolutionary cause in Europe had not gone unnoticed by Harney. Reviewing the situation in the *Northern Star* of 1 January 1848, he pointed out that the example of the Swiss in ridding themselves of reactionary Catholic influence late in 1847 had had profound effects in Italy and Germany; and Austria's domination was tottering in Hungary as well as in Italy. His analysis of the French situation, deriving much from Engels's on-the-spot reporting, was even more acute. The Reformers would be voted down by "Guizot and Co." and would then increase their public agitation. When the government attempted to repress that agitation, resistance would be provoked and the revolution would begin.

[1] *Northern Star*, 11 December 1847.

How much closer to the historical currents of the day than
the majority of Englishmen Harney was is indicated by the fact
that on 18 February, just four days before the Paris uprising
began, Lord John Russell asked in his Budget speech for an increase in the military forces—a course dictated by fear of an
invasion from a France firmly ruled by Louis Philippe. There
were but few isolated reports which foretold the French revolution; and the Foreign Office as well as the general public seems
to have considered the position of the "Citizen King" secure.[1]

The event which all European revolutionaries regarded as
the real prelude to Continental revolution found the Fraternal
Democrats at their usual monthly meeting in their large room
behind the "White Hart" tavern in Drury Lane. Michelot, the
French secretary, had returned for the meeting from Paris,
where the suppression of his lectures had led to student rioting,
and with Harney, "pale and quiet as usual", and the other
secretaries, sat on a podium under the flags of the nationalities
with a mingled audience of Chartists and *émigrés* filling the room.
An eye-witness later described the reaction of the meeting when
the news of Louis Philippe's abdication and the proclamation of
the French Republic was brought in:[2]

> "The effect was electrical. Frenchmen, Germans, Poles, Magyars'
> sprang to their feet, embraced, shouted, and gesticulated in the
> wildest enthusiasm. Snatches of oratory were delivered in excited
> tones, and flags were caught from the walls, to be waved exultantly,
> amidst cries of 'Hoch! Eljen! Vive la Republique!' Then the doors
> were opened, and the whole assemblage . . . with linked arms and
> colours flying, marched to the meeting place of the Westminster
> Chartists in Dean Street, Soho. There another enthusiastic
> fraternization took place, and great was the clinking of glasses that
> night in and around Soho and Leicester Square."

The excitement of that evening was not confined to these areas.
Preceded by mounted men, a large crowd paraded the main
thoroughfares shouting, "The Republic forever!"; and at Sadler's
Wells the pit and gallery stopped the performance and called for
the "Marseillaise", which was played and cheered.

"The hour of conflict between the millions and their masters
is at hand," Harney had told a public meeting a few days before,

[1] Elie Halévy, *The Age of Peel and Cobden* (London: 1948), pp. 198-99.
[2] Frost, *Forty Years Recollections*, pp. 127-28.

"the rule of the bourgeoisie is doomed." Chartist response to the revolution in Paris indicated that he was not alone in regarding this event as a prelude to domestic changes. The posters which advertised a great sympathy meeting in south London read: "The Republic for France and the Charter for England"; and the speech of William Cuffay, the quiet mulatto tailor who was to be on a convict ship bound for Australia within the year, was typical of the addresses at this highly excited gathering in its thinly-veiled appeal to physical force. The meeting, and another of the Fraternal Democrats a few days later from which hundreds were turned away, also adopted a congratulatory address to the Provisional Government of France, and elected Harney, Ernest Jones, and the president of the Chartist Executive, Philip McGrath, to deliver it in person.

The following days represented the summit of Harney's experience. Revolution had finally come again to France, the centre of his ideas and aspirations; and he was now to see it for the first time as a representative of the London working classes. When the three men arrived on 4 March, Paris was still littered with the debris of revolution; barricades remained in the streets and armed workers stood guard by cannon in front of the public buildings. Their arrival coincided with the funeral procession for those who had died in the "Three Days". Enormous crowds, kept off the roadway by a single tricoloured ribbon, stood in silence as the coffins passed, followed by the members of Provisional Government, while the muted strains of "Mourir pour la Patrie" and the "Marseillaise" filled the air.

The English representatives, accompanied by the German Democrats, Schapper, Moll, and Bauer (who had participated in the abortive Blanquist rising of 1839), went to the seat of the new government in the Hôtel de Ville the next day. Greeted by one of the blue-bloused guards who, it seemed, was a member of the German Democratic Society, they were ushered in without formality and immediately received by Ledru Rollin, Garnier-Pages, and Marrast. Jones, speaking in French, vowed that the English working classes would refuse to participate in any war against France; and Harney presented a parchment address, which was hung on the wall over the Presidential chair in the Hall of Audience. Garnier-Pages, replying for the Provisional Government, "hailed with delight" their expression of English support; and Harney and his two companions brought the dramatic occasion to an end by exiting with shouts of "*Vive la République!*" [1]

Despite his prostration with illness for a week, Harney tasted other revolutionary delights. In Flocon's office at the *Réforme* he met and chatted with Bakunin; and in company with Karl Schapper he breakfasted with Henri Imbert at the Tuileries. Imbert's position provides a vivid illustration of this upside-down new world. Just three weeks before, in exile in Belgium, he had been a member of the obscure Brussels Democratic Society; now he was the governor of what had been Louis Philippe's palace, which was to be converted into a home for the aged and infirm. The three enjoyed a "most superb breakfast, served up on what *was* Louis Philippe's crockery", as Harney told the Fraternal Democrats on his return, and afterwards strolled about the palace. In Louis Philippe's council room they decided to have no banquet (great laughter) and Harney stood on the spot formerly occupied by the King's throne before it had been taken out and symbolically burned in front of the palace.

The presence of Schapper, Moll and Bauer indicated that Harney and Jones had another purpose in coming to Paris. About 12 March, Marx informed Engels that they had arrived, and that a new Central Authority of the Communist League had been elected. With the shifting of the Central Authority to Paris, and the League's new restriction to German members, the connection of Harney and Jones with the organization seems to have come to an end. In any case this was a parting of the ways with the Germans, for their attention was fixed beyond the Rhine. By late April, Marx, Engels and Schapper were actively engaged in the revolutionary movement in Germany; and with their freedom to work in the open the *raison d'être* of the Communist League temporarily disappeared. Harney, however, remained in communication with Engels throughout the year.

With his two companions, Harney returned to an England where the political ferment on the Continent was working powerfully. Even before the February Revolution, scattered disorders and rioting had necessitated the use of troops in various localities; and the persistence of the commercial crisis and widespread

[1] *Northern Star*, 25 March 1848. The account appears to have been written by Jones.

unemployment made for a receptive working class. The effect of the Continental revolutions was to accentuate the depression in trade and, at the same time, to show in the French Provisional Government's proclamation of the "Right to Labour" that a thoroughly democratic government assumed responsibility for unemployment and working-class suffering—a thoroughly pernicious doctrine in the view of *The Times*. The Metropolitan Trades Delegates committee, which claimed with some exaggeration to speak for 200,000 operatives, immediately endorsed the principle of the "Right to Labour" in England; and then coupled this with the demand for the Charter at a great gathering of trade unionists, an action headlined by Harney: "First Effects of the Glorious French Revolution".[1]

Political excitement intensified as March drew on. Lower middle class as well as working-class signatures were appended to a new National Petition; and plans for a National Convention to meet on 3 April and present the Petition were matured. And, as in 1839 and 1842, the rise in political interest was matched by a sharp increase in violence. In Manchester, riotous mobs necessitated the dispatch of a regiment of troops; in Glasgow, thousands of unemployed operatives plundered shops and temporarily controlled the streets. Nor were the outbreaks confined to the localities affected in 1839 and 1842. Towns which had remained unaffected then—Exeter, Weymouth, Plymouth, Bath, Newark —reported disorders as well as the traditional centres of violence. In hitherto placid London, above all, nightly meetings of tumultuous crowds sometimes numbering 15,000 were an added source of anxiety to an already worried government.

Once again the familiar pattern of pike manufacture, the purchase of firearms and secret drilling was emerging; but to this had been added the new element of French revolutionary influence. As they proceeded about their work, the Glasgow rioters had shouted such slogans as "Bread or Revolution!" (the cry of the barricades) and "*Vive la République!*", cheering the soldiers sent against them. Ralph Waldo Emerson, the American essayist then visiting in fashionable circles in London, noted of a great mass-meeting early in March, "The Marseillaise was sung as songs are in our abolition meetings"; and by the end of the

---

[1] Among other evidence of some swing-over of the trades to Chartism is the fact that Charles Knight, co-editor of the middle-class Radical *Voice of the People*, used the terms "trade-unionist" and "Chartist" interchangeably.

month was writing home about the "universal anxiety" that events in France would be duplicated in England.[1]

Most threatening of all were the signs of an alliance of forces which had remained alien in the past—the Irish independence movement and the Chartists. In Manchester on 21 March a gathering of some 15,000 Chartists and Irishmen was addressed by O'Connor and the revolutionary Irish leaders, Doheny and Meagher, who had come from Dublin for the demonstration. In Liverpool, from whence arms were being shipped secretly to Ireland, a combination of the two groups was taking place semi-clandestinely, a process which led finally to a concentration of troops there sufficient to conquer an Indian province.

Against this setting of imminent crisis it is not easy to fix the position or the amount of control exerted by the formal Chartist leadership. The Executive, whose positions as directors and officers of the Land Company had absorbed most of their efforts, were a collection of men of no particular abilities—not even in bookkeeping, it was to become apparent—who simply followed O'Connor; and Feargus, never notable for consistency or determination in crucial circumstances, had become even more erratic in his behaviour. Some contemporaries thought that this was due to a newly-acquired habit—a heavy indulgence in spirits. More likely the change of character attributed to brandy was really due to the insidious work of the spirochete which, it seems more than probable, was the eventual cause of his madness and death. Whatever the cause, whether excessive drinking or the onset of *dementia paralytica*, he was unable to act decisively.

Caught by the heady enthusiasm of these March days of 1848 and full of his Paris experience, Harney was scarcely more consistent in his utterances. Initially, he reverted to his former identification with Marat, adopting the pen-name of "*L'Ami du Peuple*" in the series of letters contrasting the actions of French and English democrats which appeared in the *Northern Star*. "We have been meeting, talking and writing for the last ten years and have not yet got our Charter," he told a meeting of the Fraternal Democrats. "The French, with three days work, have obtained the Charter and something more." A subsequent address of the Fraternal Democrats made his implication more explicit: every means equal to the end of "bursting their political

[1] James E. Cabot, *A Memoir of Ralph Waldo Emerson*, 2 vols. (Boston and New York: 1887), vol. II, pp. 527, 530.

and social fetters" was justifiable.[1] Yet he was no longer the uncomplicated revolutionary of the first National Convention, to whom all opposition to insurrection was cowardice. The fiascos of 1839 and 1842 had convinced him of the basic necessity for thorough organization and a concerted popular effort to achieve a successful revolution. In contrast to his ardent optimism a sober note may be discerned in his warning against rashness and emphasis on the "bounds of due discipline" within which the aroused spirit of the people must work. Harney realized as well as anyone in the movement the importance of local organization; and while he was aware that Chartist re-organization was proceeding in important centres like Aberdeen and Newcastle, he knew also that the Executive controlled not a political organization so much as a land society, and that the agitation stirring the working classes was in large part unorganized.

Once again, as in 1842, it was difficult to tell who were leaders and who were led. For the last time the Chartist movement was being confusedly swept along in a torrent of working-class protest. "Their empty pantries and shoeless children should dictate their actions," declared one speaker at the Nottingham mass-meeting which elected Harney its delegate to the National Convention. Another evoked an echo of the younger Harney by crying, "The man who had only one life and feared to give it was not worthy of living in the land!" When a vote of thanks was given to the Mayor for the use of the Town Hall a voice added, "It will be ours in a fortnight." But the veteran of fifteen years in the radical movement who took his seat when the Convention met in London on 4 April had heard such speeches before, sometimes from his own lips. He could also remember the mass-imprisonment of Chartist leaders and the reaction of working-class indifference which had followed the speeches. Certainly it was in no simple state of mind that he joined the forty-six other delegates in the John Street Institute.

Of the Chartist marshals of the "Old Guard" only four had survived the barren political steppes of the years since 1839 to appear in the Convention of 1848: Harney, Bronterre O'Brien, Richard Marsden, the Preston weaver, and John McCrae, who had represented Ayrshire in 1839 and was now Dundee's delegate. There was also O'Connor, the Napoleon of the movement—whose Land Plan some working-class leaders regarded as

[1] *Northern Star*, 25 March 1848.

Chartism's Moscow; and for the first time since 1839 Scottish delegates had returned across the border to sit in a Chartist convention in force. Some localities represented were new—Exeter, Plymouth, Cheltenham and Totnes—and Ireland had a voice in Bernard McCarthy, a leader of the Irish Confederation who was allowed a seat after being accepted as a London delegate.

The tone of the delegates' opening speeches caused the government-sponsored *Voice of the People* (a penny journal which Harriet Martineau and Charles Knight, both popularizers of the classical economists, had been hired to edit) to label the members "vain, empty, bellowing and hired braggadocios, who feed upon the delusions which they propagate". It was quite true that no more than four or five delegates spoke in the moderate manner that the "*Voice of the Profit-Mongers*"—Harney's sarcastic re-baptism—found so admirable; a majority of the members advocated a resort to force as an ultimate measure. Yet even the most extreme speakers were far milder than Harney, Rider and Taylor had been in 1839; and, paradoxically enough, the general attitude of the Convention toward the middle classes was friendly.

From the first, Harney bent all his efforts toward plans for organization. In the meetings prior to the date selected for presentation of the National Petition, 10 April, he strongly supported Ernest Jones's plan to create a solid base for extending the Chartist agitation. Unanimously accepted by the Convention, Jones's plan assumed the rejection of the Petition and concerned itself with subsequent steps to be taken. Following the rejection, provincial mass-meetings were to be held on 21 April to elect a new and more representative "National Assembly" which would remain in permanent session and "concert action". More immediately, the delegates agreed that the Petition would be carried to the House of Commons by a great procession proceeding from a mass-meeting at Kennington Common. All this seems reasonable enough in cold print; but a truer indication of the heat of the delegates' feeling is to be found in O'Brien's resignation at a public meeting in Lambeth on 9 April. No physical coward, Bronterre told the crowd that the delegates would go too fast due to the pressure of distress in their districts—and the government was too strong for the working classes. The "Schoolmaster of Chartism" was groaned off the platform.

Both the propertied classes and the government were in accord with Bronterre's view of the seriousness of the situation.

That there was a revolution fixed for 10 April was common talk in these circles; and the government had reacted accordingly. With the example of the results of dilatory action in 1839 and 1842 before him and aware of the contagiousness of the revolutions which had engulfed the Continent, the Home Secretary, Sir George Grey, had taken elaborate precautions not only in London but all over the country. The yeomanry regiments had been called up; special constables enrolled and in the most seriously disturbed areas armed with cutlasses; and troops concentrated in a way made possible by the network of railways which had grown up since 1839. The army, as Harney wrote a year later, was "seated like a spider in the centre of its web, on the diverging lines of iron road".[1] Another new means of central control, the electric telegraph, was seized by the government on 9 April and its use limited to those with a personal cachet signed by the Home Secretary. This action, in conjunction with a proclamation in London and more than sixty other localities forbidding meetings on 10 April, indicates a fear of spontaneous uprisings. If such fears existed, the efficiency and dispatch with which precautions had been taken, as well as the technological advances which had made it possible, left the government in a position far different from that which had worried General Napier nine years before.

The government's preparations and its prohibition of the meeting and the procession to Westminster placed the Convention in a difficult position. "Every hour the strength of our adversary, and our own weakness, became more and more apparent," Harney wrote subsequently. "There was no longer any mistake that, if we meant to proceed with the procession, it would be a fight from the moment we left Kennington Common in the direction of the Houses of Parliament, and for which the people were not prepared."[2] While there were a few hotheads who wished to precipitate a conflict, by the day fixed for the presentation of the Petition there was a pretty general agreement among the delegates that the procession would be cancelled, and events now confirmed their decision.

When the Convention met briefly on the sunny morning of 10 April before proceeding to Kennington Common, they were

[1] *Democratic Review*, October 1849.
[2] Letter in *Northern Star*, 2 February 1850. Little of the proceedings of 8-10 April appeared in the press at the time, for obvious reasons.

III. Bronterre O'Brien

IV. Feargus O'Connor

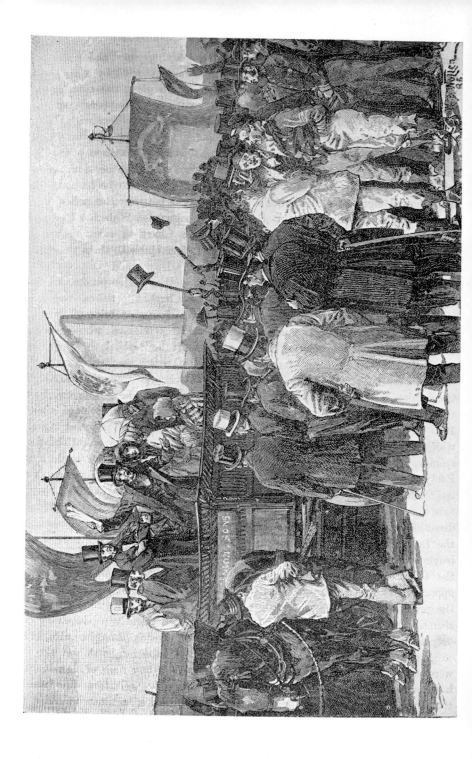

faced with a massive mobilization of government force and the propertied classes. Writing late in March, Emerson had acutely observed, "One thing is certain: that if the peace of England should be broken up, the aristocracy here—or, I should say, the rich—are stout-hearted, and as ready to fight for their own as the poor . . ." [1] Harney, on his walk from his home in Brompton to the John Street Institute, could scarcely have avoided seeing many of the 150,000 special constables, including the future emperor of France, who had volunteered. And the 9,000 soldiers and marines and four batteries of field artillery brought into London, though kept out of sight near such strategic positions as the bridges, could not have escaped the notice of the Chartists. The barricaded public buildings, behind the windows of which stood armed government servants; the commandeered ships on the Thames; the news that the Duke of Wellington was directing operations: these were arguments that needed no elaboration, and the delegates quickly decided to abandon the forbidden procession.

So far as they knew, however, the ban on the Kennington Common meeting was still in force, and this they determined to defy. Accordingly, Harney, O'Connor, Jones and the Chartist Executive, in a wagon preceded by another bearing the huge bulk of the National Petition, drove to the Common accompanied by a procession of 10,000—one of many converging from different parts of the city. Kennington Common, according to the reporter of the *Morning Post*, was filled with a great crowd of at least 80,000 men, wheeling and marching about in the brilliant sunshine under trade-union flags, tricolours and such threatening banners as "And Guizot Laughed"—a reference to the reported mirth of the French minister when he read a demand for his impeachment just before the February Revolution.[2]

The government had meanwhile decided to allow the meeting to proceed undisturbed provided the procession was cancelled, and had taken the precaution of seizing the bridges, thus sealing off the Chartists on the south bank of the Thames. The only time that day when violence seemed imminent was when the giant

---

[1] Cabot, *A Memoir of Ralph Waldo Emerson*, vol. II, p. 531.

[2] Estimates of the number of demonstrators on the Common vary even more than is usual in such cases. O'Connor's figure was 250,000; that of *The Times*, 25,000. The *Evening Sun* agrees with the top estimate of the *Morning Post*, 150,000. So with the estimates of the number of special constables sworn in: *The Times's* figure was 150,000; O'Connor's, "upwards of 70,000".

figure of O'Connor was seen leaving the Common accompanied
by a police inspector. " 'They have got him!' " the cry went up,
and for a moment the issue hung in the balance.[1] But Feargus
had simply been summoned to a conference with the Metropolitan Police Superintendent, Colonel Mayne, where he was
told that the meeting would be permitted if the procession was
cancelled—a proposal which O'Connor quickly accepted.
According to one observer of these events, the crowd received
this news with relief; and while the meeting split into sections to
be addressed by the delegates, the Petition was humbly taken
over Battersea Bridge and deposited at the House of Commons.

"The corrupt daily press would say that in abandoning the
procession they had retreated," Harney told the large contingent
of Irish Confederates who were his audience, "but they had only
retreated, as the ablest generals had done, to come again, perhaps in another shape and another form." [2] The latent threat in
this and other speeches pried up no cobblestones, however; nor,
obviously, were they intended to lead to this result. A dismal
rain completed the government's work that day; the sodden
participants were allowed to filter back across the bridges late
in the afternoon; and the 10th of April came to a gloomy end.

While it had not been the Convention's intention to assay a
trial of force, the mobilization of the propertied classes and the
government had given that effect to these events. The "corrupt
daily press" made the capital out of 10 April which Harney had
anticipated. Three days later the relieved laughter of the upper
classes was renewed by a report of the House of Commons' committee that had examined the Petition. It claimed to have found
but 1,975,000 signatures, many of them dubious, and not the
5,706,000 boasted of by Feargus. Instead of salvaging the salient
fact that the Petition still represented an impressive document of
public opinion, Feargus proceeded to compound the effect of the
report. In a ridiculous and melodramatic series of events, he
lost his temper and challenged a particularly carping M.P. to a
duel, was hauled into the House by the Sergeant-at-Arms, and—
with his opponent—forced to apologize.

The events of 10 April and the jeering reception of the
National Petition were seen by Harney and others in retrospect
as heavy blows; but at the time Chartist strength showed no sign
of waning. From all parts of the country came resolutions of

---

[1] Frost, *Forty Years Recollections*, p. 137.   [2] *Northern Star*, 15 April 1848.

support for the Convention; and in the May issues of the *Northern Star* a full page was necessary for the small local reports of Chartist meetings—an indication that the basically essential organization was proceeding. There were other, more ominous, indications of activity as well. It is doubtful that the propertied classes' attitude in the days after 10 April was shared by Sir George Grey in the Home Office. Reports of drilling and the sale of arms continued to reach him, and on 21 April troops had to be sent to Dudley and Barnsley. Even more disturbing were the reports of joint demonstrations of the Irish and the Chartists in Sheffield, Liverpool and Whitehaven—a trend which culminated in mid-April in Dublin when a mass-meeting was held to form a league between the "producing-classes of both countries", at which John Mitchell, a leader of the militant United Irishmen, spoke for the Charter. Still another Dublin meeting on the 24th, attended by two delegates from the National Convention, adopted the Six Points.

The government's answer to these threatening manifestations was a "Gagging Act"—the Crown and Government Security Act—which provided rigorous penalties for incitement to violence and made sedition a transportable offence. But the most effective instrument in destroying the working-class political movement was provided by the Chartist leaders themselves. As in previous times of crisis when united action was the imperative need, the Chartist leadership split into factions. In part, the reason for discord was embodied in the familiar question which had rent the movement before: should the Chartists unite with the middle-class Radicals or should the movement remain independently proletarian? More immediately damaging in its effect, however, was a new issue—that of a concerted attempt by both moderates and extremists to oust O'Connor from the position of dominance he had occupied so long. The resultant dissension mortally wounded the movement.

Even before the first meeting on 1 May of the National Assembly, the more representative body which had been elected by mass-meetings late in April, it was apparent that a majority of the Chartist leaders had drawn the conclusion from the events of 10 and 13 April that legal action could succeed only by collaboration with those who had already achieved a measure of political power. Before its dissolution the National Convention had passed a resolution approving overtures to the middle

classes which went at least half-way—and already in existence
was a powerful middle-class Radical movement to respond to
these overtures. Led in Parliament by Richard Cobden, John
Bright, and the indestructible old Radical, Joseph Hume, the
exponents of a "Little Charter" of moderate aims—a rate-paying
suffrage, the ballot, triennial parliaments and a redistribution of
seats—hoped to capitalize on the popular political ferment to
continue the transference of power to the manufacturing and
commercial classes which had begun in 1832. More specifically,
their aim was "administrative and financial reform". That there
was a great ground-swell of sentiment for a union of the classes was
abundantly attested by the number of mass-meetings in which
the two groups had joined forces to push their common aims.

It was in these circumstances that the National Assembly convened on May Day amid intense interest. Yet the very meeting
of this body indicated that a split had already opened in the
Chartist ranks, for Feargus had advocated a boycott of the
Assembly, doubtless aware of the intention of the delegates to
end his control. The difference between him and the moderate
delegates was not that of middle-class collaboration—O'Connor
had become as thoroughly convinced of its necessity as the
majority of the Assembly—but rather these delegates' desire to
rid themselves of a man whom they had come to consider an
incubus. The Assembly "Montagnards" had additional differences. The attack came first from the Left, such London exponents of physical force as young Vernon being joined by the
Scottish delegates. The latter showed a remarkable change from
the days of 1838–39, when the Edinburgh moderates had condemned O'Connor's proletarian extremism. Now the shoe was
on the other foot: O'Connor was condemned as an exponent of
union with the "great upholders of that system of political
economy which ground the working classes to the dust".[1] These
"Socialists first, and Chartists second", as Feargus labelled them,
proposed that he be jettisoned and that Chartism should re-form
itself into a new social-democratic confederation which would
include Ireland. Although they were voted down by a majority
of three to one, the incident was a significant one in being the
first specific proposal in a Chartist convention of a democratic
organization with socialist aims.

Although the delegates showed their agreement with O'Con-

[1] *Northern Star*, 6 May 1848.

nor's views by their adverse vote, as well as by a disavowal of the London extremists' demands for a resort to force, the election of a new Provisional Executive made their determination to change leadership unmistakable. Feargus was proposed and defeated; his following on the old Executive was not even nominated. But the battle was only joined. It was quickly apparent that the "Lion of the North" still commanded a loyal following among the national rank-and-file, as the flood of letters which inundated the *Northern Star* indicated. A chastened Assembly repudiated any hostility to O'Connor and the latter, having demonstrated his still-existent popularity, graciously made his peace with them. The harm had been done, however. Both Chartist unity and O'Connor's power had been undercut, with divisions in Chartist associations over the issue taking place throughout the country. The metropolitan press had reported the schism until, as Harney wrote, "it tired of the superfluous effort of destroying the effect of the Assembly".[1] Though the delegates had developed a careful reorganizational plan for the movement, this never seems to have got beyond the paper stage except in London; and when the Assembly dissolved itself on 13 May it was clear that Chartism was drifting while the captains fought.

Harney had taken no direct part in these events. O'Connor had indicated to him that his participation in the Assembly would mean the end of his editorship of the *Northern Star*; and he had acceded to this ultimatum. Doubtless pecuniary reasons played a part in his decision; and, as he wrote later, there was his loyalty to the increasingly erratic man who had done so much for him. Yet this did not mean that he had sacrificed his independence of principle. To the desire of the "Lion of the North" to lie down with the middle-class lamb he was as cool as to the Assembly's expressions of class-compatibility. The views he expressed were, in fact, identical with those of the Scottish "Socialist-Chartists". The real purpose of the Hume-Cobden group, he wrote, was to use the Chartists to frighten the government into shifting the main burden of taxation from the middle classes to the landed interest. By helping the bourgeoisie, the working class would once again find itself duped as in 1832.

This developing argument was rendered an abstraction by the action of Richard Cobden late in May. When O'Connor accused Hume in the House of Commons of procrastinating in his

[1] *Ibid.*, 27 May 1848.

M

presentation of a motion on the "Little Charter", Cobden rose and in a cutting reply unconditionally divorced himself from any connection with the Chartists led by O'Connor in the agitation for an extension of the suffrage. When Hume's motion was finally debated in July, Cobden attempted to conciliate Chartist opinion but it was too late. Feargus had reacted furiously, calling for obstructive action against middle-class meetings; and the Provisional Executive had echoed his demand: Chartists should unmask the "new movers" and "tear the flimsy veils off their vague and meaningless resolutions" at their meetings. Once again the suspicious courters had sheered off at the verge of marriage. Harney could not refrain from pointing the moral: Cobden's actions "must satisfy the most credulous as to the real designs of the bourgeoisie".[1]

The moderates had failed; legalistic means to the achievement of the Chartists had led to an impasse. The inability of the Chartists and the middle-class Radicals to reach a *modus vivendi* to further their joint aims meant the closing of an alternative course. The immediate effect was to confirm the extremists in their argument for stronger measures and to further influence frustrated men like Ernest Jones who were already leaning in their direction. As in 1839, it was the innings again of those who advocated violence—but this was to be the last innings of Chartism as a mass-movement.

[1] *Northern Star.*

CHAPTER VIII

From Green Flag to Red

"A set of grim, dirty and discontented men, trudging with a hang-dog air through the streets, with a hideous sort of mystery as to what may be in their heads or in their pockets constitute a scene perfectly abhorrent to the taste of the genuine, business-like Londoner, dividing his time between his counter and his fireside."

SO *The Times* described an enormous column, six men abreast and a mile and a half long, which suddenly appeared and silently marched through London's main thoroughfares on the night of 29 May. In the north at Bradford the day before a force of 2,000 bludgeon-wielding operatives had routed a greater number of police and special constables. The military force necessary to put them down reads like a battle order: two infantry companies, two troops of dragoons, the West Yorkshire Yeomanry Cavalry, and the Yorkshire Hussars. "Let us do the Chartists justice," remarked *The Times* with reluctant admiration. "If fighting with pluck against special constables and the police could make a revolution, those who fought at Bradford ought to have succeeded." Such events must have given pause to those who thought Chartism had been buried on the 10th of April. It was rather in the summer of 1848 that the movement's life-blood drained away when, driven to desperation, the extremists tried to mount their forces and revolt. The first attempt, in June, was crushed by governmental action before it had gained any semblance of unity; the second, occurring in a void of popular sympathy in August, had been destroyed from within prior to the date set for insurrection.

In spite of the extraordinary powers vested in him by the "Gagging Act", Grey had followed a policy of letting the Chartists talk themselves out after 10 April, hoping that the faint signs of improvement in the home trade would soon extend to the foreign trade and that fuller stomachs would bring cooler heads. But the fighting in the North in May and the growing rumours that violence would follow the simultaneous meetings scheduled for 12 June—which had been called by the Provisional Executive to protest against the Prime Minister's declaration that the people did not want the Charter—put an end to this policy. With an increasingly vociferous chorus of the "respectable" press calling for repressive measures, the Home Office instructed magistrates to arrest "seditious" speakers; large meetings were to be considered a menace to public order *per se* and proceeded against. The nightly gatherings in the metropolis first felt the weight of this edict. On the evening of 4 June mass-meetings at Bishop Bonner's Fields, Victoria Park and Bethnal Green were broken up, precipitating street fighting which lasted all night near the Green. Within the next few days the leaders who had been addressing the metropolitan gatherings were seized—Jones, Vernon, Sharpe, Fussell and Williams, one of the leaders of the old Democratic Association.

The evidence against Jones and Vernon could have convicted no one in normal times; but their trial early in July took place in a witch-hunting atmosphere. The middle classes, frightened by the extremism of those with whom they had just been trying to unite, made common cause with the upper classes; the Radical *Morning Advertiser* joined with the Tory *Morning Post* in demanding strong action. And accentuating the fears caused by talk of incendiarism and arming came the news of the extremely bloody street fighting in Paris late in June which had resulted from the abolition of the National Workshops. The parallel seemed plain: England was the "Thermopylae of Europe", the Attorney General told the jurors; they would defend her from the chaos affecting the Continent by finding the defendants guilty. Jones and the other defendants did not have a hope under these conditions.

Of the inevitable result, Harney declared bitterly that the prisoners had been found guilty not of sedition but of the "Communism" and "French terrorism" so frequently mentioned by the prosecution. "If men are to be indicted as Chartists and convicted as Communists," he wrote, "they may begin to ask themselves why they should stop short at advocating political reform." [1] There was something of prescience in this remark. Jones, no socialist when he went to prison, returned to working-class politics after two years convinced, like Harney, that the economic system must be basically altered. "Imprisonment had

[1] *Northern Star*, 15 July 1848.

had the effect of propelling him from Chartism to Red Republicanism," another of the defendants, Fussell, declared on his release in 1850.[1]

The influence of French events, so marked in the trial of Jones and the other defendants, had already accounted for the destruction of the Fraternal Democrats as an organization with foreign members in May. In the same way that the government had used the "Gagging Act" against Chartist extremists, a new Alien Act, which gave Grey almost a free hand in deporting émigrés from England, was used to break Chartist connections with foreign revolutionaries. The pervasive fears aroused by the memory of French internationalism permeated the debate on the bill. The Marquess of Lansdowne spoke of a report that 50,000 Frenchmen were ready to assist in an English insurrection; the Earl of Malmesbury quoted a speech by Harney which "alluded to the willingness expressed by foreigners to assist in any struggle that might be considered necessary in this country".[2] That the French government, even prior to the reaction following the June uprising, had pursued a strict non-interventionist policy does not seem to have been apparent to the debaters. *Punch*, increasingly a mirror of the propertied classes in these months, reflected their feeling in a cartoon about the Alien Act which showed a Frenchman with a torch and placards reading "Sedition", "Communism" and "Treason" being kicked into the Channel by John Bull. The meeting room of the Fraternal Democrats in Drury Lane was closed to them; and, very likely at the request of the refugees themselves, their connection with the society formally came to an end.

Once started, the mechanism of repression ground on. Under pressure from those who saw an analogy in the role of the ultra-radical press in Paris and in Britain—"prime movers of the work of Satan", as one clerical pamphleteer labelled them[3]—the government suppressed the *North British Express* in Edinburgh and moved against Joseph Barker's *The People*. However, despite such attacks on the *Northern Star* as that of Joseph Hume, who wanted Harney "scouted from society", it remained untouched —though Feargus wasted no time in settling a libel suit based on one of *L'Ami du Peuple's* attacks on a witness in the Jones affair.

---

[1] *Red Republican*, 13 July 1850.   [2] *Hansard*, 3rd series, vol. XCVIII, pp. 137-38.
[3] *The French Revolution of 1848, Reviewed in the Light of Prophecy* (Dorchester: 1848), quoted in *Northern Star*, 1 July 1848.

More oblique, but equally damaging in its effect on Chartism, was a parliamentary committee's report on the Chartist Land Plan late in July. Alexander Somerville, the Anti-Corn Law League's "Whistler at the Plough", was to state a few years later that Cobden had hired him to collect evidence against the Land Company to blacken O'Connor's character.[1] Though O'Connor's personal honesty was affirmed by the committee—he was, in fact, some £3,298 out of pocket—it was evident that the management of the Company had been extremely inefficient and irregular. As constituted, the Company was illegal; and it was recommended that the shareholders wind it up. The wide publicity given to the fact that only 250 out of almost 70,000 subscribers had been settled on the land was bad enough; what was worse was O'Connor's ingenuous explanation to his readers that having hoped only for an "infant scheme" he had found himself, like Frankenstein, with a "monstrous creature" on his hands. That creature had absorbed the savings of many, and it was unlikely that they thought better of either O'Connor or the movement he stood for as a result.

Fresh rumours of simultaneous risings in England and increasing unrest in Ireland accompanied the last act of that unhappy summer, on which the curtain fell on 14 August. So alarming had the situation grown across the Irish Sea that the government suspended the Habeus Corpus Act for Ireland on 22 July; and the situation in heavily Irish Liverpool was so threatening as to cause the propertied classes to petition for their inclusion in the suspension. Unified organizations of Irishmen and Chartists were also reported in Bolton and Manchester, and events showed these groups were also acting in concert in Ashton-under-Lyne. A considerable number of Irishmen were involved in the preparations for revolt in London; and, according to one contemporary, this represented a union with "Young Ireland".[2]

Subsequent trial testimony indicates that the conspiracy had national ramifications. Moreover, in London at any rate, an elaborate organization was in existence and the rising set for 15 August had been carefully planned. The revolutionaries were divided into brigades and divisions, each with a definite function: e.g. one division was to erect barricades at Seven Dials,

---

[1] Somerville, *Cobdenic Policy the Internal Enemy of England* (London: 1854), Ch. V.
[2] Frost, *Forty Years Recollections*, p. 148.

from which point Drury Lane would be seized; more barricades would then go up at St. Mary's-in-the-Strand and at Temple Bar, and so on. Cartridges, fire-balls, and grenades had been cached; and in more than one account mention is made of a mysterious chemical which, mixed with water, was to set London alight—perhaps an indication of the influence of science on revolutionary profiteering. According to the plan found in one of the conspirator's rooms, the number of participants in London was 1,200, not an impossible figure.[1]

The government was aware of all this from the beginning, the conspiratorial movement having been thoroughly infiltrated with spies and *agents-provocateurs*. "I was not a Chartist, but merely joined them for the purpose of obtaining information," brazenly testified the leader of the "Wat Tyler Brigade" in Greenwich. "I wished to ingratiate myself with these people that I might betray them." [2] The Lancashire plotters were led by a man who became the chief witness for the Crown a month later; and Thomas Powell, whose testimony against Cuffay, Ritchie, Fay and the other London leaders led to their being sentenced to transportation for life, admitted that he had taken an initiatory part in the arming. When Lacy, one of the London leaders, returned from the manufacturing districts with the word that the risings would take place on the night of the 15th, the government was informed and struck with mass-arrests in Liverpool, Oldham, Manchester, and Bolton. Cuffay's group was seized in the "Orange Tree" public house in Bloomsbury at their final conference. Over 100 Irishmen at Seven Dials and another armed force of men near Westminster were already assembled when the police arrived. Only at Ashton-under-Lyne, where the revolutionaries rose a day early and controlled the town for a time, was it necessary to use the military.

Had this *émeute* come off as planned, still another sanguinary incident would have been written into the annals of 1848, but it could have amounted to no more than that. Cuffay's plot found its analogy not in the February Revolution of 1848 but in Blanqui's abortive outbreak in 1839. The revolutionaries, as in the Chartist plots of January 1840, had cut themselves off from

[1] There were thirty brigade leaders at the last meeting, and, according to one witness, thirty members of his brigade awaited their leaders' return. If all the brigades were of this size, the number of revolutionaries would have been about 1,000.

[2] *Northern Star*, 30 September 1848.

popular support; they had also chosen a time to strike when general political excitement was ebbing. There is evidence to show that, even at the height of popular agitation four months before, the élite of the working classes, those with a vested interest in the *status quo*, would probably have stood with the propertied classes in the event of violence.[1] By August, the hopes of Cuffay and his fellows for a mass-rising following their example were doomed by the growing indifference of all ranks of the working classes.

Before the end of the year the Ashton revolutionary leaders were on their way to join the London conspirators in the Australian penal colony; and in the sweeping arrests and trials which followed the summer's violence such veteran Chartist leaders as James Leach and John McDouall, both members of the Provisional Executive, and Harney's old friends, George White of Birmingham and John West of Stockport, were sent to prison. The familiar exhaustion had succeeded the fever of political excitement; nothing was to be seen of the thousands who had thronged to public meetings. "I am bound to say that the old ship is about to float," wrote O'Connor optimistically from Scotland in October; but the remark is more enlightening as to the state of the ship than as evidence of a rising tide, for his reception had been unenthusiastic.[2] What local organizations remained split into factions, and even the staunch few who had carried the movement through the passive mid-'forties found public meeting places closed against them. "When trade is good, political agitation is a farce," wrote Harney in September; yet even this consolation was lacking. The improvement of economic conditions was not to be apparent until 1849. Trade was not good, yet, as he admitted, "Popular indifference was never more clearly manifested than at this very time. . . . Chartist organization has become the merest name—the very shadow of a shade."[3]

In analysing the Chartist debacle of 1848, Harney came to the conclusion that their organization had not been equal to the crisis. The Chartist leadership had channelled some of the tre-

---

[1] See, e.g., dispatches from the Home Secretary expressing gratification at the volunteering of operatives as special constables in Manchester and Birmingham, 8, 15 April 1848, in H.O. 41/19.

[2] *Northern Star*, 28 October 1848. *Cf.* Anon., *Memorandum of the Chartist Agitation in Dundee* (Dundee: 1889), p. 79.

[3] *Ibid.*, 2 September, 28 October 1848.

mendous but inchoate political enthusiasm of March and April into the movement for the Charter, only to have the dissension in the Assembly destroy their unity. Then the "over-ardent Chartists", seeing their hopes dwindling, had undertaken a hopeless struggle and sacrificed themselves. These events had revealed an even more disheartening truth. As *L'Ami du Peuple* wrote frankly on the first day of 1849:

> "It is a terrible fact, that after so many years of 'Reform' and 'Chartist' agitation, multitudes of men, whose every interest would benefit by the triumph of Chartism, are yet ignorant of or indifferent to the Charter. This is true not merely of the agricultural workers, but also of a considerable proportion of the town population."

Nor had the utter failure of the working-class movement and the "triumph of the bourgeoisie" been limited to England. As the months passed after the February Revolution in France, the course of events there had come as a painful revelation to Harney. From the height of optimism, symbolized by that moment in the Tuileries when he had stood with Imbert and Schapper on the spot once occupied by Louis Philippe's throne, a series of rude shocks had brought him to the depths of disillusionment. The first effect of universal suffrage had not been a programme of social and economic reforms, but the election of a chamber dominated by bankers, landlords, army officers and others of the propertied classes, who—as he clearly discerned at the time —were intent on sabotaging Louis Blanc's *Ateliers Nationaux*. Equally distressing to him had been the Provisional Government's attitude toward other revolutions. Instead of the crusade for European freedom he had confidently hoped for, the first action of the Foreign Minister, Lamartine, had been to allow Belgian and German legions to arm openly in France and then having assisted them to their respective frontiers, to disavow them "after the unfortunate enthusiasts had committed themselves to destruction".[1] With the crushing of the June Revolution and the establishment of a virtual dictatorship under General Cavaignac the ruin of his sanguine hopes was almost complete. Their final destruction came with the presidential election of Louis Napoleon—the "contemptible lackey who took up a bludgeon on the 10th of April against the oppressed English people"—by an overwhelming majority in December 1848, an event Harney had prophesied two months before. The spectacle

[1] *Ibid.*, 10 June 1848. *Cf.* Mehring, *Karl Marx*, p. 154.

of what had happened in France in those few months, he wrote, was "calculated to almost break the heart of those who regarded the 24th of June as the dawn of democratic freedom, happiness and glory".

The events of 1848 convinced Harney, and the extreme section of Chartism of which he was the spokesman, that if an independent English working-class movement was to survive it must be socialist as well as democratic. The failure of the working class in France demonstrated that universal suffrage could as easily be an instrument of reaction as of social revolution, if the people exercising their political rights were ignorant of their social rights. "Only by the immediate reorganization of society could they have ensured their triumph," he wrote after the June blood-letting which broke the Paris proletariat. And only by providing a focus for the most vital drives of the English working class could Chartism be revived. Otherwise the political field would have to be abandoned to the doctrines and leadership of the Manchester School.

As with most events, others drew converse conclusions from the fate of Chartism and the French Revolution in 1848. The failure of political agitation to lead to social amelioration gave a new impulse to the alternatives of trade-unionism and the co-operative movement. Not only did many of the thousands who had signed the National Petition and cheered Chartist speakers now turn to industrial action, but within the Chartist organiz-ation a deep cleavage took place. The basic issue in the following two years was the old problem of collaboration with the middle class. What was new about it was the fact that O'Connor, who had destroyed those who espoused a policy of collaboration at times in the past, became its foremost exponent. What was new also was that those who fought a union with the middle classes put forward a positive opposition programme. The year 1848 saw the end of Chartism as a mass-movement, but in the intel-lectual ferment which followed those who refused to admit this emerged as Britain's first social-democratic party—a develop-ment in which Harney played the leading role.

Three years after the upheaval of 1839 industrial unrest had again assumed a formidable political form in the General Strike of 1842. A like lapse of time after the popular excitement of 1848 witnessed some Chartist leaders formally burying their move-ment. The main reason for this wasting away of Chartism was

simply put by an obscure old Leicester radical in a letter to the
Northern Star in the spring of 1849. Hundreds of young men in
Leicester had been Chartists, he wrote, "but as soon as they got
employment they totally forgot their political duties. It appears
to me that if they can get as much by working fourteen or fifteen
hours a day as will keep body and soul together they are perfectly
satisfied." [1] Needless to say, the improvement of working-class
conditions as the benefits of an expanding world market and
British industrial supremacy filtered down was not instantaneous.
Doubt is permissible about Lamartine's glowing description of
the changes wrought in London since a previous visit twenty
years before in 1830: slums had been converted into bright, airy
districts and English operatives had been transformed into a
strong, healthy, clean-limbed race. In this Elysium, all were
contented except Chartist demagogues and romantic aristocrats.
The Times also indulged itself in this sort of myopic description,
advising the newly-arrived Louis Blanc to walk past the glittering
shops in Regent Street and observe the blessings of a happy
English conservatism.

With fanatical sophistry—to paraphrase Lamartine—Chartist
demagogues insisted that there was more to the picture. Harney
advised Blanc to extend his researches beyond Regent Street:

> "[V]isit the purlieus of Westminster, the rookeries of St. Giles's,
> the dens of sin, and shame, and sorrow, of want, and wretchedness
> and woe abounding in Clerkenwell, Southwark, and the Tower
> Hamlets . . . Norwich, Manchester, Liverpool and Glasgow will
> exhibit still more appalling illustrations of the 'blessings' *The Times*
> vaunts of." [2]

Mayhew's famous articles in the *Morning Chronicle*, which began
in the latter part of 1849, revealed more of the misery behind the
façade of Regent Street; and *The Times*, in a less patronizing
mood, worried about the "30,000 naked, lawless children" who
roamed Lamartine's hygienic streets.

But improvement is a comparative term, and though the
"hopeless, helpless, chronic destitution, which crushes the
sufferer down to a little more than vegetative existence" continued to exist in such districts as Bethnal Green,[3] conditions
were improving. Sir George Grey's trust in increased trade as
the best antidote to political agitation was being amply borne

---

[1] George Wray, in *Northern Star*, 3 March 1849.
[2] *Ibid.*, 9 September 1848.   [3] Frost, *Forty Years Recollections*, p. 224.

out. The reports of disturbances to the Home Office in 1849 were concerned less with Chartists than with riots between Irish railway workers and English operatives. Harney might write, "By Heavens! the patience—or rather, the suicidal apathy—of the masses is wonderful and pitiable!" [1] but he was aware that a mass agitation was impossible in the "flush of prosperity" which was ameliorating the conditions of the factory-workers in 1849.

There remained, however, an immediate task which had to be undertaken if the next flood-tide of political excitement were not to leave them stranded again. In an article printed by Harney in October 1849 this task was clearly set forth: the mobs of operatives who rushed forward in times of economic crisis must be indoctrinated with a knowledge of social-democratic ideas which would not be dissipated when the "day of suffering" had again come and gone. [2] That the conditions which produced political agitation would recur, Harney did not doubt. The cyclical nature of trade had not escaped the notice of the men who suffered from it, and when Harney wrote that the principal causes of the frightful misery of depression years still existed in the competitive system, which would inevitably bring about once more the glutted markets, short time, falling wages, and "ultimately general destitution of the proletarians", there was nothing startling in this to his readers. [3] In short, he and his section of the Chartist movement were proposing a social-democratic propaganda which would bear its fruit in the sharp economic crises their experience had convinced them would recur.

Harney's social and economic ideas were in direct disagreement with those of O'Connor; and the conflict between their ideologies was to underlie the history of Chartism until its resolution in 1850. Feargus had long recognized and written of the tendency toward monopoly in a capitalist society, but he was sincerely convinced that socialism in any form was an impracticable and dangerous solution. "The principle is at variance with the ruling instinct of man, which is selfishness, self-interest, self-reliance, and individuality," he wrote late in 1848. [4] Accepting competition and private property as the economic basis of

---

[1] *Northern Star*, 8 December 1849.

[2] The article was signed "One of the Men of the Future", and was probably written by George White. A very interesting minor figure of Chartism, White was to die a pauper in the Sheffield workhouse in 1868.

[3] *Northern Star*, 8 December 1849; *Democratic Review*, December 1849, pp. 243-44.

[4] *Northern Star*, 23 September 1848.

society, he had called for the fostering of a large class of "small and well-remunerated capitalists" as the answer to the narrowing of ownership—this was the rationale of the Land Plan. The Land Company's failure did not lead to any modifications in his old belief that it was to the working man's interest to uphold capital, for "they could not all be capitalists".[1] His view in 1849 was, in fact, indistinguishable from that of such stalwart exponents of classical economics as his fellow M.P., Joseph Hume; and certainly an element in the increasing heat of his fulminations against the "Socialist-Chartists" in 1849 and 1850 was the desire to maintain the "respectability" of his position.

O'Connor's economic views were more than palatable to the middle-class radicals with whom he was attempting to unite the remnants of Chartism. How acceptable they were to the working classes in 1849 is another matter. Though the ardent defender of *laissez-faire*, Francis Place, thought in the late 'thirties that the majority of operatives were infected with "pernicious views" toward property, it is possible to find working-class statements espousing the co-operation of capital and labour even in the blackest days of the 'forties.[2] The élite workers who were benefiting from the increase in industrialization—e.g. the skilled mechanics—already had an interest in preserving the existent economic system. As Harney noted in 1849, those of the working classes who were well paid were not only indifferent to ideas of social-democratic reform but were, if anything, disposed to hostility toward them. Whatever the belief in middle-class economics in 1849, however, the stimulating effect of improving material conditions in their spread can scarcely be underestimated. If men enjoy employment and the prospect of betterment they tend to become defenders of the economic system which provides these things.

This was to be the way of the future, but it was not yet apparent in the first few years after 1848. In the minds of the social-

---

[1] *Ibid.*, 11 September 1841.

[2] See, e.g., a very interesting anticipation of Marx's analysis in a declaration in 1842 of the Manchester Mechanics—a council of six pro-Chartist trade unions—which, after stating that the tendency of English society was toward a state of affairs in which there would be only two classes, the very rich and very poor, with the consequence of bloodshed and anarchy, concluded with a plea for co-operation between capital and labour to prevent this inevitable result (*English Chartist Circular*, vol. I, no. 2). *Cf.* declarations of the Irish Democratic Confederation in London (*Northern Star*, 18 September 1847); report of moral force Chartist conference in Leeds in 1841 (*Leeds Times*, 13 November 1841).

democrats led by Harney the principles advocated by O'Connor were middle-class shibboleths already proved false by history. That they could not all be capitalists, Harney admitted; but his contention was that society should be so organized "That Capital, the offspring of Labour, shall be its servant and not its master." [1] The instrument for such a change could only be the state; the means to its achievement was nothing less than the nationalization of public resources, utilities, and non-producing factories and workshops. For the origins of this programme, part of which took a specific form by 1850, one must look as much to English as to Continental sources. Although the ideas of Louis Blanc, who had arrived in England in August 1848, had a greater circulation in 1848–49 than those of any other foreign socialist, his influence is to be noted mainly in the producers' co-operatives of the Christian Socialists at a later date. And while it is true that Harney was aware of the specific socialist programme of Marx and Engels as put forward in the *Communist Manifesto*[2] the idea of state-socialism had long been endemic in England, though it had taken no organized political form. It remained to be seen if it took form in the National Charter Association.

The struggle between the old Chartism and the new assumed the familiar guise of disagreement over the issue of political collaboration with the middle-class Radicals. Following the failure of Hume's "Little Charter" movement of 1848, those Radicals led by Richard Cobden whose main concern was the reduction and transfer to non-commercial class shoulders of some of the burden of taxation, had tried to separate the issues of tax-reform and suffrage-extension. By March of 1849 it was apparent that this policy had failed; and a new organization, the Metropolitan Financial and Parliamentary Reform Association, made its debut by calling for a "large extension of the suffrage"— which meant, in effect, a rate-paying franchise. Headed by Sir Joshua Walmsley, the Parliamentary Reformers included Hume and a majority of the Radicals in the Commons, as well as Lord Dudley Stuart in the House of Lords, while Cobden remained

---

[1] *Northern Star*, 26 February 1848.

[2] Engels did an English translation of the *Communist Manifesto* for Harney in May 1848 (Mayer, *Friedrich Engels*, p. 92). The seventeen demands of the German Communist Party, promulgated by Marx and Engels in Paris a few weeks after the February Revolution, are echoed in the "Manifesto of the Red Republicans of Germany", printed in the *Democratic Review*, July 1849, pp. 66–70, by Harney.

cautiously aloof. It was in the conflict over the relationship of the National Charter Association to this group that the incompatibility between the two wings of Chartism became open.

After his usual period of ambivalence, Feargus embraced the cause of the Parliamentary Reformers. In the summer of 1849, while protesting that he would never abandon a single point of the Charter, he appeared on platforms with Walmsley, Hume and Lord Dudley Stuart, reiterating his support for an alliance and his willingness to "accept their rights in instalments". The propaganda line was plain, being in fact a reversion to the pre-1832 position: i.e. the common enemy of the middle and working classes was the land-owning aristocracy. Feargus made much play with this idea, stressing the idea that the union of the two classes which he desired was not an alliance between capital and labour, but between "mental labour on the one hand and manual labour on the other".

O'Connor's adherence to the Parliamentary Reformers meant that the formal organization of Chartism, such as it remained, was being swung behind the movement toward union, for with the imprisonment of the leading members of the Provisional Executive in 1848 he had once again gained control. A new "Executive residing in London" was packed with his satraps from the old Land Company; though Harney and two other Fraternal Democrats sat on this body, they were in a minority.

Harney lost no time in expressing his opposition to O'Connor's actions, and in so doing began a conflict which ultimately became a contest for Chartist leadership. The grounds of his disagreement constantly repeated throughout his struggle with Feargus and the pro-middle class Chartist wing, were both political and economic. Once again the unlaid ghosts of the Reform Bill agitation of 1832 made their appearance. Walmsley and his adherents to the "Little Charter", Harney wrote, wished to extend the suffrage only so far as to swamp the House of Commons with representatives of the "Manchester School". Their policy was "to make use of the proletarians to establish bourgeois supremacy".[1] That they would extend the franchise to the point where their control might be challenged from below seemed ridiculous to Harney; the economic and social interests of the middle classes were irreconcilably opposed to those of the

---

[1] *Democratic Review*, February 1850, p. 350. *Cf. ibid.*, June 1849, pp. 16–17; *Northern Star*, 30 December 1848, 29 December 1849; *Red Republican*, 26 October, 1850.

working classes. To the argument that the triumph of the Radical reformers might bring some benefits to the working classes, he replied scornfully,

> "The antecedents of these men, and their well-known devotion to the doctrines of the political economists, sufficiently answer that question. They were the bitter enemies of the Ten Hours Bill, they have always defended the worst features of the New Poor Law, and the reader will not have forgotten Cobden's fierce hostility to the Bakers' Protection Bill [limiting working hours] in the last session of Parliament." [1]

What it came down to was this: without social democracy, political democracy would be fruitless; the Radical reformers opposed the former while giving only conditional acceptance to the latter. Harney's answer to the advocates of class-union remained as it had been throughout his political career: "*From the ranks of the Proletarians* must come the saviours of industry." [2]

Harney had a policy; it was to become apparent that he had a following; but his minority position on the London Executive left him without an organization. There remained but one instrument at hand to organize the anti-collaborationist and social-democratic sentiment of Chartism—the Fraternal Democrats. Still under the ban of the Alien Act, the society had lost its international representatives; but it had already served as a rallying-point for the Chartist ultra-radical wing. Beginning early in 1849 the Fraternal Democrats set about expanding this function. At a banquet sponsored by the society on the first anniversary of the French Revolution the participants heard men who might form the nucleus of a social-democratic party speak for a union of Socialists and Chartists. G. J. Holyoake called for such a step as an old Owenite, as did Walter Cooper, a working-class lecturer of Scottish birth. Among other leading speakers were Robert Buchanan, until recently the publisher of the Socialist *Spirit of the Age*, and Bronterre O'Brien, whose warm praise of Harney ended a coolness which had lasted almost a decade. Ideologically, if not from the viewpoint of mass support, the meeting was a significant one: Owenites had heretofore stood aside from the political objectives of the Chartists.

Internationalist sympathy had also been strongly expressed at this meeting and it was on this issue that O'Connor, increasingly

---

[1] *Democratic Review*, February 1850, p. 351.
[2] *Northern Star*, 10 November 1849.

annoyed with his editor's recalcitrance about union with the Parliamentary Radicals and anxiously observing the drawing together of socialist and democratic elements, chose to bring Harney to heel. Early in March he wrote a rambling disquisition on those who wished to swamp Chartism with a "republican party" and expressed an old aversion by warning Chartists away from "foreign questions", which, it soon developed, meant Continental socialism. The confusion of such issues with Chartism, he wrote, would alienate those to whom they were becoming respectable.

Harney had no difficulty in recognizing the object of this attack. His answer to O'Connor was a blunt rebuttal of Feargus's isolationism and a repetition of his views on the middle class. He also printed two letters from Chartist localities which rebuked O'Connor. They had been in the movement as long as Feargus, the Nottingham Chartists declared, and they did not depend on him for their ideas. "The world is our country," they wrote, and all working men should fight together against the "international ruling class". And why should they worry about what the middle classes thought? Feargus felt that he had been betrayed. In a self-pitying and sometimes incoherent discourse carried on over a period of three weeks in the *Northern Star* he demonstrated his increasing identification with the class he had associated with since 1847. The truculence of the working class had always been his greatest difficulty, he complained; and, expressing what was doubtless an old grievance against Harney, the doctrines preached in the *Northern Star* had been "flashed in his face in the House of Commons". Finally, after asserting that the paper should no longer be a foreign organ, he offered to resign as the "acknowledged leader of Chartism" if he were so requested.

The end of this wearying exchange was anti-climactic. O'Connor's resignation threat, which once would have evoked a flood of letters of support, was greeted indifferently. In fact, the entire disagreement seems to have been carried on in a vacuum of apathy—but what response there had been was militantly internationalist and anti-middle class. Possibly because of this, more likely because of the real affection between the ageing, increasingly unstable leader and his young challenger, Harney was not asked to resign. In the following months, however, he experienced a growing difficulty in preserving the *Northern Star's*

N

excellent foreign coverage and in keeping its columns open to such exiles as Mazzini, Blanc and Arnold Ruge, the former left-wing leader of the Frankfurt Parliament. His direct editorial power, already weakened, was almost at an end; and it was obviously only a question of time before he would be forced to knuckle under or resign. The realization of this, as well as the need for an organ to express the opinions so repellent to Feargus, had a more immediate result. In June 1849 he launched a three-penny, forty-page monthly, the *Democratic Review of British Politics, History and Literature,* his first independent journalistic venture since the London *Democrat* of 1839.

A comparison of the *Democratic Review* with the London *Democrat* is an illuminating one for the changes which the decade separating them had worked both in Harney and in his readers. One basic conviction underlying the editorial policy of the two journals remained the same: only through the capture of political power could the working class achieve emancipation, and the main obstacle to that end was the middle class. But gone were the belief in the necessity for forcible revolution, the exhortations to "Arm! Arm! Arm!", and disingenuous articles on military tactics. And a more significant contrast is to be found in the social-democratic character of the new journal. In a vague form this had been implicit in the London *Democrat,* as it had been in the Chartism of 1839; now it was explicit.

The precise nature of "Socialism" remained undefined in the *Democratic Review.* Though in his prospectus Harney declared that the new journal would stand for land-nationalization and the substitution of co-operation for competition in manufactures and commerce, the *Review* was a forum for socialist thought, rather than a propagator of one particular socialist view. With the reaction on the Continent and the hostility of the greater part of the British press making it nearly impossible for the socialist *émigrés* to make their voices heard, the new journal provided what was almost their only outlet. These two factors gave the *Review* its unique character of providing a cross-section of collectivist thought in the post-1848 period.

His dual editorial capacity made Harney even more important to the emigration than he had been before 1848. Although his control of the *Northern Star* had lessened, he was still able to reprint articles from the *Review* and thus give them a wider circulation. No English working-class leader had had such close

contact with the Continental socialists before 1848; and with
their flight from repression in 1848–49 this contact was renewed
and widened. One of his contemporaries later wrote that the
first inquiry made by the political refugees on arriving in London
was as to Harney's whereabouts—doubtless an exaggerated
statement, but with an element of truth. Louis Blanc early became his friend and Claudius Johannes, a Frenchman standing
politically somewhat to the left of Ledru Rollin, acted as the
Review's Paris correspondent for a time.

That the renewal of his connection with the emigration occurred first with such men doubtless accounts for the dominance
of the French socialist in the early issues of the new journal.
Marx did not arrive in England until August 1849 and Engels
still later in the year, and their influence began to make itself
apparent only in 1850. With a catholicity of selection which was
to seem treasonable to the two Germans later, Harney not only
gave pages to such men as Louis Blanc, with some of whose
ideas he sympathized, but to those with whom he disagreed.
The Fourierist, Victor Considérant, fell in the latter category;
and Harney, after printing an article by him which stressed non-
violent means and the "irresistible artillery of ideas" could not
forbear from remarking mildly, "I fear that our Phalansterian
friend is somewhat Utopian." Only one German socialist document appeared in the early issues of the *Review*—the "Manifesto
of the Red Republicans of Germany", a sharp contrast to the
French socialists' moderation in its militant assertion of the
proletariat as the standard-bearers of revolution and the state as
the instrument to achieve supreme power "over all economical
and social relationships".[1]

Less militant, but equally interesting, were Harney's English
contributors. Robert Isham,[2] one of the slowly-coalescing social-
democratic group, wrote a series of articles on public ownership
of the soil, incidentally illustrating the gap between the radicalism of the post-Napoleonic and the post-1848 periods by attacking Cobbett, the idol of an older generation, for his defence of
private property. Still another series of articles, evidently by a
journeyman, gives a vivid picture of what the great Victorian
building boom meant to the builders. There is a thoroughly

[1] *Democratic Review*, July 1849, pp. 66–70.
[2] Isham, later the manager of the Working Printers' Association, a Christian
Democratic producers' co-operative, wrote under the pen-name "Terriginous".

modern ring to his protest against the masters' attempt to break
down the building trades through the use of piece-work rates, the
violation of jurisdictional boundaries, and an increasing special-
ization of jobs which meant a growing use of semi-skilled and
unskilled labour. In a remarkable anticipation of Ruskin and
William Morris, he expressed the effect on a craftsman's pride of
the pressures of capitalist production in the creation of shoddy
houses. "Our houses are not built for use, but like the razors, to
sell," he wrote. "The spirit of commerce, transformed into a
fiend, destructive and cannibal, renders the work of our hands as
useless and ephemeral as our lives are joyless and devoid of
hope." [1]

The class-consciousness and protest against the values of the
"educated classes" which permeated the *Democratic Review* extended even to its historical articles. Thus a brief biography of
Caesar became a means to belabour historians as the "hirelings
of aristocracy" who wrote as their masters wished—a judgment
not entirely lacking in truth. And Harney's comments on such
current history as the frequent accouchements of the Queen
made fine fare for republicans: the newly-born Prince Arthur
was greeted as "a royal burden, from whom the greatest and
most potent monarch in the world has condescendingly allowed
herself, in her magnanimous deference to natural law, to be relieved". [2] A parody of the Prince Consort's chorale for the same
occasion further illustrates the *Review's* irreverent attitude toward
the institution of monarchy: [3]

> "Bring forth the babe! From foreign lands
>   Fresh royal vampires come to greet
> This new one in its nurse's hands—
>   For royal mothers give no teat.
>
> *   *   *   *
>
> Bring forth the toy of princely whim
>   And on your knees fall down and pray,
> For ought we not to *pray for him*
>   Who'll *prey on us* enough some day?"

---

[1] "John the Workman", *Democratic Review*, February, April 1850. I have been
unable to identify the author.

[2] *Democratic Review*, July 1850, p. 48.

[3] *Ibid.*, p. 50.

The readers of the *Democratic Review* numbered "some thousands of the best informed and most devoted of the veritable Democrats of Great Britain", according to Harney, and as the journal paid its way for most of its sixteen-month existence, this figure was probably not an exaggeration. If a circulation of 2,000–3,000 is accepted, the number of those who sympathized with Harney's views to the extent of threepence a month was small, but it was a significant proportion of the total of active Chartists, whose number was steadily dwindling. The strength of the party against which the *Review* spoke was, however, growing swiftly in the summer of 1849.

"What it took the Anti-Corn Law League seven years to accomplish has been done by their successors in a month," the Radical *Weekly Dispatch* claimed in late June, referring to the packed audiences of the middle class and working men at the Parliamentary Reformers' meetings in London. Such influential working-class leaders as Thomas Cooper and Thomas Frost, the Croydon Chartist, had joined the London Executive in plumping for a joint effort for a rate-paying franchise and financial reform; and, after a temporary shift in direction, O'Connor had returned to the fold. The *Weekly Dispatch* had reason for its optimism in reporting that the Radicals and the Chartists were at last united; and the effect of events on the Continent in the summer of 1849 gave an added stimulus initially toward common action.

The "respectable classes" had regarded the revolutions of 1848 with fear and loathing, but the main revolutionary struggle of 1849—that of the Hungarians for their independence from Austria—received a support from these classes extraordinary in its enthusiasm. A minority of public opinion, made up of a section of the Tories and finding a spokesman in *The Times*, did not share this feeling; but their voices went almost unheard in the excitement of July and August. This is the more surprising in that up to this time public indifference had given a tacit approval to the counter-revolution on the Continent. There were a number of reasons for this reversal of feeling. The invasion of Hungary by Austria and Russia, coming as it did almost immediately after the suppression of the gallantly defended Roman Republic by Louis Napoleon's army in June, crystallized what seems to have been a widespread and growing uneasiness at the overwhelming victories of the forces of reaction and the extremity of the counter-revolution. In addition to the liberal repugnance for the despotism symbolized by Russia and Austria, the incursion of the Czar's troops into Central Europe revived the fears of Russian expansionism. Hungary, in the highly-coloured prose of the *Nonconformist*, was the "living breakwater to oppose the swelling flood of barbaric absolutism with which Russia, in alliance with Austria, seeks to inundate and overwhelm Western Europe". There was the fact too that the Hungarian revolutionaries were "respectable". They were not, as one of the leaders of the agitation, Lord Dudley Stuart, carefully pointed out to his audiences, "Red Republican insurrectionists", but had risen to defend a constitution much like the British.[1] Finally, there was the best of all economic reasons: the Hungarians were "devotedly attached" to the principles of Free Trade—it was Austria which was protectionist—and the extension of Liberal, Free-Trading nations in Europe would be vastly to England's benefit.[2]

The combination of these factors made an irresistible appeal to the English classes which had been estranged by the extremism of 1848. Beginning with a mass demonstration for the Hungarians in Glasgow on 4 July, the movement quickly spread to most of the major cities of Britain. The majority of these mass-meetings were called through the requisition on mayors of the propertied classes and were heavily attended by operatives. In London, the centre of the agitation, the Parliamentary Reformers dominated the agitation in its initial stages, with Cobden lending his powerful influence; and their association with a cause so intensely popular promised fruitful results when domestic reform succeeded the pro-Hungarian demonstrations. What happened instead was that the agitation produced a new rift between the middle-class Radicals and the working class—an effect for which Harney was mainly responsible.

Though disclaiming any intention of creating a division in the agitation, Harney, with the help of the Radical publisher, G. W. M. Reynolds, split the London operatives away from the

[1] *Northern Star*, 28 July, 15 September 1849.

[2] *Cf.* speeches of Stuart and J. Wyld, quoted in *ibid.*, 15 September, 4 August 1849. The power of this economic argument had not escaped some Continental revolutionaries. See, e.g., the Polish leader, General Bem's plea for British aid in 1848, on the grounds that a free Poland would be a source of cheap grain and an "infinite market" for British consumer goods and capital (railway) investment (*ibid.*, 6 May 1848). The equation of national freedom, liberalism and free trade is to be found in the Risorgimento as well. (See Kent Roberts Greenfield, "Economic Ideas and Facts in the Early Period of the Risorgimento (1815–1848)", *American Historical Review*, XXXVI (1930), pp. 31–43.)

Parliamentary Reformers' leadership within a month. The
wedge which he used was a demand for English military intervention. While the middle-class Radicals were positive enough
about the arguments for government recognition of Hungary,
their strong pacifist element was opposed to war. What Cobden
proposed was private action to force the Russians to seek peace.
"Russia can't carry on two campaigns beyond her own territories
without coming to Western Europe for a loan," he declared to a
great London meeting on 23 July. "And if any London bankers
offered such a loan, the Peace Society would raise . . . a storm
of public opinion against them." [1] His policy might be described
as "*laissez-faire* interventionism"—an embryonic form of the
policy which was to send a private army to aid Garibaldi eleven
years later. To Harney, this careful line placed between recognition of an independent Hungary and war seemed nonsense;
recognition would mean war, and the belief in the success of any
steps short of military intervention was "moonshine". Cobden's
argument about Russian inability to carry on two campaigns fell
into the same lunar category. As to an economic boycott by
bankers, Harney wrote, Nicholas would experience no difficulties
in this respect: "What moneymonger cares one jot for the liberty
of Hungary or any other country?"

Still asserting his desire for a united agitation, Harney fought
his battle from the floor of the public meetings. Called by the
crowd at the great gathering of 23 July, at which Cobden, Lord
Dudley Stuart, and more than twenty M.P.s sat on the platform,
he delivered a pro-war speech which evoked tremendous applause. At another meeting of 1,500 in Marylebone sponsored by
the middle-class group a week later precisely the same thing
happened, this time with a "forest of hands" raised in support of
Harney's demand for war if it were necessary. It was apparent
that the Radicals had lost control of the agitation to the person
described by *The Times* as a "domestic agitator" and "noisy
belligerent". They were, furthermore, being tarred by the red
brush. "Our Marylebone Radicals have caught the war-fever
from Ledru Rollin, Mazzini, Kossuth and the heroes of Baden
. . . ," *The Times* commented sarcastically. "Lord Dudley Stuart
and Mr. Julian Harney, Mr. Monckton Milnes and Mr. Hetherington, in conclave assembled, have had the glory of adding
another point to the People's Charter . . . 'fraternity with all

[1] *The Times*, 24 July 1849.

democracies'." [1] The Radicals lost no time in disassociating themselves from such company. Harney was denounced by the Radical press as a "usurper", and the pro-war party excoriated. But though the Stuart group continued to sponsor meetings, the movement had gone beyond their control.

The reason for Harney's success lay in the state of popular working-class feeling toward the Hungarian question. One moderate weekly, after labelling Harney the leader of the popular war-party, admitted that there were hundreds of thousands who shared his views, and concluded that it was "perhaps fortunate that the power of declaring war does not lie with public meetings".[2] In response to invitations from the provinces, Harney spoke at demonstrations in Nottingham, Sutton-in-Ashfield, Loughborough and Ashford; mass-meetings calling for war occurred in Derby and Leicester, as well as in London; and by mid-August there was some evidence that the war-spirit was infecting the middle classes. The course of events in Hungary had by that time emptied this mass-enthusiasm of meaning: Kossuth fled on 11 August and the Hungarian general, Gorgey, surrendered two days later. "The Cossacks are victorious! Woe to Europe!" wrote Harney in despair.

The Hungarian agitation had not brought English diplomatic action, much less military intervention; but it had important consequences nevertheless. The agitation had revealed and fostered anti-Russian feeling; and this, together with the Turkish refusal in October to surrender the Hungarian and Polish refugees who had taken asylum there on the demand of Austria and Russia—a stand backed by Palmerston with a British fleet— was another link in the chain of events leading to the Crimean War. The domestic effect of the agitation, though less important, was not negligible. The Radical-pacifist denunciation of the war-party had provided another cause for working-class suspicion of their protestations of common interests, and, as during the Crimean War, constituted one reason for the alienation which persisted.

[1] *Democratic Review*, August 1849, p. 83. *Cf. The Times's* agreement, 26 July 1849. What the effect of the Peace League's pressure might have been is of course conjectural. Harney's German correspondent (probably Engels) wrote early in 1850 that the Austrian emperor had been deprived of a loan "through the exertions of Mr. Cobden", but that Russia and Prussia got money for military purposes by borrowing for "railroads" (*Democratic Review*, March 1850, p. 398).

[2] *Spirit of the Times*, quoted in *Northern Star*, 8 September 1849.

These events had also resulted in Harney's re-emergence as a popular leader. The insularity of the working class in the early and mid-'forties was not characteristic of the post-1848 period; and with this growing interest in foreign affairs, Harney, whom one contemporary described later as "more conversant with foreign politics than any man I ever knew" [1] at last came into his own. Up to this time, his reputation as the leading Chartist internationalist had been limited for the most part to the émigrés and their sympathizers. Now, his leadership of a cause which had engaged more working-class interest than any event since the Chartist excitement of 1848 vastly enlarged that reputation. But his expenditure of energy had cost him his usual price, and very ill with the throat ailment which had given him particular trouble throughout 1849, he went to Ayrshire in September to recuperate. During the month he remained in Scotland his policy of opposition to O'Connor and Chartist collaboration with the Parliamentary Reformers took a definite form.

It was plain on his return that Harney had determined to challenge the Chartist leadership, still dominated by O'Connor, and force a decision on the Chartist rank-and-file. His programme, reiterated once again in the *Northern Star* and the *Democratic Review*, was that which he had drawn from the lessons of 1848: Chartism could be revived as a mass-movement in the future only if it adopted a socialist as well as democratic programme. There was no use in "singing small" about their real aims in order to avoid offending the Radical reformers, union with whom would in any case mean the destruction of an independent working-class party. The social and economic aims of the two classes were fundamentally opposed, he declared once again, and it would be impossible for Chartists to "serve two masters, or that which is the same thing—to advocate two distinct systems". [2]

To accomplish his ends, Harney turned once again to the plan which the Hungarian agitation had held in abeyance. In October, the Fraternal Democrats were reorganized with the avowed aim of preparing the English working class for their "deliverance from the oppression of irresponsible capital". They would not hinder the Parliamentary Reformers, Harney wrote,

---

[1] J. B. Leno, *Aftermath* (London: 1892), p. 61. Leno, one of the younger Chartist generation, was just rising to prominence in the movement in 1849.

[2] *Northern Star*, 15 December 1849.

nor rival any reorganized Chartist party. At the same time the Fraternal Democrats welcomed the signs of renewed democratic activity shown by the formation of Bronterre O'Brien's "National Reform League"—an organization with aims much like their own—and the reorganization stirring the ranks of Chartists and socialists. The coalition of forces foreshadowed some months before also began to emerge, as Harney made frequent appearances on public platforms with Bronterre and Lloyd Jones, probably the most respected Owenite leader. And while the Fraternal Democrats had disavowed any intention of rivalling the Chartist party, this did not mean that they had forsworn capturing it—which they now set out to do.

Whether due to the stimulus of this activity on the left or because they felt that their power in the proposed union with the Parliamentary Reformers would be nugatory without a following, the old Executive began to take steps to revive Chartism in November. That revival was necessary was painfully obvious: the national organization, as the *Northern Star* admitted, had ceased to exist so far as any real support was concerned. Also obvious was the basis of re-activation espoused by the O'Connorites—a juncture with the middle-class Radicals, which leading articles in the *Star* were now casually referring to as having taken place. Their first step was taken at a London conference summoned in December to launch a new agitation, when the policy of a concerted action with the Parliamentary Reformers for limited objectives—accompanied by protestations of loyalty to the Six Points—was carried over the opposition of Harney and his delegation. The last word had not been said, however; the conference adjourned with no explicit plan of union with the Reformers and the struggle moved into the arena of public meetings.

Only one provincial delegate had attended the conference, though delegate meetings in Aberdeen and the West Riding had pledged their support to re-activation of the movement. But reaction to the conference was surprisingly strong. In late December and the first months of 1850 reports of re-organization meetings in the provinces gave the *Northern Star* some semblance of its old appearance. In London, the new agitation was to get under way at a public meeting on 14 January, and it was here that the fundamental difference within the Chartist party began to be resolved. In a furious exchange, Thomas Clark, the spokesman for the O'Connorite forces, clashed with Harney over the issue of collaboration with the Radicals. The issue then was adjourned to the pages of the *Northern Star*.

Personal controversies had always been a feature of periods of Chartist decline, but for venomous polemics nothing had ever matched the exchange of letters that followed. Clark revived every charge which had ever been made against Harney and gave birth to some others. Harney, no new hand at this sort of thing, made such germane points to the argument as Clark's having lolled about in a luxurious director's office during the palmy days of the now-defunct Land Company, too proud and indolent to reply to humble stockholders. Out of this flood of vituperation the opposing views emerged sharply. Clark asserted that Chartism was finished, and that co-operation with the middle classes held the only hope for the future. Harney replied that the subservience of Chartism to the Parliamentary Reformers would benefit no one but the latter. When O'Connor echoed Clark's attack on Harney's class-consciousness—"the violent language of poor gentlemen who are too proud to work, and too poor to live without labour"—Harney resigned from the Provisional Executive to force a decision, an action followed by the O'Connorites under pressure from the London and Birmingham Chartists. The sole remaining member of the Executive, G. W. M. Reynolds—still debating which way to jump—then recalled the Metropolitan Conference to decide the issue.

The result was a resounding victory for Harney. Of the nine members elected to the new Provisional elective, he and four other Fraternal Democrats constituted the majority. The Clark-O'Connor faction lost out entirely and the most important hurdle in capturing the Chartist organization had been taken. There remained but one other, a Chartist national election for a permanent Executive. Harney had already received letters of support from fourteen localities; and the faithful George White, freshly released from his tenth imprisonment, had pledged him the support of the Leeds Chartists. During the next two months, Harney was indefatigable, speaking to crowded audiences in Manchester—where James Leach and John West, also just out of prison, had swung the movement to him—and in Macclesfield, Stockport, Rochdale and London. Fraternal Democrats were to be found making leading speeches and occupying chairs at other London meetings, and Harney also had the aid of

Bronterre and the Owenite, Walter Cooper, whose names stud the reports of these weeks. Still another accession of strength came with the freeing of the London Chartists sentenced in 1848, whose imprisonment had, as one declared, converted them into "Red Republicans".

The tone of all these meetings was forthrightly socialist as well as Chartist, the dominant theme being attacks on capitalism. So favourable was the response that that reliable weather-vane of public opinion, G. W. M. Reynolds, finally made his decision and began to advocate socialism publicly. Of Reynolds, a contemporary later observed, "It was as a charlatan and a trader rather than as a genuine politician that . . . [he] was generally regarded by the Chartist rank-and-file";[1] but in these months he was in great demand as a speaker in the provinces and constituted a valuable ally. A more dramatic illustration of the socialist trend is to be found in the reception accorded O'Connor when he damned Harney and Reynolds as "Red Republicans" and denounced socialism and communism at a public meeting. In a pitiful scene, he was told flatly that, while they owed much to his past efforts, his usefulness was at an end—a judgment which evoked loud cheers.

It had been apparent since their quarrel of the preceding March that the separation of Harney and O'Connor was inevitable unless their differences were resolved. O'Connor's attack, coupled with his sympathy for a new "National Charter League" —formed by Clark and the other leaders of the old Executive with the avowed purpose of union with the Parliamentary Reformers—provoked the final break. After Clark had written a long letter in the *Northern Star* attacking Harney and the Chartist movement, Harney was refused space to reply and resigned, thus bringing to an end a connection which had lasted since 1841, when he had become the *Star's* Sheffield correspondent. The step was a painful one. It meant the severance of a friendship which dated back to the young and hopeful days of the Central National Association, when Harney had first known the bluff and charming Irishman—then, with his great days before him; now, with a lunatic asylum just two years away. There is no reason to believe that the deep regret expressed by both at

---

[1] Adams, *Memoirs of a Social Atom*, vol. I, p. 235. *Cf.* Harney's comment on Reynolds's "thirst for notoriety at the time of the Trafalgar Square demonstration in 1848" (*Northern Star*, 26 August 1848).

this parting was not sincere; but their aims had become irreconcilable.

The national election showed that the Chartist rank-and-file had also repudiated their connection with O'Connor. The Fraternal Democrat-dominated Provisional Executive was elected as the new National Executive without opposition. "Hearty cheers for the Red Republicans," wrote the Bradford Chartists; and from the northern centre of the movement, the Yorkshire and Lancashire Delegate Council, came a unanimous vote and a strong resolution of support. O'Connor had signified his availability as a candidate, but no organized support for him was reported. In the month following the election the new National Executive resuscitated the Metropolitan Delegate Council with another Fraternal Democrat as chairman, and the campaign which Harney had begun with the reorganization of the Fraternal Democrats just eight months before was finished.

The Chartist movement had emerged as Britain's first avowedly social-democratic party—that is, a party which aimed at the achievement of socialist measures through political means. A "declaration of social rights" immediately adopted by the National Executive called for the nationalization of the land, mines and fisheries, the extension of state credit to all, a "just and wise system of currency and exchange", national secular education, and humane provision for the destitute. The last point was made more explicit by the Metropolitan Delegate Council, which added a policy of public works for the unemployed. These specific aims must be attributed to the old "Schoolmaster of Chartism", Bronterre O'Brien, as a comparison with the programme of his National Reform League shows. His following was, in fact, instructed by him to support the new National Charter Association in preference to their own organization.

Harney summed up the change with a justifiable satisfaction. In the past, he wrote, those Chartists who espoused socialist programmes had been denounced as "utopian" and "dangerous". But time had brought them to two alternatives: a retreat from the Charter into "*bourgeois* idealism" or the broadening of the political agitation to include socialist aims. The adoption of the declaration of social rights had shown which alternative had been chosen. "Chartism and Red Republicanism must henceforth be regarded as synonymous terms," wrote one observer;[1] and, fittingly enough, the journal which Harney launched in June as an organ of the new Chartism was named the *Red Republican*.

Ernest Jones's release early in July 1850 meant another strong addition to the social-democratic forces. Jones's already considerable popularity had been greatly enhanced by his sufferings in prison, and the effect of two years of solitary confinement on him had been, as with most of the Chartist prisoners, to deepen his radicalism. In his first speech, given at a congratulatory dinner of the Fraternal Democrats, Jones declared that they must show the people that the Charter meant social rights: "bread, beef, and beer". When, four days later, he rode through densely packed streets of cheering Chartists in Halifax beside Harney, the only other leader invited by the Lancashire and Yorkshire Chartist delegates, it must have seemed to both that a new dawn of Chartism had broken. Delegates from twelve localities, and a crowd estimated by the *Northern Star* at 30,000 listened on the next day to a series of speeches which reiterated the message of the Halifax address to Jones: "The war of classes, sir, is now no longer a mere war of politics, but a war between capital and labour." The change between 1848 and 1850, Harney declared, was symbolized by the change in the Chartist flag colour; when Jones went to prison it had been green—now it was red. The irony of the moment was mercifully hidden from the jubilant crowd: Jones's release meant the beginning of the last deadly struggle within the Chartist movement.

[1] Howard Morton (Helen Macfarlane?), *Red Republican*, 13 July 1850.

CHAPTER IX

Defeat

VIEWED as a development in working-class thought, the transformation of Chartism into a social-democratic party is significant in itself. The estimation of its contemporary significance is more difficult: what, after all, did Chartism amount to in 1850? Measured by the standard of subscribing members, almost nothing. At no time since 1842 had the National Charter Association numbered more than 2,000; by 1850 only 500 members were being carried on its books. Some 50 localities seem still to have had active associations; but, as Christopher Shackleton, secretary of the West Riding delegates, reported in October, "The number of enrolled and paying members are exceedingly few. The local lecturers tell the same old tale to the same old faces, to the surfeit of both. . . . The numbers who attend our great gatherings for the most part give no assistance beyond shouting at the said gatherings." [1] Of London, the same could be said; the eight localities which sent delegates to the Metropolitan Council could scarcely have averaged thirty members each. Entire areas where associations had once existed had reverted to silence. "We cannot speak as to the state of Chartism in the south and south-west of England. We believe there is little or no organization," Harney replied vaguely to one inquiry. [2]

On the other hand, Chartism had never been a movement capable of measurement in terms of subscribing members. With 2,000 or less members in 1848, perhaps a thousand times that number had signified their adherence to the Six Points. Shackleton's report, if it illustrates organized Chartism's decline, also shows that "great gatherings" of Chartist sympathizers still occurred. And a tour by Jones in the Autumn of 1850 corroborated this. The "largest crowds since 1848" flocked to hear him —though they did not join their local associations when he had gone. The N.C.A. was unable to support one full-time lecturer at £2 per week; yet it was undoubtedly true that, as Harney

[1] *Red Republican*, 19 October 1850.   [2] *Ibid.*, 24 August 1850.

wrote, "In the manufacturing districts the Chartists, although at present a rope of sand, are very numerous." [1]

The contradiction in an organization dying for want of pennies and the widespread sympathy for its aims sometimes shook Harney's optimism. "The let-alone system is in the ascendant," he commented in February. But such pessimism was rare. Organized Chartism was now avowedly socialist and this knowledge sustained his hopes. "They are blind," he wrote, "who cannot see that instead of retrograding in their political knowledge and reforming aspirations, the working classes have been advancing until now the vast mass of those who were Chartists—purely and simply—are Chartists and much more." [2] There was a further encouragement to Harney in the younger men coming into the movement, who were almost without exception social-democrats and ardent internationalists. Typical of these were J. B. Leno, a typographer, and Gerald Massey, a poet of some talent, who organized the "Democratic and Social Propagandists" in response to the *Democratic Review's* call for propagandist cells. Lecturing gratis about London, this organization formed a direct link with a later generation of working-class leaders: their discussions at the "Windsor Castle" public house in Holborn influenced Odger, Applegarth, Howell, Davis, Henriette and others, trade-union leaders of the next decades, according to Leno's account, and some of their members figured prominently in the Reform League of the 1860's. Leno himself provides a direct link between the Fraternal Democrats and the First International, of which he was a Council member.

Nor was this young group which looked directly to Harney for leadership limited to London. A propagandist association straight from the loins of the *Democratic Review* existed in Renfrewshire; as did a similar organization in Cheltenham under the leadership of W. E. Adams, later editor of the influential Newcastle *Weekly Chronicle*. Adams has left a vignette of the feelings of such young men in 1850: what made them Fraternal Democrats as well as "Chartists and something more" was their passionate aspiration for a better world; and Harney's *Friend of the People*—which succeeded the *Red Republican* in the winter of 1850 —provided the gospel for the group. "No paper then published so satisfied our longings for an ideal," Adams recollected. [3]

---

[1] *Democratic Review*, December 1849.   [2] *Northern Star*, 2 March 1850.
[3] Adams, *Memoirs of a Social Atom*, vol. I, p. 262.

These few but dedicated supporters of the Adams type were surprisingly widespread. In 1850, more than twenty localities stretching from Aberdeen to Plymouth had chapters of Fraternal Democrats. This was in actuality the "few determined men to make a start" which the *Democratic Review* had called for; and their potentiality as propagators of the new movement was not proportionate to their numbers. Such activists had always become leaders when the working class threw up their massmovements.

Thus though there was sufficient cause for pessimism in the non-participation of the great mass of the working class in Chartism in 1850, the situation did not seem entirely discouraging to Harney. An indeterminable number remained Chartist in sympathy; part of the old cadre remained loyal; and a vital young cadre had been recruited. And while the two latter groups provided the main support for the new organ of social-democratic Chartism, the *Red Republican*, they were not its only subscribers. According to the alarmist *Scottish Press*, Harney's new journal circulated by the hundreds in Edinburgh, and its dangerous doctrines were the "Political Confession of Faith of vast numbers of the people". A government report on the mining districts in 1850 gives some indication of where other copies of his publications found their way. Journals conveying the "worst doctrines" had always circulated in the colliery towns, the report declared, but the new feature of this press was its extremely bitter class-consciousness and its open adoption of the principles of Socialism. It was unwise to treat these papers lightly: they were "conducted with an ability quite capable of making them attractive" and their appeals to class prejudice found ready access to the minds of their readers.[1] As the upsurge of papers in 1848–49 which advocated such doctrines had already subsided and the new working-class journals were almost entirely advocates of factory reform, trade-unionism and co-operation, Harney's journalistic efforts must bear a considerable part of the report's opprobrium.[2]

---

[1] *Report of the Commission appointed under the provisions of the Act 5th and 6th Victoria, c. 99, to inquire into the operation of that Act and the state of the population in the mining districts, 1850* (London: 1851), quoted in *Quarterly Review*, vol. 89, pp. 536–37 (September 1851).

[2] Among the casualties in 1849 were the *Spirit of the Age*, Uxbridge *Spirit of Freedom* (edited by Leno and Massey), *Commonwealth*, *Progressionist*, *Reformer*, *Plain Speaker*, and *New World*. Typical of the new journals were the *Champion* (Manchester),

o

There was no question about the *Red Republican's* editorial policy fitting the report's description. First appearing on 22 June 1850, after a gratifying response to the appeal for funds which Harney and the Fraternal Democrats had made, the new penny weekly added to the defiance of its title—"A most imprudent name!" commented Harney—by its banner, which depicted a red cap resting atop a crossed spear and fasces. The contents were equally militant.

> "Will they charge us with being 'enemies to order'?" Harney wrote in his first leading article. "We shall prove that their order is an 'organized hypocrisy'. Will they charge us with contemplating spoliation? We shall prove that they themselves are spoliators and robbers. Will they accuse us of being 'bloodthirsty democrats'? We shall prove our accusers to be remorseless traffickers in the lives of their fellow creatures. . . ."

Commenting on the fear expressed in respectable circles about universal suffrage leading to the domination of society by the operatives, the *Red Republican* replied bluntly: "As regards the working men swamping the other classes, the answer is easy:— *other classes have no right even to exist.*"

This was simply a re-statement of the Babeuvian (and Biblical) doctrine that "he who will not work, neither shall he eat"; but from the first issue a new influence was apparent in the *Red Republican*, both in Harney's writing and that of his mysterious contributor, "Howard Morton". The new influence had also become marked in the *Democratic Review*, beginning with the January 1850 number. Though Harney continued his impartial editorial policy, the writing of Blanc, Mazzini, Cabet and Ledru Rollin figuring largely in the columns of both journals, it was evident that the reunion of Marx and Engels and the renewal of their friendship with Harney had borne fruit. Engels probably occupied more space in the *Democratic Review* in 1850 than any other foreign contributor—"probably", for the reason that much of what seems stamped by his viewpoint and style was unsigned. The similarity of analysis to other contemporary writings of Marx and Engels,[1] a comparison with Engels's previous articles

Frame-Work Knitter's Advocate, Herald of Co-operation (Manchester). One exception: the *Weekly Tribune*, a communist paper.

[1] *Cf. Democratic Review*, February 1850 and *Plan of Campaign against Democracy*, devised by Marx and Engels and endorsed by the Communist League in March for transmission to Germany (Mehring, *Karl Marx*, p. 202; Mayer, *Friedrich Engels*,

in the *Northern Star*, a unique command of "ultra-radical English", the closeness of contact between Harney and Engels: all these point to the young German as the author of both the "Letters from Germany" and "Letters from Paris" which appeared in the *Democratic Review* after January.[1] Though the German letters were postmarked Cologne, this is hardly conclusive evidence of the location of the writer. In the case of at least one important daily, the Tory *Morning Chronicle*, it was common knowledge that its "Paris Correspondent" was a French socialist refugee who wrote his on-the-spot news from Fitzroy Square.

A similar problem of identification lies in the identity of "Howard Morton", whose articles in the *Red Republican* occupied only less space than those of Harney and Gerald Massey.[2] That a real Howard Morton existed seems highly questionable. Despite the obvious power and penetration of the writer and his intimate knowledge of the inner politics of Chartism, his name does not appear in the Chartist press in any other connection, although it is apparent that he lived in Manchester. And, though Morton's non-participation in active politics is by no means proof of his non-existence, his absence from the Marx-Engels correspondence is even more peculiar. Much of Morton's writing may be collated almost verbatim with the *Communist Manifesto*, which was not to appear in English until November 1850, and it seems unlikely that Engels—who moved to Manchester in that month—would not have looked up a man who expressed his own and Marx's ideas so literally.[3]

p. 121); correspondent's views on the Schleswig-Holstein question in *Democratic Review*, August 1850 and those in *Neue Rheinische Zeitung's* discussion in 1848 (Mehring, *op. cit.*, pp. 168–69; etc.).

[1] Other possibilities are Carl Schapper, and the devoted follower of Marx and Engels, Conrad Schramm. But Schapper was in prison during the first months of 1850 and the style makes Engels a more reasonable choice than Schramm. Marx can definitely be ruled out, except indirectly: he had no facility with English.

[2] Massey signed his poetry; his articles appeared over the pen-name "Bandiera". It was through his poetry that Massey made those connections in the fashionable literary world which carried him out of the radical movement. Harney wrote to W. E. Adams in 1884 that after a famous critic had read Massey's poetry in the *Red Republican* he got him into the *Athenaeum*; the poet's "beautiful verse and face got him into society"; and, eventually, he was granted a government pension. Massey immersed himself in Egyptology and the study of the occult during his later years.

[3] *Cf. Democratic Review*, September 1850, p. 125; *Communist Manifesto* (Harold Laski, ed., *The Communist Manifesto: Socialist Landmark*, London: 1948), p. 125; *Red Republican*, 22 June, 13 July; *Communist Manifesto*, pp. 126, 143; *Red Republican*, 14 September, *Communist Manifesto*, pp. 143–44; etc.

The possessor of an intimate knowledge of the *Communist Manifesto* with the initials "H. M.": who could this be but Helen Macfarlane, the admired acquaintance of Marx and Engels and translator of the first printed English translation of the *Manifesto*, which appeared in the four November 1850 issues of the *Red Republican*? Of MacFarlane almost no contemporary reference is to be found, though from her signed articles on Carlyle in the *Democratic Review* it is possible to gather that she was a remarkable person—an ardent feminist, thoroughly emancipated and advanced in her expression; well-read in philosophy and an admirer of Hegel; and evidently a travelled woman as well, having witnessed the Vienna revolution in 1848. If her identity as "Howard Morton" is accepted, it is evident that one of the most vigorous minds in the last period of Chartism was a feminine one. Her writings, more especially the concrete social proposals for England which she put forward,[1] gain an added interest from her close connection with Marx and Engels, for they were never explicit about such proposals.

Marx's analysis of the French Revolution of 1848 also appeared in the *Review* in a series of long paraphrases which were probably the work of Engels. The extraordinary quality of Harney's periodicals, as well as the radical catholicity of his editorial policy, is illustrated by the fact that another version of these events by Louis Blanc appeared in some of the same issues as "Citizen Charles Marx's". The few thousands who bought the little journal could, for threepence, contrast the analyses of two of the most fertile minds of the time. There is no question about the version preferred by Harney; Marx's articles, with their attempt to grasp underlying forces, were the "real criticism" of the French Revolution, just as the *Communist Manifesto* was the "most revolutionary document ever given to the world".

When it came to the two Germans' analysis of English working-class affairs, however, Harney's attitude was significantly different. There was a doctrinaire abstraction at times in their approach to English problems which bordered on the inhuman; and Harney, solidly rooted in British working-class empiricism, was incapable of such aloofness. To take one instance—Engels's observations in the *Democratic Review* on the virtual abrogation of the Ten Hours' Bill by a court decision. Reasoning on orthodox "Marxist" lines, he pointed out that the destruction of this

[1] See, e.g. *Red Republican*, 12 October 1850.

hard-won regulation would hasten the inevitable economic cataclysm which would free the proletariat.

> "Working men of England," he concluded. "If you, your wives, and children are again to be locked up in the 'rattle boxes' for thirteen hours a day, do not despair. This is a cup which, though bitter, must be drunk. The sooner you get over it, the better. Your proud masters, be assured, have dug their grave in obtaining what they call a victory over you."[1]

Whatever the truth, if any, in the long-range view,[2] there was cold comfort here for those whose working day would be lengthened.

Such impersonal solace remained entirely foreign to Harney's habit of thought, though Engels's influence on him early in 1850 may be found in his phraseology. In writing of the role of the middle-class Radicals, for example, Harney observed: "That the moderate reformers will have their triumph and the money-mongers their turn, we do not doubt. It appears to be in the nature of things that such should be the case. They have a mission to fulfil, that mission being to destroy the feudal aristocracy." What the proletariat should ensure was that bourgeois ascendancy should be as brief as possible, and this could be accomplished only through a social democratic propaganda which would prepare the people to push forward from the bourgeois victory.[3] Yet if the language owes something to Engels the idea expressed does not. Harney's entire effort in the past year had been based on these assumptions. Such compatibility of views, added to the fact that Harney had a mass-following of sorts (which Marx and Engels did not) and journals through which they could make themselves heard, made him an invaluable ally whom the two Germans assiduously cultivated. But his pragmatism—his deeper insight into English working-class affairs and solider grasp of what action was necessary—stood as a bar to their domination of him. Certainly his decision to attempt the formation of a new party that would encompass the forces which were sapping Chartism's strength—a policy which brought him into direct conflict with Marx, Engels and

---

[1] "F. E.", in *Democratic Review*, March 1850.

[2] *Cf.* Marx, in the Address of the International Working Men's Association, 1864, where he states that the Ten Hours' Act was the "victory of a principle; it was the first time ... the political economy of the middle class succumbed to the political economy of the working class" (G. M. Steckloff, *History of the First International* [London: 1928], Appendix, p. 444).

[3] *Democratic Review*, February 1850, p. 352.

Ernest Jones in 1851–52—was both more creative and more realistic than their view.

The National Charter Association had adopted socialist aims early in 1850, yet it was far from representing an organic fusion with the "general believers in association"—that is, the remnants of Owenism, and the co-operative societies now enjoying a period of rapid growth. Also indifferent to political action were the trade unions, whose organization of the workers' élite was proceeding rapidly. By the summer of 1850 Harney had come to the conclusion that the only hope for the survival of an independent working-class party lay in uniting these forces, particularly the trade unions, with the National Charter Association. In the Chartist Convention of 1849 it had been Harney who prodded the members into sending delegations to the metropolitan trades, as well as strongly advising the inclusion of trades' members on the National Executive. "Men of the Trades!" he wrote in August 1850. "On you mainly depends whether the political serfdom and social slavery of your order is to continue."

He had no illusions about the immediate political effectiveness of such a central party. Well aware that the great periods of Chartism—in 1838–39, 1842, and 1848—had all been characterized by economic crises, he believed that no mass-revival of the political movement would happen until the next "revulsion of trade".[1] But he was convinced that such conditions would inevitably recur, and when that time came the trade-union and co-operative movements would be subordinated to the real working-class task of achieving political power. Meanwhile, the Chartists should not alienate, but act as closely as possible with, the exponents of industrial action. It was this conviction that dominated his efforts in the next two years and led to the final struggle with Jones.

In pursuing his objective, Harney employed two approaches. The first of these was to convince the trades' leaders that direct industrial action would prove ineffective without political power. The *Red Republican* devoted a large amount of space to strike news —of which there was a great deal in this period—while constantly emphasizing the lesson that "the long purses can always beat the hungry guts". Nor was his effort to win trade-union friendship limited to propaganda. In the London Typographers'

[1] *Red Republican*, 19 October 1850.

VI. The Chartist "Orange Tree"

THE RED REPUBLICAN:

EQUALITY, LIBERTY, FRATERNITY.
EDITED BY G. JULIAN HARNEY.

No. 21.—Vol. I.]   SATURDAY, NOVEMBER 9, 1850.   [Price One Pe

German Communism.

MANIFESTO OF THE GERMAN COMMUNIST PARTY.

(Published in February, 1848.)

The following Manifesto, which has since been adopted by all fractions of German Communists, was drawn up in the German language, in January 1848, by Citizens *Charles Marx* and *Frederic Engels*. It was immediately printed in London, in the German language, and published a few days before the outbreak of the Revolution of February. The turmoil consequent upon that great event made it impossible to carry out, at that time, the intention of translating it into all the languages of civilized Europe. There exist two different French versions of it in manuscript, but under the present oppressive laws of France, the publication of either of them has been found impracticable. The English reader will be enabled, by the following excellent translation of this important document, to judge of the plans and principles of the most advanced party of the German Revolutionists.

It must not be forgotten, that the whole of his Manifesto was written and printed before the Revolution of February.

A frightful hobgoblin stalks throughout Europe. We are haunted by a ghost, the ghost of Communism. All the Powers of the Past have joined in a holy crusade to lay this ghost to rest,—the Pope and the Czar, Metternich and Guizot, French Radicals and German police agents. Where is the opposition which has not been accused of Communism by its enemies in Power? And where the opposition that has not hurled this blighting accusation at the heads of the more advanced oppositionists, as well as at those of its official enemies?

Two things appear on considering these facts. I. The ruling Powers of Europe acknowledge Communism to be also a Power. II. It is time for the Communists to lay before the world an account of their aims and tendencies, and to oppose these silly fables about the bugbear of Communism, by a manifesto of the Communist Party.

CHAPTER I.

BOURGEOIS AND PROLETARIANS.

Hitherto the history of Society has been the history of the battles between the classes composing it. Freemen and Slaves, Patricians and Plebeians, Nobles and Serfs, Members of Guilds and journeymen,—in a word, the oppressors and the oppressed, have always stood in direct opposition to each other. The battle between them has sometimes been open, sometimes concealed, but always continuous. A never-ceasing battle, which has invariably ended, either in a revolutionary alteration of the social system, or in the common destruction of the hostile classes.

In the earlier historical epochs we find almost everywhere a minute division of Society into classes or ranks, a variety of grades in social position. In ancient Rome we find Patricians, Knights, Plebeians, Slaves; in mediæval Europe, Feudal Lords, Vassals, Burghers, Journeymen, Serfs; and in each of these classes there were again grades and distinctions. Modern Bourgeois Society, proceeded from the ruins of the feudal system, but the Bourgeois régime has not abolished the antagonism of classes.

New classes, new conditions of oppression, new forms and modes of carrying on the struggle, have been substituted for the old ones. The characteristic of our Epoch, the Era of the Middle-class, or Bourgeoisie, is that the struggle between the various Social Classes, has been reduced to its simplest form. Society incessantly tends to be divided into two great camps, into two great hostile armies, the Bourgeoisie and the Proletariat.

The burgesses of the early Communes sprang from the Serfs of the Middle Ages, and from this Municipal class were developed the primitive elements of the modern Bourgeoisie. The di of the New World, the circumnavigation of gave the Middleclass—then coming into new fields of action. The colonization of A the opening up of the East Indian and Markets, the Colonial Trade, the increase modities generally and of the means of ex gave an impetus, hitherto unknown, to Com Shipping, and Manufactures; and aided th evolution of the revolutionary element in decaying, feudal form of Society. The old way of managing the industrial interest by of guilds and monopolies was not found su for the increased demand caused by the oper of these new markets. It was replaced by t manufacturing system. Guilds vanished bef industrial Middle-class, and the division of between the different corporations was succee the division of labour between the workmen and the same great workshop.

But the demand always increased, new r came into play. The manufacturing system turn, was found to be inadequate. At th industrial Production was revolutionised by nery and steam. The modern industrial was developed in all its gigantic power instead of the industrial Middle-class we find trial millionaires, chiefs of whole industrial the modern Bourgeois, or Middle-class Cap The discovery of America was the first step t the formation of a colossal market, embrac whole world; whereby an immense develo was given to Commerce, and to the means o munication by sea and land. This again upon the industrial system, and the develo of the Bourgeoisie, the increase of their C the superseding of all classes handed do modern times from the Middle Ages, kept pa the developement of Production, Trade, and communication.

We find, therefore, that the modern Bour are themselves the result of a long process of lopement, of a series of revolutions in the m Production and Exchange. Each of the dep industrial evolution, passed through by the r Middle-class, was accompanied by a corresp

strike of 1850 he won their gratitude by speaking at public meetings on their behalf, and was able through his foreign connections
to expose the French strike-breakers who had been brought to
London as the "black-leg" employees of a Paris firm with close
London connections. The result was declarations of support for
the London strikers from a "General Extraordinary Assembly"
of the "Founderie-Typographie-Française" and the Brussels
Typographers—an example of the international aspect of the
conflict between workers and employers fully emphasized by the
Red Republican. But the dominant theme of Harney's labour
coverage was the repetition of the necessity for political organization. "Trades organizations may mitigate but they cannot up-
root existing evils," he wrote. "For the working classes there is
but one way of righting their wrongs, that of obtaining mastery
of the state." This, in brief, was his judgment on the co-operative
movement as well.

The other means by which he sought to achieve his objective
was more direct. In August, Harney organized a "Democratic
Conference", which continued to hold discussions until the end
of the year. Initially, the Conference seemed promising. The
socialist and co-operative part of a new party had already
achieved a measure of union with the formation of the "Social
Reform League" several months before, which included delegates
from Owenite societies and the Christian Socialist "Society for
Promoting Working Men's Associations". Though non-political
in its inception, the Social Reform League sent four representatives to Harney's Conference. Bronterre represented his National
Reform League and the Fraternal Democrats also sent delegates.
Numerically, those organizations were small; but the Metropolitan Trades Council, two of whose delegates to the Conference were also active Chartists, claimed a membership of
17,000. Also represented were the "respectable classes" in
Thornton Hunt, son of Leigh Hunt, a self-styled "communist"
and editor of the *Leader* (a journal sympathetic to the Christian
Socialists); and Robert Le Blond, a council-member of the
Parliamentary Reformers with "very advanced views". In short,
leaders of elements of trade-unionism, co-operation, socialism
and Chartism sat at these meetings. Harney's attempt to weld
some form of central party from them was the anticipation of a
process which was only to reach fruition in the twentieth century.

The attempt was premature; by the end of the year the

Conference had failed, though it had gone so far as to adopt a name for a new party and at one time a majority had voted for fusion. An inability to agree on the N.C.A. being the dominant party in the organization was one reason for this result; another was the opposition of Jones, O'Connor and other Chartist leaders. Doubtless an additional factor was the forced withdrawal of the main driving force in the Conference, for in early December, as Jenny Marx informed Engels, "poor Harney" was dangerously ill and a serious operation on his throat was necessary. Finally, there was the necessity of concentrating the organized Chartist forces against a last effort by O'Connor and the Clark faction to set up a rival Chartist organization.

O'Connor's action was a pitiful affair from beginning to end. An anti-socialist move backed by the Manchester Chartist Council's demand that the "stigma of Redism" be eradicated from Chartism, the Manchester Conference had been repudiated before it met in January 1851 by the majority of active Chartists. Only four localities had sent delegates and one of Harney's lieutenants, G. J. Mantle, succeeded on the meeting's fifth day in carrying a resolution of support for the National Executive. "It is really enough to make a Quaker kick his mother to see the absurd and ridiculous manner in which the popular mind is now governed," Feargus wrote with a flash of his old temper;[1] but the enfeebled "Lion of the North" was now down and even his own jackals, Clark and the other ex-directors of the Land Company, attacked him a few months later. The final repudiation of the anti-socialist wing came with the meeting of a Chartist Conference in March 1851.

While Harney's Democratic Conference had failed in its attempt to amalgamate the forces for a new party, this failure did not extend to its programme. Three main points had been agreed on: the Six Points as a statement of political aims, land nationalization, and a revision of the laws hampering producers' co-operatives. This programme formed the crux of the Chartist policy approved by the Convention; and the overwhelming majority of the delegates strongly supported a union of "Social Reformers" and Chartists. Underlying the ten-point programme adopted were two assumptions: it was the first duty of the state to provide for the welfare of the whole body of the people; and this could be done only through the redistribution of wealth.

[1] *Friend of the People*, 1 March 1851.

Widely printed in the respectable press, the new programme represented a final victory for Harney and the forces of which he was the leader. The Chartists, commented *The Times*, were assimilating political democracy and industrial socialism in the same manner that had been attempted in France in 1848—a judgment which echoed Harney's judgment: "Henceforth Chartism is *Démocratique et Sociale*." Furthermore, the programme had a national imprimatur. The Convention of 1851 was more representative in character than any Chartist meeting since 1848, sixteen provincial localities, including three in Scotland, having sent delegates. As the foremost exponent of the new policy, Harney's prestige had never been higher. Perhaps one of the best indications of this was that supreme accolade to leadership, the use of his Christian name in the christening of defenceless children: such unfortunate labels as "Feargus O'Connor Frost (Smith)" had been succeeded by "Julian Harney Kossuth (Smith)".

Nor was this prestige limited to Chartism. During the period of his struggle to make Chartism socialist, he had devoted almost as much attention to the foreign refugees, whose numbers in London continued to swell. By 1851 he stood in the same relationship to the socialist exiles as did Lord Dudley Stuart with the more "respectable" republican exiles—that is, as their foremost English friend. Of this small world of former leaders plotting for their assumption of power in the revolutions they still believed were imminent only glimpses may be seen in 1849 and 1850, due to the repressive influence of the Alien Act and the consequent secrecy of their actions. Though the government's attitude toward the exiles was tolerant, their meetings were kept under close surveillance by a branch of Scotland Yard under Sergeant Sanders. It is likely that foreign agents also kept an eye on their national exiles in London, as Harney wrote indignantly in 1850; German refugees were shadowed by Prussian spies and English informers, their houses watched, and note taken of those who visited them. He was a little less than frank in his heated denial of any connection between British democrats and the refugees, however, being himself engaged with Marx and Engels at this time in an abortive attempt to unite all of the refugee socialist leaders in a "World League of Revolutionary Socialists".

There was, moreover, a steady pressure from conservative

English opinion, stimulated by newspaper dispatches from Berlin and Paris hinting darkly at revolutionary plotting, to expel the refugees. Just prior to the opening of the Great Exhibition in 1851, the conservative press became slightly hysterical about such rumours and succeeded in manufacturing an "Exhibition Revolution" out of whole cloth. "Men of action" were to enter England from the Continent; and wide circulation was given to a report in the *New York Herald* that shiploads of American socialists (including Horace Greeley, editor of the rival *New York Tribune*) and Irishmen were on their way to join the Chartists and "European Red Republicans" in an English revolt. Ledru Rollin capped this charade by denying the rumours and then strongly implying that any action against the French exiles would be punished when they returned to power in France. In spite of pressure for the re-enactment of an Alien Act the government remained calm, however, being well aware through its contacts with the French, Prussian and American police that the main "invasion" of the Exhibition summer was to be the pickpockets and confidence-men of two continents. All this was silly enough, but there was a more serious side to governmental action, information on the refugees' activities being passed on to foreign governments by the Home Office.

As in 1855 and 1858, the bulk of support for the refugees came from the working-class Radicals. A classic example of working-class sympathy for the revolutionary causes on the Continent and of the class-differences which divided English public opinion on this subject was the "Haynau incident" of September 1850. An Austrian marshal, Haynau had crushed the Hungarian revolution with a brutality which had made him an archetype of the reaction; and when it was reported that he was to visit England, Harney appealed to the working class to protest, though without much hope. Events provided a welcome surprise. When the marshal visited Barclay and Perkins' brewery on Bankside, work stopped and the brewery men welcomed their guest by dropping a truss of hay on him and chasing him into the street, heavily pelted with manure. Here a crowd of lightermen and coal-heavers took up the pursuit. Down Bankside ran the marshal, his clothes torn, his moustachios being violently pulled, covered with fresh volleys of dung thrown by the angry mob shouting, "Down with the Austrian butcher!" After being routed out from a temporary refuge in the dustbin of "The George" public house, Haynau finally found protection upstairs, from whence he was eventually rescued by a strong force of police and rowed to safety across the Thames. He left England within a week.

Harney lost no time in drawing the moral from this incident. In an exultant three-page leader, he wrote in part, "The hunt of Haynau . . . proclaimed at once the progress of the working classes in political knowledge, their uncorrupted love of justice, and their intense hatred of tyranny and cruelty." [1] The identification of class-consciousness with foreign revolutionary sympathy that underlay this affair was pointed up in a jingle chanted in the streets of Southwark in the following days, which was reprinted by the *Red Republican*:

> "Turn him out, turn him out, from our side of the Thames,
> Let him go to great Tories and high-titled dames.
> He may walk the west-end and parade in his pride,
> But he'll not come back again near the 'George' in Bankside."

The conservative press was as quick to draw the same conclusion. The attack on Haynau, according to the *Quarterly Review*, was "an indication of foreign influence even amongst our own people", and evidence of the spread of socialist and communist doctrines. While this was more than Harney claimed for the incident, the brewery-workers' action evoked a great popular response. Public meetings in Nottingham and Manchester sent their congratulations, and at a demonstration organized by the Fraternal Democrats and addressed by Harney and Engels hundreds were turned away from Farringdon Hall. The "acclamations of democracy" predicted by Harney were expressed also in congratulatory messages from Paris and the "New York City Industrial Congress", the latter conveying their compliments on the "very striking reception" tendered Haynau through the *Red Republican*.

Channelling this working-class sympathy into financial help for the *émigrés* was a more difficult matter. Most of the refugees, particularly those "political Ishmaelites", the Poles, lived in terrible poverty, and Harney's unremitting efforts to collect money for them were never very successful. The "Democratic Refugee Committee" which he founded in June 1850 to aid socialist refugees was unable to compete with the resources of the middle-class Italian and Polish funds for non-socialist *émigrés*; but it did

[1] *Red Republican*, 14 September 1850.

serve as a propaganda counter-weight to the middle-class committees' and the government's pressure on the refugees to
emigrate to America. This, Harney declared, was part of a
conspiracy to clear the really revolutionary Poles from Europe
—and certainly government expenditures for refugees' passages
indicate that it wished to clear them from England. The connection was not missed by the conservative press. When the last
remnant of the Polish Legion which had fought in the Hungarian
rebellion arrived in Liverpool in 1851, their refusal to continue
to America was roundly condemned as the result of a Chartist
plot.

As the most articulate exponent of English working-class internationalism and the ardent defender of the radical *émigrés*
against conservative enmity in England, Harney occupied a
unique position among the exiles by the beginning of 1851. His
reputation in the Chartist movement and his possession of one
of the few socialist papers remaining in Europe led the radical
exiles to court his influence. But it was an impossible situation in
which to retain everyone's friendship: impartiality meant antagonism in the atmosphere which was developing. As the
months passed and the prospect of new revolutions on the Continent grew dimmer, the differences between the exiles were
exacerbated. Their futility becoming more apparent, the leaders'
ideological disagreements were magnified, and, like hawkers
competing for the attention of an indifferent public, their voices
became shriller. In spite of their differences, the refugees had
for a time presented an appearance of unity to the public eye,
but by the early months of 1851 even the semblance of unity had
disappeared. With the formation of the "Central European
Democratic Committee" under the joint leadership of Mazzini,
Ledru Rollin, Arnold Ruge and the Pole, Albert Darasq, in the
later summer of 1850, the bourgeois republican elements among
the refugees had coalesced, and Rollin and Louis Blanc approached an open break.[1] At almost the same time, Marx and
Engels, in splitting off from the majority of the Communist
League, in effect declared their opposition to both the republican and socialist sections of the *émigrés*.

---

[1] Ledru Rollin headed the largest section of French *émigrés*, the *Société de la
Révolution*; Blanc spoke for the utopian socialists; and condemning both groups for
their moderation was the *Commune Révolutionnaire*, a Blanquist minority led by Felix
Pyat and Barthelemy.

In view of the divisions now opening among the refugees, Harney's speech at a New Year's banquet sponsored by the Fraternal Democrats and attended by delegates from all sections of the emigration was really wishful thinking. He advised his "foreign brethren" to so unite "as to present one grand phalanx of opposition to the common foe". Engels, in replying to this speech, made plain his and Marx's view that revolution would come only as the "result of a long struggle, consummated by a new generation of men"—a belief which smacked of apostasy to the majority of the emigration, still desperately dreaming of imminent action. In close contact with Marx and Engels, Harney could scarcely have been unaware of their contempt for "bourgeois democrats" and those who believed in the human will, rather than economic factors, as the prerequisite of revolution. What he evidently did not realize was that an ideological difference, or for that matter, impartiality, would be sufficient to estrange them. The megalomania from which all of these leaders suffered was particularly apparent in Marx and Engels. This may be labelled "intellectual certainty"; but the evidence of certainty was sometimes a spiteful and contemptuous intolerance. Harney, in attempting to maintain his connection with all of the democratic emigration, was guilty in the two Germans' eyes of nothing less than "betrayal" and was consigned to the limbo of the unenlightened.

One of the most fertile sources of grievance was the maddening catholicity of Harney's editorial policy. While printing "The Last Stage of Bourgeois Society", for example, the product of Marx's faithful follower, George Eccarius, Harney also gave space to the addresses of the Central European Democratic Committee and appeals for funds by Mazzini. To Engels this was the equivalent of himself supporting the Parliamentary Reformers. "The humbug which Harney is carrying on with Mazzini and Co. is getting too bad," he wrote to Marx in February; Harney would have to be put on the "right track".[1] The "right track" was even at this time a rather tortuous line, for it meant that Harney should also eschew contact with his old friend, Carl Schapper, who had remained with the majority faction of the Communist League, and the extreme left of the French emigration. What they were asking, in short, was that Harney should sacrifice his entire émigré acquaintanceship to follow them into

[1] 5, 12 February 1851, *Briefwechsel*, vol. I, pp. 141, 146.

the isolation which was fast enveloping them. In London by this time what might be called the "Marxist party" was really but some half-dozen men.

The retention of Harney's friendship was felt to be vital by Marx and Engels, but it now became apparent that this would have to be on his terms. When Harney spoke at a public meeting co-sponsored by the Fraternal Democrats and several sections of the emigration, and thus "gave character to the meeting", as Marx expressed it, the split began to open. Harney's appearance with Schapper was likened by a bitterly resentful Marx to Engels appearing with Thomas Clark; and with a satisfaction which under the circumstances seems somewhat disingenuous, he concluded that their role of isolation was a fine one. Engels agreed, and in a reply which has been frequently quoted, wrote:

> "One realizes more and more that the emigration is an institution in which everyone must necessarily become a fool, a donkey and a scurvy knave unless he withdraws from it completely and contents himself with being an independent writer who doesn't bother his head even in the least about the so-called revolutionary party." [1]

In the context of events, this sounds more like the rationalization of unpleasant facts than philosophical detachment. The two Germans continued to bother themselves a good deal about *émigré* politics, as their correspondence concerning their final break with Harney shows. The occasion for the final rupture was the anniversary of the February Revolution. Louis Blanc had decided to split publicly with Ledru Rollin by holding a rival banquet on 24 February, and for this purpose he had united with Schapper's faction and the Blanquist minority, and solicited Harney's aid. Marx's acid etching of these preliminaries conveys better than any paraphrase the atmosphere of this small, intense London refugee world in the post-1848 period, with the passionate involvement in the trivial of these increasingly isolated revolutionary leaders, and the importance attached to Harney's influence. After some preliminary remarks about Blanc—of whom Engels had recently written, "The frivolous dwarf's vanity of the super-clever Louis Blanc is developing in a way which really stamps the conceited man as a pure idiot" . . .—Marx warmed to his task of describing Harney's action and character:[2]

[1] Quoted in Mehring, *Karl Marx*, p. 208.
[2] Marx to Engels, 23 February 1851, *Briefwechsel*, vol. I, pp. 152–55.

"He has by no means been content to take part at the meeting of these people. No. He has made their banquet of the 24th February, which without him would have been a complete failure, into a London event. Already a thousand tickets have been sold. . . . Harney has sold the largest part of the tickets, as Jones told me the day before yesterday. O'Connor, Reynolds, and hundreds of Chartists are taking part. Harney has drummed them together. He is on his way all day carrying out the orders of Louis Blanc, as Jones told me also. . . .

"Jones declared to me that in view of my explanations he would probably . . . not be present at the banquet. What makes his decision uncertain is very rational. If he doesn't come he loses his popularity as, thanks to Dear [Harney] this banquet has become a Chartist matter. . . . Jones disapproves of Dear's behaviour. . . . He attempted to excuse it by saying that if the Chartists did not take part in either of the two banquets, they would be accused of political apathy or of antipathy against the foreign revolutionaries. I answered him, then Harney should have held a Chartist meeting in celebration of the lousy 24th of February instead of making himself into a pedestal for a dwarf and half a dozen camels . . .[1]

"Harney has got himself involved in this affair, first because of his need to have great men to admire, which we have often made fun of in the past. Then, he loves theatrical effects. He is certainly a popularity-seeker—I don't wish to say *vaniteux*. He is without doubt strongly ruled by the phrase and is developing very rich vapidities. He's stuck deeper in the democratic mud than he wishes to admit. He has a double spirit: one which Frederick Engels made for him and another which is his own. The first is a sort of strait-jacket for him; the last is himself *in puris naturalibus*. But there is yet a third familiar spirit—that is, his good wife. She has great partiality for *les jants jaunes a la Landolphe*[2] and Louis Blanc. She hates me, for example, as a frivolous person who might become dangerous to her 'property to be watched upon'. I have definite proof that this woman has got her two long plebeian hands in the pie here. How much Harney is possessed by this familiar spirit and how sly and narrowly Scots she is you can judge from the following. You will remember how, on New Year's Eve, she insulted Helen Macfarlane in the presence of my wife. Later she told my wife with a smiling face that Harney had not seen Mrs. Macfarlane for the whole of the evening . . . Harney was stupid and cowardly enough not to let her get her own back for the insult, and so breaks, in the most undignified way, with the only collaborator on his spouting rag who had original ideas—a rare bird, on his paper. . . ."

"Detachment" is scarcely the characteristic quality of this

[1] I.e. Blanc and the "Windmill Street Gang"—Schapper, the former Prussian officer Willich, etc.
[2] Blanc's lieutenant, a man of very agreeable manners.

bilious gossip. What is most apparent is the writer's outraged pride, by which, for example, Mary Harney's influence and Harney's vanity, rather than any political convictions, are assigned as the real motive for his actions. There is much truth in the description of Harney: of vanity he had a good share, and he was doubtless impressed by the great names of those who sought his help. But such a remark of Marx's as "I am tired of this incense with which Harney never tires surrounding *les petits grandhommes*" [1] indicates that other vanities existed to be wounded. The main point, however, is not that Marx and Engels wished admiration—which they got in generous measure from Harney —but that they wanted an obedient conformity to their position on all matters. Anything less was treasonable.

The actual parting of the ways was surrounded by violence. Harney, after speaking briefly at Ledru Rollin's banquet, made a leading speech at Highbury Barn, where some thousand Chartists, Frenchmen, Poles, Germans and Hungarians had gathered to hear Blanc, Schapper and others. Two of Marx's faithful supporters were thrown out of the meeting, followed by cries of "Spy! Spy!", and badly beaten in the courtyard. Harney's failure to intercede on their behalf appeared to them the "betrayal of old tried party comrades"; he had made himself the supporter of their direct enemies, as Marx wrote bitterly to Engels, and thus "had thrown his considerable weight for them as against us in Germany".[2] There are indications that Marx continued to hope for Harney's re-conversion for a time, though he was already pinning his hopes on Ernest Jones. But the friendship begun when young Engels entered the *Northern Star's* office at Leeds eight years before had come to an end in the courtyard at Highbury Barn—a fact which Harney does not seem to have realized immediately. Three months later, at a tea-party where Robert Owen was celebrating his eightieth birthday, a slightly inebriated and very friendly Harney came up to Marx and asked after Engels. So far as can be told, this was the last time he talked to Marx until their paths crossed in Waterloo Station a quarter of a century later.

It is likely that a similar tragi-comedy would have been played out sooner or later in any case. Harney was not without ideological intolerance himself, as his fervent participation in the

---

[1] Marx to Engels, 11 February 1851, *Briefwechsel*, vol. I, p. 145.
[2] 26 February 1851, *ibid.*, p. 163.

weeding out of Chartists from the party in the past had shown. But the absolute loyalty to their ideas which Marx and Engels demanded was foreign to him for the simple reason that he considered all of the emigration, despite their differences, one party. With the socialists his sympathies were closest; and to him Marx, Blanc and Schapper were all going in the right direction. In spite of the similarity of ideas which had caused Marx to write of the "spirit which Frederick Engels had made" for Harney, the latter had never become a "Marxist". He spoke with great admiration of Marx; he spoke with equal admiration of Marx's ideological enemy, Proudhon. To Harney, both men were humanitarians and socialists, not leaders of intellectual sects or political cliques. It was this "indiscrimination" which led Marx and Engels to label Harney "Hip Hip Hurrah" in their correspondence following the schism, and which would probably have caused their estrangement at some not-distant time.

Considering the unpopularity and lack of following of the two Germans, Harney's separation from them meant rather an access than a loss of prestige in the emigration. In the Ledru Rollin-Louis Blanc rivalry he had maintained a scrupulous impartiality, and he retained the friendship of both men. His relationship with the majority of London Germans had become even closer through his support of Schapper, and his long championing of the Poles assured him their loyalty. Thus, in April 1851, Harney had reached a pinnacle of influence in his relationship with the foreign revolutionaries which matched his position in the Chartist party. It was his personal tragedy that both were lost causes; from this point his career as a public man is a story of decline.

By May of 1851 it was plain that the Chartist Convention's new programme was having no revitalizing effect on the roots of Chartism. "It has been asserted that Chartism exhibits the spectacle of a head without a body," Harney wrote. "This is in some measure true. But whose the fault? . . . Only from below can the movement be reborn." [1] Those below seemed interested in almost everything except Chartism, however. The operatives of one Manchester factory subscribed £21 for a statue of Sir Robert Peel and £60 had come in Bradford working-class pennies for the Great Exhibition—but the N.C.A. was unable to pay the rent of a small office. Cardinal Wiseman's plot to

[1] *Friend of the People*, 3 May 1851.

P

"impose a foreign yoke" on the British nation through the subtle stratagem of dividing England into bishoprics (the "Papal Agression" of 1850) had generated intense working-class excitement at the same time that one former Chartist leader was writing off his movement as "A handful of men clinging yet to a forlorn hope".[1] And, in spite of his optimistic words about Chartism being *"Démocratique et Sociale"*, Harney had changed the name of the *Red Republican* to the *Friend of the People* in December 1850, admitting that the original name had excited active prejudice amongst some sections of the working classes.

More basic to the weakness of Chartism was the preoccupation of the working classes with trade-unionism and the co-operative movement. Harney had already realized this in 1849 and 1850; and, in a striking article written early in 1851, he summed up his conclusions as to the tactics which would have to be employed if an independent working-class party was to survive. A certain recurrent pattern of political agitation, succeeded after failure by industrial action, could be traced from the time of Peterloo, he wrote.[2] Such a period of reaction was taking place at the present time; social, rather than political reform, in the form of Labour Associations (the producers' co-operatives of the Christian Socialists), co-operative societies, and trade unions, had engaged the masses. To ardent reformers convinced that the proletariat should first achieve mastery of the state, the success of these movements was anything but gratifying. But there it was: what was to be done about it? To fight them would be unwise, and their effect was beneficial in spreading the principles of social reform. When political agitation revived, the people would be better prepared to struggle for the "Abolition of Classes" and the "Sovereignty of Labour", along with Universal Suffrage.

That political agitation would revive he was certain: it waited only on the inevitable recurrence of commercial crisis. He was convinced also that a government which represented only property would, in the event that they gained too much power, refuse legal protection to the co-operators and "legislate into impotency" the trade unions—with the consequence that the working classes would be forced once again to take up the fight for political control. The role of the Chartist party in the mean-

[1] W. J. Linton, *English Republic*, 1851, p. 83.
[2] *Friend of the People*, 25 January 1851.

time should be to retain the friendship of co-operators and
trade-unionists, and, if possible, to combine all three groups in a
new party. It was this conviction that had already motivated
Harney's efforts in the Democratic Congress and had led to the
inclusion of a co-operative plank in the Convention's programme
of 1851; and this belief dominated his efforts throughout the
year.

There were some indications that such a new party might
be organized. The trades were generally indifferent; but the
Metropolitan Trades Delegates had endorsed universal suffrage,
and two of their leaders—Delaforce and Murray—continued to
play an active part in London Chartism. Moreover, one of the
most powerful of the trades' leaders, William Newton, the organizer of the "New Model" Amalgamated Society of Engineers,
had appeared on Chartist platforms in 1850 and had publicly
declared his support of the social and political aims of the
movement. Nor were these indications limited to the trades.
It was true that the majority of the upper- and middle-class
promoters of the Christian Socialist movement were anti-democratic. Their propagandist, Charles Kingsley, described Harney
as part of the "smoke of the pit"; and Frederick Maurice, the
Church of England clergyman to whom the others gave ultimate
obedience, believed democracy possible only on the basis of
slavery. Yet Thornton Hunt, a powerful supporter of Christian
Socialism through his editorship of the *Leader*, was desirous of
just such a union of Chartist and socialist forces as that engaging
Harney's attention; and such working members of their co-
operative associations as Gerald Massey and J. B. Leno were
also of one mind with Harney. "We believe that political power
is essential to consolidate or even give fair vantage ground to
co-operative associations," declared Massey.[1] Finally, there was
the co-operative retail movement, growing most rapidly in Yorkshire and Lancashire. If Samuel Kydd, a member of the Chartist Executive, may be believed, this movement represented no
basic challenge to political action: he had known many old
Radicals and Chartists who had been members of co-operative
retail stores for more than twenty years without losing any of
their political ardour, he wrote; they had, in fact, been among
the staunchest.[2]

It can be seen that there were some grounds for Harney's

---

[1] *Ibid.*, 28 February 1852.   [2] *Northern Star*, 31 January 1852.

belief that a steady effort on the lines he suggested might be successful. He never had the opportunity to prove it. Whatever
chance his policy had was negatived by the last fatal schism in
the Chartist body, when Ernest Jones took a position of irreconcilable opposition to the trades and co-operative movements. The two men were agreed as to the necessity for the
conquest of the state by the working classes; it was with regard
to the immediate tactics to be pursued by the Chartist party
that they disagreed. To Jones, co-operative societies "increased
the numbers of the most dangerous class—the aristocrats among
their own body";[1] and so with the "aristocracy of labour", the
trade unions. Jones said, in short, that the working-class political
movement could be kept alive only by fighting the industrial
movements which were sapping its strength; to which Harney
replied that in co-operation with those forces lay their only hope
of survival.

There were personal factors involved as well in their estrangement, which became open in 1852. Marx and Engels, implac-
ably hostile to Harney following his "apostasy", desired nothing
more than to see Jones become the unquestioned leader of
Chartism, and they encouraged—if they did not inspire—his
attacks on co-operation and the trades.[2] Jones himself strongly
desired power; he could be ruthless in his intolerance. And
Harney was scarcely the self-effacing type; he had never been
distinguished by his moderation in the treatment of political
enemies in the past. Neither ever made a secret of his ability
to lead the movement, and that they could have continued to
share the steadily decreasing power of Chartism is doubtful in
any event. As in the relationship of Harney and Feargus, it
was only their mutual affection which prolonged the friendship
of the two men.

Together, they might at least have united the waning movement, but it was obvious immediately after the National Convention of March–April 1851 that they were pulling apart.
After an abortive attempt to launch a new stamped paper with
the two as co-editors, Jones determined to continue printing his
weekly *Notes to the People*, which he had begun for the purpose
of publishing his prison-poetry. But, as Jones was to point out

[1] *Northern Star*, 2 November 1850.
[2] *Cf.* letters of 5 May 1851; 4 February, 18 March 1852; *Briefwechsel*, vol. I,
pp. 193, 317, 331.

VIII. Snig's End, Gloucestershire, in 1850; the Site of O'Connor's Chartist Land Delusion

IX. JULIAN HARNEY IN 1850

with great heat under reversed circumstances a year later, there was no room for two papers in the movement. The success of one could only be at the expense of the other, as the demise of the *Friend of the People* in July showed. For the first time since 1842 Harney was without a public organ in which to express himself—a particularly unfortunate circumstance in view of Jones's now having one.

The end of the *Friend of the People* had been announced from Mauchline, where illness had taken Harney in June. During the summer and autumn he found enthusiastic audiences of Chartists who flocked to hear him on a tour of southern Scotland. It is significant, however, that the greatest cheers evoked by his speeches were for his references to Kossuth, the Hungarian leader who was to be idolized by the British public; and enthusiasm for Kossuth buttered no Chartist bread. Crowds cheering; the petty debts of the Chartist Executive remaining unpaid—Harney finally drew the reluctant conclusion from his tour that the N.C.A. as an organized national party was at an end. Arriving in Newcastle in December, he confessed in a public letter that he thought it could not be revived and refused to stand as a candidate for the annual election of the Executive.

With the election of the new Executive, any semblance of Chartist unity or strength which remained was dissipated. Many of the leaders of note declined nomination, and Jones, who headed the poll, received but 900 votes. To this proof of the mortification of the Chartist body was added evidence of the schizophrenic state of its head, for in the first meeting Jones resigned in protest against the inclusion of pro-middle-class members such as Holyoake, and after the addition of new members under rather questionable circumstances, the Executive was almost evenly split between pro- and anti-middle-class members. The old war-horse of Chartism, the *Northern Star*, which changed ownership at this juncture, provided additional evidence of disintegration by declaring, "Away with the name of Chartist, it is offensive to both sight and taste." And the final symbol of this process was to be found in the complete breakdown of O'Connor, who, after a series of pitiably comical scenes in the Court of Chancery (which had begun to masticate the remains of the Land Company) and the House of Commons, made a brief trip to America to avoid a Commission of Lunacy, and on his return was taken to Doctor Tuke's asylum in Chiswick hopelessly insane. Harney and Jones, attacked by Holyoake for "abandoning Chartism", in reality held whatever hope of survival of a working-class political party there was in their hands. But Harney's launching of a new *Friend of the People* in February 1852, when Jones had already asked for support of his new organ, the *People's Paper*, indicated that their efforts would be in opposite directions.

His new paper was not yet a month old when Harney summed up his opinion of Chartism and proposed a new movement. "Chartists are numerous, but the Chartist *body* is no more," he wrote. "Surviving driblets of the once vast stream only serve to show the extent of the drouth." But what was the remedy? "My belief is that for Chartism there is no future existence save in a *new birth*," he declared. "Any attempt to galvanize the dry bones of a worn out past must, as in the case of such attempts already tried, prove to be labour in vain." The "*new birth*", as it emerged from subsequent articles, was to be a third force. Two forces were already in existence in those, like Thornton Hunt and Holyoake, who wished for a union with the middle-class Radicals and their representatives in Parliament; and others, like Jones, who believed in the continuance of the old Chartist technique of an "outside agitation". Harney's projected party would draw its strength both from old Chartists and those Radicals who would support the Six Points, while at the same time trying to achieve a coalition with the trade-unionists and co-operators. To achieve the latter, there were political lessons at hand, as he took pains to point out. The failure of attempts in Parliament to remove legislative restrictions on co-operative associations and the defeat of the great Amalgamated Engineers strike of January–April by a combination of employers were proof that only by the achievement of political power could they deal with the capitalist order which made the laws and controlled the economic system. The iron trades had the best organization in the country, Harney declared, and if they were wary of some of the charlatans in the Chartist movement, let them come forward and take the power out of their hands.

This last remark was a reference to the refusal of the Engineers to give Ernest Jones a hearing at a public meeting in January, due to their fear of prejudicing their cause by connecting it with Chartism. The incident confirmed Jones's conviction that the trades were a force hostile to the political movement. In the same month, he made his opposition to co-operation (as then functioning) clear in a series of debates with Lloyd Jones in Manchester. When the Christian Socialists and Amalgamated Engineers launched a plan to set up a co-operative iron-works as an answer to the employers in February, he bitterly attacked it, and thus brought the basic divergence of views between himself and Harney into the open. Harney told Jones that this was an attack on democracy—in a struggle of Labour against capital their ranks should be closed—and asked him to refrain from the hostility "which would make enemies of men whom it was desirable to have as friends and fellow-labourers in the cause of political justice".[1] And Jones once more reiterated his belief that the fallacy of trade-unionism should not be perpetuated: "The aristocracy of labour must be broken down." [2] It was clear that the two were basically opposed as to future action; and any possibility of their reconciliation was now rendered impossible by Harney's acquisition of the *Star* under circumstances which Jones regarded as the "crowning infamy" of their relationship.

A faithful barometer of the state of Chartism to the last, the *Northern Star* had declined steadily in circulation from 21,000 in 1848 to 1,200 in 1852, despite the efforts of its publisher, Mac-Gowan. In April, Harney announced that he had bought the *Star*, which would be merged with the *Friend of the People* under a new name, the *Star of Freedom*. Jones's reaction to this was a splenetic outburst in which he accused Harney of outbidding him in order to destroy his still-projected *People's Paper*. "He must well know two such papers cannot at present exist together," he wrote angrily.[3] Harney's reply, backed by a letter from MacGowan, was devastating. Jones had been offered the paper first, and Harney only after this. Did he have to have Jones's "leave to politically exist" or to resume an editorship he had held before Jones was ever heard of? asked Harney; then launched into a full flood of invective about the "charlatanism of adventurers of the 'Esq.' order" who aped in private the aristocrats by whom they were scorned and flourished at the expense of the poor. This acrimonious quarrel—described by Marx with what

[1] *Friend of the People*, 24 April 1852.
[2] For Jones's account of the disagreement, see *Notes to the People*, vol. II, pp. 860–62.
[3] *Ibid.*, pp. 1013–15. *Cf.* his flyleaf attacking Harney, *An Appeal for the Judgment of the People* (London: 1852), Howell Collection, Bishopsgate Institute.

seems to have been complete unself-consciousness as "on the level of German emigrants' polemics"—and the launching of Jones's *People's Paper* on 8 May meant that the last internal struggle of Chartism had begun.

Jones now proceeded to follow in O'Connor's footsteps of the preceding year by calling a Chartist conference in Manchester, which set up a rival Executive of three: himself and two henchmen, Gammage (later the first historian of Chartism) and Finlen. Even before the conference strong opposition to it had been expressed, Jones being roundly condemned at a meeting of the West Riding delegates for the "disastrous effects" of his attacks on trade-unionism and co-operation. Only six localities were represented at the conference, and its actions were repudiated by 13 out of 19 of the West Riding localities, who affirmed their support in the old National Executive. The Metropolitan Delegate Council, dominated by Jones since March, split on the issue; and the Newcastle Chartists also condemned Jones's action. It was apparent that a large reservoir of support remained to be tapped by Harney.

Harney's hopes were centred in William Newton, the organizer of the powerful Amalgamated Society of Engineers. With the failure of the Engineers' strike, Newton determined to enter politics as a Labour candidate for Tower Hamlets, an action strongly supported by the *Star of Freedom*. The two men found no difficulty in seeing eye-to-eye on social reforms, Newton calling for the management of machinery and land for the benefit of the working classes, legislative protection for co-operators, and state-help for the unemployed. In what might have been a paraphrase of Harney's viewpoint, he stressed the point that labourers would not achieve a fair share of their production until they were represented in Parliament. Newton's entry into the arena of politics and his broad social views were in fact a refutation of Jones's attacks on a selfish "aristocracy of labour" intent only on its own immediate gains, and Harney saw in him the real hope of the new labour party which would keep what had been the Chartist movement from extinction.

The General Election of 1852 was a decisive event in Harney's life. While its effect was temporarily to coalesce the group of leaders in whom he felt the future of the working-class movement lay, it also brought home to him in a shocking fashion the state of popular feeling. The *Star of Freedom* supported five

candidates who espoused a wide extension of the suffrage, as
well as Newton. At the last moment, Harney acquiesced in the
demands of the Bradford non-electors and, though arriving too
late to make any speeches, went to the hustings. The result was
his humiliation in losing the show of hands. To expect more
under the circumstances was doubtless foolish on his part, but
his reaction was one of extreme disgust and bitterness. His
description of the affair conveys something of his feeling:[1]

"What a wretched spectacle to see a multitude of grown men
shouting, cuffing, fighting, struggling under a July sun with,
apparently, all the frantic fury of demons let loose, some for the
'yellow', some for the 'blue'; one side for 'our Protestant institutions', the other half for half a bellyful of 'cheap bread' . . . In the
name of common sense . . . of what interest to the poor and unenfranchised are these fights of rival churches and rival oppressors?
Will the people never learn that the rich and privileged, whatever
their party and sectarian designations, are really of one mind in
politics and religion, and engaged in one unholy compact to rob
the millions of their rights and their substance in this world, and to
keep them in terror-stricken bondage in the world to come?"

Harney's last appearance on the hustings had been on another
memorable July day just five years before, when he had bearded
Palmerston and won an overwhelming popular decision. The
contrast with his fiasco at Bradford need not be stressed: it was
one thing to deplore working-class apathy, another to be struck
in the face by it. And Jones's victory on the show of hands at
Halifax could not have assuaged his feelings.

The election had been equally disastrous so far as the other
democratic candidates were concerned. Tom Duncombe, the
old friend of Chartism, had been returned for Finsbury, but all
the other candidates had lost, Newton being returned at the
bottom of the poll. The new Parliament, wrote Harney, was "the
very incarnation of bourgeois baseness . . . the most mindless,
soulless, heartless crew of shams, tricksters, counterfeits and im-
posters ever got together since Parliaments had real existence".
Nevertheless, the election had had one fortunate result in convincing others beside Harney of the necessity for organization,
and during the next two months the framework of the "new
party" emerged in the form of support committees for the *Star
of Freedom*. Newton headed the organization in London, with
the Christian Socialists Isham and Walter Cooper, and A. E.

[1] *Star of Freedom*, 17 July 1852.

Delaforce of the Metropolitan Trades Delegates, also becoming members. Democratic associations in Halifax, Bradford and Nottingham pledged their support; and the London Committee called for local organizations in other towns. This was, in effect, the call for a new party including the trade unions and co-operatives, with the *Star of Freedom* standing in the same relationship to it as had the *Northern Star* to Chartism.

Early in September, in a long and moderately phrased letter in the *Star of Freedom*, Newton made the objective of the new party explicit. A "National Party" should be formed on the basis of one point: Manhood Suffrage. Such a programme would be able to muster the formidable force that the Anti-Corn Law League had organized through its single-mindedness, he argued; and, in the same way that the abolition of the Navigation Laws and sugar-tax had followed the Leaguers' victory, so would the other Five Points follow the attainment of one. Furthermore, such an agitation would receive Parliamentary support; he had the written assurance of several M.P.s to this effect. Newton concluded by calling for a public meeting to launch the new organization.

Harney, though disagreeing with Newton about limiting the "National Party's" programme to the one point of Manhood Suffrage, clearly stood behind him, as did Thornton Hunt and Robert Le Blond. Holyoake was also favourable toward such a new party, though he had been the foremost working-class propagandist of the Parliamentary Reformers. If to these men are added such Chartist, co-operative or trade-union leaders as Delaforce, Isham, Walter Cooper, Massey, Leno, Pettie and others, it is apparent that the potential support of the new party was not negligible. And this was now reinforced by the adherence to Newton's plan of the recently activated Northern Political Union in Newcastle, in which the same combination of forces were to be observed: the miners' organizer, Martin Jude; the former Chartist leader, James Charlton; and the young Radical, Joseph Cowen, Jr.—all, incidentally, good friends of Harney.

What is most significant—and paradoxical—about the majority of these men was their combination of Socialist idealism with political "Liberalism". Hunt, for example, labelled himself a "communist" (which meant a believer in co-operation), but he was also one of the most consistent exponents of union with the

Radical middle-class. Newton's social views were anti-capitalist, yet he was now suggesting an alliance with the most advanced political section of that class. Holyoake probably foreshadowed the "Labour rump" of the Liberal party more clearly than the others, but his sympathy with the Manchester School was accompanied by strong co-operative views. The "National Party" which was projected was for the most part in its economic view antagonistic to capitalism; in its political views, desirous of co-operation with the middle-class Radicals. To accomplish the latter, and to achieve Universal Suffrage, their economic aims would have to be relegated to a secondary position and cleansed of class antagonism. The importance of this group of leaders makes their acceptance of this necessity important: the change in thought which they and their obscure "National Party" exemplified marked another step of all but the minority under Jones into the Liberal camp.

After an inconclusive contest at a public meeting between the "new movers" and Jones—who accused them of being part of a middle-class plot working through Newton to destroy Chartism —the meeting which Newton had called for took place in Finsbury. Harney appeared with Hunt and Le Blond and in a coldly favourable speech killed what he had struggled so long for. The movement to create a new National Party was premature, he said; a popular agitation was not possible for the moment. Newton had taken the initiative in the matter, and he should take the next steps. He himself, concluded Harney, would be willing to follow the young men, though he would not take a leading part in the movement.

What had happened was another of the fatal schisms which had plagued all of these attempts. Newton had apparently found public response too slight to pursue the idea further. He had not appeared at the Finsbury meeting nor had he figured in any public meetings in September and October. Harney obviously thought Newton, with his great prestige in the iron trades, the keystone of any new structure; without him he was unable to swallow Holyoake and Hunt—the more so since Hunt's *Leader* had recently attacked "Red Republicanism". While he was willing to include some "truly Radical M.P.s" in the new party, his hatred of the Manchester School remained unabated. The main reason for his defeatism, however, was the apathy which had smothered the whole proceedings. Harney was tired; his speech at the Finsbury meeting was in fact his swan-song so far as the working-class movement for which he had struggled in one form or another for so long was concerned. The Bradford election experience in July had left a deep scar on him; the general behaviour of non-electors all over Britain almost convinced him of the fruitlessness of further effort. From this abyss of hopelessness, the attempt of August–October had briefly lifted him—only to have the lack of response of the working classes provide final crushing proof of the new party's futility.

The sea of working-class indifference closed over the *Star of Freedom* in November. Jones's *People's Paper*, though circulating less than 3,000 copies weekly, had captured the support of the majority of Chartists who remained; the *Leader* and *Reynolds's Weekly Newspaper*, then claiming a weekly sale of 50,000, had siphoned away the co-operative and trades' readers who bought weekly newspapers. Harney had cut himself off from the old organization, such as it was, and had failed to reach the new audience to which Newton's committee had appealed in August. And finally, he had turned his back on Hunt and Le Blond. What was left? The fact was that no working-class political movement as such remained outside of the few stragglers under Jones, and with the demise of the *Star of Freedom*, Harney's political career was almost totally eclipsed.

Harney's last attempt to publish a newspaper—the weekly *Vanguard*, which began publication in January 1853—came to an end with the cruellest blow he had yet suffered. In February Mary Harney died in Mauchline. "Where I first saw and loved, I for the last time gazed upon and mourned her," he wrote, and in a long epitaph, he revealed something of the character of this beautiful woman and his own feeling:[1]

> "At this hour, with bodily infirmity, depression of spirits, a mesh of difficulties, a future, gloomy, uncertain, impenetrable weighing upon me, sorely and sadly I feel the want of her admirable counsel. . . . All that in me may be worthy she possessed, but with this great difference, that her worth, wisdom and virtues were unclouded, unalloyed, by my weaknesses, errors of judgment, and faults of temper."

Mary Cameron's death symbolized the break with his past

[1] *Vanguard*, vol. I, p. 84.

which had already occurred in his political career. Still only
thirty-six, Harney was to live longer than he had yet lived; and
though not vigorous, he was entering an age which should have
been his prime of life. The fact was that every step he took from
this time carried him away from the main currents of English
politics. In a valedictory which appeared in the last number of
the *Vanguard*, he wrote that his main interest and hope in the
future lay not in English politics but in the progress of Continental democracy; yet even here the rising tide of middle-class
Radicalism was nudging him out of contact with the foreign
refugees. It was the "respectable" classes who took the main
role in pro-refugee organizations in 1853, with their societies to
aid Mazzini and Kossuth; and even if Harney had not been
cool toward these bourgeois leaders, the associations supporting
them had no desire for the help of a man so thoroughly identified
with "Red Republicanism" as Harney. There was also the
harsh truth that without a newspaper and an organization his
influence was worth little.

The ultra-radical section of the emigration was itself deter-
iorating both in morale and numbers, as their hope of revolution
on the Continent melted away. Like Harney, many had believed revolt would come when Napoleon tried to establish
complete control, but the acceptance of his *coup d'état* of December
1851 put an end to that. A small minority turned to plotting
the assassination of Napoleon (as early as March 1853 the omnipresent Sergeant Sanders found an infernal machine in a
refugee's house). But the bulk of the *émigrés*, having lost their
hope of an early return to their countries, were settling into
English life. Harney's old friend, Carl Schapper, one of the
fieriest of the German revolutionaries in the past, had become a
publican in Long Acre; and it seems that the indefatigable Sergeant Sanders—to revert to him once more—had a pint with
him and Willich there on occasion. Such an atmosphere of
petit-bourgeois respectability meant the destruction of another of
Harney's *raisons d'être*.

The foreign colony, with which his connection had long been
so close, was not only being absorbed to some extent by English
society, but was emigrating to America in increasing numbers.
The final acceptance of the permanence of the conservative victory on the Continent was the main motive in this exodus; and
the English government's policy of financial aid for the political

refugees to emigrate made it possible.[1] In the six years after 1852 the numbers of the emigration were halved by departures for New York. Harney was not immune to this reaction of hopelessness, nor to the desire to make a new start which was causing his own countrymen as well to leave England in great numbers. "At times, we lose heart in our struggle, though we never lose faith in our principles, nor in their ultimate triumph, only it may be so long first," he wrote in 1852. "What wonder that we are sometimes driven to echo the cry, 'Let's Emigrate'." [2]

"Only it may be so long"—a great deal was summed up in that short phrase. A world of social justice would come one day (or what had all of his efforts been for?); meanwhile, what was he to do? The causes, both domestic and foreign, which had absorbed much of his youth and all of his adult life were, temporarily at any rate, lost. How quickly a working-class leader and journalist could drop from the public eye when bereft of an organ of publicity was shown by his almost complete absence from notice in the Radical press. In July, the Fraternal Democrats made what seems to have been their last public utterance and a few months later, in the intense excitement which followed the outbreak of the Russo-Turkish War, Harney appeared with Duncombe at a public meeting which demanded an English declaration of war on Russia. Other than in these reports, no mention was made of him.

There remained but one more incident to complete this fateful year for Harney. On 28 November, at a joint meeting of democratic Poles and English operatives in Holborn, Harney's proposal as chairman was the signal for an outburst of hostility between his supporters and Jones's Chartists. Finlen declared that Harney, as an unworthy representative of English democracy, ought not to be allowed to represent foreign democracy—a statement accompanied by shouts at Harney of "dry-bones", "renegade", "traitor", and counter-cheers. The meeting then degenerated into a brawl, and only with the arrival of the police was order restored. Harney had been struck several times and had been forced to give way to a French chairman—as Marx

---

[1] Assistance to enable refugee emigration was rendered with considerable circumspection from Secret Service funds. That the assistance was utilized is attested by a bill for passages submitted to the Home Office in May 1852 for the sum of £1,380. (See H.O.: O.S. 45/4,302, correspondence between Foreign Office and Home Office, 9, 19 January, 6 May 1852; bills and letters of 23 April 1852.)

[2] *Star of Freedom*, 24 July 1852.

wrote with great relish to Engels, "Thus the nemesis for Father George Julian Harney".[1]

The "stupid Poles" (Marx's term) had supported Harney in this fracas, as well as a section of the English operatives, but the incident was a painful one for all that. It was plain that Harney's estrangement from the Jones faction limited his usefulness to the refugees. At a more sedate meeting on the following night, graced by the presence of Ruge, Herzen, Ledru Rollin and Worcell, Harney was not present. There had been years in the past when he alone had organized banquets to commemorate the Polish Revolution; now that the Russo-Turkish war had, in the words of this meeting, brought the "hour of deliverance" near for the Poles, Hungarians and Italians, Harney was either not asked, or refused to attend. The incident was trivial, but its implications were tragic enough. There was, in short, no room for Harney in London, and in December he left for Newcastle, where his young middle-class Republican friend, Joseph Cowen, Jr., had offered him an editorial position on the new weekly he was launching. Harney was not to live again in London until he returned to Richmond thirty-five years later.

*   *   *

He had, perhaps, wanted too much. In an eloquent statement of his ideal society, Harney had written in the middle of his struggle to unite the main forces in working-class life into a new party:[2]

> "It is not any amelioration of the condition of the most miserable that will satisfy us; it is justice to all we demand. It is not the mere improvement of the social life of our class that we seek; but the abolition of classes and the destruction of those wicked distinctions which have divided the human race into princes and paupers, landlords and labourers, masters and slaves. It is not any patching and cobbling of the present system we aspire to accomplish, but the annihilation of that system, and the substitution instead of an order of things in which all shall labour and all enjoy, and the happiness of each guarantee the welfare of the entire community."

To desire the overthrow of English capitalism at a time when it was entering a period of unprecedented growth made disappointment inevitable. This can be said looking back on it, but

---

[1] 2 December 1853, *Briefwechsel*, vol. I, p. 515.
[2] *Red Republican*, 12 October 1850.

the experience of the 1830's and 1840's had given Harney no such knowledge. What he predicated the success of a social-democratic party on was the recurrence of the economic crises he had experienced. These did recur, but in a much less acute form. Meanwhile there was a material bettering of working-class conditions, an improvement attributed to the system he fought against. From Lovett, through Thomas Cooper, to O'Connor, the path of Chartist leaders had led into the middle-class Radical camp, and it was, in a larger sense, the path of the Chartist movement. Harney, after a political life which more than that of any other Chartist leader's exemplified an intransigent hostility to the middle-class, had been unable to follow, and so cut himself off from one vital part of British political life.

What he had tried to do was to weld Chartism into an advance-guard which would maintain its identity and carry on a social democratic propaganda to prepare the working classes for their accession to power, when the mechanism of distress made a mass movement possible again. Realizing that industrial activity had succeeded political activity for a time, he had also attempted to unite with the political elements of the co-operative and trades-union movements, so that when they failed—as he thought they inevitably must through the legal obstruction of the propertied class—and turned once more to the struggle for political power, an organization for this purpose would be in existence. These were the tactics which he pursued from 1849 to 1853.

Whether there was any chance of their success is extremely doubtful. Such events as the passage of the Industrial and Provident Societies Act in June 1852, a great step toward the legalization of co-operative societies, particularly with reference to protection of their funds, robbed him of one of his most effective arguments. Here was the propertied class aiding working-class industrial action—another of the appeasements by which they relieved working-class pressures throughout the century. And Jones's opposition—which, as Harney abandoned the old N.C.A., became the policy of Chartism—negated Harney's last attempt to put his theories into practice. Who was right, assuming that any policy to keep an independent working-class political movement alive would have succeeded?

Certainly Jones's strictures on the dangers of co-operation becoming an extension of "joint-stock shop-keeping" have been shown to be not without foundation. But his objections to Harney's policy in 1851–52 had largely evaporated by 1853, at which time he was calling for what was in effect a Chartist-Trades party. Marx, who supported Jones's views at the time of the split between the two Chartist leaders, virtually paraphrased Harney's arguments about the co-operative movement little more than ten years later in the address he drafted for the International Working Men's Association; and that Association itself was composed of the "aristocracy of labour" which Jones attacked in 1852. If these views were right in 1853 or 1864, were they wrong at the time Harney promulgated them?

These are questions only of theory, and answers can be only speculative. Possibly no tactics would have preserved an independent working-class political party. But Chartism after 1848 has its significance as an intellectual movement, though it had lost its mass-following; and it is worth noting in this connection that Harney's grasp of events and the tactics he suggested anticipated Jones's and Marx's. In spite of his strong romantic bent, he was far from the empty-headed spouter etched by Marx and Engels. He was, in fact, anticipating by a half-century those empirical British working-class leaders who were finally to attempt to build a non-Marxist socialist state.

Moreover, though the Chartist organization had died, the ideas to which he had contributed so greatly during the decline of the movement persisted, to re-emerge in the 1880's. Nor had the efforts of the hundreds of thousands of anonymous Chartists who had marched under the banner of the Six Points and social justice been for nothing. As Harney summed it up in a prescient valedictory on the movement in October 1852:

"Chartism itself will survive the wreck of parties and the ruin of politicians. Apparently it has fallen into contempt, and is nearly consigned to oblivion; but in truth its spirit has begun to exercise an influence over the country's politics; and all parties in turn have come to acknowledge the potency of that democratic opinion. . . ."

CHAPTER X

Retreat

HARNEY'S departure from London in December 1853 was symbolic—the first step in a journey which took him away from the main current of British politics and, finally, from England itself. There was, in truth, little of working-class politics to leave behind. Feargus O'Connor, who more than any man had epitomized Chartism, was tranquilly suspended on a water mattress in Doctor Tuke's asylum slowly sinking into a happy idiocy and death, mercifully unaware of the litigious aftermath of his Land Company.[1] Though Ernest Jones was attempting to revitalize the organization in a "Labour Parliament", the Chartist cortex, like O'Connor's, was almost dead and the movements at the extremities were without meaning. And going to Newcastle was symbolic in another sense as well for Harney. It meant an alliance with middle-class Radicalism, personified by the young republican, Joseph Cowen, Jr.

The strongest bond between Harney and Cowen was their mutual sympathy for the European nationalist movements. Newcastle had compelling associations from the past for Harney —much had happened to him there since the Christmas Day in 1838 when he had first arrived half-frozen on top of a stage-coach—but the Tyne district had a more immediate appeal as a field for action, being regarded in London as the focal point of the English agitation for "European freedom". For this, Cowen could take much credit. If his father had not invented a process whereby clay could take the place of cast-iron in certain types of

---

[1] O'Connor had gone back to live in a happier past. In a painful scene at the time of his interview by a Lunacy Commission in April 1853 in the garden at Doctor Tuke's, he was unable to talk of current events, but strode up and down singing with his great voice the song which thousands had sung on his release from York Castle a dozen years before:

The Lion of Freedom has come from his den,
We'll rally around him again and again,
We'll crown him with laurel, our champion to be,
O'Connor—the patriot for sweet liberty.

According to Doctor Tuke, "everything was with him *couleur de rose*" (*Reynolds's Weekly Newspaper*, 17 April 1853; *Lancet*, quoted in *ibid.*, 26 August 1855).

pipe and thus made a modest fortune, it is possible that the son's republican enthusiasm might not have seemed so respectable, nor his influence have been so considerable on Tyneside. But young Cowen himself, in spite of his black clothes a size too large, his contempt for "society", and his friendships with working men, managed to keep within the pale of respectability by application to the family clay-works. He was known as a plain, unconventional man who eschewed "Esquire" and spent much time on foreigners; but his industry assured him the Victorian imprimatur: as one local eulogist put it, "To his honour, be it recorded, *he never neglects his business*." [1] Yet he was a good deal more than this, being in a moderate way an active European revolutionary.

Cowen's efforts were not limited to his activities on behalf of the *émigrés* in England, which brought Hungarian and Polish refugees to settle on Tyneside and gained him the friendship of Mazzini, Kossuth and other revolutionary leaders. Following in the English tradition of personal intervention when government failed to act—typified in the past by Byron and Lord Cochrane and in 1860 by the "private excursion to Mount Vesuvius" of "English tourists" in aid of Garibaldi—the odd bourgeois in the ill-fitting clothes used his firm's name in letters of recommendation for Polish "commercial travellers" on the Continent; barrels of his fire-brick arrived in Danzig and were relieved through an elaborate clandestine organization of inflammatory pamphlets; and, evidently, he knew something of the plotting which led to Orsini's unsuccessful attempt on Louis Napoleon's life in 1858. [2]

The young manufacturer had not drunk at such pure radical springs as had Harney, however, nor had he experienced the poverty which made Harney's attitude toward the *status quo* what it was. While they were one with regard to foreign questions, the disparity of their backgrounds was reflected in their views on domestic policy. Harney was a social-democrat; Cowen, in spite of his support of the *Red Republican* in the past, remained a republican in the Mazzinian tradition. To Harney, the "Republic" meant a social as well as political democracy; with Cowen the term connoted a latter-day Athens of duties and

---

[1] *Northern Examiner*, 11 January 1856.

[2] Secret correspondence with the Poles (Cowen Collection, Newcastle Central Library). The correspondence is fragmentary and appears to have been treated with heat, perhaps to make invisible ink show. Jane Cowen recorded in her diary (Cowen Collection) that her father destroyed most of his dangerous correspondence following news of Orsini's arrest.

virtues. Like Mazzini and Carlyle, Cowen was a moralist, and one hears echoes of both men in his writing. "Capital has its duties as well as its rights, and there ought to be closer than a mere money-bond between 'masters' and 'men'." [1] Yet his status *was* that of the "master", and a prudent, if paternal, attitude toward the application of his belief left him sometimes not far from the Manchester brethren he detested. After all, "sweetmeats *did* often kill the baby", and "Charity sapped the reliance of the working population", to paraphrase the aphorisms in his youthful scrapbook. It was with this complex young man, later to become a Radical M.P. and a power in reform movements, that Harney worked closely for two years.

The arrangement was mutually beneficial. Cowen needed expert editorial help for his new monthly, the *Northern Tribune*, which first appeared on 1 January 1854; Harney was unemployed and doubtless glad to accept the £1 weekly he received for his labours—a common salary for a provincial editor, if a sad come-down from the £4 he had been paid by Feargus on the *Northern Star*. His direct influence on the *Tribune's* editorial policy was secondary. A local editor, remembering Harney from 1839, saw his hand in the "mad barricade style of composition and Robespierre political logic" of the *Tribune* and advised that he "put himself or be put under restraint";[2] but it is difficult to see what excited this choleric outburst. It was the moderate republicanism of W. J. Linton, the ex-Chartist engraver and journalist who published the magazine at his remote house in the Lake District with the aid of a disciple or two, which dominated the *Tribune's* pages. This brand of republicanism, also characteristic of the "Republican Brotherhood", a short-lived organization launched by Cowen and Harney in 1855, found its model not in the French Republic of 1793 but the Puritan Commonwealth; its patron saint was Oliver Cromwell, not Robespierre. As its adherents admitted, however, the achievement of the English Republic lay far in the future—and Harney, to whom arguments about political systems had always seemed unimportant compared with the actual exercise of political and social power by the working class, did not defend his revered Revolution in print.

In any case, the pall of working-class apathy in domestic ques-

---

[1] *Northern Tribune*, vol. I, p. 63 (February 1854).
[2] North and South Shields *Gazette*, 3 November 1854.

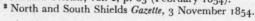

tions made such discussions academic. Unrest had by no means disappeared, as riots and mass-meetings in Devon, Birmingham and London protesting the high price of bread in 1854 and 1855 attested; and wage-cuts in 1855 resulted in the familiar spectacle of thousands of operatives fighting police and yeomanry in Warwickshire. Nor had the class-hostility of the 'forties been transmuted; fine clothes were sufficient to provoke manhandling in the Hyde Park demonstrations against a Sunday-closing bill in 1855.[1] But these outbursts aroused little interest, for in March 1854 Britain declared war on Russia and popular attention was absorbed by events in the Near East. With this event, the *Northern Tribune* became the organ of the ultra-radical war party in Newcastle.

In its initial enthusiasm for the war the British public was almost united. The glory of Waterloo was remembered; the carnage which had sickened the Duke of Wellington was not (though enthusiasm led few to recruiting offices and one gets the impression from British casualty lists that the war was fought by the Irish). All classes shared the sense of a righteous crusade against Russian aggression, and the sober protesting voices of Cobden and Bright were drowned out in the exhilarating idealism expressed by Tennyson's "Maud". Through a familiar process, the Turks were rationalized into the defenders of liberalism; Turkey became the European bastion against despotism; and if the general public was even vaguer about war aims than the cabinet headed by Lord Aberdeen—who thought the war an act of folly—patriotic fervour was for the moment enough.

One section of popular opinion, however, the revolutionary war party, had very definite ideas about what the object of the struggle with the "loathsome Nicholas" should be. "The hour is now striking for the unavoidable national struggle", proclaimed the Polish Central Democratic Committee—a belief echoed by the rest of the emigration who, united at least in this, saw the war as the long-awaited opportunity for a general European uprising of the suppressed nationalities and the overturning of the conservative victors of 1848–49. "What now glitters in the desperate grasp of Turkey is not the old dented scimitar of Othman, but the brilliant lightning of revolution," Victor Hugo

---

[1] An amusing cartoon in *Punch* (24 November 1855) depicts a Cockney dandy saying to a friend: " 'Go and walk in Hyde Park? Oh, ah!—I dessay!—and get pelted for a Haristocrat?—No thank'e—Not if I know it.' "

wrote in the *Northern Tribune* from his exile in Jersey; and Marx, stirred to a similar poetic flight, believed the conflict would result in revolution coming forth "in shining armour and sword in hand, like Minerva from the head of the Olympian".[1]

The English exponents of this view were a heterogeneous lot, ranging from old Chartists to the amorphous group of middle-class reformers who were whiling away the tedium of the domestic political doldrums by their efforts in the exiles' cause. The greater part of the extreme war party's support came from the working class; and the veteran ex-Chartist leaders now had what was to be their last innings in a common cause, only Bronterre O'Brien opposing the war on the ground that it was a ruling-class device to distract the working class from its grievances. London was one centre of the agitation to encourage a Polish rising; Newcastle, due to the efforts of Harney and Cowen, was another. In both, there was an element of middle-class Radical participation; but the Manchester School's hostility to the war prevented them from making political capital out of joint action.

"The people have been deluded into believing the war would favour the nationalities," Cobden told the House in July 1854. Harney had reluctantly arrived at the same conclusion a month before. Austria's alignment with the allies, though she did not engage in overt hostilities, meant the early blighting of Harney's hope that the Aberdeen cabinet would encourage a Polish rising for independence, thus setting off revolutions in Hungary and Italy. Mazzini, in his furious reaction to what he considered the government's pro-Austrian policy, broke away from the unanimous support for the war which had hitherto united the *émigrés*, and by the following year had come to a position in most respects indistinguishable from that of Bright. Harney's reaction, and that of the Radical working class, was equally outraged, but it took another form. Public meetings of working men began to pass resolutions condemning the ministry, and the use of the terms "treason" and "connivance" became common in the Radical press's references to the conduct of the war. The terms were evidence of the persistent propaganda of David Urquhart, now finding an audience because of government policy; and Harney and Cowen were faced with a double task—to stimulate

---

[1] Karl Marx, *The Eastern Question*, edited by Edward and Eleanor Marx Aveling (London: 1899), p. 435. This book is a collection of correspondence written by Marx, and very likely, Engels, for the New York *Tribune* during the years 1853–56.

protest against the cabinet's anti-revolutionary stand, and at the same time to gain control of the Newcastle "Foreign Affairs Committee", organized by two ardent Urquhartites, George Crawshay, a Gateshead manufacturer, and Charles Attwood, brother of the Radical Birmingham banker who had presented the National Petition of 1839 to the House of Commons.

Urquhart's views, aired in person by the ubiquitous Russophobe before a large Newcastle audience in October, are interesting not only for their content but for the number of adherents they gained as the war passed from ineptitude to futility in 1854 and 1855. After a brief sojourn as an English consular official in Constantinople during the 1830's, Urquhart had spent the ensuing years crying the alarm about Russian expansionism. The first aim of Russian policy, he declared, was domination of Constantinople and the Straits; this accomplished, they would turn to the domination of Europe and Asia through the creation of satellite states.[1] All this has a prophetic ring, but the seer had become obsessed by his vision: Urquhart found Russian influence everywhere. The Welsh Chartist rising of 1839 had been a Russian plot; Palmerston was the "paid tool of St. Petersburg"; every European cabinet was a nest of Russian-dominated mercenaries.[2] Marx, who respected and utilized Urquhart's diplomatic research, was scarcely exaggerating this phobia when he wrote ironically of the outbreak of cholera in Newcastle late in 1853, "If I shared the opinions of Mr. Urquhart, I should say that the Czar had dispatched the cholera morbus to England with the 'secret mission' to break down the last remnant of what is called the 'Anglo-Saxon spirit'."[3]

[1] Urquhart, whose views on Russia have been given a fresh interest by contemporary developments, has only engaged the attention of one full-length biographer, Gertrude Robinson, in her *David Urquhart* (Oxford: 1920). For special studies, see G. H. Bolsover, "David Urquhart and the Eastern Question", *Journal of Modern History* (December 1936), and Sir Charles Webster, "Urquhart, Ponsonby, and Palmerston", *Journal of English History* (July 1946).

[2] *Cf.* David Urquhart, *The Crown of Denmark Disposed of by a Religious Minister through a Fraudulent Minister*, published anonymously (London: 1853), pp. 36–37; *The Progress of Russia*, 5th edition (London: 1853), preface to 3rd edition. An M.P. for a brief period, Urquhart, who had been discharged from the foreign service by Palmerston in 1837, tried to have him impeached in 1848 on grounds of treason. Urquhart had very nearly not lived so long: Major Beniowski, Harney's old associate of the London Democratic Association days, almost throttled him in front of the Carlton Club in the early 'forties after Urquhart had labelled him a Russian spy.

[3] Karl Marx, *The Eastern Question*, p. 140. The day of bomber-carried potato-bugs and germ warfare, Communist version, was yet to come.

At the time of Urquhart's arrival in Newcastle his attitude toward the war was, in some respects, that of Harney and Cowen. "With Mr. Urquhart we denounce the cry of 'peace at any price'," wrote Harney. "With him we wish to see the war carried on honestly and thoroughly for the destruction of Russian ascendency." [1] The two men were prepared to go as far as Urquhart in condemning the cabinet as "treasonable", but with this the difference in their attitudes toward the war became irreconcilable. Harney and Cowen believed the government was not honestly pursuing victory because of its failure to arm the Poles and raise a European revolution; to Urquhart, "treason" meant the actual secret support of Russia by Palmerston and others of the cabinet—the war was a Russian-inspired hoax. But where Harney, whose reaction to Urquhart hovered between exasperation and amusement, really took issue with him was over the role that European national revolutions could play in the destruction of Russian power. Under the fantastic shadow cast by the Russian bear on Urquhart's mind, the revolutionaries were also tools of the Russians. Kossuth had served them as effectively as the "traitor" Gorgey; Mazzini was a Muscovite agent.

Urquhart's almost mesmeric influence over such solid citizens as Charles Attwood and Crawshay should not surprise observers of the modern American scene. These men had been convinced by him that every diplomat's closet contained a Russian and respectable statesmen were doing the work of St. Petersburg. And it is only mildly surprising to read Attwood's comment on his idol: "He is one of those natural lords and rulers of the human race whom it is vain to look for but at intervals of distant ages . . . etc." Being a successful man of business constituted no guarantee that he could not also be a fool about other affairs. What is somewhat puzzling, however, is that Urquhart's considerable following in Newcastle included a large working-class element, for the Russophobe made no secret of the fact that he was a "Tory of the time of Queen Anne" and that part of his messianic task was to lead England back to that Eden. [2] Un-

---

[1] *Northern Tribune*, vol. I, p. 391 (December 1854).

[2] This sense of destiny, shared in a properly subordinate way by Attwood, accounts for the note of solemn nonsense which permeated their relationship—as in Attwood's account of their first meeting in 1838: to Attwood's question as to how he proposed to "save" England, Urquhart replied, "With twelve men, of whom you are one" (Birmingham *Mercury*, 7 July 1855).

doubtedly his monomania carried conviction to some. In 1840 he had split the Chartists in Newcastle and had some success with those in Glasgow and Carlisle; and in the winter of 1854, as Harney admitted, " 'The faith as it is in Urquhart' " had a respectable number of adherents on Tyneside.[1]

From the belief that the war was a Russian-inspired hoax to the advocacy of the withdrawal of British troops from the Crimea was but a short step, and before the beginning of 1855 the Urquhartites had become a peace organization. Despite his disgust with the failure of the cabinet to put arms in the hands of the Poles and his growing sense of futility, Harney was unwilling to abandon his support of the war. In the bitter infighting which followed over control of the Foreign Affairs Committee Attwood was no match for his experienced opponent and by March the Urquhart faction had been repudiated and resigned. Harney's victory anticipated the concerted attack made on Urquhart's national organization later in the year, mainly by Chartists, the outcome of which permitted Harney to write, "The Urquhart hubbub is disposed of, the bubble is no more." [2]

He had gained control of the Committee, yet the struggle seems hardly to have been worth the effort. The Committee could usually find someone at Westminster to present its petitions, but their demands were not even dignified by a response. Defeated on many questions, the coalition ministry proved obdurate in its war policy, even when Louis Napoleon threatened to arm the Poles in the last months of the war. It was quite apparent by the spring of 1855 that the efforts of the extreme war party to influence the government were hopeless. A widespread sympathy existed for the Poles and other nationalities, but the general feeling was that it was both untimely and inexpedient to push their cause while the war continued.

The ineffectuality of ultra-radical opinion brought home to Harney once again the necessity for domestic reform. "The Deluge seems to be at hand, 'the time is ripe and rotten for a change'," he wrote wishfully in March. The governing classes had been weighed and found wanting—an opinion repeated in Marx's aphorism a few months later: "War passes supreme judgment on social organizations that have outlived their vitality." [1] But while the ineptitude with which the war had been waged was being used by the unenfranchised to attack the argument that power was being exercised by those "fit to govern", the harvest time for this attack lay in the future. The immediate result of the stalemate before Sebastopol—and Gladstone's doubling of the income tax—was to multiply the adherents of Bright's demand for peace. Harney's urgent call for a renewal of popular agitation for universal suffrage did not stir a ripple of interest. It was, in fact, a last desperate affirmation of belief, for with the March issue the *Northern Tribune* ceased publication, a victim of working-class indifference.

The "Republican Brotherhood", organized by Harney and Cowen early in the year, suffered from the same apathy. Other than in exciting the loyal citizens of Newcastle to circulate handbills condemning their "rabid and seditious attacks on the British monarchy", the Brotherhood attracted almost no attention. An effort to combine all of the democratic and socialist clubs in the Tyne area during the summer met with some small success, but the importance of this lay also in the future, when the same elements, united under Cowen's leadership in the Northern Reform Union, exercised a considerable influence in the reform agitation of the 1860's. It was only too plain that Harney had once again enlisted in a lost cause. The source of his income during the summer of 1855 is not evident; what was evident was that he had reached the end of another *cul-de-sac*. Thus a series of events which began in late September and burgeoned into a minor *cause célèbre* found him ready to cut the few remaining ties which bound him to England. The origin of these events lay in a public letter written by Felix Pyat, a leader of the extreme left *Commune Revolutionnaire* in London, which attacked Queen Victoria's recent visit to England's ally, Napoleon III, and threatened the "bloody usurper and assassin of December 2nd". Within a month, the repercussions of the letter's appearance had taken Harney to Jersey.

Despite the element of the comic in what followed, the consequences could well have been serious for all of the political refugees enjoying British sanctuary. Pyat's letter went almost unnoticed in England, but its re-publication in *L'Homme*, the journal of the French exiles in Jersey, set off a chain of incidents which resulted in the expulsion of *L'Homme's* staff, and, as a

[1] *The Eastern Question*, p. 576 (*New York Tribune*, 24 September 1855).

result of their protest, Victor Hugo and thirty-four other refugees to Guernsey and London. The suspicious promptitude with which placards had appeared in St. Helier with an English translation of the letter which made the most of what was, in any case, not overly delicate in the original;[1] the deliberate incitement of mob-action by a secret group including a French official in St. Helier and the omnipresent Sergeant Sanders, the Metropolitan Police refugee expert; and communications between the French and English governments on the one hand and instructions from the Home Office to the Lieutenant Governor in Jersey on the other: all this makes it sufficiently clear that *L'Homme's* publication of the letter was seized upon as a pretext by the government to expel the refugees.

Moreover, under the pressure of Louis Napoleon's increasingly angry demands for action against the French *émigrés*, it would seem that the government entertained the idea of re-enacting an Alien Act. Certainly Palmerston, now the Prime Minister, was not averse to such an action. The *Morning Post*, generally believed to be a mouthpiece of his, had been sending up trial balloons about an Alien Act since August, and three years later in peace-time he was to attempt the passage of strong measures against the refugees under less pressing circumstances.[2] Considering their ignorance of the government's dispatches, the Radicals' diagnosis of the real motives behind the expulsion was remarkably accurate; and even the pro-government *Times* immediately assumed that French pressure was responsible for the action. The result was a great outcry in England from Liberals and working-class Radicals against the violation of the traditional right of sanctuary for political refugees and the threat of an Alien Act, the effect of which was to effectually block any steps by the cabinet.

Meanwhile, as the envoy of the Newcastle Foreign Affairs Committee, Harney had arrived in St. Helier in time to see

---

[1] E.g. "You [the Queen] have had your knee kissed by thirty Arabian chiefs *under* your garter. . . . Yes, you have sacrificed all! . . . even CHASTITY!" To render "*la pudeur*" as "chastity" was, Harney noted on the margin of one of the placards, "A wrong translation" (*Translation of the Insulting Letter to the Queen*, Cowen Collection).

[2] Napoleon's appeasement in late 1855 was particularly urgent because of his desire to bring home troops from the Crimea, which constituted a threat to Palmerston's policy of continuing the war. For the communications between the two governments regarding the refugees and an Alien Act, see F.O. 27/1094 and 27/1105, October 1855.

Hugo and his compatriots sail in a driving rain for what they considered but a temporary refuge in Guernsey and London. He found that sober second-thoughts had begun to afflict the local inhabitants, many of whom had shown little enthusiasm for the demonstrations against the "Red Republicans" from the first. ("An officer offered a sovereign to a workman to be the first to throw a stone; the workman refused," one observer reported of the "attack" on *L'Homme's* office which preceded the expulsion.)[1] Loyalty to the Queen may have been a dominant Jersey characteristic, but jealousy of any encroachments on the island's legislative body, the "States", was even stronger; and uneasiness about the arbitrariness of the action taken by the Lieutenant Governor—an appointive official whose position was evidently regarded in England as a sinecure for deserving brigadiers and in Jersey as having only nominal powers—soon took overt form. Defending the Governor's and his own action, the Constable of St. Helier made heavy weather of it in the States. "We all know they [the refugees] insulted us. Have they not carried their red flag in our streets?" he asked with considerable irrelevance, adding, in a pungent comment on Jersey justice, "Had we brought the offenders before the court, it would only have been acting a comedy, which would never have an end."[2]

If it had been Harney's intention to rally support in Jersey for the exiles, his work was already being done for him in the typically devious local manner. A few weeks after his arrival he journeyed to Guernsey and, in a ceremony widely reported in the English liberal and ultra-radical press, presented an address to Hugo from the Foreign Affairs Committee pledging the support of the Tyneside working class. Hugo's thanks to "*notre courageuse co-religionnaire*" were undoubtedly heartfelt: Harney epitomized one section of a popular support which had forcefully indicated that English sanctuary for refugees was a matter that deeply concerned them. The whole affair was no more than a minor incident, perhaps; nonetheless it was an admirable display of liberal idealism in a Europe over which the forces of reaction had been uniformly victorious. So far as Harney's future was concerned, his part in the display had the paradoxical effect of taking him another step from English politics.

He was now thirty-eight, ill, tired, and once more adrift. Jersey must have seemed to him a soothing refuge, green and

[1] *Reasoner*, 11 November 1855   [2] Jersey *Weekly Times*, 19 November 1855.

fertile and ruled by laws and customs which teetered always on the thin edge of satire. One aftermath of the Hugo expulsion illustrates the tendency for the serious to lapse into the farcical on the island. As the Chevalier de Châtelaine indignantly informed the public, "Evangeline", the "saint-like daughter of Longfellow's muse", had shared the fate of the expelled refugees. The *Nouvelle Chronique*, which had been printing his translation of the poem into French, had suppressed the lines: "After your houses are built, and your fields are yellow with harvests,/No King George of England shall drive you away from your homesteads." This editorial ruthlessness could only mean one thing, wrote the Chevalier: "The journal thought fit to suppress so incendiary a passage, no doubt by command from headquarters." [1]

In 1855, Jersey could have served even better than pre-Reform England as the whipping-boy for a Jeremy Bentham. The laws, part English, part Norman, and thoroughly anachronistic, and the vaguely defined relationship between the local legislature and the "Sovereign in Council", provided an inexhaustible mine for lawyers. Coupled with this antique legal machinery was the inveterate local litigiousness expressed by the aphorism, "An Englishman goes on holiday; a Jerseyman goes to court." Periodic attempts to codify or modernize the law had failed because of the resistance of the seigneurs, who retained some feudal rights and controlled the States and the Royal Court, or because of insular jealousy when the reform was bruited in the form of an Order in Council. As an anonymous writer of doggerel pointed out in regard to a particularly crying abuse: "You may think this not fair, but the States, Sir, know best,/And the States will remain *statu quo*, Sir." [2]

Harney knew something of this. Nine years before in the *Northern Star* he had printed letters from Jersey in which the writers heaped vituperation on each other over issues which seemingly never died. But in his initial contact with Jersey he probably felt the common bewilderment of Englishmen at the customs of the island. Palmerston, for example, conning the Channel Islands correspondence in 1854 in his capacity as Home Secretary, found that a debtor had been in a Jersey gaol since 1845, and asked in some astonishment if there was no Insolvent Debtors Act there. Even Engels, whose German background

[1] Letter in the Jersey *Weekly Times*, 1 December 1855.
[2] Jersey *Independent*, 23 February 1856.

made him not unfamiliar with the peculiarities of small principalities, was struck by this small appendage of Britain. "There is much humour in the posthumous feudal setup and the whole mess is incredibly comical," he wrote to Marx from the island in 1857. "A modern lawyer as seigneur and the shopkeepers of St. Helier as vassals. The masquerade is quite a joke." [1]

But if the legal system and land-laws badly needed reform, Jersey was not unique in this, and it possessed charms which almost justified the hyperbole of guide-book authors. Madame Hugo had found the country superb and the food cheap and abundant on her arrival in 1852; and though subsequent events give more than a trace of irony to her original impression, Jersey had seemed to her pre-eminently a land of freedom. "Passports are papers of which the meaning is not understood," she wrote. "Everybody comes and goes as suits his particular fancy." [2] To complete this exile's paradise, residents were taxed only with a nominal police rate, and there were no duties, tolls or stamps.

What this meant to Harney is not difficult to imagine. There was little in England for him to go back to—not even a living, so far as one can tell. While he had had no intention of remaining in Jersey when he arrived to aid the refugees, a bout of fever and general exhaustion kept him there until the new year, and when he had recovered he stayed on. The opportunity being offered him to edit the small, twice-weekly Jersey Independent, he accepted, probably with alacrity. Like Newcastle, Jersey may have seemed a *cul-de-sac*, but there was at any rate a garden at the end of it— the pleasant old tree-lined Royal Square, which could be gazed upon while consuming the excellent and inexpensive "beakers of burgundy" of which he was fond.

Even if the exact date of Harney's accession as editor of the *Independent* were lacking, it would be possible to date it closely from changes in the paper. In July a new and clearer format was introduced; the news content, both foreign and local, was increased; and the familiar vigorous and polemical style imposed itself on the leading articles. As early as April, one "Anglo-Caesarean" had inveighed against the persecution of an Italian exile; after 5 July (when Harney took up the reins) a regular correspondent calling himself "Englishman" made his appearance, and in company with another new regular, "Argus",

[1] 29 October 1857, *Briefwechsel*, vol. II, p. 235.
[2] Quoted in F. T. Marzials, *Life of Victor Hugo* (London: 1888), p. 150.

began to attack abuses at home and abroad. The style and view-point of this trio irresistibly suggest editorial ventriloquism. The *Independent* had been an earnest paper, but dull; now it became the most controversial and readable English-language newspaper in St. Helier, and in two years Harney's shrewd professional guidance made it the island's first daily.

The *Independent* was, as all of Harney's papers had been, a crusading journal. The duty of a newspaper, he informed his readers, was to "enlighten and lead the masses", as well as to collect and disseminate news. "Hitherto, plain-speaking—on the side of Truth and Freedom—had not been the rule in Jersey", he wrote in an early issue. "It is time, however, that a fashion so commendable should be introduced." "Fair Play" and "Constant Reader" now joined "Argus" & Co. in commending the editor when a proper response from his readers was not forth-coming—a claque that did not always escape the attention of the *Independent's* rivals.

The Jersey newspapers, which enjoyed a total weekly circulation of 16,000 in a population of 50,000, pandered to the appetites of an audience whose penchant for violence ("the hit on the nose", as the bilingual writers for the English-language papers put it) burdened the calendars of the Royal Court. "Personal abuse flourishes with a vigour worthy of Yankeedom," wrote one observer.[1] Harney lost no time in inhaling this bracing atmo-sphere, taking a projected visit of the Queen as an opportunity to comment judiciously on the fawning attitude of the "Jersey *Timeserver*" (the Jersey *Weekly Times*) and the "old fogies' journal, the superannuated *British Press*".

As the hot summer of 1856 wore on, he read of the Guards' triumphant return from the Crimea, their passage down White-hall in showers of flowers thrown by elegant ladies and their review at Aldershot by the Queen—irreverently likened to "one of Astley's female equestrians" in her tight red costume by *Reynolds's Weekly Newspaper*.[2] Harney wasted few words in

[1] J. B. Payne, *A Gossiping Guide to Jersey* (London: 1862), p. 197.

[2] 20 July 1856. "She certainly did her best to assume a martial appearance. But it would not do. Nature is, at times, too strong even for kings and queens. . . . The courtiers were crestfallen; they felt that they had made a blunder in permitting the preposterous exhibition. . . . Never, we venture to say, was a more unqueenly figure seen on horseback. The violent colours of the royal garb brought out in strong relief the squatness of the royal person. It is said that the Queen's advisers had the utmost difficulty in dissuading her from marching through London at the head of her troops."

mourning the opportunities lost in the war. The *Independent's* leading article on the evacuation of the Crimea featured instead the last Englishman to leave—a thoroughly intoxicated member of the Land Transport Corps retrieved from a ditch by six Cossacks. Harney suggested that he should rent himself out to English Teetotal Societies as a "shocking example".

Other echoes from lost causes reached Jersey, such as the tumultuous welcome by a London crowd of 10,000 of John Frost, the leader of the Welsh Chartist rising of 1839, on his return from Van Dieman's Land; but it is doubtful that Harney regretted not being in the centre of things. His happiness in his retreat is apparent not only in the relaxed humour of the *Independent's* leaders, but in the round of small activities which were to be typical of the next six years. His reputation, as well as the consistently radical attitude of the *Independent* toward foreign affairs, ensured him a standing with the considerable local *émigré* colony; to the Poles he was a heroic figure (". . . remember me to the Immortal Harney", wrote the Polish leader Constantine Lekawski to Joseph Cowen some years later).[1] It was natural when a distinguished refugee such as the famous Hungarian violinist Remenyi visited Jersey that the *Independent's* editor should preside over a fine dinner in his honour at the "Pomme d'Or" and give the toast to the "speedy liberation of Hungary". Such incidents shook no thrones, but they were pleasant.

His prestige was not limited to the *émigré* colony. By the time Engels, in ill health, visited Jersey in October 1857, Harney had become a leader of the radical party on the island—which, in the pre-1789 stage of Jersey's political development, meant the middle classes of St. Helier. In a letter to Marx soon after his arrival, Engels wrote of Harney:[2]

"He has acquired a strange appearance with a large, pitch-black beard, somewhat like the greasy Jew's who travelled in the small boat which landed us from the steamer—certainly an improvement. He regards his Jersey politics from the humorous point of view, saying he got a 'great deal of fun' from it, etc. . . . Later I went drinking with him and had him tell me about the local constitution, etc.; there was no talk of bygone days. For the moment he seems damn'd glad to have retired from high politics to his little kingdom of the blind. As a one-eyed man he is king of the opposi-

---

[1] 16 April 1867, Cowen Collection.
[2] 6 October 1857, *Briefwechsel*, vol. II, pp. 229–30.

tion: on his right the first grocer, on his left the first tallow-chandler in the town. . . . For Harney the whole history of Jersey is divided into two periods: that before and that after the expulsion of the toads. Both periods are distinguished by the fact that nothing happened in them."

The relative, if patronizing, forbearance shown in these remarks did not last long. A fortnight later he added to his original impression of Harney:[1]

"He is terribly stupid and feels most comfortable here in his petty critical [*spiessbürger*] role. . . . Naturally, he expects the English workers to do something sooner or later, but that something is by no means of a Chartist nature. Anyway, all this is only theoretical phraseology with him, and it would certainly be unpleasant to him to be uprooted from his little agitation here. He is very busy, but busy doing nothing."

Ignoring the tone of acidity reserved for those who did not see eye-to-eye with the two Germans, it is evident from Engels's description that Harney had contentedly resigned himself to his idyllic backwater. Without taking the petty politics of the island very seriously, he was enjoying himself. "Our Royal Court scenes, our States' debates, our political meetings, our newspaper polemics at least 'keep us alive'," he wrote subsequently.[2] Doubtless he would have minded very much being uprooted: where, after all, was he to go and how was he to live? Marx might live in great poverty, but, unlike Harney, he at least had a "Lieber Fred" with a Manchester mill to turn to in adversity. What really distinguished Engels and Marx from Harney, however, was their impenetrable sense of dedication and awareness of their historical importance. They were imbued with the fervour of the apostles of early Christianity; Harney was like a tired Roman reformer.

As to the basic question involved—Harney's loss of faith in an independent English working-class movement under the conditions then existing—it is not too much to say that his understanding of domestic political feeling was more acute than that of the two Germans. The trend in English working-class radicalism was away from an independent and class-conscious movement to the collaboration with the middle classes which issued in the Gladstonian Liberal party. It was this drift which

---

[1] 19 October 1857, *ibid.*, pp. 231–32.
[2] Jersey *Independent*, 13 September 1860.

constituted "high politics" in the late 'fifties so far as the Radical working class was concerned; not, as Marx and Engels wished it to be, working-class preparation for revolutionary changes in the economic crisis they believed was imminent. The events of 1858, when a sharp commercial slump had hit Britain, were to show whose "theoretical phraseology" was closer to reality.

Though Harney's preoccupation with local abuses seemed to Engels an abdication of his radical role it is more than doubtful that it represented anything of the kind to the established order in Jersey. The local Working Men's Association offered little scope for his reform efforts, being dominated by the local clergy and subject to lectures on such subjects as "Early Irish Music"; and Harney had turned his organizing zeal to the service of the class which suffered most from seigneurial domination and the anachronistic legal system—the "vassals" of Engels's satirical description. The "Reform League", which came into being in September 1856 under Harney's aegis, was composed mainly of merchants, small ship-owners, bank employees and the like; and the main object of their attacks was the monopoly of power exercised by the old families of the island.

This organization of the Radical middle class existed under one name or another during the entire period of Harney's stay in Jersey. Although it represented a powerful body of local opinion, its usefulness was impaired by the tendency of its leading members, in the rare event of their becoming Deputies in the States or Jurats (judges) of the Royal Court, to forget their grievances with those in power in the sharing of it. And while the *Independent* became known as the "eloquent organ of the reform party" so far away as Guernsey (twenty miles), it was as well for Harney that he retained a humorous objectivity about local politics, for the sober fact was that his support of candidates was, more often than not, fatal to their political ambitions.

Although the franchise was very limited in Jersey, this did not preclude election appeals to public opinion any more than it did in England. During the canvassing period accusations of treachery filled the newspapers; the town, even to the rather odd statue of George II in the Royal square, was placarded with a truly Italian political exuberance; and the Royal Court received a fresh batch of suits for libel—a contingency that seems to have deterred none of the defendants, possibly because so many were also plaintiffs. (One trick fruitful of lawsuits was that of issuing

placards which recommended a list of men for office, the majority
of whom were notorious local criminals—and among whom, of
course, was listed one's opponent.) Yet when the ranks of the old
families were threatened, they sank their differences and solidly
supported their order.

But if the "radicals" of Jersey were for the most part precluded from direct political action, they were still able to resort
to "bold clamour and abuse" (as the staid Jersey *Weekly Times*
put it); and in their new champion on the *Independent* they had
gained a craftsman with a long apprenticeship in this sort of
thing. Never hesitant in selecting the largest game, Harney chose
for his attack on the vested interests of Jersey the first lawyer of
St. Helier, François Godfray, who besides symbolizing the dominant vice of litigiousness on the island was also a great land-
owner, a prominent member of the States, a banker, and a
seigneur with a number of fiefs. Not yet a month in the editorial
chair, Harney began baiting this formidable Norman bull by
likening those whom he took to court to the unfortunate victims
of "Godfray's Cordial", a narcotic proprietary-medicine with
which Lancashire working-class mothers had been wont to
"quiet, stultify, and ultimately dose out of existence" their fret-
ting children.

This sport did not divert Harney's attention from the existence
of a serious grievance, however. In Jersey law, the feudal lords
and the Crown retained a claim to a year's possession of land
and its corn-rents when a tenant died without direct heirs; and
cases involving payments for inheriting or alienating property
were decided in the court dominated by seigneurs. Against this
system the Reform League and Harney tirelessly inveighed; and
after the omnipresent Godfray had "stultified" some poor tenants
in what they regarded as a particularly outrageous fashion in
1858, their clamour reached a peak. Shedding its skin, the
Reform League emerged with fresh vigour in the apt guise of the
"Anti-Feudal League"—an appearance which caused Godfray's
Le Constitutionnel, the most conservative paper in a scarcely
radical press, to hint darkly of the *rougées*, demagogues and followers of Voltaire behind it. The seigneur was no better than
Dick Turpin, Harney replied with gusto, and he would label
Godfray's action theft, if called before the Royal Court. The
opportunity was almost immediately offered him: hauled into the
court by the irate feudal lord on a charge of calumny, he was

unable to convince the bench of seigneurs that he had merely referred to Godfray as an "abstraction", and the suit began its tortuous journey through the antique Jersey legal machinery, to be quashed a few years later. But despite this irrepressible element of low-comedy, the end to which the "bold clamour" of the *Independent* and the Anti-Feudal League continued to be directed was achieved by the appointment of a Royal Commission to inquire into the Jersey land-laws in 1860.

Such teapot-tempests were a far cry from the revolutionary days of 1838–39, yet in a sense Harney was playing the same role as a catalyst for the forces of discontent. It is almost necessary to be a glacialist to discern movement of any kind in the Jersey society of these years, yet movement there was, and Harney was almost invariably involved in it. Certainly there was no lack of survivals evocative of the *Ancien Régime* to serve as objects for satirical attack. English conservatism of the time seems feverishly Jacobinical when compared with its Channel Island counterpart. In the matter of religion, for example, while the secularist lecturer, Charles Bradlaugh, had his slight difficulties with British audiences, in Guernsey his appearance was sufficient to cause a mob to pursue him to the quay shouting, "Pitch the infidel into the sea!" And echoes of a yet more distant past are to be heard in the accusations of witchcraft made by local citizens against a neighbour in a trial before the Royal Court so late as 1862.

Little wonder, then, that Harney was considered "*un grand Sans-Culottes anglais*" and worse in this semi-medieval (and rather endearing) society, where the term "Enlightenment" connoted opprobrium. Usually the attacks on him were merely verbal, though one editorial opponent "demanded satisfaction" after a particularly virulent interchange in which he had been bested by Harney's exposure of his past travels in France with a boa-constrictor. The tack generally taken was to condemn him as an atheist—one local journal triumphantly revealed to its readers that Harney possessed Voltaire's *Philosophical Dictionary*—and a Chartist revolutionary. His dangerous friends of the past and his trial for seditious conspiracy at Lancaster in 1843 were sufficient proof that he was plotting, through the medium of the *Independent*, to establish on the ruins of the Jersey constitution and Norman nationality a social republic *à la Marat*, declared the editor of *Le Constitutionnel* in 1858—ingenuously revealing the reason for his pique in concluding: "Hitherto his impostures have succeeded only too well in making dupes."

Harney was not mollified by this indirect compliment, and his reply may serve as an example of the virile polemics by which he had so quickly made himself one of the most controversial figures on that strange island. *La Prostitutionnel*, he began roundly, had raised the religious and Chartist questions in order to obscure the issue of Godfray's thieving and usurious conduct. Even if it were true that he was

> "a Mohammedan, a believer in Brahma, Vishnu and Siva; a Buddhist, a disbeliever in the blessed miracles of 'Brother Peter', and an atrocious atheist to the gospel according to St. Pusey. . . . That he was with FROST at Newport, with SMITH O'BRIEN at Ballingary, with ROBESPIERRE in the Jacobin Club, with JACK CADE on London Bridge, with WAT TYLER on Blackheath . . ., in the 'sedition of the Gracchi', and the revolt of the Ten Tribes when that 'Chartist' shout was raised, 'To your tents, O Israel!' ",

this had nothing to do with Godfray's spoliation of his victims. *That* was the "damn'd spot" which was not to be washed out by the "filthy contents of his utensil, the *Constitutionnel*". Bronterre would have been proud of his pupil's dismissal of the rival editor as a "lying and scurrilous Jesuit, a disgrace to the profession to which he belongs, a sacerdotal ruffian who exhibits all the instincts of a Spanish inquisitor".

Sandwiched between these enlivening bouts of abuse may be found a dignified testament by Harney which reveals much of the gradual shifting of his political attitude in these years. In an open letter to Godfray, he wrote:

> "Far from being ashamed of having been connected with the Chartist movement, I feel proud in avowing that I have asserted the rights of the industrious but unrepresented classes of Great Britain. . . . You set your creatures to talk about what you and they are profoundly ignorant of. Were I to discuss Chartism with you, and you were to begin by explaining your ideas of that 'ism', I am certain that you would exhibit the most thorough ignorance of principles which have not only been agitated by the working men of England and their friends, but which are in the course of gradual but certain adoption by the Legislature; and which in time will be grafted upon, and become part and parcel of the British Constitution." [1]

This belief in the slow but inevitable passage into law of the

[1] Jersey *Independent*, 18 December 1858. The property qualification for M.P.s had recently been abolished.

Six Points differed from his revolutionary outlook in 1839 as working-class radicalism in 1858 differed from that of twenty years before. Harney was, in fact, illustrating by the change in his life and attitudes a historical trend which Engels, with his contempt for the change, was only to realize later: the English working class would become more bourgeois before it became less so. In Harney's writing in the *Independent* it is possible to trace the effect of a gradually increasing material well-being on the working classes, in the adoption of middle-class standards and the general abandonment of the class-struggle doctrine.

Harney's material well-being had increased a good deal more than most of his class. As a leader of the radical *petit-bourgeoisie* in St. Helier, he had found at last a snug backwater which offered security and amusement and prestige of a sort, even if it was far from the mainstream of events. He had doubts at first: his Christmas 1856 greeting to old friends in England conveys an unmistakable sense of isolation; and in his lonely walk about St. Helier on that rainy Christmas Eve—not speaking to an attractive young woman through shyness, and finally having a drink by himself in a pub—there is more than a suggestion of the rootlessness of the *émigré*. But these were passing uncertainties. Presumably, a man could remain a bachelor in St. Helier only by strength of will. As an observer in the late 'forties noted, "St. Helier is, *par excellence*, the retreat of old maids. Out of 2,400 souls, there are 1,300 unmarried adult females. There are only 400 men in the town." [1] Whether the woman Harney married was an old maid or not, she was evidently a person of some intelligence, possessing as well the invaluable trait of admiring her husband. And sometime during the next few years Harney also adopted a son.

In their house on one of the steep streets overlooking the lovely harbour of St. Helier, Harney sank deeper into Victorian respectability. Evidently Marie Harney had brought a *dot* into the marriage, for the rosewood ottomans, Chinese porcelain and damask curtains of their home were not the sort of thing a provincial newspaper editor's salary would buy. The contrast between this and the rooms in the noisome alleys of Blackfriars and Southwark of his youth was as great as the gap between "George Julian Harney, Esquire", the signature he now adopted, and the deliberately class-conscious way he had signed his name to the

[1] *Northern Star*, 22 May 1847.

manifestos of the East London Democratic Association: "George Julian Harney, Labourer". Just a decade before, when Henry Vincent, the fiery orator of the early days of Chartism, had assumed the gentlemanly grace, Harney had condemned "political mountebanks who take the style and title of ESQ." as traitors to their order. "In the course of my little time I have seen some strange turnings and twistings," he had concluded, "and, doubtless, I shall see more yet." [1] Ages of swift change are apt to be prodigal of such ironies.

Harney was not alone in typifying the fading of a militant proletarianism under the influence of developments in the 'fifties. The commercial crisis of late 1857 and 1858 which sent a rejuvenated Engels hastening back to England from his cure in Jersey—"I now feel in splendid form in this general collapse," he wrote to Marx[2]—did not deter Ernest Jones from his attempt to wed the remnant of Chartism with the middle-class Radicals whom he had so bitterly assailed a few years before. Jones had finally given way to the despair over the prospects of an independent working-class party which had overwhelmed Harney some years earlier. Engels declared exultantly to Marx as the economic crisis became more acute, "In 1848 we thought our time was coming and in a certain sense it was, . . . this time it is really coming and everything is at stake." [3] The fact was that nothing happened in the way of a revival of a class-conscious movement and Jones succeeded in his aim of carrying the majority of those Chartists who remained into the middle-class camp in his conference of 1858.

Within the short period of five years, first Harney, then Jones, had as Marx put it—"sold out". The two leaders who had tried to resuscitate Chartism by making it a socialist as well as democratic movement had, in fact, succumbed to the apathy of those to whom their appeal was directed. Revolutionary socialism obviously had little appeal in a generally rising labour market; the short commercial crisis of 1857–58 led to grumbling about the government, not demands for its forcible overthrow. There was a kind of truth in Marx's judgment, however. As a contemporary wrote later, "Jones was starved into surrender";[4] and the necessities which had driven Harney from the movement need not be reviewed. Both men, the one pursuing his obscure

<hr />

[1] *Ibid.*, 7 July, 4 August 1849. [2] Quoted in Mehring, *Karl Marx*, p. 254.
[3] *Ibid.* [4] Adams, *Memoirs of a Social Atom*, vol. I, p. 161.

reforms in Jersey, the other resuming the practice of law in Manchester and attempting to enter Parliament as a Liberal-Labour member, were the creatures of the impersonal forces which Marx and Engels were trying to delineate—and to which they were often blind in the present.

All this is not to say that Harney had been transformed by a few years of easier living into a conservative or an admirer of *laissez-faire*. The economic depression of 1857–58 and the Lancashire slump a few years later during the American Civil War were both attributed by him to the inherent nature of capitalism. The crisis in Lancashire would have come just as surely without the cotton famine caused by the Union blockade, he wrote—a judgment with which latter-day historians would be likely to agree. His remarks about the "Millocracy" and "political economy" remained as acrimonious as ever; and he continued to maintain that government should be responsible for the economic welfare of its citizens. But it was no longer solely through the achievement of Socialism that government could exercise this responsibility. Though private philanthropy was unequal to the task, distress in times of depression could be eased by public works and direct relief—a pernicious enough doctrine to some Liberals, but a great modification of Harney's old "root-and-branch" belief.

His attitude toward foreign affairs had also become less outrageous to respectable opinion. This was not due to any change in his attitude, however, but to the growing acceptability of the position he had taken for so many years. One evidence of this is to be found in the fate of Palmerston in 1858 when he attempted to bring in an Alien Act under the pressure of Louis Napoleon, who had just missed assassination at the hands of the Italian revolutionary, Felice Orsini (whose plot and bomb had been made in England). Combined with the bellicosity of the semi-official French press, Palmerston's action was sufficient to cause a great popular reaction and his fall from office.

The intensity of interest in the Italian struggle for independence and unity in 1859–60 doubtless owed much to the stultification of reform efforts at home. Mazzini's cause, with its emphasis on "liberty" rather than "equality", furnished an ideal meeting-ground for all classes of liberals; and Garibaldi became a symbol of democratic liberties to the English working classes. The result of this unanimity of feeling was an extraordinary enthusiasm, demonstrated in the impressive sums subscribed for the revolutionaries, and in the even more remarkable (and typically Liberal) form of a private army, the "English Brigade".[1]

Though he condemned the Liberal opposition to the idea of formal military intervention in Italy and turned a lack-lustre eye on Cavour, Harney found little to criticize in the English response. The Irish reaction was something different. Harney's growing distaste for a nationality whose grievances he had warmly championed in the past may be dated from the intervention in the Italian conflict of the Irish volunteers, some 1,000 strong, who went to the defence of the Church and Rome. While excoriating this evidence of Popish domination and strongly supporting the Italian cause in the *Independent*, Harney also found time to organize a Garibaldi fund, and was able to bring Victor Hugo back to St. Helier in triumph to speak at a money-raising banquet. This occasion, no more and no less significant than scores of meetings for a similar purpose that year, showed once again Harney's unchanging conviction that events on the Tagus and Arno—or the Tiber—should concern Englishmen as much as events on the Thames. During all of these quiet years in Jersey the *Independent's* banner motto might well have been John Donne's dictum about the interconnection of all men. And this belief was not limited to lip-service on Harney's part, as the "tolling of the bell" represented in the first cannon-fire on Fort Sumter in 1861 was to show.

Of the Republic now faced with its supreme test, Harney, in the flush of his youth twenty years before, had declared to an Aberdeen working-class audience: "America is still the hope of the nations—the terror of their oppressors; on her, from the first hour of her independence, has the eye of patriotism been fixed . . . in her we find a surety for the final and universal enfranchisement of mankind." [2] Subsequent events had left him less sanguine than some of the defenders of the Republic.[3] The Mexican

---

[1] To avoid the provisions of the Foreign Enlistment Act, the Brigade was disguised as an excursion to visit Mounts Vesuvius and Etna. The "excursionists" were furnished with the "means of self-defence" and a uniform costume to "ensure their recognition" of each other (Jersey *Independent*, 3 September 1860. The financial records of the Brigade are to be found in the Howell Collection, Bishopsgate Institute).

[2] *Northern Star*, 17 October 1840.

[3] E.g. *Reynolds's Weekly Newspaper*, which in its attempt always to uphold the United States as the *summum bonum* of republican virtues, sometimes became involved in a tortured apologetics suggestive of nothing so much as the compulsive rationalization of Soviet policy by modern Communists of other nations.

War—"a stain upon Republicanism and sore discouragement to the advocates of democratic institutions"—had tempered his admiration; the sublimation of the socialist and free-land ferment of the 'forties in the homestead movement had dashed his hope that the real American revolution was at hand. "Bourgeois liberalism" was the proper description of American democracy, he wrote in 1849.

But the real worm in the Republic's heart was the institution of slavery. Ernest Jones might declaim in the mid-'fifties that "Liberty has spread wherever the Stars and Stripes have been lifted";[1] Harney, observing the pressure of the slavery states for expansion in Cuba and Central America, was not so certain. There were white as well as black slaves in the United States, he wrote, but the institution of negro slavery was a threat even to "*bourgeois* idealism". "The slaveholders are the worst enemies to Liberty and Mankind that exist on the face of the Earth, and have done more to prevent the triumph of Washington's principles than all the despots and armies of Europe combined," he declared bitterly in the *Independent*.

In spite of these faults, however, America still remained in 1861 to him, as it did to the majority of European liberals, the "hope of the nations"—the great example of a working democracy. Consequently, he believed, the ruin of the American system of government would be a fatal blow to the cause of general freedom. Quoting Lincoln's words, Harney asked his readers to consider the fundamental question posed by secession: " 'Must a government of necessity be too strong for the liberties of its own people, or too weak to maintain its own existence?' " If the rebels were successful, the answer could only be that democratic institutions were incapable of enduring when threatened by basic internal disagreement. The effect of Southern success, he wrote, must be to drastically retard the development of free institutions everywhere. The Tiber had become the James and the Mississippi.

Such a belief was common to the greater part of the English working class and to a small but influential body of liberals led by Bright, Cobden, and W. E. Forster. The existence of this feeling was crucial in the initial phase of the Civil War: it was democratic sentiment which sustained the Union cause in England until, after the passage of more than a year, Lincoln's

[1] *People's Paper*, 1 December 1855.

"Emancipation Proclamation" made it possible to appeal to the Nonconformist conscience on the issue of slavery. Those supporting the Union were faced by a formidable opposition. A majority of the free-trade mercantile class were pro-Southern, as were the anti-democratic aristocracy and fashionable society in general—and, it is possible, a portion of the working class engaged on war work for the Confederacy.[1] To the governing classes could be added such powerful sympathizers (for one reason or another) in the cabinet as Lord John Russell and Gladstone. Moreover, the overpowering voice of *The Times* and all save a small minority of the press was countered by only a handful of important journals. But Palmerston, once again Prime Minister, stood against "mediation"—i.e. intervention— for a number of cogent reasons; and one may hazard the guess that he was fortified in his course by the mass-opinion of the unenfranchised, to which he was attentive in his way.

The Jersey microcosm faithfully represented the state of opinion in England, the *Independent* being alone among the island press in supporting the Union. When, in the winter of 1861, an American naval vessel intercepted the British ship *Trent* on the high seas and seized two Confederate representatives on their way to England, the *Independent* stood with the minute pro-Northern press against the violent demands for action which swept the British newspapers. Nor did the series of Union defeats in the summer of 1862, and Gladstone's public declaration in November that Jefferson Davis had made a nation—an utterance widely interpreted to mean that the cabinet had decided to recognize the Confederate States—shake his resolution in defending the Union cause.

He was aware that this was not only a thoroughly unpopular policy with the forces that mattered in Jersey, but a dangerous one as well. The feeling aroused by the Civil War was extraordinarily deep in England. As Thomas Hughes, the Christian Socialist, told a Massachusetts audience a few years later, "Our political struggles do not, as a rule, affect our social life, but during your war the antagonism between your friends and the friends of the rebel states often grew into personal hostility. . . .

---

[1] Gladstone's notorious interventionist *gaffe* in October 1862 was cheered by a crowd of Jarrow ship-workers (Newcastle *Weekly Chronicle*, 8 October 1862. W. E. Adams, later editor of the *Weekly Chronicle*, claimed that this was the only verbatim report of the speech).

I heard, over and over again, men refuse to meet those who were conspicuous on the other side." [1] Henry Adams, who spent the war years in London with his father, the American Minister, never forgot the freezing hostility with which they were treated by London society and a social atmosphere in which "Lincoln's brutality and Seward's [the Secretary of State's] ferocity became a dogma of popular faith". [2] And so in Jersey. Harney had been in conflict with the proprietor of the *Independent* for some time about his editorial policy, refusing either to change his views or be silent, and the series of attacks which he wrote on Gladstone's speech provoked a final breach.

The attitude against which Harney had fought his losing battle and the way in which his intransigence was regarded even by his less rabid critics found expression in the elegy which appeared in the *Independent* after his dismissal.

"From this day forth our readers will perceive a difference in our treatment of the American Struggle," a leading article began. ". . . All dispassionate observers of American events must recognize it with the definiteness of a Divine Decree that the North is already doomed to be disappointed in its efforts to re-conquer the South. . . . We cannot help seeing that an almighty blow is to be dealt at that big bloated Yankee idolatry which worshipped the dollar."

The ex-editor's "warmth of heart or narrowness of mind" had prevented him from seeing this obvious truth; he had been blinded by an abstract ideal.

With the certainty expressed by this writer about the war's outcome there would have been few to disagree in the winter of 1862. It speaks a good deal for Harney's integrity and courage in refusing to compromise his support of the Northern cause that he too was by no means convinced of the inevitability of a Union victory. "All the Jersey papers now sing to the same tune:— 'Let the American Republic be dismembered for the greater glory of England,' " he wrote to Charles Sumner, the senator from Massachusetts, shortly after his dismissal. "This I hold to be as stupid as it is brutally selfish, as the Future, *should the South prevail*, will prove." [3] After a life which had been a succession of

---

[1] Hughes, *Vacation Rambles* (London: 1895), p. 389.

[2] *Education of Henry Adams*, English edition (London: 1919), p. 131. He adds a penetrating comment: "All London society needed the nervous relief of expressing emotion, for if Mr. Lincoln was not what they said he was—what were they?"

[3] 10 December 1862 (Houghton Library, Harvard University). Italics mine.

struggles for lost causes, there was a peculiar perversity in the fact that he had now become a fatality in a winning cause.

Obviously, there was no comfort in this for Harney at the time. Since the winter day in 1855 when he had arrived in Jersey fatigued and unwanted, the years had been happy ones. Those years had also seen him grow into middle age, losing what connections remained with his old life. For an unemployed journalist approaching fifty the prospect was not bright. The alternative that remained was one against which some of his most acrid attacks had been levelled in the past—that "monstrous doctrine preached by non-producers to producers", emigration. After some doubts about whether to respond to the persuasion of friends to come to Australia, he decided to try America; and when his furnishings had been auctioned there remained but one event to keep him in the temporary haven of which he had become so fond.

Early in the year his friends had begun to collect a testimonial for Harney, and at a farewell dinner in April he was presented with a gold watch and fifty gold sovereigns—sovereigns which, he punned, he preferred to all those of Europe. Despite such efforts, the dinner was a pathetic affair, with the dead ring of the past already echoing in the eulogies of his efforts in England and Jersey. The most poignant speech of the evening was that of a Polish exile, Schmitt, who in a voice full of emotion presented "their dear friend Julian Harney" with an address signed by the Polish colony which reviewed his tireless efforts since the 'thirties on behalf of Poland. Above any Englishman, he had personified their struggle, Schmitt declared. There could have been little question in the minds of his listeners as to the justification of the claim by which Harney concluded his brief speech of thanks: "He had always been a democrat, he was one now, and he hoped he should remain one until the day of his death."

More than twenty years before, Harney had set forth his conception of a working-class leader as a "tribune of the people"—a defender of the under-privileged and an enemy of abuses. Such he had continued to be in these Jersey years, as his name faded from the pages of English working-class history. In a national sense he had ceased to be a significant figure even before he came to the island; whatever significance he retained there was as one of the obscure and idealistic men whose efforts are noted only in total. Forgotten except by a few in England, but remembered at any rate by the Poles and by the tallow-chandler and grocer at whose expense Engels had made merry, Harney sailed with his wife and son from Liverpool in May 1863. He was only forty-six, but his life as a public figure and moulder of opinion was over.

CHAPTER XI

Looking Backward

THE unemployed Radical journalist who first gazed on New York in the early summer of 1863 was no bright-eyed immigrant with an unbounded faith in the Mecca of Europe's oppressed peoples. That there were those whose careers after arriving in America were made-to-order for a Samuel Smiles would not have been denied by Harney. He himself knew two such men: M. M. Trumbull, a Civil War general and Collector of Internal Revenue in the Grant administration, who as a young Chartist in the 1840's had been stirred to emigrate by the *Northern Star's* reports of American democracy; and James Charlton, an ex-Chartist leader from Newcastle who had become the manager of a middle-western railway. But he was aware that success was not the invariable fortune of those pouring across the Atlantic. Years later, he described Andrew Carnegie, then triumphantly perambulating Britain in a four-in-hand carriage flying the Stars and Stripes, as "One of those delightful 'self-made men', who take care not to hide their light under a bushel; who tell you, 'I went steerage to America, and was glad to get a job at a quarter a day, . . . and now see what I have achieved!'" But, Harney concluded, "We are never told how many scores, hundreds, or thousands of other men have been exploited—devoured body and bones—to make that one 'triumphant' man." [1] He might also have pointed to the fact that at the time of Carnegie's tour the striking workers of the Carnegie Steel Company were fighting a sanguinary battle with blacklegs and the private police of a company founded by still another ex-Chartist success, Alan Pinkerton.

The experience of his first weeks in New York did nothing to alleviate Harney's doubts about his new refuge. Soon after his arrival he attended a meeting of "Copperheads" (Northern sympathizers with the Confederacy) at which Fernando Wood, an ex-mayor of New York and "as near perfect a mob-orator" as the experienced *émigré* had heard, made an outright plea for

[1] Newcastle *Weekly Chronicle*, 16 July 1892.

violence against the Union which evoked frantic cheers from his predominantly Irish audience. A few weeks later the same element participated in the great New York anti-draft riot in which negroes were lynched, some thousand people killed or injured, and troops were necessary to restore order. The spectacle of Irishmen—only recently released from what they and Harney had regarded as English bondage—demonstrating for the slave-owners' cause could only mean a deepening of Harney's disillusionment.

To account for the jaundiced eye with which he came to look on the "high pressure and anything but model Republic"—as he had described it with momentary bitterness in 1860—there was also the fact that he was and remained an unwilling exile. Doubtless this was a handicap in his climbing the ladder as Trumbull and others had, but it left him a mordant and entertaining, if not always scrupulously fair, observer of the American scene. And even as a somewhat disillusioned idealist, Harney could scarcely have chosen a worse time to live in the United States. With the tremendous expansion that followed the Civil War went a series of scandals which reached from the lowest rank of Boss Tweed's ward-heelers in New York to the highest levels of the national government, involving even those close to the President. To Harney it seemed an "age of corrupt and shameless politicians, an age too of social corruption, by which I mean an almost all-pervading lust for dollars, dollars to be gained or filched, speculated for or plundered".[1] The Civil War, he wrote later, had bloodily cured one evil; but in the very effort another disease in American national life had received a great stimulus. Millionaires were now able to buy, or at least to dominate and manipulate governments; social life had degenerated to the lowest form of the "cash nexus".

Harney was by no means unique in this reaction to post-Civil War America (as the *Education of Henry Adams* testifies). His revulsion from what he considered the dominance of the commercial ethic in American life was typical of other old Chartists who had emigrated. "There are some very good laws," an obscure correspondent of Jones's *People's Paper* had commented a few years before, "but the Americans are such an avaricious people that profits are their whole study." W. J. Linton, the republican engraver who settled in Connecticut, came to the

[1] Letter in *ibid.*, 28 March 1874.

conclusion that "America is no country for the poor man" [1]—
a judgment echoed in the writing of Thomas Devyr, the Newcastle Radical editor who had fled arrest in 1839. The latter
added a more cynical comment on the rampant bribery and
vote-buying he had observed in his long American sojourn.

> "You need not claim, if there is unbounded plunder to scramble
> for, the masses of England will be one whit better than the masses
> of the United States," he wrote to Joseph Cowen. "There [in
> America], under the sway of Universal Suffrage, a system has been
> engendered that *excludes every virtuous man from power* as effectually as
> he could be excluded in England." [2]

That all of these critics found no real use for their talents in
American society doubtless accounts in part for the bitterness of
their tone; but there was no scarcity of evils to shock men who
had long looked to America as the exemplar of the democratic
virtues.

Harney's talent was journalistic, and the letters on the
American scene which he wrote to the Newcastle *Weekly Chronicle*
indicate that he might have made a new, if lesser, name for himself as the American correspondent for an English newspaper—
a position he deeply desired. His coverage of the "Jefferson
Borden Tragedy", for example—a case involving a mutiny on
an American ship, in which he was able by strenuous efforts to
save a young English participant from hanging—provides a
model of trial-reporting. But his abilities were instead wasted
on another kind of paperwork. Evidently through the efforts
of the Boston liberals who, according to Holyoake, gave him a
warm welcome as a "fiery patriot", he became a clerk in the
Massachusetts State House. His life soon settled into a placid
routine of commuting daily to his den there, which went on with
few interruptions for fourteen years.

Holyoake later wrote that Harney's non-participation in
American politics was a disappointment to the Boston liberals.
Even if this were true (and Holyoake must be accepted with
caution) it is difficult to see how a virtually unknown Englishman, in a section of the country where Anglophobia had
reached a frenzied pitch because of British sympathy with the
South, could have hoped for much political success. What
effect would Harney's accent have had on a crowd of Boston

---

[1] Quoted in W. E. Adams, *Our American Cousins* (London: 1887), p. 294.
[2] Letter dated 7 July 1860, Cowen Collection.

S

rishmen? These handicaps aside, it is doubtful whether Harney wished to take the plunge once again. Politics had not treated him kindly—and there was the fact that it was not a new life that he wished, but an eventual return to England. Meanwhile, to live quietly in his house full of the portraits of the revolutionary heroes he had known or admired, to indulge his passion for literature, and to be an observer rather than a participant, must have seemed a not unattractive prospect for a man so buffeted by society in the past.

Throughout these years, Harney maintained a connection with England through correspondence, sending Massachusetts labour and education documents to such recipients as A. J. Mundella, the Radical M.P., and Marx, and becoming a member of the National Reform League and the First International. George Howell, the labour leader and historian, was also the recipient of considerable information from Harney, another evidence of a continuing wish on his part to serve British labour even in exile. Visitors from England occasionally came to Boston: Harney dropped by the poet James Russell Lowell's house to reminisce with Thomas Hughes, the exponent of "muscular Christianity" who had become an M.P., about Christian Socialist days: and in company with Wendell Phillips, the "Silver Tongued Demosthenes of New England", he showed the secularist Charles Bradlaugh around town. But his absence from the scene of events made his interest in English affairs, other than industrial struggles, more passive after the achievement of the Second Reform Bill in 1867. "Compared with the stormy Chartist times, 1838–48, your politics have been in my estimation 'As moonlight is to sunlight, and as water is to wine'," he told the readers of the Newcastle *Weekly Chronicle* in 1873.

The Boston into which Harney's existence quietly merged was in the autumn of the great New England literary renaissance which had made the city the centre of American intellectual life. Emerson was still to be observed walking about the streets, "amazingly youthful despite his years", as Harney observed; and he heard Oliver Wendell Holmes and others at the Lowell Institute. On a trip to nearby Amesbury, he visited the Quaker Abolitionist and nature poet, John Greenleaf Whittier, whose poems he had once printed in the *Northern Star*, answering his eager questions about old Chartist leaders and European revolutionaries. In Cambridge, still park-like with its pleasant tree-lined streets, he finally settled in a house close to Longfellow's. It is not apparent whether he ever told the poet of the memorable second banishment of his "Evangeline" from Jersey.

This society of cultivation and intellect was not all of Boston, however, and the other aspect did not escape Harney's satirical attention. Being "star-spangled and yankee-doodled to death" by the excess of patriotism at concerts led him to mild complaint; and the exuberant American tendency toward "bigness" —exemplified by an enormous concert conducted by Johann Strauss at which the "Anvil Chorus" was rendered by "2,000 instrumentalists, 100 Boston firemen beating on a like number of Birmingham anvils, and a chorus of 20,000 which expanded their mouths from here to yonder"—left him dazed but undaunted. Anticipating H. L. Mencken's strictures on Southern California, Harney looked more wryly on other manifestations of American energy about him. As he wrote in retrospect,

> "That portion of the earth's surface termed the United States is very largely a land of cranks. If anyone has a new quack medicine, a new quack government, or a new quack social system to introduce into the world, the States constitute 'his happy hunting ground', and of course, in such experiments, Boston is the 'hub of the universe.' " [1]

There was much that was defensive about such criticisms. As with many exiles who fail to root themselves in a new society, his attachment to his home-country grew stronger with separation; and the Anglophobia about him heightened this reaction. His feeling sometimes took the form of deploring the anti-English conditioning that American children imbibed from their history books, or the aggressive demands for recognition that he heard. At other times it expressed itself in an excess of sensitivity about the behaviour of visiting Englishmen. "That British complacency which makes our countrymen so beloved wherever they go" and the writers and lecturers who came over and made themselves foolish for dollars mortified him in a way not unfamiliar to expatriates observing their countrymen abroad. Occasionally his sensitivity took a ridiculous form, as in his criticism of the English journals which had given Americans the idea that Englishmen habitually referred to their homeland as

[1] Newcastle *Weekly Chronicle*, 27 November 1897.

"Hingland", a certain London suburb as "Ampstead", and a part of the national diet as "weal-pies".

But his main reaction to American society was to be found in a growing disquiet at the abuse of democratic institutions. The quondam mob orator who had found his following among the *sans-culottes* of Bethnal Green and Spitalfields now began to look with some misgivings at the professional demagogues who, with the aid of an unscrupulous press, wielded such power over the "town mobs" of the United States. Harney's fear of the irrational city crowd or of an intolerant majority was not incompatible with a faith in democracy—as Thomas Jefferson and John Stuart Mill testified—but it was another evidence of the modification of his views.

As he grew into old age the simple blacks and whites of his youthful faith no longer satisfied him, though he was in no sense ashamed of his past. William Lovett, writing scathingly in his autobiography of Harney's violent behaviour at the time of the Convention in 1839, added a footnote before the book's publication (1876) to the effect that he had since redeemed his folly and violence by his intelligent writings and moderation. Harney replied in the Newcastle *Weekly Chronicle* that he could not accept the compliment; he "still called a spade a spade". As to the events of 1839, he commented:

> "When I look back upon the past, when I remember the wrongs and sufferings of the working classes, far from being able to reproach myself with 'violence', I am astonished at my moderation; considering as I do that the wrongs referred to would have satisfied a degree of 'violence' far beyond anything my recollection enables me to charge for my own account." [1]

It is difficult to escape the conclusion that the modifications in Harney's political views corresponded to some degree with the changes in Boston society in these years. His friends were of the educated class, including a lawyer, a fine-book publisher, and an art critic connected with the Boston Museum of Fine Arts; and it was in this company that he watched the slow submergence of the old order by the great influx of Irish immigrants who came to Boston. "The cultivated gentlemen of the Athenaeum and the Historical Society", as he described them, found them-

---

[1] 2 December 1876. Harney deplored Lovett's bitterness toward O'Connor, but praised both his *Autobiography* and the recently published *Life of Thomas Cooper, Written by Himself*—an indication of the trustworthiness of these volumes as Chartist sources.

selves exercising less and less influence as time passed. Harney's attitude toward the Irish had begun to change with the Irish volunteers' support of the Pope against Garibaldi, and their part in the New York anti-draft riots did not reverse the process. For the political bosses he had come to detest, the newly-arrived immigrants made easy game; and the Irish influx also meant an increase in the influence of the Roman Catholic Church, an institution he regarded to the end of his life with undiminished hatred as an enemy of civil liberties. All in all, the growing power of the Irish and the "machine-politics" which thrived on them were not things he could regard with equanimity.

Years later, Holyoake was to write that Harney had come forth "naked and unashamed" as a "full-blown Tory" during his American stay.[1] This judgment, as with some others from this source, does not deserve too much credence.[2] Stiffening in the Liberal mould as he aged and recasting his memoirs accordingly[3] (as well as creating a Holyoake hagiology), he defined Harney as a Tory because the latter wrote home disparagingly of America and was pro-Turkish at the time of the Bulgarian atrocities. If this is accepted as a definition of Toryism, Harney was indeed "full blown". But it is quite obvious from his correspondence in the Newcastle *Weekly Chronicle* that his disparagement of America was that of an outraged democrat, not an opponent of democratic institutions. And, until the Turco-Bulgarian affair of 1876, he admired Gladstone and considered the Liberals as the lesser of two evils. What Liberal would have cavilled at Harney's description of Disraeli as an "adventurer leading a phalanx of obstructives"?

[1] Holyoake, *Bygones Worth Remembering* (London: 1905), p. 111.

[2] *Cf.* two judgments by contemporaries well qualified to judge: J. M. Ludlow, the Christian Socialist and co-operator, wrote in a private letter in 1904: "Holyoake himself I cannot make up my mind about, after all the years I have known him . . . his inaccuracy of statement is such that if he said he had dined off a mutton chop the chance would be ten to one that it was more probably a beefsteak" (quoted in C. E. Raven, *Christian Socialism, 1848–1854* [London: 1920], p. 62). Lloyd Jones, also intimately connected with Holyoake, had anticipated Ludlow, writing in the Newcastle *Weekly Chronicle* (19 July 1879): "When the public know Mr. Holyoake's literary ways they will, I think, be disposed to test his accuracy before they give absolute credence to his statements." Harney himself, in the 1890's, was apt to be irreverent in discussing the "Grand Old Man of Co-operation" as well as picking holes in his discussion of the Chartist period—activities which led to a note of asperity in Holyoake's replies, though the two men remained good friends.

[3] *Cf. Sixty Years of an Agitator's Life*, written between 1881 and 1892, and *Bygones Worth Remembering*, which appeared in 1905.

Gladstone's famous pamphlet attacking the Turks' brutal suppression of Christian-nationalist risings in the Balkans, *The Bulgarian Horrors and the Question of the East,* altered this. The Gladstonian view, which temporarily expressed English popular opinion, was that the Turks should be driven from Europe; its corollary was support of Russia as the champion of the Balkan Christians. It was this aspect of the agitation that aroused Harney, who remained as inveterately Russophobic as anti-Catholic, to reply to Gladstone in a pamphlet of his own, *The Anti-Turkish Crusade.* Support for the Russians, he wrote, would assure the domination of the Balkans and the Straits by the most dangerously despotic and imperialistic nation in Europe. The advanced Liberal belief in Russian disinterestedness seemed to him the most sanguine of self-delusions, "seeing that the march of Russian aggression has never ceased for centuries—temporarily arrested in Europe it is continued in Asia, year by year, and is now likely to be resumed in Europe". One could scarcely find a more succinct résumé of Russian imperial policy in the late nineteenth and early twentieth centuries. There were other flashes of prescience in this trenchant pamphlet, as in the statement that a revolutionary change in Russia would only increase the nationalism and expansionism which had been that country's policy since the time of Peter the Great.[1] Harney's final words on Gladstone have also stood the test of time well.

> "The world knows Mr. Gladstone as an eminent statesman, a powerful orator, a brilliant writer, a man sincere, humane, and generously impulsive; at once profound and popular, whether manipulating a budget or discussing Homer, and as efficient in cutting up an encyclical as cutting down oaks at Hawarden," he wrote, ". . . but I am not so sure of Mr. Gladstone's ability in the realm of foreign politics."

It was in his general comment on European affairs that the younger Harney re-emerged, passionately involved, polemical and effective. Carlyle's exultation at the French debacle in 1870 provoked him to write, "Prussian despotism is the true re-

[1] Or compare his remarks in 1852, which could be adopted verbatim today as summing up the argument of opponents of peaceful co-existence: "The only means by which Europe and Asia can be made free is by the destruction of the Russian power, which is the incarnation of the despotism of the world. All circumstances combine to point out America as the natural leader of . . . freedom, and consequently the natural enemy of Russia. Between these principles of absolutism and liberty there will be continual struggle, until one of them will be universally triumphant" (*Star of Freedom,* 19 June 1852).

ligion; the Prussian drill-sergeant is the destined redeemer of Europe; and Carlyle is the apostle and preacher of the new dispensation!" [1] But that strong feeling did not sweep away his very real ability to penetrate to the forces behind events is evidenced by his reply to the "sanguinary mountebank's" (i.e. Carlyle's) claim that French hostility had caused the war— the general view at the time. Bismarck, wrote Harney, had plotted, prepared, and sprung the trap into which " 'that sagacious prince' [as Disraeli had described Louis Napoleon] so idiotically fell".

The years so misspent in the wrong kind of paperwork came at last to an end in 1877, possibly because he had reached the retirement age of sixty, and he was free to do what had long been in his mind—to visit England. Despite the smallness of his salary, Harney had contrived to save a few hundred pounds, and with his wife he arrived in England in 1879. It was sixteen years since they had sailed from Liverpool for New York, and almost a quarter of a century since he had lived in England. The returned exile felt, as he said, "a stranger in his own land".

There were few familiar faces to greet him. The "guide, philosopher and friend" of his youth, Bronterre O'Brien, had died in 1864 after eking out his last miserable days as a loafer in Fleet Street, "shabby, snuffy, beery", opening discussions in pothouses for a few shillings and his night's liquor. [2] Another old companion, John Arnott, once the general secretary of the National Chartist Association and a Fraternal Democrat, had last been recognized by W. E. Adams in a half-starved old man begging in the Strand years before. Ernest Jones, with whom Harney had long since made up his differences, had gone to a Manchester grave in 1868, mourned by a great concourse of admirers. Harney, reading this news on his morning walk to the State House in Boston, had been "almost blinded by emotion". Aware that Jones had died just when it seemed probable that his ambition of sitting in Parliament as a labour member would be realized, he wrote, "I turned sick at the thought of this riddle of existence." [3] The attrition of time had removed others of his old acquaintances as well. William Lovett, the foremost spokesman of moral-force Chartism, and John Frost, the leader of the

---

[1] Newcastle *Weekly Chronicle*, 7 January 1871.
[2] Adams, *Memoirs of a Social Atom*, vol. I, p. 210.
[3] Letter in *Social Democrat*, 1 July 1869.

Welsh rising had died within days of each other a few years before. Of the delegates who had met with millennial hopes in the National Convention of the Industrious Classes in 1839, only one other member, Henry Vincent, still lived.

Yet some links with the past remained very much alive. Harney and his wife encountered the Marxes in Waterloo Station on their way to a vacation in Jersey—the only reference to that encounter being the cryptic remark of Marx, a chronic misogynist so far as Harney's wives were concerned, that they were relieved to find Mrs. Harney was travelling first-class, for though a good woman she was "not just the person for those who are travelling to cheer themselves up".[1] A warmer welcome was given Harney by Louis Blanc, whom he visited in Paris. Extremely young still in appearance, Blanc had retained his youthful optimism as well, though Harney thought he discerned an air of sadness about him. The Third Republic had acclaimed his return and then forgotten about him—a fate which all of the French veterans of 1848–49 had suffered, Harney observed. It was the "more compromising" younger politicians who ruled France.

His sombre reflections were not limited to the fate of revolutionaries. Like many émigrés, Harney had tended to idealize the homeland from which circumstances had banished him. But the devil of the commercial ethic was in Eden, too. He found that England as well as America was dominated by the "pandemonium of commerce, in which . . . to be rich—no matter by what fraud and swindling, 'rings' and 'corners' riches are gained —is to be honoured in this life, with a good set-off by the churches for heaven in the next; but in which to be poor is to be damned".[2] The poor still existed; and the poor had paid the price for the nation which had got rich out of steam. "There was one sight that impressed one painfully," he wrote later of the participants in a Hyde Park mass-demonstration, "—the stunted height and ill-formed build of thousands of the workers and onlookers." Looking at undersized English factory-hands and thinking of the navvies who had built the first English railroads, Harney asked, "Where are the armies of stalwart men that tramped over and changed the face of England forty years ago?" His observations

---

[1] Marx to Engels, 14 August 1879, *Briefwechsel*, vol. IV, p. 486.
[2] Newcastle *Weekly Chronicle*, 18 August 1883. Except where specifically noted, subsequent quotations of Harney are taken from letters and columns which appeared in the *Chronicle*.

abroad well qualified him to answer: "Transplanted, I fear, to other lands, cast out by England to build up Australia, New Zealand, Canada, and, mainly, the United States. . . . And still the cry is 'Emigration!' England is to be saved by further depleting her of her best blood."

Harney's reaction to late-Victorian social mores was no less vehement. "It is not pleasant to have to confess," he wrote, "but the truth is that England is, *par excellence*, the land of cant and humbug. Queen Victoria rules over the Britannic Empire, but Mrs. Grundy rules over British society." There were other foibles of his countrymen on which he turned a more benevolent irony. "The perseverence of Englishmen in taking their pleasure gravely, under the most adverse meteorological circumstances," he observed, "cannot be too highly commended, especially by doctors and undertakers." In the eighteenth century, Montesquieu had attributed *le mal anglais* to the English climate; Harney's explanation was even more convincing: "Foreigners, in reflecting on the alleged tendency of the English, beyond other nations, to commit suicide, fail to take into account the dispiriting effect of looking into the London 'comic' papers."

Renewed acquaintance with England made Harney look back on America more tolerantly. The Americans were, after all, "our kith and kin, of all foreign nations the closest to us in blood, language and religion", he told the readers of the Newcastle *Weekly Chronicle*. But he had no wish to leave England again, and when he sailed with his wife for New York in 1879 it was with the hope of a quick return. The fulfilment of his hope was delayed for five years, when he returned once more to visit such old Chartist comrades as remained and make a sentimental pilgrimage to the places of his youth. There is much in this second return that conveys the painfulness of time passing. Thomas Cooper, the firebrand of 1842, who after a number of violent conversions and backslidings had finally ended as a Christian lecturer, was too blind to recognize Harney, but sprang up and embraced his old colleague when he heard his voice. A similar incident in an old weaver-friend's cottage near Thrums could have done little to lessen the sense of "being a stranger in one's own land" that Harney had felt on his first return. When he gave his name, the weaver started and exclaimed, "Why, I had no thoct ye were leevin'; I heard lang syne ye were deid!" Most poignant of all was his return to Ayrshire, where more than forty years before he had climbed the hill familiar to Burns and gazed on the valley of the River Doon, a scene "beautiful as Elysium"—and where he had met Mary Cameron, who now lay in Mauchline churchyard.

After a last sojourn in the United States, Harney returned permanently to England in 1888, his wife remaining in Cambridge to carry on her language school. He settled finally at Richmond, Surrey,—the same pleasant town where the fashionable young barrister, Ernest Jones, had spent his honeymoon nearly a half-century before, after being (as he noted in his diary) "Married to Jane, dashing wedding, St. George's, Hanover Square." [1] Here, despite the onset of the extremely painful rheumatoid arthritis which steadily crippled him, Harney's extraordinary intellectual vigour enabled him to make a new life once again, this time as a regular columnist for the Newcastle *Weekly Chronicle*. In his usually light-hearted writing of the 1890's almost no hint of the ailment he endured appears, and then only in satirical allusions, such as his experience of the "cure" at Droitwich. After floating for some time in the brine-baths, Harney recorded, he sat "in the buff" in the melting atmosphere of a salt-drying shed, "with some apprehension of sharing the fate of Lot's wife, and being sold to Barnum to be placed in the New York Museum along with the two skulls of Captain Cook and the sword with which Balaam desired to smite his too intelligent ass". It would have been a salt-statue well worth studying, with its strong and handsome features, mobile lips half-buried in a white beard seemingly charged with static electricity, and deep laughter wrinkles beside the nose and eyes.

The appetite for life which had always been one of Harney's dominant characteristics was now channelled almost entirely into his reading and writing. In his small room under the eaves, soon overflowing with the books he purchased from his minute income, this product of a few years of dame schools wrote a weekly literary column in which Montaigne, Beranger, Voltaire, Herodotus, Thucydides and many others were familiarly quoted, and engaged in arguments in *Notes and Queries* about minute facts in Byron's life—on which he had become something of an authority. He was fortunate in his main outlet, the Newcastle *Weekly Chronicle*, which the old Cheltenham Chartist and Fra-

[1] 15 June 1841, Howell Collection, Bishopsgate Institute.

ternal Democrat, W. E. Adams, had made into a remarkably stimulating newspaper. One competent American critic described the *Chronicle* as the "best paper in the world";[1] its foreign and domestic news-coverage, special features, and correspondence page—a mine for the student of opinion with its furious battles on such subjects as Socialism, Anarchism, Spelling Reform, and "Is Teetotalism a Species of Insanity?"—make a modern reader aware of the disastrous inverted alchemy Alfred Harmsworth and others worked on the British press.

In this spirited medium, Harney's column soon became a leading feature, as well as a place to exercise himself freely in the only way that remained. Returning from being wheeled through Richmond Park, with its chestnut trees blooming, children playing, and the unfulfilable desire to throw himself on to the grass all fresh in his mind, he could find some consolation in writing a long essay on Cobbett's *Rural Rides*, the poetry of Richard Jefferies, and White's *Natural History of Selborne*. But there was nothing escapist about his critical principle. "I am no believer in the cant of 'Art for Art's Sake', but prefer to measure the value of art by its service rendered to Humanity," he wrote with his usual trenchancy. Perhaps this utilitarian standard had something to do with his recommendation that Barrie's *Little Minister* should be published in the same manner as scholarly editions of Greek and Latin works—that is, with the original tongue and the English translation on facing pages.

Harney's writing in the 1890's is testimony to the truism that wit may be the product of pain. One might look long for a better example of delicate understatement than: "*Selections from the Table Talk of Martin Luther* is a book that, taken in itself, will disappoint some readers." He had also developed a gift for aphorism, as in likening those critics who spoke of "resuscitating Byron" to Londoners in a fog speaking of resuscitating the sun. His old turn of irony was to be found in the "no small surprise" he felt at first seeing Robert Blatchford of the "terrible *Clarion*", who looked "neat, mild, and dapper enough to be—Robespierre". Almost everything Harney touched was lightened, even an old regret—his inability to read any foreign language. After exhorting the manufacturers of international languages to hurry up, he pointed a lesson for them: "The hideous name of

[1] Paul Carus, the editor in the 'nineties of the *Open Court*, a Chicago journal with a high intellectual standard.

the last recipe—Volapuck—foredoomed it." And it was quite obvious that he had lost none of the corrosive talent he had developed from reading Cobbett and Bronterre. Of one of the host of Edward Bellamy's (*Looking Backward*) imitators who signed himself "X.Y.Z.", he remarked briefly that a more appropriate pseudonym would be "A.S.S.". Usually his caustic shafts were directed at deserving victims, such as the county councillors responsible for the breaking up of Druidical stones in Dartmoor for roadmetal—whose wooden heads Harney recommended as a more suitable material.

While his columns ranged from Ernest Newman's articles on music to Henry James's criticism of Matthew Arnold, he was particularly interested in books dealing with events of which he had personal knowledge. Adams, who considered Chartism the "greatest political movement we have known in this country since the Revolution", printed reminiscences of survivors of those days—Lloyd Jones, Gammage, Holyoake and more obscure men—and constantly exhorted Harney to write a history of the movement. Judging from the correspondence columns of the *Chronicle*, there was a rather wide, if vague, knowledge of Chartism in the 1890's, and a common agreement that the movement had put into motion the political changes of the last half of the century. Harney's excellent memory, aided by a good collection of early Radical literature, fitted him to deal with the subject in a way that no one else could have done. The idea was in his mind for years, and he went so far as to collect materials in the British Museum and the Newcastle Central Library in the 'eighties; but the project got no farther than a few fragments, tantalizing in their immediacy to the events described and their clear generalization.

For this unhappy circumstance, there was a reason other than his crippling illness. He was too absorbed in the present to find time for a sustained effort dealing with the past. Sitting in his quiet room surrounded by books and portraits, Harney wrote with deceptive resignation in 1891, "I would fain ride the rest of my days in smooth waters"; but it is quite obvious from some of the political columns which issued from his peaceful haven that nothing was more remote from his thoughts. An incurable controversialist to the end, he could not resist the opportunity of stimulating the furious arguments which raged for weeks in the *Chronicle's* correspondence page, to be quenched finally by

Adams after his pleas for moderation of language had gone un-answered. The main stimulus for these savage battles of the pen, into which Harney flung himself so ardently, was his anti-Gladstonism. The "Grand Old Man" venerated by Liberals was variously described by his impious critic at one time or another as the "Grand Old Mountebank", the "Grand Old Maniac", the "Grand Old Sequah"—a reference to the West-Indian quack-healer then enjoying a vogue in England, and, after his retirement, the "Grand Old Politically Defunct". Of Gladstone's writings, which he had once found admirable, he now observed, "We read, we yawn, we collapse," and recom-mended the Victoria Cross for those who finished his articles on theology.

To account for Harney's antipathy for the Liberal leader is to sum up his reaction to the politics of the 'nineties. Though he had begun to have his doubts about Gladstone during the Turco-Bulgarian affair, it was the "Grand Old Anarch of the British Empire" whom he came to detest so heartily. For the militant imperialism then at its zenith, Harney had nothing but distaste. "I take no stock in the British any more than any other nation's exploitation of the African continent," he wrote. "The pretence of spreading civilization is a lie to mask the inhuman greed of the so-called 'civilizers'." But his distaste was equally acute for the "Little England" school, of which he considered Gladstone the spokesman. Instead of getting rid of colonies as costly encum-brances, Harney wished to see them held to England by "links of justice" in a co-operative, mutually beneficial system with com-mon English freedoms.[1]

His opposition to Gladstone's policies found its strongest expression over the question of Irish independence. The passage of the second Home Rule Bill by the House of Commons in 1893 appeared to him "The Great Betrayal", and for the first time in his long life the spectacle could be observed of Harney praising the House of Lords, when they vetoed the bill. Some reasons have been suggested for this striking change from his youthful belief that Ireland was the "Poland of the West", to be liberated by any means, the chief of these being his conviction that an independent Ireland would actually be a priest-dominated Ire-land. By the 1890's this belief had been reinforced by his

[1] Speech at Tiverton, 1847, quoted in Snell, *Palmerston's Borough*, p. 86. Harney wrote to Snell in 1894 that this still represented his attitude toward the Empire.

increasing uneasiness about England's future security. "It is not disintegration, but closer union that the British Isles need," he wrote in 1897. Nor was he alone among old Chartists in opposing Home Rule on military grounds. Adams thought of Irish independence as a "secession" which would leave a hostile country on England's flank.

Harney's uneasiness about the future of Britain was not limited to her military security. The doubts which had afflicted him when he first returned to England in 1879 and witnessed the effects of the waning of British commercial supremacy had not lessened with the passage of years. In the things that she did best, he wrote, England was being outstripped by her foreign competitors. The illustrations for English periodicals, for example, were being sent to Germany, where they could be done more cheaply by new processes. In a penetrating review of the course of the British economy written in 1896, he glanced back over the preceding half-century and drew some pessimistic conclusions. British agriculture had been destroyed by Free Trade, he wrote, with the result that the country had become dependent on its commercial efficiency for its very life. But in enjoying a virtual monopoly of world trade, British manufacturers had neglected to keep up their progress in machine-design and technical training; they had lost their flexibility in foreign markets, even refusing to learn the languages of their customers,[1] and through their inertia were losing profitable domestic markets. Meanwhile the Germans, showing all the qualities which made for commercial greatness, had progressed rapidly. The sceptre of British trade supremacy was passing to Germany, Harney concluded gloomily, and he saw no action by which this could be prevented.

But at least the swamping of the internal market by foreign goods could be prevented by Protection, he argued, thus taking another stand against Liberal policy. The problem came down to a simple question: could one nation, enjoying no particular natural advantages, afford a Free Trade policy in a protectionist world? Free-Traders of the mid-century, he reminded his readers, had believed that England's example would be followed by every nation within a few decades, making them so beneficially interdependent that armies would disappear and wars

---

[1] Engels had made the same point four years before in print. (*Socialism, Utopian and Scientific*, tr. by Edward Aveling [London: 1892], note, p. xxxiii.)

become the memory of an irrational past. But it had been the American post-Civil War example of high tariffs and not that of English Free Trade which the leading manufacturing nations had followed, as well as the British colonies. As an ideal, Free Trade was admirable, but—as the Radical working class of the 1830's and 1840's had held—it should be practised only reciprocally. Chartists, Harney recalled, had opposed the Anti-Corn Law League not only because its agitation distracted the working class from the Charter, but because they believed that Free Trade would destroy English agriculture, and ultimately, if practised with countries which excluded English goods by tariffs, lead to unemployment and the flooding of the home market with cheap foreign goods. The first of these consequences had already proved true; Britain's monopoly of world trade had delayed the reckoning of the last. But, he asked, what would happen now that their monopoly had ended?

Harney was obviously in the anti-Gladstone camp in holding these views—a fact that led more than one indignant Liberal to accuse him of having "ratted from the Radical party to the Tory". It is difficult to say which party-affiliation implied in this accusation made him angrier. "Radical" still connoted to him the *laissez-faire*, Free Trade, anti-union principles personified by such men as Daniel O'Connell in the past. Yet it is true that his social criticism was also apt to take an anti-Liberal guise, just as it had in the period of Chartism. Primarily, this was due to his disgust at working class acceptance of Liberal leadership. Support of a party capable of such actions as voting solidly against Keir Hardie's demand in Parliament in 1893 for government aid to those out of work at a time when unemployed demonstrators were being repressed by force on Tower Hill and the Embankment, or howling their approval when the chair silenced Sidney Webb for attempting to introduce an Eight Hours' Day resolution at a Liberal Federation meeting, seemed to Harney sheer infatuation.

In their attitude toward social questions, the Tories were no better, though they were at any rate free of "that gigantic hypocrisy, the 'Nonconformist Conscience' ". What lay at the bottom of his disgust for both parties was their failure to do anything about the still widespread inequity and misery of English life which continued to exist in spite of the enormous wealth brought to the country by industrial expansion and trade.

What mattered Gladstone's Home Rule or Balfour's Irish County Councils, he asked during the trade recession of the early 'nineties, when men fruitlessly walked London streets looking for work? Conditions were better than those of the past, but sweated industries such as the nail and chain makers still existed, the truck acts continued to be evaded, and the gap between the denizens of Mayfair and the "Black Country slaves" remained as wide as ever. "O! noble lords and honourable gentlemen", he asked, "can you not give us one session devoted to that Condition-of-England Question which to Thomas Carlyle, fifty years ago, seemed the only question worth a sensible man's thoughts, but which question is still unsolved?" During the great celebrations of 1897 the old Chartist voice stubbornly reiterated its question: "Amidst all the Jubilee hubbub, may I ask what is being done for Slumland and its wretched inhabitants? How contemptible most of the questions that engage the attention of Parliament compared with the 'spreading ulcer' of East End destitution."

Labour's industrial efforts to solve the "Condition-of-England Question" were thus followed by Harney with warm interest. Nothing for years had given him more hope for the future of the working class than the fraternity shown by the simultaneous striking of stevedores and lightermen with the dockers, he commented in an article on the Dockers' Strike of 1889.[1] The international demonstrations for the Eight Hours' Day in 1890 and 1891 seemed to him a "sunburst illuminating the European and American world", and welcome evidence that the "Old" and "New" Unionism were joining forces. His unabated hostility to the profit-system made him a protagonist of nationalization of the coal mines and transportation, for nationalization of the mines would mean not only the eradication of "non-producers" and the ensuring of a fair wage to the miners, but the replacement of a policy of exploitation by one of conservation in the management of the precious resource.

Toward the political organization of labour Harney's attitude was more conditional. It was not the socialist demands of the Independent Labour Party, expressed in the programme of 1895, that accounted for his reservations. He admired such men as Keir Hardy, Tom Mann, Ben Tillet and H. M. Hyndman, and cheered the launching of the *Social Democrat* in 1897 by

---

[1] "The Revolt of the East End", Newcastle *Weekly Chronicle*, 26 September 1889. The article was also extensively quoted in the *Labour Elector*, 28 September 1889.

Edward and Eleanor Marx Aveling. It was good that Socialism "as it was in the days of Marx and Engels" should be expounded, he wrote; adding, in a remark reminiscent of his two departed friends, that the "undoubted ills of our present social system could not fail to become worse, until unendurable, and an explosion occurred". What accounted for a certain coolness on his part toward the I.L.P. programme was its inclusion of a provision binding members to follow party directives in voting on candidates. This aroused all the fears engendered by his observation of American politics; the spectre of a tyrannical caucus dictating to individuals rose once again. Economic collectivism was one thing, political collectivism another; and Harney's personal experience had developed in him what sometimes amounted to almost an obsessive horror of encroachment on personal liberties by intolerant majorities.

Such doubts accounted only in part for the pessimism which sometimes entirely submerged his habitual attitude of cheerful irony—a mood which caused him to write, "Men are such fools as to rejoice when a child is born; they should weep." His pessimism was that of a man who had lived long enough to see how hollow the fulfilment of hopes can sometimes be. In a moving passage written in 1893, he conveyed much of his feeling:

"When I was young, as Coleridge says, the reform and regeneration of the world—at least of this little world of ours called Britain—seemed by no means a labour of Hercules, but comparatively easy of performance and attainment. The prescription to effect the desired cure was simplicity itself. The people were ignorant, suffering under social wrong, and unrepresented in the council of lawmakers. Give them knowledge and recognize their rights as men and citizens, and the march of regeneration would be swift and sure; all that was oppressive would be overthrown, and triumphant Justice would take the place of extirpated Wrong. Had it not been said and firmly believed—'For a people to love Liberty it is sufficient that they know it; to be free, it is sufficient that they will it'?
"When I was young!
"And now?
"When I look around, seeing what I see, knowing what I know of passing events, I would fain drink of the Lethean stream fabled by poets, that I might forget the past, and be oblivious, or at least indifferent to the present."

The youthful Harney could not have been more imbued with

T

the ideals of the French Revolution and the Enlightenment if he had matured in a Paris, rather than a London, slum. His journey through the nineteenth century had changed all that. To what use had the free press, fought for so hard by a few idealists, been put; to what use the democratic suffrage, now almost achieved? Harney asked. In his blackest moods, he felt that Lammenais' belief in the perfectibility of man through such media had been fatuous. Writing more than forty years before, Harney had shown a remarkable foresight in prophesying that, even with the removal of taxes on newspapers, the press would remain bourgeois in principle due to middle-class control of advertising patronage. "Then, as now, large capitalists will have an immense advantage over those possessed only of small means," he had written. "They will be able to produce the largest and cheapest journals, and command the largest circulation. The 'biggest penny-worths' will be the most attractive to multitudes of working men, who 'care nothing for politics'." The prophecy had proved true, in his opinion; their achievement had been as " 'Dead Sea fruit that tempts the eye and turns to ashes on the tongue'." Freedom of the press had turned out to be profit for the limited companies. The commercial press would not willingly do anything to offend a possible patron by commission or omission; and—the real Dead Sea fruit—the mass of working men did nothing to support a paper which spoke for them, if its anti-working-class rivals contained better "tips" or was more expeditious with its "winners".

The working classes' appetite for trash and their political inertness seemed to Harney, as to other old Chartists like Thomas Cooper, evidence of a loss of moral fibre. Not politics and education, but the music-hall, football and bicycling absorbed their interest—a change symbolized by the large room in Bolt Court, Fleet Street, where the National Convention of 1839 had met: it had become a sporting club. "I see no evidence of any increase in solid intelligence and that practical knowledge without which freedom is a fraud and popular franchises only useful to the traders in politics and traffickers in votes," he wrote gloomily in marking these changes. Evolution was not always advance. Electric lighting might succeed gas; but what would be read by it? In religious matters, he remarked caustically, the "crowds of fanatical dupes" had simply changed their names. Where once it had been the Scottish Free Kirk or the Mormons, now it was

"General Booth and his Salvationists, with their hideous cater-
wauling on street corners".

There was, in truth, much to arouse doubts of the future in his
last days. The great outburst of anti-British feeling in the United
States during the Venezuela boundary dispute of 1895 was not
calculated to allay his apprehensions, believing as he did that
America would inevitably supersede Britain as the dominant
world power. The "progressive advancement of mankind" in
which he had so passionately believed in his youth appeared more
than ever an illusion in a world where unthinking violence
seemed daily to gain in strength. The assassination of the French
president by Anarchists in 1894, the Jameson Raid and the
Kruger Telegram, the ominous growth in armaments and the
sharpening of international exchanges—Harney was not alone
in observing these evidences of the culmination of the Century of
Progress with an extreme pessimism.

An agnostic to the last, there was no religious refuge for him
to retreat to: life had to be judged in itself. And there were
fewer and fewer contemporaries with whom he could share
judgments. He experienced the ultimate sadness of old age repeatedly in the 'nineties, J. B. Leno, Samuel Kydd and Thomas
Cooper "passing away", as he wrote, "like bubbles in the stream
of time". Engels, whom Harney had found "just as modest and
ready for self-effacement" in 1894 as he had been when they first
met in the *Northern Star's* office in Leeds over a half-century
before, died in 1895—a shock to Harney, for whatever bitterness
had entered their friendship had long vanished.[1] There were
also the uncelebrated men who had filled the ranks of Chartism.
A letter in the Newcastle *Weekly Chronicle* recalling his red cap
and his singing and dancing at Winlaton in 1839 moved Harney
to reply: "My amusement has been dashed by an emotion I will
not attempt to represent by words, in reading the names of
Winlatonians, all of whom are now dead. They were genuine
men, they were 'true grit', they and others who might be named.
I loved and honoured them as friends 58 years ago, I love and

---

[1] In a review of Marx's *Revolution and Counter-Revolution in Germany in 1848*, which
appeared in the Newcastle *Weekly Chronicle* in 1896, Harney wrote retrospectively:
"To many, the name of Karl Marx as the editor of *Das Kapital*, the prophet pioneer
of Militant Socialism, is a name of terror; but those who knew him personally can
entertain only pleasant recollections of one of the most warm-hearted, genial, and
attractive of men." This affectionate judgment is scarcely borne out by Marx's
comments on Harney in his correspondence with Engels.

honour them still." Of the old leaders there remained only
Holyoake, whom he saw occasionally; Linton, far off in Connecticut; and Gerald Massey, immersed in Egyptian mythology
and spiritualism.

Harney's isolation was not only that of a man outliving his
contemporaries, but his whole world as well. The river filled
with a "forest of masts" of East and West Indiamen at which he
had peered through the balustrade of old London Bridge as a
small boy was now busy with steam-vessels, and beneath it an
electric underground ran from the City to Waterloo. He had
seen the Brighton stage-coach depart when railways were unknown; now he read of automobiles making the trip. During his
lifetime, London had been transformed from an eighteenth- to a
twentieth-century city.

Looking backward from this new world, what did he think of
his life and the causes to which he had given his youth and young
manhood? It seemed to him a Sisyphean task that he and others
had attempted. Yet he had no regrets for his participation in the
struggle. "If we can do but little toward regenerating the
world," he wrote, "we may try to remove some of the grains of
the mountains of misery always at hand, working and hoping. . . ." Byron, a poet he had treasured since boyhood, remained to him a symbol of his own life—"dear to Pessimists who
see the wrong rampant which they know they cannot conquer,
but which they will not tamely endure". The refusal to endure
wrong had made him an Ishmaelite: a picturesque figure in its
own habitat, he wrote, but not a role to bring success in England.
Yet, given another opportunity, he would not have exchanged
the role.

There was a final irony to his life. In a society which had given
such a distorted form to the things he had struggled for, he was
no longer an Ishmaelite. He enjoyed a certain celebrity in
socialist and secularist circles in London, being interviewed for
their press; and a steady stream of visitors seems to have visited
the small room in Kingston.[1] On his eightieth birthday a testimonial fund of £200—which included such diverse subscribers
as the Bury Social Democratic Association, Joseph Chamberlain,

---

[1] Mr. M. Kavanaugh, Whiteway Colony, Stroud, has written to me of visiting
Harney in company with Holyoake in 1897. "I knew a number of the Chartists and
Owenists," he recollects, "and all I knew looked upon Harney not only as one of the
most courageous, but also one of the most intelligent men of the day . . . from
what others have told me he was a much bigger man than is generally recognized."

Robert Applegarth, an assortment of lords, and "Bunker Ned" (6*d*.)—was presented to him. A great number of congratulatory messages had come from all over England, as well as from such distant points as Paris, Lisbon, Goa, Melbourne and Chicago.

In his speech of acceptance on this occasion, Harney summed up his attitude toward Chartism, the movement which had, in some ways, represented the real climax of his life. After placing Lovett "first in honour" among its leaders, he went on: "It may be said that the Chartist agitation—which had for its object the reform of Parliaments—was so much energy wasted. I think not. The Chartist influence extended beyond the Six Points, and to it we largely owe the extirpation of innumerable, some of them abominable, abuses, and a great widening of the bonds of freedom." So far as he was concerned, however, he had lost the simple faith which had activated the men of that movement, still under the spell of the French Revolution. "I do not attach supreme importance to any form of government," he said. "All forms have had their uses and merits at particular times. But all have failed to bring us even near to that perfectibility of man, which was the beautiful dream of so many good men and so many eloquent writers a little over a hundred years ago." The Age of Reason, the Age of Progress, the Age of Anxiety and Doubt: Harney's life had spanned all three.

Although during the following months he became bed-ridden and found it necessary to dictate his columns to a young friend, Harney's lust for the life of the intellect—expressed in his wish to be sentenced to confinement in the British Museum for a few years—remained unimpaired. There were so many questions left unanswered. Why, for example, had John Henry Newman taken one way and his brother Francis exactly the opposite? Toward the "spiritual" in general he preserved a steady rationalism, retaining a certain sensitivity to the ludicrous in formal religious systems which his long life had developed. In what was his last article, he was obviously delighted in reviewing the *Memoirs of Madame Blavatsky*, a volume purportedly written by the spirit of the founder of Theosophy on a typewriter sealed in a box in Boston, to pass on so choice a quotation as her reason for marrying one Bertinelli years before her death: it was to "avoid his astral companionship, which he had promised if I failed to connect myself with him by this act".

Harney would have been happy to know that some readers

were probably still laughing at his column when he died in great pain on 9 December 1897. This last of the great early-Victorian working-class leaders had always given as much of himself to England as she would take, but she had not been a generous mistress. And it is the fact that the face of society had been turned most stonily against him when he had insisted on pointing to its disfigurement that gives a deeper meaning to the simple philosophy he had finally adopted as his own—a few lines from Byron which might well serve as his epitaph:

> I wish men to be free
> As much from mobs as kings—
> from you as me.

There were other mobs in Victorian England than those of the working class.

Harney's deepest impulse had been to devote himself to bettering the life of his class—and he had been one of the few to realize that this was an international, not just an English, affair. His personal tragedy was that his fellow men stopped listening to him after a period in which he spoke as eloquently and meaningfully as any leader of his time. He has been considered a revolutionary born out of his time, a latter-day Marat mouthing slogans of the French Revolution. Perhaps it is true that he was born in the wrong epoch. If so, it was not too late but too soon. And in looking back on the long struggle of the British working classes to achieve their rightful portion of the fruit of labour and the dignity as human beings that goes with it, the man who expressed their aims before they had finally become those of a major political party in the twentieth century deserves a better fate than obscurity. The good as well as the evil that men do may well survive their passing.

Bibliography

The following bibliography is not an exhaustive treatment of the sources of Chartism. Secondary sources have been repeated from footnotes when they were of importance, and unacknowledged works of which general use was made have been added. However, periodicals and MSS. materials have been detailed more fully in the hope that this may be of some usefulness to students of the period.

As to Harney, four biographical articles, all evidently based on personal interviews with him, were valuable as a source for his obscure youth; and G. D. H. Cole's study of Harney in his excellent *Chartist Portraits* considerably lightened the preliminary spadework. Chartist and other memoirs and such contemporary comment as that found in the Marx-Engels correspondence—a lively and self-revelatory exchange which certainly merits translation for a wider audience—threw some light on his character. Yet in the end the detailing of Harney's life and times attempted here depended mainly on the periodicals and newspapers listed below. One wishes only that all the leading figures of the time had shared the pack-rat habits of Francis Place and Joseph Cowen, Jr., who, whether through a sense of historicity or ingrained habits of saving, rarely threw away anything written or printed.

MSS. COLLECTIONS AND PRINTED CORRESPONDENCE

Autographed Letters, volume in Goldsmiths' Library, University of London.

COWEN COLLECTION .(Newcastle-upon-Tyne Central Library)

Foreign Affairs Committee of Newcastle-upon-Tyne: correspondence, minute book, posters, etc., 1855–56.

Northern Political Union: correspondence, 1858–59.

People's International League: circulars, 1847.

Personal correspondence of Joseph Cowen, Jr.

Polish Hungarian Central Relief Committee: newspaper clippings, the *Refugee Circular*, 1851.

Republican Record, January, March, 1855.

HOWELL COLLECTION (Bishopsgate Institute)

Ernest Jones's diary, 1840–47.

Extracts from Jones's diary, 1839.

G. J. Holyoake's diary, 1835–1905.

George Howell's MS. biography of Ernest Jones; clippings, pamphlets on Jones.

Personal correspondence.

LOVETT COLLECTION (Birmingham Public Library)

London Working Men's Association: addresses, correspondence, flyleafs, newspaper clippings, etc.

Personal correspondence.

Prospectus of the East London Democratic Association, circular, 1837.

PLACE (ADD.) MSS. (British Museum)

27,819: Historical narrative of the formation of the London Working Men's Association, proceedings of the society, etc.

27,820: Continuation of above; proceedings of the Birmingham Political Association.

27,821: Continuation, 1839.

34,245: Letter-books of the National Convention, 1839.

37,773: London Working Men's Association minute book, 1836–39.

PLACE NEWSPAPER COLLECTION (British Museum)

Set 56, vol. I: Newspaper clippings and narrative of the early Chartist movement.

HOME OFFICE PAPERS (Public Record Office)

40/44: Disturbances (correspondence). Lancaster, Bolton, Leicester, Middlesex, 1839.

40/46: Disturbances (correspondence). Montgomeryshire, Northumberland, Norfolk, Surrey, Hertford, Northampton, Essex, 1839.

40/49–50: Disturbances (correspondence). Warwickshire, 1839.

40/53: Military correspondence and Chartist intercepted letters.

40/57: Scottish and Welsh miscellaneous correspondence, 1840.

40/59: Miscellaneous correspondence, 1841–55.

41/14–20: Disturbances (entry books), 1839–67.

41/26: Disturbances (correspondence), London, 1820–48.

41/30: Socialists (correspondence on Secularists).

44/32: Miscellaneous correspondence, 1839.

48/33: Law officers' reports and correspondence, 1839–40.

49/8: Letters to law officers, 1834–43.

61/22: Metropolitan Police correspondence, 1839.

65/10: Letter book, Birmingham, 1839–42.

79/4–5: Entry books, private and secret (contain warrants for opening of private mail, etc.), 1819–55.

99/10: Letter Book, Channel Islands, 1851–60.

FOREIGN OFFICE PAPERS (Public Record Office)

27/1094: Domestic, France, 1855.

27/1105: Domestic, various, 1855.

"The Chartist Correspondence", *Sheffield Free Press Serials*, no. 13. Sheffield, 1856.

Marx, Karl, and Engels, Friedrich, *Briefwechsel*. 4 vols., Berlin, 1929.

PERIODICALS AND NEWSPAPERS, EDITED BY HARNEY OR CONTAINING
CONTRIBUTIONS FROM HIM.

London *Democrat*: 13 April–8 June 1839. Jointly edited by Harney
and J. S. Coombe. Harney's active connection was limited to the five
weekly issues from 13 April.

Northern Star and Leeds General Advertiser: 1837–44, changed to
Northern Star and National Trades Journal, November 1844; to *Star of
Freedom* in May 1852, ceased publication in November 1852. Harney
was Sheffield correspondent from August 1841 to September 1843,
when he became sub-editor. By 1845 he had become in effect editor,
a position made formal in October 1845 and lasting until his resignation in May 1850. He acquired the paper (*The Star*) in April 1852
and continued it as the *Star of Freedom* until it failed in November.

Democratic Review: June 1849–May 1850. Monthly, owned and
edited by Harney.

Red Republican: June–December 1850, changed name to *Friend of the
People.* Weekly, owned and edited by Harney.

Friend of the People: 1st series, December 1850–July 1851; 2nd series,
February–April 1852, when absorbed in *The Star* by Harney's purchase of latter. Weekly, owned and edited by Harney.

Vanguard: January–March 1853. Weekly, owned and edited by
Harney.

Northern Tribune: Newcastle-upon-Tyne, January 1854–March
1855. Monthly until January 1855, then weekly. Edited by Joseph
Cowen, Jr., Harney was second editor.

Jersey *Independent*: Twice-weekly until 1858, then daily. Edited by
Harney July 1856–November 1862.

Newcastle *Weekly Chronicle*: Edited by W. E. Adams. Correspondence from Harney appeared intermittently from 1873 until
1890, when he became a weekly columnist. This connection lasted
until his death in 1897.

Notes and Queries: Casual correspondence from Harney on a great
variety of subjects from 1878 to 1896.

PERIODICALS AND NEWSPAPERS, CHARTIST AND WORKING CLASS
RADICAL

British Statesman: 1842–43. Edited briefly in 1842 by Bronterre
O'Brien.

Bronterre's National Reformer: 1837.

Champion: 1836–40. Edited by J. Whittle; anti-O'Connorite.

Charter: 1839. Edited by William Carpenter. London Working
Men's Association viewpoint.

Chartist: 1839. Strong moral force.

T*

Democrat and Labour Advocate: 1855. Edited by George White.

English Chartist Circular: 1839–41. Non-controversial. Valuable for theoretical Chartist discussion. Edited by William Carpenter.

English Republic: 1851–55. Edited by W. J. Linton. Republican.

Labourer: 1847–48. Jointly edited by O'Connor and Ernest Jones. Land Plan organ.

London *Dispatch*: 1836–39. Owned by Henry Hetherington 1836–37. London Working Men's Association viewpoint.

London *Mercury*: 1836–37. Edited by John Bell, jointly with Bronterre O'Brien, April–August 1837. Merged with London *Dispatch*, September 1837. Intellectually, the most lively of early Chartist newspapers.

Northern Liberator: 1837–40. Newcastle-upon-Tyne. Edited originally by Augustus Beaumont. Strong physical force viewpoint.

Northern Star: 1837–52. See above, or notations in index.

Notes to the People: 1851–52. Owned and edited by Ernest Jones. Valuable for late Chartist period.

Operative: 1838–39. Edited by Bronterre O'Brien.

People's Paper: 1852–58. Edited by Ernest Jones. The essential source for Chartism's decline. Contains much material by Karl Marx.

Plain Speaker: 1848–49. Edited by Thomas Cooper and Thomas Wooler. Moderate Chartist.

Poor Man's Guardian: 1830–35. Leading organ of the unstamped struggle. Owned by Hetherington, edited for most of its existence by Bronterre O'Brien.

Reasoner: 1846–61. Edited by G. J. Holyoake. Secularist and moderate Chartist. Absorbed the *Northern Tribune* in March 1855.

Republican: 1848. Edited by G. M. Harding. Moderate republican.

Reynolds's Political Instructor: 1849–50. Editor, G. W. M. Reynolds. Contains illustrated sketches of Chartist leaders, 1850. Merged with:

Reynolds's Weekly Newspaper: 1850–. Indispensable for ultra-radical activities of 1850's.

Social Economist: 1868–69. Contains allusions to Chartist leaders' deaths: e.g. Ernest Jones, George White.

Southern Star: 1840. Edited by William Carpenter; jointly, for a brief period, with Bronterre O'Brien. Moderate Chartist.

Spirit of the Age: 1848–49. Edited by Alexander Campbell as organ of the Metropolitan Trades' Delegates until November 1848, socialist and democratic; dominant interest in co-operative movement under editorship of G. J. Holyoake after purchase by W. H. Ashurst.

Weekly Tribune: 1849–50. Socialist.

Working Man's Friend: 1832–33. Unstamped, published by James Watson.

OTHER PERIODICALS AND NEWSPAPERS

(years given are those of which use was made)

Constitutional: 1858, 1860. St. Helier, Jersey. Ultra-conservative.

Leader: 1851–52. Advanced liberal. Valuable for reports on efforts at union between working and middle-class radicals.

Morning Chronicle: 1839, 1842. Whig until 1847, then Peelite. Contains unusually full accounts of riots and Chartist trials.

Nonconformist: 1842. Edited by Edward Miall. Very useful for Sturgeite viewpoint and attempts at Chartist-Radical coalition.

Punch: 1848. Interesting in its reflection of changing attitude of governing classes.

The Times: Less grey, more shrill than now; an invaluable source for "respectable" opinion.

Voice of the People: 1848. Charles Knight's and Harriet Martineau's short-lived weekly devoted to the conversion of Chartists to "political economy".

Weekly Dispatch: Middle-class Radical.

BIOGRAPHICAL ESSAYS ON HARNEY

Anon. (G. W. M. Reynolds?), "George Julian Harney", *Reynolds's Political Instructor*, 16 February 1850.

Aveling, Edward, "George Julian Harney: A Straggler of 1848", *Social Democrat*, January 1897. Like the others in this group, important mainly for reminiscences of Harney's youth. A "racy sketch" in the words of its subject.

Cole, G. D. H., "George Julian Harney", in *Chartist Portraits*, London, 1941.

Gould, F. J., "A Literary Chat with George Julian Harney", *Literary Guide*, March 1895.

Mortimer, Geoffrey (pseud., probably J. M. Robertson, editor of the *Free Review*), "Julian Harney, the Last of the Chartist Leaders", *Free Review*, March 1896. "Full, excellent, and accurate", according to Harney.

BIOGRAPHIES, MEMOIRS, GENERAL HISTORIES, PAMPHLETS

Adams, Henry, *The Education of Henry Adams.* London ed., 1919.

Adams, W. E., *Memoirs of a Social Atom.* 2 vols., London, 1903.

Adams, W. E., *Our American Cousins.* London, 1887.

Anon., *Memoranda of the Chartist Agitation in Dundee.* Dundee, 1889.

Anon., *Quelques Révélations sur le "Docteur" Taylor ainsi que sur M. George Julian Harney.* Pamphlet, Jersey, 1858.

Anon., *Revelations on the Subject of "Doctor" Taylor and Mr. George Julian Harney.* English translation of preceding, Jersey, 1858.

Beer, Max, *A History of British Socialism.* 2 vols., 7th ed., London, 1948.

Buonarotti, *History of Babeuf's Conspiracy for Equality.* Translated by Bronterre (J. B. O'Brien). London, 1836.

Calman, A. R., *Ledru Rollin après 1848.* Paris, 1921.

Clark, Thomas, *Reflections upon the Past Policy and Future Prospects of the Chartist Party; also a Letter Condemnatory of Private Assassination, as Recommended by Mr. George Julian Harney.* Pamphlet, London, 1850.

Cole, G. D. H., *Chartist Portraits.* London, 1941.

Cole, G. D. H., *A Short History of the British Working-Class Movement.* Revised ed., London, 1948.

Cole, G. D. H., and Postgate, Raymond, *The British People, 1746–1946.* Revised ed., New York, 1947.

Collet, C. D., *History of the Taxes on Knowledge.* Thinkers Library ed., London, 1933.

Conklin, R. J., *Thomas Cooper the Chartist.* Manila, 1936.

Cooper, Thomas, *The Life of Thomas Cooper, Written by Himself.* London, 1872.

Dechêne, Abel, *Les Proscrits du Deux Décembre à Jersey.* Paris, 1917.

Devyr, Thomas, *The Odd Book of the Nineteenth Century.* Greenpoint, New York, 1882.

Dolléans, Edouard, *Le Chartisme.* 2 vols., Paris, 1912.

Driver, Cecil, *Tory Radical; the Life of Richard Oastler.* New York, 1946.

Duncombe, Thomas H., ed., *The Life and Correspondence of Thomas Slingsby Duncombe.* 2 vols., London, 1868.

Engels, Friedrich, *The Condition of the Working Class in England in 1844.* London, 1892.

Engels, Friedrich, and Marx, Karl, *The Communist Manifesto.* With an appreciation by Harold Laski, London, 1948.

Faulkner, H. U., *Chartism and the Churches.* New York, 1916.

Frost, Thomas, *Forty Years' Recollections.* London, 1880.

Gammage, R. G., *History of the Chartist Movement.* 2nd ed., London and Newcastle-upon-Tyne, 1894.

Gillespie, Frances, *Labor and Politics in England, 1850–1867.* Durham, North Carolina, 1927.

Groves, Reg, *But We Shall Rise Again: a Narrative History of Chartism.* London, 1938.

Hammond, J. L. and B., *The Age of the Chartists.* London, 1930.

Harney, George Julian, *The Anti-Turkish Crusade: a Review of a Recent Agitation, with Reflections on the Eastern Question.* Boston, Mass., 1876.

Holyoake, G. J., *Bygones Worth Remembering.* 2 vols., London, 1905.

Holyoake, G. J., *Sixty Years of an Agitator's Life.* 2 vols., 2nd ed., London, 1893.

Hovell, Mark, *The Chartist Movement*. Edited and completed by T. F. Tout, Manchester, 1918.

Hughes, Thomas, *Vacation Rambles*. London, 1895.

Hunt, Thomas, *Chartism, Trades-Unionism, and Socialism*. Pamphlet, London, 1840.

Jones, Ernest, *An Appeal for the Judgment of the People*. Pamphlet, London, 1852.

Jones, E. R., *The Life and Speeches of Joseph Cowen, M.P.* London, 1885.

Kingsley, Charles, *Alton Locke*. 3rd ed., London, 1890.

Kingsley, F. E., ed., *Charles Kingsley: His Letters and Memories of His Life*. 2 vols., London, 1877.

LeCras, Abraham, *Manorial Rights in Jersey*. Pamphlet, Jersey, 1856.

Leno, J. B., *The Aftermath*. London, 1892.

Linton, W. J., *European Republicans: Recollections of Mazzini and His Friends*. London, 1893.

Linton, W. J., *James Watson: a Memoir*. Manchester, 1880.

Linton, W. J., *Memories*. London, 1895.

Lovett, William, *Chartism: a New Organization of the People*. London, 1841.

Lovett, William, *Life and Struggles of William Lovett*. 2 vols., 2nd ed., London, 1920.

Maccoby, S., *English Radicalism, 1832–1886*. 2 vols., London, 1935, 1938.

Martin, B. Kingsley, *The Triumph of Lord Palmerston*. London, 1924.

Marx, Karl, *The Eastern Question*. Edited by Edward and Eleanor Marx Aveling, London, 1899.

Marzials, F. T., *Life of Victor Hugo*. London, 1888.

Maurice, F., ed., *Life of Frederick Denison Maurice*. 2 vols., London, 1884.

Mayer, Gustav, *Friedrich Engels*. London, 1936.

Mehring, Franz, *Karl Marx, the Story of His Life*. London, 1948.

Morris, M., ed., *From Cobbett to the Chartists, 1815–1848*. London, 1951.

Napier, William, *Life of Sir Charles J. Napier*. 4 vols., London, 1857.

O'Brien, J. B., *Life and Character of Maximilian Robespierre*. London, 1838.

O'Connor, Feargus, ed., *The Trial of Feargus O'Connor and Fifty-Eight Others at Lancaster*. London, 1843.

Palmerston, Lord, *Speech of Lord Viscount Palmerston to the Electors of Tiverton on 31st July 1847*. Pamphlet, London, 1847.

Payne, J. B., *The Gossiping Guide to Jersey*. London, 1862.

Raven, C. E., *Christian Socialism, 1848–1854*. London, 1920.

Rosenblatt, Frank, *The Chartist Movement in Its Social and Economic Aspects*. New York, 1916.

Rostow, W. W., *British Economy of the Nineteenth Century.* Oxford, 1948.

Rothstein, Theodor, *From Chartism to Labourism.* London, 1929.

Ryazanoff, D., *The Communist Manifesto of Karl Marx and Friedrich Engels.* London, 1930.

St. André, Jules C., *Five Years in the Land of Refuge.* London, 1854.

Saville, John, *Ernest Jones: Chartist.* London, 1952.

Slosson, P. W., *The Decline of the Chartist Movement.* New York, 1916.

Snell, F. J., *Palmerston's Borough.* London, 1894.

Solly, Henry, *James Woodford, Carpenter and Chartist.* 2 vols., London, 1881.

Somerville, Alexander, *The Autobiography of a Working Man.* London, 1854.

Somerville, Alexander, *Cobdenic Policy, the Internal Enemy of England.* London, 1854.

Stekloff, G. M., *History of the First International.* London, 1928.

Stubbs, C. W., *Charles Kingsley and the Christian Socialist Movement.* London, 1899.

Taylor, John, *The Coming Revolution.* Pamphlet, Carlisle, 1840.

Urquhart, David, *Constitutional Remedies.* Newcastle-upon-Tyne, 1854.

Urquhart, David, *The Progress of Russia.* 5th ed., London, 1853.

Urquhart, David, *Recent Events in the East.* London, 1854.

Webster, P. C. G., *Records of the Queen's Own Royal Regiment of Staffordshire Yeomanry.* Lichfield and London, 1870.

West, Julius, *A History of the Chartist Movement.* London, 1920.

Wheelbarrow (M. M. Trumbull), *Articles and Discussions on the Labor Question.* Chicago, 1890.

Williams, David, *John Frost, a Study in Chartism.* Cardiff, 1939.

INDEX

Aberdeen, 100, 102, 162, 194, 201
Aberdeen, Lord, 237–8
Adams, Henry, 260
Adams, W. E., 200, 271, 274–6
Agents-provocateurs, 61, 63, 175
Agricultural workers, and Chartism, 33*n*., 177
Alien Acts, 173, 184, 209, 243, 256
Alston, W. C., 87–8
America, attitudes toward, 127–8, 153, 257–60, 264–5, 267, 269, 270*n*., 273
American Civil War, and English opinion, 258–61
Anarchism, 275, 283
Anti-Corn Law agitation, 95, 103, 106, 109–11, 117, 119, 143, 146, 152, 226, 279
Anti-Turkish Crusade, The, 270
Applegarth, Robert, 200, 285
Arming, Chartist, 42, 47, 63–4, 66–8, 70, 75, 91, 160–1, 167, 175
Army, and Chartist violence, 71, 73–5, 80, 82, 83*n*., 84–5, 91, 93–4, 114–15, 118, 160, 164–5, 167, 171; loyalty of, 48, 52, 63, 82–3
Arnott, John, 271
Ashford, 192
Ashton-under-Lyne, 174, 176
Attwood, Charles, 239–41
Attwood, Thomas, 5, 21*n*., 30–1, 39–40, 70
Aveling, Edward and Eleanor Marx, 280–1
Ayr, 40, 45

Babeuf, Gracchus, 14, 29, 130, 135, 143–4
Bairstow, Jonathan, 105
Bakunin, Michael, 159
Balfour, Arthur, 280
Barnsley, 84, 167
Barthelemy, 212*n*.
Bath, 109, 160
Bauer, Heinrich, 137, 142–3, 158–9
Beaumont, Augustus, 25, 42*n*.
Bedlington, 73–5
Bell, John, 17–20
Bellamy, Edward, 276
Bem, General, 190*n*.
Benbow, William, 70
Beniowski, Major, 62–3, 88, 90, 92, 239*n*.
Bernard, James, 17–21
Birmingham, 11, 21, 67–71, 80–1, 87–9, 91–2, 96, 101, 109, 119, 195

Birmingham Political Union, 30–1, 35–6, 39–40, 43, 54, 59, 76
Blanc, Louis, 155, 177, 179, 182, 186–7, 202, 204, 212, 214–17, 272
Blatchford, Robert, 275
Bolton, 85, 174–5
Boston (Mass.), 265–9
Bradford, 48, 92–4, 108, 197, 225
Bradlaugh, Charles, 252, 266
Bright, John, 109, 168, 237, 258
Bristol, 4, 40
Brougham, Lord, 7, 24
Buchanan, Robert, 184
Bulgarian atrocities, 269–70
Burdett, Sir Francis, 5
Burns, Robert, 126
Burns, Robert (son), 94
Burrit, Elihu, 153
Bury, 48
Byron, Lord, 2, 123, 127, 130, 274–5, 284, 286

Canterbury, 32
Cardo, William, 41, 90*n*.
Carlile, Richard, 5–6, 8
Carlisle, 40, 48, 72, 74, 85, 90*n*., 92, 104
Carlyle, Thomas, 126, 270–1, 280
Carnegie, Andrew, 263
Caroline, Queen, 2
Castlereagh, Lord, 9
Catholicism, attitudes toward, 217–18, 269, 278
Central European Democratic Committee, 212–13
Central National Association, 17–21
Charlton, James, 100, 226, 263
Charter, Little (1848), 168–70, 182
Charter, People's, 35, 120
Chartism, Scottish, 39, 94–6, 100–4, 122, 163, 168, 209, 221; *see also* localities
Chartist Land Plan, 131–2, 146–9, 161–2, 174, 180–1, 195, 221
Chartists, female, 47, 72
Cheltenham, 163, 200
Civil War, *see* American Civil War
Clapham Sect, 3
Clarion, 275
Clark, Thomas, 152, 194–5, 208
Class-struggle, concept of, 62, 96, 102, 130, 144, 181*n*., 183–4, 198, 204–5, 218, 225, 231, 249–50, 254
Cleave, John, 37–8, 65
Cobbett, J. P., 56
Cobbett, William, 16, 29, 107, 131–2, 148, 187, 275–6

295